Education
with the Grain of the Universe

The C. Henry Smith series is edited by J. Denny Weaver. Volumes to date have been released by Cascadia Publishing House (originally Pandora Press U.S., a name some of the earlier series books carry) and frequently copublished by Herald Press in cooperation with Bluffton University as well as the Mennonite Historical Society. Bluffton University, in consultation with the publishers, is primarily responsible for the content of the studies.

1. Anabaptists and Postmodernity
   Edited by Susan Biesecker-Mast and Gerald Biesecker-Mast, 2000

2. Anabaptist Theology in Face of Postmodernity:
   A Proposal for the Third Millennium
   By J. Denny Weaver, 2000

3. Fractured Dance:
   Gadamer and a Mennonite Conflict over Homosexuality:
   By Michael A. King, 2001

4. Fixing Tradition: Joseph W. Yoder, Amish American
   By Julia Kasdorf, 2002

5. Walker in the Fog: On Mennonite Writing
   By Jeff Gundy, 2005

6. Separation and the Sword in Anabaptist Persuasion:
   Radical Confessional Rhetoric from Schleitheim to Dordrecht
   By Gerald Biesecker-Mast, 2006

7. Searching for Sacred Ground:
   The Journey of Chief Lawrence Hart, Mennonite
   By Raylene Hinz-Penner, 2007

8. Practicing the Politics of Jesus:
   The Origin and Significance of John Howard Yoder's Social Ethics
   By Earl Zimmerman, 2007

9. Peace to War:
   Shifting Allegiances in the Assemblies of God
   By Paul Alexander, 2009

10. Songs from an Empty Cage:
    Poetry, Mystery, Anabaptism, and Peace
    By Jeff Gundy, 2013

11. Education with the Grain of the Universe:
    A Peaceable Vision for the Future of Mennonite Schools,
    Colleges, and Universities
    Edited by J. Denny Weaver, 2017

Education
with the Grain of the Universe

A Peaceable Vision for the Future of
Mennonite Schools, Colleges, and Universities

Edited by J. Denny Weaver

Foreword by
Susan Schultz Huxman

The C. Henry Smith Series
Volume 11

Cascadia
Publishing House
Telford, Pennsylvania

Cascadia Publishing House orders, information, reprint permissions:
contact@CascadiaPublishingHouse.com
1-215-723-9125
126 Klingerman Road, Telford PA 18969
www.CascadiaPublishingHouse.com

Education with the Grain of the Universe
Copyright © 2017 by Cascadia Publishing House,
a division of Cascadia Publishing House LLC
Telford, PA 18969
All rights reserved.
Library of Congress Catalog Number: 2017040099
ISBN-13: 978-1-68027-008-2; **ISBN 10**: 1-68027-008-7
Book design by Cascadia Publishing House
Cover design by Dawn Ranck Hower with cover artwork by Greg Luginbihl
as photographed by Kent Sweitzer

All Bible quotations are used by permission, all rights reserved and, unless otherwise noted, are from *The New Revised Standard Version of the Bible*, copyright 1989, by the Division of Christian Education of the National Council of the Churches of Christ in the USA.

Library of Congress Cataloguing-in-Publication Data
Names: Weaver, J. Denny, 1941- editor.
Title: Education with the grain of the universe : a peaceable vision for the future of Mennonite schools, colleges, and universities / edited by J. Denny Weaver.
Description: Telford, Pennsylvania : Cascadia Publishing House, [2017] | Series: The C. Henry Smith series ; Volume 11 | Includes bibliographical references and index.
Identifiers: LCCN 2017040099| ISBN 9781680270082 (6 x 9" trade pbk. : alk. paper) | ISBN 1680270087 (6 x 9" trade pbk. : alk. paper)
Subjects: LCSH: Mennonite universities and colleges. | Mennonites--Parties and movements. | Mennonites--Theology.
Classification: LCC LC586.M4 E38 2017 | DDC 371.071--dc23
LC record available at https://lccn.loc.gov/2017040099

23 22 21 20 19 18   10 9 8 7 6 5 4 3 2

*To the memory of
Ronald L. Friesen,
Gregg J. Luginbuhl,
James H. Satterwhite, and
J. Richard Weaver,
professors who taught with "the grain of the universe"*

CONTENTS

Foreword by Susan Schultz Huxman   12
Editor's Preface   15
Introduction   17

Chapter One: The Story of Jesus: "The Grain of the Universe"
J. Denny Weaver • 25

PART ONE: THEOLOGY AND ETHICS

Chapter Two: True Evangelical Scholarship: Metaphysics and Mennonite Education
Justin Heinzekehr • 61

Chapter Three: Salvaging Mennonite Theological Education: Imitating Black Faith as It Imitates Christ
Drew G. I. Hart • 74

Chapter Four: From Goshen to Delano: Toward a Relational Mennonite Studies
Felipe Hinojosa • 87

Chapter Five: Mennonite Education, Pluralism, and the Dialogical Nature of Truth
Benjamin Bixler • 99

PART TWO: THE BIBLE

Chapter Six: Biblical Interpretation in an Anabaptist Perspective: Canon as Choir
Laura L. Brenneman • 117

Chapter Seven: Divine Violence and the Old Testament
J. Denny Weaver • 125

Chapter Eight: Reading the Apocrypha
Jackie Wyse-Rhodes with Afterword, Anabaptist Use of the Apocrypha, by J. Denny Weaver • 141

PART THREE: ECCLESIOLOGY

Chapter Nine: Making Peace with Ourselves: Mennonite Peace Education and Intrachurch Conflict
Hannah E. Heinzekehr • 155

Chapter Ten: Thinking of Myself as Your Servant is a Bad Idea: Mennonite Education and the Problem of the Servant Leadership Paradigm
Malinda Elizabeth Berry • 164

Chapter Eleven: Why the Anabaptist Academy Should Go to Church
Gerald J. Mast • 181

Chapter Twelve: Searching for Self: Community as Conduit for God's Deepest Transformation
Sarah Ann Bixler • 194

PART FOUR: LITERATURE FROM THE MARGINS

Chapter Thirteen: Learning to Listen in Greg Bechtel's "Smut Stories"
Daniel Shank Cruz • 213

Chapter Fourteen: Mennonite and Mormon Women's Life Writing
Rebecca Janzen • 223

PART FIVE: PEACE AND CONFLICT STUDIES

Chapter Fifteen: Peace Studies and International Law
Lowell Ewert • 245

Chapter Sixteen: Only Just War: The Broken Logic of Necessary Evil and Functional Violence
Rudi Kauffman • 256

PART SIX: LOCAL APPLICATIONS
Chapter Seventeen: Restorative Justice in Schools
Lonna Stoltzfus • 283

Chapter Eighteen: Forgiveness
J. Denny Weaver • 294

Chapter Nineteen: Teaching the "Pacifist's Dilemma"
Zachary Walton • 304

Chapter Twenty: Bringing Christian Students to Peace with Darwin
Angela Horn Montel • 320

Conclusion 331
Bibliography 335
Index 351
The Contributors 359

FOREWORD

A wise professor once told me: *"It is more important to ask hard questions than to provide easy answers."* This collection of essays—first presented at an academic interdisciplinary conference at Bluffton University and supported by the C. Henry Smith Trust Fund—is committed to enunciating a "peaceable vision for the future of our Mennonite schools." Wisely, it resists pat answers—as enticing as that might have been for each of these astute scholars. Taken together, these thoughtful, provocative essays, carefully edited by J. Denny Weaver, are an anthem to the pedagogical model of asking hard questions, of stimulating inquiry and invitation and furthering the conversation on important educational questions of our time, including these: How is Jesus relevant in our schools? What meaningful peace witness can Mennonite education provide?

I think readers will be most impressed by the tough questions, peculiar perspective, and aspirational sights that this volume of scholarship knits together. The collection is tailored to help lively interdisciplinary discussions in our Anabaptist educational institutions and our congregations. The take-aways are fulsome (encourage big gulps), imperative (demand attention), and challenging (are we ready for this?).

Tough Questions (in the spirit of humility)

In the spirit of humility, these scholars ask readers to contemplate difficult questions, such as: Why do Mennonites, known for brokering peace around the world, have such trouble making peace with themselves? Is it more important for Mennonites to be born into the right family (white, German heritage) than to walk in the footsteps of Jesus? Why do Mennonite scholars choose dialogue partners that look and think like them? How can we take sustenance from our traditional storyline while at the same time allow new flavors to change our "saltiness?" Perhaps the most perplexing question for Mennonite scholars is this one: Why in 2017 are we still having to explain what a Mennonite is and what we believe even to other scholars? There are other more pointed questions related to biblical interpretation (What do we do with all the divine violence in the Old Testament?), organizational dynamics (Why do Mennonites have a tendency to misappropriate servant leadership?), and Anabaptist history (Our Anabaptist forebears used the Apocrypha and Scripture with no distinction. Why don't we do that today?),

Peculiar Perspectives (from the margins)

In the spirit of nonconformity, many of these authors unpack the tension, dare I say the oxymoronic pairing, between "Mennonite" ("priesthood of all believers") and "theology" (foundational, systematic authority). Mennonites are more about "orthopraxy" (actual lifestyle) than orthodoxy (rigid belief system)," but this peculiar clash is celebrated here. A palpable nonconformist "big tent" perspective is embraced by the authors even as Anabaptist essentials are articulated.

The result is some well-examined irony. For starters, the title of the book turns convention on its head. We often think of Mennonites and other peace churches in their counter-culture ways as working "against the grain." But the title is *Education with the Grain of the Universe*. And the book shows at every turn how Jesus made peace with His environment. He modeled restorative justice not retributive justice. And so should we. The effective underlying argument of the book is this: Mennonite education is actually in conformity with the life and teachings of Jesus. It is really other mainstream denominations who are often nonconformists or out of step with the Gospels. Jesus was more about "kindom" ("wounded healers" committed to living in community) than kingdom (power, hierarchy, control).

On other topics irony also reigns supreme, such as the observation that "students should go to church to discover how truly flawed and disastrous the church actually is." The rationale offered is that if we expose students to the difficulty of our church history, they actually will be more "energized," than "scandalized" by the failures of the church! Now that's turning convention on its head!

Aspirational Sights (as followers of Jesus)

In the spirit of Isaiah 54:2, these essays "enlarge the place of our tents, stretch our curtain wide. They do not hold back; they lengthen our cords as they strengthen our stakes." They welcome all (stretch the curtains) and affirm Anabaptist values of peace and discipleship (strengthening stakes). They conclude that church should be a "safe harbor" and "adventure." That we should not get hung up on distracting issues (creationism versus evolution; God or science). We should hold these views together with integrity. That we should not see the Sermon on the Mount ("turn the other cheek") as some passive "do-nothing" stance but as a "take-charge" modeling of active nonviolence. That this country stands in need of a peace witness that Mennonite education can provide as it tells Jesus' story as one that is principally a rejection of the sword.

As I was traveling recently through what some might call the heart of "Mennonite country" (Lancaster, Pa.), I saw a barn with a handcrafted sign: "Know Jesus. Know Peace." I smiled. Simple, Profound. Aspirational. In the oral mode it invites us to see from an ironic, peculiar angle: "No Jesus. No Peace." As an interrogative, the sign challenges us to confront: "Do you really know Jesus? Know Peace? The scholars in this collection of essays wrestle earnestly and even eloquently with the words of this sign.

—*Susan Schultz Huxman, PhD*
President, Eastern Mennonite University;
Professor of Communication

EDITOR'S PREFACE

This book reflects a conference that met at Bluffton University October 16-18, 2015, with additional co-sponsors: the Mennonite Historical Society and the C. Henry Smith Trust. Given the contribution of the Smith Trust, it is fitting that the book from this conference appear in the C. Henry Smith Series. A generous grant from the Smith Trust supported both the conference and the publication of this book in the Series that bears Smith's name. All involved—Bluffton conference planners, book authors, myself as Series editor—wish to express great gratitude to the C. Henry Smith Trust.

The content of this manuscript makes it an exceptional fit for the C. Henry Smith Series. Smith was a vigorous advocate of education and of peace and nonviolence with a Mennonite but ecumenical orientation. This manuscript fits Smith's agenda in multiple ways, and it is appropriate and symbolically meaningful to include this volume in the C. Henry Smith Series. Several more historically oriented papers from the conference are published in the April 2017 issue of *Mennonite Quarterly Review*. History was another of C. Henry Smith's interests.

Under the aegis of the Smith Trust, the work of many people came together to produce this book. I am grateful to Gerald Mast, chair of the conference planning committee, for the invitation to edit what became the book in hand. As I explain a bit farther in the Introduction, editing this book constituted the continuation of a project that Gerald and I co-edited and published in 2003 as *Teaching Peace: Nonviolence and the Lib-*

eral Arts. I have long believed that when theology and ethics are understood as observations that draw truth from the narrative of Jesus, these Jesus-based discourses can be shown to address any issue faced or taught in Mennonite education. And since Christians believe that Jesus reveals the Creator God, the actions of Jesus who reveals God indicate the grain of the universe that God created. Thus this book presents education with the grain of the universe.

I owe many thanks to the seventeen other authors whose work appears in this book. They willingly submitted to my sometimes seemingly demanding editorial requests that stemmed from my effort to produce a book with a developing and integrated argument. I am also grateful for the understanding of those potential authors with whom I spoke initially but who then concluded that their particular contribution would not fit the book as it developed.

Chemistry professor Mark Ediger and science historian Michael Shank offered wise advice for my comments on science in the Introduction to Part Six. Scholar and pastor Ron Adams evaluated the entire manuscript. As he has done for me on other projects, Ron made a number of insightful suggestions that improved the final product. Since a fish is an ancient Christian symbol, it is fitting that a fish ornament the cover of this book on education that begins with the narrative of Jesus. The late Gregg Luginbuhl, emeritus professor of art at Bluffton University, created the exquisite piece on the cover, which has long hung in my living room. Kent Sweitzer, photographer par excellence, produced the photograph of this art that graces the cover. Finally, mentioning the lead-off writing last, a profound thanks to Susan Schultz Huxman, President of Eastern Mennonite University, whose Foreword put the crowning touch on this volume.

Having the opportunity to develop this volume that expresses my understanding of how the narrative of Jesus can address the many issues we face in the world around us has made working on this manuscript a joy. Each day since the conference that produced the initial manuscripts that have grown into this book, I have been eager to get to my study in the morning and to continue this work of love. Speaking of love, most of all I owe thanks to my wife Mary, who respects my need to express this kind of love alongside my love of her.

—*J. Denny Weaver, Editor, C. Henry Smith Series*
Summer 2017

INTRODUCTION

J. Denny Weaver

This moment, still early in the twenty-first century, offers stimulating and important challenges for the future of Mennonite education. For one thing, there is evident interest in things Anabaptist in ecumenical circles beyond Mennonites. I observe that interest in the wider academic community that I encounter at national meetings. And I sense that interest with the pastors I encounter in my work with the Wisconsin Council of Churches. There is an opportunity here for Mennonite education done with an ecumenical spirit.

One dimension of this interest in things Anabaptist, particularly in peace theology, comes from the growing disillusionment about the seemingly endless wars in which the United States is engaged. This country stands in need of the peace witness that Mennonite education can provide at all levels.

At the same time, issues of sexuality challenge the church within and threaten the witness the church can pose to the wider world. One issue concerns sexual immorality and the sexual abuse of women by male authority figures and men in leadership positions. Mennonite Church USA, the largest of the Mennonite denominations in the United States, is still struggling with how to respond to these sinful stories, both past and present. Schools face this issue as much as other church institutions. The case of John Howard Yoder is only the most prominent of such stories. How the church solves this question will have significant impact both within the church as well as without for the witness the church offers to a watching world.

Further, Mennonite Church USA is struggling with questions of inclusion of people who are LGBTQ, whether to affirm marriage of same-sex couples, and whether pastors should perform these marriages. This conflict presents an opportunity for education in Mennonite institutions to model acceptance and reconciliation. However, since Mennonite colleges are already teaching conflict resolution and have affirmed equality in hiring, it is not clear at the moment how willing a fragmented church may be to follow the lead of the educational institutions.

Mennonite schools also have an opportunity for modeling of a different kind. Gone are the days when Mennonite schools served primarily Mennonite students. Among the colleges, Bluffton University has long had more students who do not come from a Mennonite background than Mennonites. But the numbers for other schools as well are changing. Mennonite high schools and colleges are attracting students not of Mennonite background but who are interested in a high quality, religious-based education. Maintaining a clear peace-church-oriented outlook in an ecumenical manner and with clear regard for the issues of sexuality and power dynamics may be the most important challenge facing Mennonite education as it seeks to flourish in the twenty-first century. In a way, carrying out this task on our campuses constitutes a miniature version of modeling a peace outlook amid a violence-prone nation.

The chapters of this book propose an approach to education for the Mennonite future that addresses these challenges. The intent is to describe an approach to Mennonite education that sets it up to engage the world from within a clear orientation in peace and social justice but does so from an ecumenical framework accessible to any Christian.

This orientation is established in Chapter 1, which sketches the narrative of Jesus. Since all Christians profess Jesus, beginning the discussion with the narrative of Jesus is intrinsically an ecumenical orientation. Although the implications will unfold slowly and throughout the book, my suggestion for orientating education is actually a way to read the story of Jesus that opens the narrative to the discussion of virtually any subject in the school and college curriculum, present or future.[1]

A book on Mennonite education or education for Mennonites necessarily has two dimensions or faces two directions. One dimension concerns the content of teaching in Mennonite schools. What precisely belongs in the curriculum of a Mennonite school? I suggest, for example, that courses in the Bible should make clear the way a nonviolent perspective emerges from the entire narrative of Jesus, and these schools should be teaching about conflict resolution and restorative justice.

Closely related to the discussion of content is the question of pedagogical methodology, namely how should teachers in Mennonite schools teach. As a first point, I suggest that teaching should reflect a nonviolent, invitational approach to student learning rather than an authoritative, top-down approach. In practice, the issues of content and methodology overlap. Without making an effort to separate the two questions, chapters in this book move between these two poles of discussion.

In 2003, Gerald Mast and I co-edited *Teaching Peace*,[2] a book which demonstrated how an assumption of nonviolence could shape disciplines and conversations across a liberal arts curriculum. The volume in hand constitutes a kind of *Teaching Peace: Volume II*. The assumption of the current volume is that living within the story of Jesus, which makes visible the grain of the universe, has the potential to influence thinking in virtually any discipline of the school or university curriculum.[3] That orientation was assumed but not particularly explicit in the previous volume, whose chapters dealt with a wide range of disciplines. The book in hand makes explicit the footing of Mennonite education within the narrative of Jesus. For those who found that dimension lacking in the previous work, consider the current book as "Volume I" and read *Teaching Peace* as "Volume II"!

Establishing the orientation in the narrative of Jesus is the function of Chapter 1. The narrative of Jesus is not a narrow foundation. On the contrary, the chapter identifies a number of issues of education for Mennonites that emerge directly from the narrative of Jesus, while following Parts of the book extend the discussion greatly.

The chapters of Part One carry the discussion further in theology and ethics. Chapter 2 fills a lacuna in Mennonite theologizing by using process theology to project a nonviolent God that reflects a modern cosmology. Chapter 3 challenges Mennonites to engage and learn from Black Theology. Exploring the importance of understanding Mennonite history from the perspective of Latinos and Latinas occurs in Chapter 4. The last chapter of Part One embodies the dialogue posture necessary in approaching other religions in the modern context of pluralism and relativism.

Part Two offers suggestions for interpreting the Bible from the margin. The violence in the Old Testament poses a challenge to biblical interpretation from a nonviolent or peace church peace perspective. Part Two offers two approaches. Chapter 6 suggests seeing the canon as a choir with multiple voices and recommends giving special attention to the smaller or marginal voices. Chapter 7 points to a nonviolent strand alongside the violent texts of the Old Testament and argues that the story of Jesus indicates the side of the conversation that points most truly to the character of God and the reign of God. The third chapter in this Part notes that the Bible itself has a margin, namely the Apocrypha, and shows how reading these so-called marginal writings helps interpret the rest of the canon.

The chapters of Part Three deal with problems in the communal ecclesiology embraced by Mennonites. The first chapter of the section discusses the irony that Mennonites cannot make peace with themselves concerning the question of inclusion of people who identify as LGBTQ. Chapter 10 provides an important critique of the frequently referenced "servant leader" paradigm. Chapter 11 discusses what can be learned from the church's failures. Finally, Chapter 12 deals with the neglected idea of the development of the self within the churchly community.

Part Four displays learnings from readings of literature written from the margins. Chapter 13 uses a reading of stories out of chronological order to offer a suggestion on dealing with the debate about LGBTQ inclusion. Chapter 14 shows what the writings of women on the margins of the Mennonite and Mormon churches teach about their religious roots.

The chapters of Part Five deal with applications. Chapter 15 displays the potential contribution of international law to teaching for peace and nonviolence. The last chapter of Part Five uses empirical data to challenge the idea that just war logic actually results in less violence and war.

Part Six contains four chapters that address significant issues of in contemporary North American society, namely the pervasive faith in violence and the widespread, public distrust of certain findings of science. The four chapters display how individual teachers and practitioners can make an impact on these problems. In Chapter 17 we see how teachers and administrators can apply the practice of restorative justice in a public school system. The following chapter shows the role of forgiveness in the health of individuals and its potential role in restorative justice. Chapter 19 shows how to lead students to challenge "the pacifist's dilemma" and thus to begin to question the pervasive assumption in United States society about the efficacy of violence to solve problems.

One particular facet of the distrust of scientific findings occurs in the areas of evolution and determining the age of the earth. Chapter 20 gives suggestions for teaching skeptical students about the compatibility of evolution with the Bible.

The chapters of this book by no means say everything that could be said about Mennonite education and how it can development on into the twenty-first century. However, there is enough material here to show the potential for development in many areas. May the conversations flourish concerning the future of Mennonite education with the grain of the universe. When the character of God the Creator is revealed in the story of Jesus, any discipline may discover and work with that grain. The scope is limited only by the imagination of those who come to the discussion.

Notes

1. The exceptions to "virtually any subject matter" would be things related directly to the military—how to build weapons, how to lead assaults, killing in hand-to-hand combat, and so on.

2. J. Denny Weaver and Gerald Biesecker-Mast, eds., *Teaching Peace: Nonviolence and the Liberal Arts* (Lanham, Md.: Rowman & Littlefield Publishers, Inc., 2003).

3. The phrase "grain of the universe" is from John H[oward] Yoder, "Armaments and Eschatology," *Studies in Christian Ethics* 1 (1988): 58. But whereas Yoder wrote that "It is the people who bear crosses [that] are working with the grain of the universe," I have adapted the phrase to say that those who live within and are shaped by the narrative of Jesus are working with the grain of the universe.

Education

with the Grain of the Universe

CHAPTER ONE

THE STORY OF JESUS: "THE GRAIN OF THE UNIVERSE"

J. Denny Weaver

A Narrative Orientation

Mennonites are first of all Christians. I suggest that education for Mennonites should begin where Christian faith begins, namely with the story or narrative of Jesus' life. Since all Christians claim Jesus, this beginning point is intrinsically an ecumenical one. And as we will see, the fact that Jesus' identity came from a story is what sets the stage for wide-ranging Mennonite education that reflects that story.

The Earliest Version

The early church identified who Jesus was by telling his story.[1] Even though the Gospels come first in the New Testament, the earliest identifications of Jesus by narrative is in six statements or sermons in the book of Acts (2:14-36; 3:12-26; 4:8-12; 5:29-32; 10:34-43; 13:16-41). Here the apostles were explaining the authority by which they acted.[2] These six statements all used the same outline to tell the Jesus story.

Common to these statements were an initial statement about the fullness of God's time or quotes from the Old Testament or an allusion to Israel's history. This beginning intends to show that the event of Jesus was expected or was the continuation of an ongoing story. The six statements then all say that Jesus was killed by people in Jerusalem but God raised him. The speakers include themselves as witnesses to the events and conclude with response from the hearers. Sometimes included were details of Israel's history or mention of signs and wonders performed by Jesus, his burial, or references to the presence or work of the Spirit.

These statements display that the early church identified Jesus by recounting the narrative of his life. We can know that telling this story followed a set outline because Paul repeats the outline in 1 Corinthians 15, when he uses the story to argue for a general resurrection. Before he repeats the story, he says "I handed on to you as of first importance what I in turn had received" (15:3).

Meanwhile, the point to emphasize here is that the resurrection is the culmination of the story. Theologically, resurrection is why Christians proclaim Jesus to be Lord, the highest name for Jesus in the New Testament. Paul wrote to the Romans that Jesus was "declared Son of God with . . . power by resurrection from the dead" (1:4).

The Gospels were written some decades after the events recorded in the book of Acts. They expand the outline of Jesus' story found in Acts and used by Paul. If God is truly present in and revealed in Jesus, then the Gospels give some indication of what the reign of God looks like on earth, in Jesus' life.

Any summary of this narrative and selections from it are necessarily selective. The vignettes used here were chosen from the story of Jesus with a view to showing how the reign of God made visible on earth challenges injustices. These stories and the implications drawn from them can then serve as the beginning of a foundation for Mennonite education. Implications drawn in this chapter come rather directly from the story. In following Parts of the book, implications and applications are developed beyond the biblical text itself.

A Narrative Orientation: The Gospels

Jesus' Birth

What we know about the life of Jesus comes from the New Testament, primarily from the Gospels. The Gospels of Matthew and Luke each have a story about the birth of Jesus. Matthew's version contains the familiar story of the wise men who came to visit the baby born in Bethlehem, followed by two years in Egypt to escape the threat from King Herod. Luke's Gospel contains the well-known story of the visit by shepherds, and eight days later, the baby was circumcised and given the name Jesus. Mary and Joseph took him to Jerusalem for a dedication ceremony in the temple, and then they returned to Joseph's hometown of Nazareth.

Although popular paintings and manger scenes show both shepherds and wise men gathered around the manger, these accounts cannot be harmonized. But for present purposes, the two accounts agree on elements that are significant for the development of theology. Both stories locate the baby Jesus in the historical world at an identifiable time in the history of the Roman empire and Roman occupation of Palestine. Both stories situate his birth in Bethlehem and both place his growing up years in Nazareth. Both versions identify Jesus as a descendant of King David. These items all identify Jesus as one who belongs to the historical world that we live in. Most importantly, they identify Jesus as a Jew, a man who was heir to and a continuation of the story of Israel, the people whose beginning the Bible links to the patriarch Abraham.

Jesus Announces His Mission

In Luke's Gospel, Jesus began his public ministry with a rather dramatic reading and announcement in the synagogue at Nazareth (Luke 4:16-39). He read the section listed in our Bibles as the first one and a half verses of Isaiah 61:

> The Spirit of the Lord is upon me,
> > because he has anointed me
> > > to bring good news to the poor.
> He has sent me to proclaim release to the captives
> > and recovery of sight to the blind,
> > > to let the oppressed go free,
> to proclaim the year of the Lord's favor.

When Jesus had finished the reading, he announced, "Today this Scripture has been fulfilled in your hearing."

These words signal the character of the reign of God that Jesus proclaimed and embodied. Good news for the poor, releasing captives, healing the blind and freeing the oppressed, indicate that his mission had clear social and economic components, which would challenge the status quo of his society.

Where Jesus stopped reading from Isaiah also signaled something important. He broke off the reading just before Isaiah wrote of proclaiming "the day of vengeance of our God" (61:2b). I read Jesus' stopping place as an indication that the rejection of violence was an intrinsic characteristic of his career and thus of the reign of God.

A New Community

Jesus' message was that the reign of God had come. Jesus preached that message himself. And when he sent out his followers to preach, sometimes the twelve and another time seventy, their message was that the "kingdom of God has come near" (Luke 10:1-16; Luke 8:1; Matt. 9:35-10:15). We might say that he was creating a new community to carry on the mission of making the reign of God visible. In his teaching and in his person, Jesus was making the reign of God present to people. The vignettes in this chapter indicate the character of this new community. Wherever they are, followers of Jesus are the continuation of this community created by Jesus, and a continuation of Jesus' mission to witness to the reign and rule of God.

Healing and Forgiveness of Sins

The Gospels contain many stories of people that Jesus healed. Healing gives visibility to the restorative power of God's reign, including healing from sin. Along with healing, he also forgave sins. These healings inspired the common people, but raised opposition among the religious leaders. When Jesus forgave the sins of a paralyzed man whom he also healed, the scribes and Pharisees accused Jesus of blasphemy. Only God can forgive sins, they claimed (Luke 5:17-26). In actuality, Jesus was threatening the temple establishment, through which the priestly class made a lot of money from the sacrifices in the temple. If people could find forgiveness from Jesus without paying for a sacrifice in the temple, that threatened the sacrificial system itself, and its demise would cost the rulers a lot of money.

Chapters in Part Five to follow expand the discussion of forgiveness, punishment, and theology.

Restoring Life

The Gospels contain stories in which Jesus restored people to life who had died. One such account involved the only son of a widow, who was weeping. Jesus felt sorry for her, and raised the son (Luke 7:11-17). Another time a synagogue leader came and begged Jesus to come and heal his twelve-year-old daughter who was dying. She was dead by the time Jesus arrived, and bystanders laughed when Jesus said that she was sleeping. But he took her by the hand and said, "Child, get up." She got up, and he suggested that they feed her (Luke 8:40-56).

The stories of healing make an important point about the God revealed in Jesus. The God of Jesus does not kill and take life. God gives life and restores life. This restoration of life is one dimension of the nonviolence of God who is revealed in Jesus.

Interaction with Sabbath Laws[3]

Jesus healed in direct defiance of one interpretation of Sabbath law as practiced by the scribes and Pharisees. As told in Luke 6:6-11, on one such occasion, in the synagogue where he was teaching on the Sabbath was a man with a "withered hand." Since the condition was not life-threatening, some interpreters held that healing on the Sabbath would violate a provision in the legal code against unnecessary labor on that day. These scribes and Pharisees knew what Jesus might do and hoped to catch him in a violation.

Jesus knew their plan, and orchestrated a deliberate confrontation. He invited the man to stand by him where everyone could see what would transpire. Jesus asked those watching, "Is it lawful to do good or to do harm on the Sabbath, to save life or to destroy it?" Then he looked around at his audience, making eye contact to ensure that he had their attention. And with every eye on him, Jesus commanded the man, "Stretch our your hand." He did, and was healed, but the religious leaders were furious. However, the majority of people would probably have agreed with Jesus' view of healing on the Sabbath.

In another instance of Sabbath healing, when he cured a woman who had been bent over for eighteen years, he was charged by the president of the synagogue with violating the Sabbath. Jesus defended his action by saying that the woman deserved healing on the Sabbath from her eighteen-year-long bondage just as much as did the ox or donkey that were untied from the manger on the Sabbath and led away for water.

With that answer "his opponents were put to shame, and the entire crowd was rejoicing at all the wonderful things that he was doing" (Luke 13:17).

With his healing, Jesus was not rejecting Sabbath law or Judaism per se. In fact as a Jew he honored the Sabbath. Jesus defied one particular interpretation, but his view likely represented the Jewish majority. He was honoring the day as one of joy, healing, and restoration while simultaneously challenging an oppressive application.

Confronting Racism and Sexism

When Jesus interacted with with Samaritans and Gentiles, the challenge to racism of these actions is sometimes missed. His interactions with women also challenged aspects of the role of women in a patriarchal society.

John 4:1-39 tells of a time Jesus and his disciples traveled from Judea in the south to Galilee in the north of Palestine. He passed through Samaria. Since there was mutual antagonism between Jews and Samaritans, some Jews would have gone out of their way to travel north on the east side of the Jordan River. Thus the presence of Jesus and the disciples in Samaria was already a remarkable event. When they reached the village of Sychar, Jesus rested by the village well while the disciples went into town to buy food. Meanwhile, a village woman arrived at the well, and Jesus asked her for a drink.

Upon their return, the disciples were astonished that he was speaking with a woman. No reason is given for this surprise. Some commentators have linked it to Leviticus 15:19-24. This text declares a menstruating women ritually unclean along with anything that she has touched, which would include the drinking vessel. In any case, Jesus interacted with a Samaritan who was a woman, and he accepted a drink from her jar. While many levels of meaning can be developed from this story, the point to draw out here is that Jesus was willing to put himself in the position of a minority in Samaritan territory and to cross boundaries of race or ethnicity and gender.

Jesus' parable of the Good Samaritan (Luke 10:29-37) also contains a challenge to racism. The term *good Samaritan* has passed into our everyday language as merely a way to designate a helpful person who does more than is expected. But the parable has a more profound message. In the run-up to the parable, a lawyer had asked Jesus what he must do to be saved. And Jesus answered, "You shall love the Lord your God with all you heart, and with all your soul, and with all your strength, and with all your mind; and your neighbor as yourself." But then the lawyer tried to test Jesus and make himself look good by asking, "Who is my neighbor?"

In answer, Jesus told the story we call the Parable of the Good Samaritan. It was the Samaritan who aided the wounded man while the Levite and priest walked by on the other side of the road. We can only speculate on the basis for their actions. But to sense the impact made by the story, consider that the lawyer would be seeing himself as the wounded man. In light of the mutual antagonism between Jews and Samaritans, it would be a shock for the lawyer to acknowledge that those he assumed to be upstanding folks would pass by, while the Samaritan he looked down on or distrusted emerges as the good neighbor.

In terms of inclusion of all ethnicities, another story of particular interest concerns Jesus' interaction with a Gentile woman (Matt. 15:21-28; Mark 7:24-30). She is frequently identified by Mark's designation as a Syrophoenician woman. As a Gentile she may have been one of the wealthy minority foreigners living in territory occupied by the Romans. And like the Samaritans, she was outside the focus of the mission that Jesus gave the disciples. Jesus had gone north of Galilee into the area of Tyre and Sidon in Phoenecia, where he hoped to stay incognito. But the woman discovered where he was staying and pleaded for him to help her daughter, who was possessed by a demon.

Jesus' initial response was to declare, "I was sent only to the lost sheep of the house of Israel." In other words, Jesus' understanding of his mission did not include Gentiles, and he dismissed her plea. But she got down on her knees and begged. Jesus replied sharply, this time with an epithet: "It is not fair to take the children's bread and throw it to the dogs." Since dogs were scavengers and thus considered unclean, Jesus was rejecting her entreaty with what was arguably an insult. The woman was not deterred.

She countered, "Yes, Lord, yet even the dogs eat the crumbs that fall from the masters' table." Her retort led Jesus to change his mind, and on the basis of her great faith, he promised that her daughter would be healed. This story is the only account in the Gospels in which an interlocutor got the better of Jesus—and it was a woman and a Gentile. It is a story of another boundary that Jesus confronted and crossed.

As a Jew, Jesus was the bearer of the covenant between God and Israel. But with Jesus, it became clear that the God of Israel was the God of all peoples. Jesus was not a new beginning of God's people that left Israel behind. Rather, with Jesus, the covenant was expanded and Israel as God's people was reconstituted as a way of being that could include all peoples. It became Paul's mission to invite Gentiles into this covenant that now included all peoples. Linking Jesus to the covenant with Abraham means that the Jewish flesh of Jesus has universal implications; it welcomes all peoples into the people of God.

Economics

Jesus had several things to say about money. When he announced his mission, the reading included bringing "good news to the poor." Quoting from Isaiah shows Jesus' familiarity with the Old Testament, in which writings by the Prophets frequently condemn greed and exploitation.

Jesus' proclamation of "good news for the poor" certainly fits with these prophetic words.

It also needs to be stressed that Jesus (and the prophets) do not condemn wealth and the acquisition of wealth in and of themselves. What is condemned is acquiring riches by exploitative or dishonest means, and hoarding wealth for its own sake. Instead, Jesus taught that those who have wealth should be generous with it. When hosting a banquet, invite those who cannot repay (Luke 14:12-14). Lay up treasures not on earth but in heaven. (Matt. 6:19-21). In other words, one should not be identified by or bound by earthly possessions. Strive to live like the birds, who "neither sow nor reap, . . . and yet God feeds them" (Luke 12:24, 27-31).

Living generously, living without worrying about food, clothing, and possessions sounds irresponsible in the context of our twenty-first century world. The words about living without worry should probably be understood in the context of the common purse of Jesus and his disciples. We know about the common purse because Judas kept it and stole from it (John 12:6).

Having a common purse meant that Jesus and the disciples pooled their money and shared expenses equally. While no one had a personal account, it also meant that no individual was ever left stranded. This idea may have been in Jesus' mind when he told the rich young ruler,

"Sell your possessions, and give the money to the poor, and you will have treasure in heaven; then come, follow me" (Matt. 19:21). Given the idea of a common pursue, this was not a suggestion that the young man become destitute. It was rather an invitation to join the followers of Jesus who supported each other and lived loosely connected to earthly wealth and possession.

The account of Jesus' interaction with Zacchaeus illustrates the condemnation of ill-gotten wealth and poses an example of restoration (Luke 19:1-10). Zacchaeus is described as "a chief tax collector, and rich." This job description meant that he worked for the hated Roman occupiers. It also permitted graft, allowing Zacchaeus to skim money from tax payments into his own accounts. Even though he was an Israelite, the local population would have despised him.

Although we do not know the particulars of their interaction, it is clear that Zacchaeus's attitude toward wealth changed through his encounter with Jesus. He announced that he would give half his wealth to the poor. And since he promised to restore money gained through fraud, most certainly he had engaged in dishonest transactions. In terms of repaying money with interest, he was practicing what today would be called "restorative justice" (more on restorative justice in a section below). When Jesus saw Zacchaeus's restoration of money gained dishonestly, he declared, "Today salvation has come to this house, since he [Zacchaeus] is also a son of Abraham."

Nonviolence

Jesus' well-known Sermon on the Mount in Matthew 5–7 spells out what it means to live out the reign of God. He spoke of blessings from God for troubled hearts, the poor in spirit, those who mourn, the meek who lack the wherewithal to make a big impact on society, the merciful, and the peacemakers. Much of the Sermon on the Mount deals with loyalty—the difference between living according to common expectations and loyalty to or serving the reign of God—statements about being faithful in marriage, avoiding divorce, not putting one's trust in worldly riches, seeking the reign of God, treating others as one would like to be treated, and much more.

One of the most striking sections of the Sermon on the Mount concerns Jesus' statements about not retaliating. He told his listeners not to reply to an evil deed with an equal evil, not to mirror evil. Thus "If anyone strikes you on the right cheek, turn the other also; and if anyone wants to sue you and take your coat, give your cloak as well; and if anyone forces you to go one mile, go also the second mile" (Matt. 5:39-42). These words follow the injunction, "Do not resist an evil doer" (5:39), and have been interpreted as Jesus' instruction to remain passive and doing nothing in the face of evil or to go even farther in the direction commanded by the aggressor. But they actually carry a quite different meaning.

Notice that Matthew talked about being struck on the right cheek. In that culture, the left hand was the unclean hand and would not be used in public. Thus the only blow that could touch the right cheek would be a back-handed slap by the aggressor. Such a slap is not designed to injure but to insult. It would come from a higher-status person insulting a lower-status person—master over slave, husband over wife, parent over child, Roman over Jew—reminding the one slapped of his or her inferior social standing.

Retaliation in this instance would seemingly justify additional violence on the part of the aggressor. But Jesus suggests that when insulted in this way, the person insulted should take charge of the situation by turning the left cheek toward the aggressor. This move would refuse the insult and invite another hit, this time by a closed fist, which would be a mark of equality.

If the aggressor does strike the target, the aggressor has lost the encounter by treating the lesser status person as an equal. But doing nothing is also a loss of face for the aggressor, since the person slapped has taken the initiative by refusing the insult. In essence, turning the other cheek is an instance of active nonviolence, an assertion of full humanity by a supposedly lesser person but performed in a way that has the potential to change a situation and avoid a violent follow up.

The setting for the statement about giving cloak along with coat—under garment with outer garment—is the debtors court. Common in Jesus' day was the poor tenant farmer who owed debts impossible to pay to a rich and exploitative landowner. The law allowed the debt holder to require something of value as collateral for the loan. For a poor person, the collateral might well be his only possession of value, namely the coat on his back that he slept in. However, the law also had a stipulation that the poor person could claim it again at night for sleeping, with the knowledge that it would be surrendered again the next morning if repayment was not possible. (See Exod. 22:25-27, Deut. 24:10-13.) Jesus suggests that when the coat is demanded for collateral, the debtor should strip off his underwear as well, hand both to the debt holder, and then leave the court to parade naked for the rest of the day. In a society where the shame of nakedness fell on the one who caused it, this act would expose the exploitative nature of the system. Again, it is a nonviolent action to expose a situation that needed changing and another instance of Jesus' concern for the poor.

Going the second mile concerned the Roman military occupiers of Palestine. Military regulations permitted a soldier to commandeer a civilian at any time and require him to carry the soldier's sixty- or even eighty-pound pack for one mile. However, to minimize the resentment of the locals for this forced labor on behalf of the hated occupiers, military regulations also limited the distance for any one requisitioned civilian to one mile. The civilian who followed Jesus' suggestion would actually put the soldier in violation of his own regulations. Since violators risked punishment, one can even imagine the tables turned entirely, with the solder begging the civilian to put down the pack before the solder got in trouble.

Immediately following these three examples in the Sermon on the Mount of ways to respond to aggression, Jesus said "Love your enemies" (Matt. 5:44). Here "love" is not a term of liking and affection. It is rather another version of the examples of ways to respond without retaliating. Jesus is telling his followers that when confronted with an enemy, they should act in such a way as to change the situation. Do something to move the situation away from a conflict and toward a resolution which preserves the humanity of the aggressor as well as the one offended.

The three examples just noted are such actions. Jesus' injunction about loving enemies is a reminder that such actions are not to be done out of an attitude of vengeance or hostility but with a view to moving the encounter to one that has a resolution—hitter may see slapped person as human, debt holder sees poor person as individual in need, soldier learns that locals are human beings.

These creative ways of responding to aggression and injustice are intrinsic to Jesus' proclamation of the reign of God. They demonstrate that followers of Jesus do not confront evil with more evil, violence with retaliatory violence but rather seek to change the situation in a way that keeps open the possibility of reconciliation. These injunctions are of a piece with healing on the Sabbath, interacting with Samaritans and women, and eventually cleansing of the temple.

Teachings of Jesus are not the only place the idea appears of not responding to evil with the same kind of evil. Paul follows Jesus' line when he writes, "Do not repay anyone evil for evil. . . . If our enemies are hungry, feed them; if they are thirsty, give them to drink; . . . Do not be overcome by evil, but overcome evil with good" (Rom. 12:17, 20, 21).

Paul repeats the idea in 1 Thessalonians 5:15: "See that none of you repays evil for evil, but always seek to do good to one another and to all." The author of 1 Peter follows suit: "Do not repay evil for evil or abuse for abuse; but, on the contrary, repay with a blessing" (3:9).

These sayings indicate that throughout the New Testament there is an ongoing appreciation of the idea of refusing to respond to evil and violence with more of the same, and instead to act in a way that changes the situation or defuses the confrontation. It is important to see that the rejection of violence is a theme throughout the New Testament.

It is equally important to stress that the belief that the use of violence is rejected in the reign of God does not dependent solely on the authority of particular biblical texts. Although these texts are important, the most authoritative source to the character of the reign of God is the life of Jesus. That life reveals the reign of God. That life makes quite clear that violence has no place in the reign of God. To this point, actions in the life of Jesus that give visibility to the way in which the nonviolent reign of God is visible in the world include healing on the Sabbath in defiance of the purity code, other Sabbath violations, his interactions with Samaritans and others considered unclean, and his pronouncing of forgiveness when the Pharisees consider that blasphemy. Additional dimensions of his teaching and nonviolent life follow.

The Temple Cleansing

Perhaps Jesus' most dramatic act of confrontation of the priestly system was what has been called the cleansing of the temple. Although this story has been claimed in support of violence, it is actually a dramatic example of nonviolent action.

Jesus had traveled to Jerusalem with his disciples at the time of the Passover. He entered the temple, where animals and pigeons were on sale for sacrifices. He overturned the tables of the money changers and the sales people and chased out the animals. John's account says that Jesus used a "whip of cords" (2:15). Combining phrases from Isaiah 56:7 and Jeremiah 7:11, Luke has Jesus say, "My house shall be a house of prayer, but you have made it a den of robbers" (Luke 19:46).

When Jesus forgave sins, there would be no need to offer sacrifices in the temple as the basis of forgiveness. His demonstration in the temple was thus an acting out of the fact that temple sacrifices were not necessary to receive God's forgiveness. Not surprisingly, such an act was perceived as a major threat by the priestly establishment and their allies, and they started to develop a plot to have Jesus killed.

Some commentators have used this account, particularly the mention of the whip, to justify violence and revolution. It is in fact nothing of the sort. Recall that healing on the Sabbath was returning the day to its proper intention of healing and restoration. Now, with this action, Jesus was reasserting the rightful purpose of the temple. The whip is not used to injure; a cracking whip makes noise, and is used to herd animals in the desired direction—in this case, out of the temple.

Confrontational Teaching

Following the demonstrative act of temple cleansing, Jesus went to the temple daily to teach. The religious leaders were looking for a way to kill him, but for a time his support among the people protected him. Because the crowds were hanging on his every word, the leaders feared a riot and were afraid to act (Luke 19:47-48, Mark 11:18).

This time of teaching contains some of Jesus' most well-known sayings and sharpest confrontations of the religious leadership. When shown a coin with Caesar's image on it and asked whether it was lawful to pay taxes to Caesar, Jesus said, "Render to Caesar the things that are Caesar's and to God the things that are God's" (Luke 20:25). They had hoped to trick Jesus into a dangerous admission, but his answer was not one with which they could find fault.

A lawyer from among the Pharisees asked Jesus which commandment was the greatest. Jesus' answer quoted from Deuteronomy 6.5 and Leviticus 19:18.

> You shall love the Lord your God with all your heart, and with all your soul, and with all your mind. This is the great and first commandment. And a second is like it. You shall love your neighbor as yourself.

On these two commands depend all the law and the prophets. (Matt. 22:36-38)

The scribes and Pharisees provide hard requirements of the law, Jesus said, but do not follow those laws themselves. Proclaiming "woe" on the scribes and Pharisees, he called them hypocrites and said that they go to great lengths to make a proselyte, but "then you make him twice as much a child of hell as yourselves." They make themselves appear very pious by tithing small things, such as herbs from the garden, but neglect more important parts of the law, such as "justice and mercy and faith." In their teaching of the law, they are like "Blind guides! You strain out a gnat but swallow a camel!" This duplicity makes them like tombs, "whitewashed" on the outside to look beautiful, "but inside they are full of the bones of the dead and of all kinds of filth."

Jesus has very sharp words about their references to the earlier prophets, who were persecuted. Although the scribes and Pharisees claimed that they would not have shed the blood of the prophets, Jesus accuses them of doing exactly that in their own time. "You snakes, you brood of vipers! How can you escape being sentenced to hell?" Since such behavior invites retribution, Jesus laments the fate of the city. "O Jerusalem, Jerusalem, killing the prophets and stoning those who are sent to you. How often would I have gathered your children together as a hen gathers her brood under her wings, and you would not!" (quotes from Matt. 23).

This account of Jesus' actions and his confrontational teaching makes clear that the reign of God that Jesus represented was different from the society in which he lived. Stated differently, the reign of God challenged injustices in Jesus' world; the reign of God posed an alternative to the way things were. In a context that prevented doing good on the Sabbath, Jesus returned the Sabbath to a day of healing and restoration. In a society where rules discriminated against ethnic minorities and identified women as second class people, Jesus raised the status of women and racial and ethnic minorities.

This selection of stories and sayings identifies Jesus as one whose life made the reign of God visible, and have evident implications for the way Christians can follow in the path of Jesus today. His death also says something about the character of his mission.

Jesus' Death

The way that Jesus faced his death makes visible the nonviolent character of the reign of God. The cleansing of the temple precipitated the plot that led to his death. Meanwhile, Jesus arranged to celebrate a Passover supper with his disciples. He knew that he did not have much longer to live. Judas left the supper to betray him (John 13:26-30).

At this meal, Jesus performed a ceremony with the disciples using bread and wine. He told them that as often as they were eating together, they should use this ceremony to remember him. Christians still follow the practice of taking bread and wine together to remember Jesus, his death and his resurrection.

From this supper, Jesus went out to pray in the Garden of Gethsemane. It was here that Jesus was arrested. Judas came out at the head of a mob inspired by the religious leadership, and perhaps including Roman soldiers (Matt. 47; John 18:3). Although Jesus had been teaching daily in the temple, this mob did not recognize him. Judas had arranged to identify him by giving Jesus a kiss.

This arrest provoked one of the disciples, identified in the gospel of John as Peter (18:10), who drew his sword to defend Jesus. He flailed away and cut off the ear of the high priest's slave. But Jesus healed the man's ear and explained to Peter that violence was not the way of the reign of God. "Put your sword back into its place; for all who take the sword will perish by the sword. Do you think that I cannot appeal to my Father, and he will at once send me more than twelve legions of angels?"

For emphasis, Jesus sarcastically scolded the crowd. "Have you come out with swords and clubs to arrest me as though I were a bandit? Day after day I sat in the temple teaching, and you did not arrest me." If you really understood me, Jesus means to say, you would know that you would not need weapons to arrest me, for violence is not my way. Besides you could easily have arrested me in the temple.

Jesus' principled refusal to use violence becomes most clear during his trial appearance before Pilate. Pilate asked Jesus if he was a king, and Jesus turned the question back on him, asking whether Pilate was asking on his own, or had others told him. Pilate said that he was not a Jew, meaning that he had no reason to answer. Then Pilate asked why Jesus' own countrymen condemned him. Jesus replied, "My kingdom is not from this world. If my kingdom were from this world, my followers would be fighting to keep me from being handed over to the Jews. But as it is, my kingdom is not from here" (John 18:36). The values and practices of the kingdom Jesus represented were different from the values and practices of Pilate's kingdom. Therefore Jesus' followers did not use violence in an attempt to protect him.

Pilate proclaimed that he found no reason to condemn Jesus. He offered the religious leaders and the mob a choice of releasing Jesus or Barabbas. The chief priests and other leaders persuaded the crowd to call for Barabbas. As the mob howled for the death of Jesus, Pilate washed his hands as a public sign that he found Jesus innocent. Nonetheless, Pilate handed Jesus over to be crucified.

Jesus was beaten and otherwise tortured and taken outside the city to a place called Golgotha. Here he was crucified, that is, nailed to a cross, which resulted in a long and painful death. For the Romans, this kind of death served to intimidate the population about the danger of rebellion against the occupation.

Joseph from Arimathea, a wealthy disciple of Jesus, collected his body, wrapped it in a shroud and laid the body in a new tomb that he had prepared for himself. A great stone was placed over the entrance to the tomb. Mary Magdalene and Jesus' mother Mary watched to identify the location of the tomb and prepared spices to use in anointing the body.

Two additional observations are important concerning the description of Jesus' death. First, notice that the account of Jesus' death has nothing in it about God needing the death of Jesus or sending Jesus to die as some kind of payment for salvation or satisfying a divine need. Rather than being needed by God, the killing of Jesus is entirely the work of forces that opposed the reign of God.

The second observation has immediate importance. The story of Jesus' death makes very clear that in the reign of God, violence is not used. The kingdom Jesus represented is a nonviolent kingdom.

Jesus' Resurrection

The accounts of the resurrection in the four Gospels differ from each other in their details. However, all Gospels agree that Jesus was raised from the dead. Resurrection is why Christians proclaim Jesus as Lord, the highest title for him in the New Testament. Lord implies deity. Resurrection means that God was present in the life of Jesus. In classic theological language, this is a statement of the deity of Jesus, or an assertion that God was present in the flesh. The resurrection of Jesus means that God was present in the life of Jesus.

That God was present in the life of Jesus means that the reign of God has already become present. Stated differently, God is working in the world even now. The resurrection is an invitation to join in that work. People who accept the invitation and choose to live in the life of Jesus are extending his mission in the world. In so doing they are joining in what God is doing in the world, and are giving visibility to the presence of the reign of God today. The life and teaching of Jesus witness to the presence of the reign of God, and to what God is doing even now in the world. Living today as a disciple of Jesus extends his mission.

Living in the story of Jesus, the church witnesses to the watching world about the presence and the character of the reign of God. However, alongside that witness to the world, the story of Jesus shines light within the church as well. The church clearly needs to submit itself and its practices to this witness. In particular I am thinking of the two issues noted in the Introduction—the church's struggle to deal with issues of unequal power dynamics and sexual abuse by men in leadership and authority positions, and the inability to resolve the conflicts around LGBT issues. Despite the respect for women displayed in the story of Jesus, the church has at times been more concerned to protect its image or important leaders than to deal with instances of sexual abuse.[4]

In the case of persons who identify as LGBT, neither has the church followed Jesus' practice of including people marginalized and discriminated against. In addition, the narrative of Jesus challenges the church's difficulty in recognizing issues of acculturation and assimilation into a violent culture, and the lack of recognition of its participation in the white privilege of American society. Chapters throughout this book touch on these issues, with major treatments in chapters by Drew Hart, Felipe Hinojosa, Hannah Heinzekehr, Malinda Berry, and Gerald Mast.

An Open-Ended Orientation

The first Christians did not identify or define Jesus in terms of timeless truths to be memorized and defended unendingly. Rather, they identified Jesus by telling his story. A story and its meaning are open-ended. Above we observed an instance of this open-endedness already in the New Testament, when Paul derived belief in a general resurrection from the story (1 Cor. 15). In Part One to follow, we will observe how New Testament writers used new language and images to express the significance of Jesus.

Further, as was clear from its recitation, telling the story has ethical implications for Christians, which puts on display the integral relationship of Christian theology and ethics. Today, Jesus is still identified by that story. And in our theologizing and drawing ethical implications in and for our context, we are engaging in the same processes as did the New Testament writers—asking what the story means and thinking about how to explain its meaning within our worldview so that it addresses issues in our world. This task is clearly open ended, just as it was for the first Christians. If Jesus is truly of God, as Christian faith professes, then there is no discipline and no area of knowledge within God's creation that is off limits for discussion as an outgrowth of understanding the meaning of Jesus for today.

Our theologizing and drawing meaning from the story of Jesus is open ended in another way as well. In these pages I have written of the narrative of Jesus. In fact, however, we have four narratives, namely the four Gospels, and they differ in their details and in the way they present Jesus' parables. Further, as our context changes, new questions arise which compel us to read these narratives again with different eyes. Thus even as we appeal to the story of Jesus for insight into our lives as followers of Jesus, we are also engaged continually in understanding the shape of the narrative itself. Although we always have a source to which to return, namely the Gospels, our task of asking what the narrative says and what it means and how to apply it is always open ended.

Mennonite education is—or at least should be—education that draws on this open-ended story of Jesus to give visibility to the way that the reign of God works in the world across a wide range of issues. That assertion is not one to establish a narrow, doctrinally based education. It is rather a statement about the stance from which Mennonite education can and should engage the surrounding society and draw implications from the story of Jesus for many issues that confront our church and our world. My proposal for education is a far-reaching approach that brings an additional layer of meaning to whatever it is that Mennonite schools teach, while simultaneously opening the door to cooperation with and learning from a wide range of fellow travelers beyond Mennonites. The remainder of this book explores dimensions of these claims.

In Several Stories

This story of Jesus' birth, life, death, and resurrection is the story that I suggest should orient Mennonite education. This story engages conversation with a number of other stories. One of these is the Anabaptist story, the historical movement in the sixteenth-century Reformation that gave birth to Mennonites. The several streams of Anabaptism had in common a rejection of the state or established church and the intent to start a new church not beholden to political authorities. In different ways, the New Testament was claimed as the authoritative source for this church. The idea was a return to the narrative of Jesus for continual renewal.

Although not all Anabaptists were pacifists, the idea of Jesus as norm made rejection of the sword a central element of debate, and eventually the pacifist side of this debate prevailed, and Anabaptism became known as a pacifist movement.[5] Mennonites as a peace church are heirs to this version of Anabaptism, as are also the Brethren, the Amish, and the Hutterites. This view of Anabaptism describes a historical stream that continues the story of a nonviolent Jesus that we find in the New Testament. Mennonite education fits within the story of Anabaptism and could be called Anabaptist education.

Locating Mennonite education in the story of Jesus' birth, life, death, and resurrection aligns that education with what God is doing in the world. But other groups also claim to work with the reign of God. Orienting Mennonite education by this story thus aligns Mennonite education in several directions, or situates Mennonites simultaneously in conversations with other Christian groups. Anchoring Mennonite education in Jesus' story means that Mennonite education is Christian education. Since all Christians profess faith in Jesus, to align education with the story of Jesus is intrinsically an ecumenical standpoint. Orienting education around Jesus thus allows Mennonites to engage with potentially every Christian tradition.

Locating Mennonite education in the story of Jesus brings forth a critique of much of what transpires in North American society, particularly in the United States. Beyond the obvious critique of continual war, this society features a pervasive individualism, economic policies that increasingly favor the wealthy at the expense of the poor and middle class, and a persistent racism that lurks below the surface. The sketch of Jesus' life just presented contains elements that challenge all of these policies and practices. With awareness of these issues, it is clear that Mennonite education should be education from the margin of American society.

As I have interpreted the narrative of Jesus, the story makes clear Jesus' rejection of the sword. I also assume that Jesus' rejection of the sword, and by extension the rejection of violence, is applicable for Christians today. Thus orienting education in the story of Jesus is education for Mennonites as a peace church. The peace church exists as a definite minority within the broad Christian tradition. Thus alongside being marginal in American society generally, Mennonite education occupies a minority theological perspective as well, a marginal perspective within the wide expanse of Christian traditions.

This position on the margin is important. At least it brings something important into view. Written by members of a religious minority, it should be expected that Mennonite theology would differ at crucial points from mainstream theology, particularly in its adherence to a rejection of violence linked to the story of Jesus. At this juncture, the critique from the margin says something both about the dominant view *and* identifies what is distinct about Mennonites. It thus ought not surprise if the way that Mennonite-oriented, peace-church educators approach and practice the various disciplines of the academic curriculum differs from the conventional approach to these disciplines.

With awareness of these issues both societal and theological, it is clear that Mennonite education should be education from the margin of American society. And that marginal orientation should give Mennonites affinity with other groups that have been marginalized by this society. Obvious examples are African-Americans, Latino and Latina Americans, and the descendants of the many indigenous and first nations peoples or natives who inhabited the continent before the arrival of Europeans. Each of these groups has both social and theological critiques that have potential parallels with Mennonite challenges to the majority society and theological traditions. The white majority of Mennonites have barely begun to recognize or embrace these affinities. In Chapter 3 to follow, Drew Hart points to the importance of this embrace.

But a marginal perspective cuts another way with Mennonites as well. For African-American and Latino/a Mennonites, the largely white Mennonite church has been the majority, with African-Americans and Latinos and Latinas on the margin of the Mennonite experience. And from the perspective of these marginal groups, the white Mennonite church looks a lot like the majority white United States society. It looks quite different than it does from inside as told in the traditional articulations of Mennonite history.[6] The majority Mennonite church is only on the verge of learning from these marginal perspectives and is just now slowly beginning to learn that its history is told more truly, as Felipe Hinojosa says in a following chapter, from the outside in rather than from the inside out. That is, Mennonite history and Mennonite theology is more truthful when the so-called marginal views are an equal and integral part of the story.

There is yet one more way to describe education oriented by the life of Jesus as education that engages the world.

Grain of the Universe

In language borrowed from the King James Bible, Christians have long professed that "God was in Christ" (2 Cor. 5:19). In other words, Jesus reveals God, which means that the life of Jesus puts on display the character of God and of the rule of God. To know what God and the reign of God are like, look at Jesus. John Howard Yoder had this in mind when he wrote that those who live in the life of Jesus who rejected violence are aligned with "the grain of the universe."[7] The universe created by God would reflect the character of the God revealed in the narrative of Jesus.

If the character of the reign of God is in the grain of the universe, that grain can be discovered outside of the visible Christian church. In that case, traces of it may be found in the actions of people other than Christians, or in practices not associated with the Christian religion per se. Upon reflection, this awareness ought not surprise. We should have no trouble believing that the reign of God is bigger and wider than the visible church. To give it a theological dimension, we can say that this working with the grain of the universe outside of the established church is the working of or the presence of the Holy Spirit in the world.

Throughout this book, these attributes are discussed for a number of areas in the academic curriculum. The first major section of the book will point to the development of theology from these perspectives and in the process point to the inseparable relationship of theology and ethics.

But before engaging the various themes and disciplines, I want to respond to three objections sometimes raised against the outlook displayed in this book.

Some Disclaimers

Separating Theology from Ethics

In other writings I have developed parts of the outlook summarized thus far, and that work has drawn some challenges. Here I respond to three such challenges.[8]

It has been claimed that identifying practices that align with the grain of the universe beyond the church visible in the wider world is separating ethics from theology, which results in ethics for Christians defined apart from the reign of God. In other words, the claim is that being able to identify practices that occur without explicit theological validation is really accepting and developing a secular ethic, and that developing tactical alliances with groups who are not Christians is practicing a secular ethic. These assertions misunderstand.

First, we need to recognize that God or the Holy Spirit is bigger than the organized church or organized Christian religion. Finding practices that work with the grain of the universe outside of Christian faith is a recognition that God's work is not limited to what Christians and the visible church can accomplish. Finding such practices entails observing where else God may be active, and then supporting that action.

Further, recognizing such practices in the wider world is not establishing a secular ethic. To claim that these visible practices reflect the reign of God means first knowing and identifying the reign of God. Thus discovering such practices is to recognize the ultimate source of what happens. It is a recognition that Jesus reveals the character of God, and a claim that ultimate validation comes from the story of Jesus, whether or not practitioners recognize it.

Reducing Theology to Ethics

A related claim is that the approach of this chapter reduces theology to right practice or ethics. In other words, it is a claim that theology has become unimportant, and that it is right behavior, apart from theology, that determines Christian identity.

Again, I reject that accusation. For one point, see my books on atonement and the character of God.[9] These volumes spend several hundred pages developing theological issues and advocating for a theology that reflects the reign of God.

More importantly, it is possible to say that the accusation has half the truth in it. In my understanding, ethics and theology are inseparable, and they each have the same beginning point. To ask who Jesus is requires telling his story, as did the early church. Theology develops when we draw meaning from or explain implications of that story further. But Christians also ask, How should we live as Christians? And again, the answer is to tell the story of Jesus. How Christians should live is derived from that story, as Christians ask how to continue it in the world today. Theology and ethics are two sides of the same proverbial coin. Ethics is the lived version of the story of Jesus that is also the beginning point of the development of theology.

In other words, theology and ethics are inseparable. In my approach, one does not exist apart from the other. To think that they are separable already assumes that theology and ethics are separable. And that is the case with the classic statements from Nicea and Chalcedon, which define Jesus as "one substance with the Father," and as "truly God and truly man." To make these conciliar declarations the foundational, unquestioned givens of who Jesus is, as the accusation apparently does, is already to posit a theological foundation that has indeed separated theology from ethics. That separation is not possible in the approach sketched above.

Reducing Theology to Nonviolence

A parallel claim is that the approach here is actually reducing theology to nonviolence. To this charge I would simply point to the previous sections of this chapter. In recounting the narrative of Jesus there was discussion of economics and racism and oppression of women and support for poor people and forgiveness as well as discussion of rejection of the sword and acting to return good for evil to break a cycle of violence. That is certainly not a description of theology and ethics reduced to nonviolence.

On the other hand, the wider discussion does concern nonviolence, but in a much different sense from the accusation. Glen Stassen and Michael Westmoreland-White define violence as "destruction to a victim by means that overpower the victim's consent."[10] This definition obviously covers the direct violence of guns and bombs. But it also includes the harm done to people by racism and by keeping women in subservient roles. It would include the harm done by criminal justice practices that focus on people of color[11] and tax policies and business practices that funnel wealth to the already wealthy and keep poor people poor. It includes the harm done to people by poverty. It would include the harm done by abusive language that belittles a child, or by the perpetuation of derogatory racial stereotypes. With this definition in mind, one can say that the focus of the reign of God is opposing violence, but violence now defined to cover the entire spectrum of ways that people are harmed by practices in society.

Against this definition of violence, nonviolence then becomes "peacemaking" that includes any nonviolent practice that opposes violent practices. Peacemaking can be understood as nonviolent struggle or nonviolent action. It can involve anything from acts of verbal persuasion to action in the court system to affirmative action in hiring to marches and boycotts and protests in the streets. This peacemaking can include active confrontation and challenge to injustice and violence, and it can include the witness of a nonviolent life in hostile environments.[12] The practices of nonviolent action are limited only by the imagination of practitioners who seek to discover ways to confront the situation at hand.[13]

A related charge is that the approach of this chapter considers nonviolence to be an abstract category defined apart from Jesus and then read back into his story. The discussion here refutes this charge as well. This chapter assumes that we read the story of Jesus and then observe that he rejected both direct and structural forms of violence. That is, he confronted and challenged practices of racism, the subservient status of women, and economic exploitation and disparity—all examples of the structural violence included in the definition of Stassen and Westmoreland-White. These challenges are in addition to the fact that neither Jesus nor his disciples started a violent revolution, and his conduct at his arrest, trial and crucifixion reflect a principled refusal to resort to the sword.

This challenge of structural violence and the refusal to use direct violence are intrinsic to his story. To describe Jesus as leading a nonviolent life is to describe the way he lived and died. And since God is revealed in

Jesus, it is apparent that nonviolence characterizes God and the reign of God and God's means of acting in the world. And then, with that idea in mind, we see evidence of it in our world. Thus rejecting violence, loving enemies, returning good for evil, challenge structural injustice and economic exploitation and racism and discrimination against women and much more are the best ways to live in God's universe. Those who live out pieces of this outlook without reference to Jesus are nonetheless sensing the grain of the universe created by the God who is revealed in Jesus.

Now to the discussion of theology and history for Mennonite education.

Notes

1. Parts of the description of the story of Jesus in this chapter are drawn from material used in a different format in J. Denny Weaver, *God Without Violence: Following a Nonviolent God in a Violent World* (Eugene, Ore.: Cascade Books, 2016).

2. The analysis of these texts follows John Howard Yoder, *Preface to Theology: Christology and Theological Method*, intro. Stanley Hauerwas and Alex Sider (Grand Rapids, Mich.: Brazos Press, 2002), 53-59.

3. This section on Jesus and the Sabbath law and the next section on Jesus and Samaritans and women are written with reference to Amy-Jill Levine, *The Misunderstood Jew: The Church and the Scandal of the Jewish Jesus* (New York: HarperOne, 2006).

4. Although his case is certainly not the only instance of protecting a powerful figure, the story of John Howard Yoder is the most obvious example. For details, see Rachel Waltner Goossen, "'Defanging the Beast': Mennonite Responses to John Howard Yoder's Sexual Abuse," *The Mennonite Quarterly Review* 89, no. 1 (Jan. 2015): 7-80. Yoder's case requires particular comment in the context of this book. As indicated in the previous note, the methodology in this chapter of identifying the outline of the narrative of Jesus in Acts and then seeing it expanded by the Gospels, with Paul and other New Testament writers developing theology from that narrative, is methodology learned from John Howard Yoder.

The methodology is in his class lectures, later published as *Preface to Theology*, but I first heard it when I took courses from Yoder in 1965 and 1969 at what is now Anabaptist Mennonite Biblical Seminary. Any methodology can be applied falsely, and no methodology alone can prevent corruption or misuse. The fact that Yoder could use this methodology in an attempt to justify his sexual predation does not in itself discredit the methodology.

Further, the synthesis of the narrative and its application are my own, and my development of the narrative into an atonement image (see my *The Nonviolent Atone-*

ment) and my use of it to argue for the nonviolence of God (see my *The Nonviolent God*) or to deal with violence in the Old Testament (see Chapter 7 of this volume) are beyond or depart from any use Yoder made of the narrative of Jesus. Thus with deeply saddened awareness of the misuse Yoder made of this methodology, I continue to work out of an orientation that I began learning and have been extending for more than forty years. As a guard against misuse of theology or theological methodology, I suggest that theology should always be done transparently, in public, and with a willingness to be corrected.

5. For a book length interpretation of this understanding of Anabaptism, see Gerald J. Mast and J. Denny Weaver, *Defenseless Christianity: Anabaptism for a Nonviolent Church*, foreword by Greg Boyd (Telford, Pa.: Cascadia Publishing House; copublished with Herald Press, 2009).

6. An example of Mennonite history from "inside" is the four-volume series The Mennonite Experience in America, published between 1985 and 1996. The chapter by Felipe Hinojosa in Part One processes this critique.

7. John H[oward] Yoder, "Armaments and Eschatology," *Studies in Christian Ethics* 1 (1988): 58.

8. A recent statement containing the challenges dealt with here is Paul Martens, "How Mennonite Theology Became Superfluous in Three Easy Steps: Bender, Yoder, Weaver," *Journal of Mennonite Studies* 33 (2015): 149-166. Martens' article can represent all such challenges described here.

9. J. Denny Weaver, *The Nonviolent Atonement*, 2nd ed., greatly rev. and expanded (Grand Rapids: William B. Eerdmans Publishing Co., 2011); J. Denny Weaver, *The Nonviolent God* (Grand Rapids, Mich.: William B. Eerdmans Publishing Co., 2013).

10. Glen H. Stassen and Michael L. Westmoreland-White, "Defining Violence and Nonviolence," in *Teaching Peace: Nonviolence and the Liberal Arts*, ed. J. Denny Weaver and Gerald Biesecker-Mast (Lanham, Md.: Rowman & Littlefield Publishers, Inc., 2003), 18.

11. For two recent statements that present indisputable evidence of institutionalized racism in the criminal justice system and police practices, see Michelle Alexander, *The New Jim Crow: Mass Incarceration in the Age of Colorblindness*, rev. ed., foreword by Cornel West (New York: The New Press, 2012); and Charles R. Epp, Steven Maynard-Moody, and Donald Haider Markel, *Pulled Over: How Police Stops Define Race and Citizenship* (Chicago: The University of Chicago Press, 2014). The report on the Baltimore police department following the death of Freddie Grey is further confirmation of these findings. See Richard A. Oppel Jr., Sheryl Gay Stolberg, and Matt Apuzzo, "U.S. to Criticize Baltimore Police Over Racial Bias," *The New York Times*, 10 August 2016, A1, A13; Timothy Williams and Joseph Goldstein, "Censure of Baltimore Revives Zero-Tolerance Policing Doubt," *The New York Times*, 11 August 2016, A1, A114.

12. Elsewhere this contrast between active confrontation and quiet witness by a lifestyle is called separation of "antagonism" and separation of "complementarity." In order for a challenge or witness to be possible, there must be some sense of separa-

tion or difference between the peace church and the social order. Whether there is "antagonism" or "complementariness" depends on context. In tolerant United States with its increasingly militarized society and silent but real racism, nonviolent confrontation often seems appropriate. In a context hostile to Christians or to the church, the key to survival might well be a stance of defenseless witness that does not pose an overt threat to the social order. For a more extended discussion, see Mast and Weaver, *Defenseless Christianity*, 57-60, 81-84.

13. For extensive lists of nonviolent actions, see Gene Sharp, *Waging Nonviolent Struggle: 20th Century Practice and 21st Century Potential* (N.p.: Porter Sargent Publishers, Inc., 2005) and Gene Sharp, *The Methods of Nonviolent Action*, The Politics of Nonviolent Action, vol. 2 (Boston: Porter Sargent Publishing, 1973).

Part One
Theology and Ethics

Part One: Theology and Ethics

In Chapter 1 we observed that the early church identified Jesus by telling the story of his life, death and resurrection. The Gospels expanded on that story. Using materials from the Gospels, I sketched that story. It displayed how Jesus confronted injustice and witnessed to the reign of God. In the process, implications for Christians today were drawn from the story. There was challenge to racism and to suppression of women, concern for poor people, teaching on ways that persons without power can respond to violence and provocation, examples of the practice of nonviolent action, forgiveness, and more. These various implications fall into the general category of ethics. The emergence of these implications from the story makes it virtually self evident that identifying Jesus by telling his story has ethical implications. Stated differently, when we tell the story, ethical guidance emerges.

Theology also develops from this story. Examples of emerging theology appear already in the New Testament. One instance was Paul's use of the outline of the narrative of Jesus we observed in Acts as the basis for his vehement argument in 1 Corinthians 15. If one believes in the resurrection of Jesus, he said, then one must also believe in a future, general resurrection of the dead, and to deny a general resurrection is to deny the resurrection of Jesus.

The significant point here is that the story itself says nothing about a general resurrection. Paul is deriving belief in such resurrection from this story. For there to be a link between Jesus' resurrection and a future resurrection of all dead, there must be a link between Jesus and all of humankind. On the basis of this assumed link, Paul states that believing in the resurrection of Jesus requires belief in a general resurrection. Here with Paul's argument for a general resurrection, we see the beginning of theologizing as the process of deriving meaning from the story of Jesus.

The New Testament also displays the beginning of the kind of theologizing that today is called Christology. When the church expanded beyond Jerusalem, the New Testament writers took the story into other worldviews and used the language and imagery of that new worldview to identify the significance of Jesus. Stated briefly, these images are the word in John 1, the high priest in Hebrews, the co-creator in Colossians 1, the new Adam in Philippians 2, and the slain and resurrected Lamb in Revelation 5-7. The first four assume a hierarchical worldview, in which the problem is how humans below are reconciled to God in the realm above. In the several images, Jesus is identified with both God at the top and humankind at the bottom of the hierarchy. The fifth image assumes a linear view of history, somewhat closer to our own, in which Jesus is the key to the direction and goal of God's history. Mention of these images shows that already in the New Testament, when the story is carried into new contexts there were multiple ways to express the meaning of Jesus.

We have now seen both ethics and theology develop from the narrative of Jesus. To ask who Jesus is requires telling his story, as did the early church. And to ask how Christians should live requires telling the story. Ethical implications emerge from the story, and theology emerges as we draw meaning from or explain further implications of that story. It becomes apparent that theology and ethics derived from the story of Jesus are inseparable, two sides of the same proverbial coin. They begin at the same point, namely the story of Jesus, and are two ways to express the meaning of Jesus—one with words and the other via the way Christians live. Describing this link between theology and ethics takes on added significance when we look back on developments in the way the church in the centuries after the New Testament came to talk about who Jesus is.

Creation of new images to express the significance of Jesus did not stop with the New Testament. In the centuries after the New Testament, the early church featured debates about the relationship of Jesus to God and how Jesus was both alike and different from humankind. What became the standard answer for many centuries to the questions of Jesus' relationship to God was first articulated by the Council of Nicea (325 CE) and repeated by the Council of Constantinople (381 CE). The church fathers were concerned to identify Jesus with God. To do so, they used the Greek word *homoousios*, which combines "same" and "substance."

With this term, they declared Jesus of the same substance or one in being with God, which asserts the deity of Jesus. This language assumed a philosophical system that defined things in terms of their fundamental or underlying substance or essence. It also assumed a three-layered universe, so that the substance of God above was the same as the substance of Jesus on earth below. In their context and cosmology, and answering their particular question, declaring Jesus to be of one substance with God the Father was a correct answer and probably the best answer.

Another observation lends additional weight to the idea of developing theology that reflects our current context. Note that a Jesus described as "one substance with the Father" and as "truly God and truly man" (Council of Chalcedon, 451 CE) has abandoned the narrative from which ethical connotations are developed. This separation of a theory about Jesus from the narrative that identified him reflects the fact that the statements came from councils called by emperors whose rule depended on the sword. These statements have allowed Christians through the centuries to profess faith in Jesus while espousing the sword that he rejected. They also allowed Christians to practice racism and slavery while ignoring the challenges to racism of the Jesus they professed to believe and to support the Doctrine of Discovery that justified in the name of Christianity the efforts of white Europeans to colonize peoples of color around the world.[1]

These observations about the accommodation of violence and racism in the statements from the councils come primarily from theologians who would challenge the majority or inherited theological perspective. Some Mennonites, including myself, but certainly not all Mennonites have pointed to the inadequacy of the inherited statements. Representatives of black theology have made the analysis concerning slavery and racism. Here is a place to emphasize interpretations from the margin as pointed to in Chapter 1. Mennonites in one way, and African-Americans in a different way, stand on the margins of the mainstream or standard theological discussions. This marginal social location enables the outsider's critique of the problems with the standard or mainstream theology. This stance on the margins is a characteristic of Mennonite theology, and it is a characteristic of black theology. Latinos might chart yet another version of theology from the margin.

We no longer live in the three-layered worldview reflected in the classic statements, and we do not assume their kind of philosophical identity. In addition, I have argued here that theology and ethics, when based on the narrative of Jesus, are inseparable, and the resulting theology and ethics should reflect Jesus' rejection of the sword. The underlying assumptions that shaped christological expression in the early centuries have long passed, but the language from the fourth century is still current, and the problems of what it accommodates still persist. It seems apparent that theologians today, and in particular Mennonites and other peace church and marginal theologians, can and should develop ways to talk about the meaning of Jesus that reflect our context and worldview, and that feature ethics as an integral dimension. In carrying out this task, today's writers will be doing what New Testament writers and what early church theologians did before them.

Another contrast between the fourth- and fifth-century context and our own highlights the importance of ethics in the theological conversation. The ancients assumed that there would be a correct answer to questions of Christology and that they could enshrine that answer in a creed. And since it was the correct answer for all right-thinking Christians to embrace, they could welcome imperial backing, the highest available political authority, to enforce adherence to the creedal belief. And for centuries the assumption was maintained that there was a correct answer, valid for all times and places and required for all right-thinking Christians to profess. The debates were about finding that correct answer.

Today, however, we have learned from philosophers that every statement of faith is contextual, every statement of faith comes out of a context and reflects the assumptions of that context. Stated another way, since all belief is contextual, there is no universally accessible source of appeal that escapes particularity and thus can coerce someone into accepting a given belief as absolutely true. For example, there is no higher authority that can compel a Muslim to accept the Bible as more true than the Qu'ran, as long as the Muslim truly believes the Qu'ran is the highest authority. This condition of recognizing that there is no ultimate, universally accepted norm of appeal has been called "postmodernity." Postmodernity means accepting the fact that our context is one of pluralism and relativism and diversity.[2]

In the face of pluralism and relativism, some thinkers have proclaimed that we have no way of proclaiming or deciding what is true, and that in fact all is relative and that it therefore makes little difference what one believes or does. As a Christian, however, I reject that claim. The fact of relativism and pluralism does not mean that there is no absolute truth. What changes is the way that we witness to what we believe is true. In the context of relativism and pluralism, the way for Christians to witness to the truth of Jesus Christ is to live by that truth, even when it is costly or dangerous. The ultimate form of this witness is martyrdom. In North America, this costly, lived witness of those who take risks might be a witness against racism in a subtly racist society. or those who continue to maintain a witness of nonviolence in our militarized society that is increasingly organized around endless war.

The absence of an absolute norm by which to coerce belief has profound implications for the way we approach those who are different or who have different beliefs or practices. The fact that there is no absolute or transcendent norm requires approaching those who are different in a spirit of openness and dialogue. It means entering dialogue with the idea that one can learn as well as witness to one's own beliefs. This approach can be summarized as a nonviolent approach to dialogue.

Chapters in Part One display these characteristics of theology. Two chapters describe efforts to produce theology for our time. Justin Heinzekehr's proposal fills a lacuna in Mennonite theologizing. Most theologizing by Mennonites has focused on Jesus and his witness to the reign of God on earth but there has been little discussion of the character of God as God.[3] Heinzekehr uses process theology to project an image of a nonviolent God that reflects a modern worldview. By comparing his own approach to education with that of mainline Protestant theologian Mark Schwehn, Heinzekehr also demonstrates the difference between mainstream and marginal orientations.

Drew Hart has recognized that with a very few exceptions, Mennonite theology has not dealt with racism nor engaged in constructive dialogue with black theology. In other words, although Mennonites are on the margins in terms of the mainstream theological traditions, this social location has not stimulated them to escape the impact of racism in the United States. In conversation with contemporary black and womanist theology, Drew Hart's project is to articulate Anabaptist theology in which anti-racism is an integral element. Given the racism that is prevalent in United States society today, Hart's project is important not only for Mennonites but for our nation. These chapters by Heinzekehr and Hart are models of the kind of theologizing that Mennonite schools should pursue.

Felipe Hinojosa's chapter is about Latino and Latina Mennonite history rather than theology, but he demonstrates the urgency of recognizing the validity of marginal perspectives. Giving the minority or marginal perspective, in this case the Latino/a perspective, equal validity in conversation with the white, majority Mennonite perspective, brings a truer historical picture of both groups.

Finally, Benjamin Bixler's call for dialogue embodies the brief description here of the dialogue required by the fact that there is no universal norm by which to coerce belief in our particular claims to the absolute truth of Jesus Christ.

Notes

1. For material on the sword, see Joerg Rieger, *Christ and Empire: From Paul to Postcolonial Times* (Minneapolis: Fortress Press, 2007), 96. For a comment from black theology, see James H. Cone, *God of the Oppressed*, rev. ed. (Maryknoll, N.Y.: Orbis, 1997), 107. For extended analysis of the way that separation of Jesus from his Jewishness by the early church fathers led to the generic Jesus of standard theology that accommodated racism and supported the western colonial enterprise, see J. Kameron Carter, *Race: A Theological Account* (New York: Oxford University Press, 2008) and Willie James Jennings, *The Christian Imagination: Theology and the Origins of Race* (New Haven & London: Yale University Press, 2010). For my longer discussion of the New Testament texts and the historical and contemporary development of Christology, see J. Denny Weaver, *The Nonviolent God* (Grand Rapids, Mich.: William B. Eerdmans Publishing Co., 2013), 153-173, as well as J. Denny Weaver, *The Nonviolent Atonement*, 2nd ed., greatly rev. and expanded (Grand Rapids: William B. Eerdmans Publishing Co., 2011), 120-126. "For a short statement on the theology behind Doctrine of Discovery, see my blog entry "The Jewish Jesus and the Doctrine of Discovery" at https://dofdmenno.org/2015/11/03/the-jewish-jesus-and-the-doctrine-of-discovery/ on the website of the project for Dismantling the Doctrine of Discovery.

2. For multi-faceted, Mennonite discussions of postmodernity, see Susan Biesecker-Mast and Gerald Biesecker-Mast, eds., *Anabaptists and Postmodernity*, foreword by J. Denny Weaver, The C. Henry Smith Series, vol. 1 (Telford, Pa.: Pandora Press U.S.; copublished with Herald Press, 2000).

3. An effort of a different sort is Gordon D. Kaufman, *In Face of Mystery: A Constructive Theology* (Cambridge, Mass.: Harvard, 1993), in which Kaufman defined Jesus as the serendipitous creativity that called humanity into existence out of the ongoing evolution of the world. Another recent discussion of God, which has affinity with early Mennonite theologizing, is Weaver, *Nonviolent God*.

CHAPTER TWO

TRUE EVANGELICAL SCHOLARSHIP: METAPHYSICS AND MENNONITE EDUCATION

Justin Heinzekehr

The Particularity of All Theology

Like all Christian theologies, Mennonite theology traces its origins in some way back to the person of Jesus. And like all Christians, Mennonites have done this theological tracing in distinct ways that emerge from specific socio-cultural locations. One difference, perhaps, is that, because of their position on the margins of Protestant history, it has been easier for Mennonites to recognize the distinctiveness of their theology compared to other mainline denominations. But in reality, mainline Christian theologies are just as distinct, just as diverse, and just as context-dependent.

It is possible, of course, to emphasize the similarities between Mennonite theology and other types of Christian theology in the interest of ecumenical relationships. This is a valid, and sometimes important, facet to emphasize. But to my mind, the more important opportunity is to draw on Mennonite theological sensitivities to illuminate some of the assumptions that might be more difficult for mainline Christians to uncover from within their own traditions. Mennonites have traditionally made these kind of contributions in the fields of Christian ethics and, to a lesser extent, systematic theology.[1]

However, Mennonites have done little thinking about how their distinct perspective might make a difference for Christian metaphysics, or reflection on the general features of reality. This chapter suggests a strategic use of process metaphysics as a way to expand Mennonite thought, and particularly Mennonite education, in this direction.

A Distinct Voice in Ethics

For a long time now, Mennonites have expressed a distinct voice in the field of Christian ethics. One major line of scholarship emphasizes the fact that Mennonite thought tends to be "nonfoundational," i.e., not based on objective, rational, abstract systems.[2] Rather, Mennonites have appreciated the importance of Jesus' cultural specificity as well as the specificity of the faith communities that model themselves on the life and teachings of Jesus. Furthermore, the thinking goes, it is precisely the nonfoundationalism of Mennonite theology that has allowed Mennonites to interpret Jesus' nonviolent ethics as a practical requirement for Christian discipleship.[3] So the Mennonite theological perspective has helped bring to light certain pitfalls of Christian ethics; the attempt to construct airtight universal systems inevitably imposes violence, or at least abstracts from the earthy nonviolence of the Gospels.

One unfortunate consequence of this line of thinking is the assumption that Mennonite theology necessarily excludes systematic or abstract types of thought. One can trace this assumption all the way back to the sixteenth-century Anabaptists, who were suspicious of formal, academic theology because it was inaccessible to lay people, disconnected from the biblical narrative, and often used to suppress the Anabaptist movement.[4]

Mennonite leaders in the following centuries carried on this suspicion of systematic theology, either through biblical fundamentalism (as in the more conservative Mennonite groups)[5] or through empirical communitarianism (in the more progressive).[6] Contemporary authors have concluded that Mennonite theology is "existential," "ad hoc," or "theopoetic,"[7] and therefore avoids the violent certainty of systematic theologies and metaphysics.

Process Thought

In reality, though, Mennonites create systems for themselves just like everyone else, and the idea that metaphysics is fundamentally at odds with the Mennonite theological project only serves to mask those systems and keep Mennonites from making the same kind of contributions to metaphysics as we have done for ethics or theology.[8] The question is, How can Mennonites engage in systematic metaphysical reflection without abstracting from the biblical or communal particularities that are so important to Mennonite theology?

There are a few schools of philosophy that offer potential resources, one of which is the process philosophy of Alfred North Whitehead and his interpreters. The strength of the process framework is that it allows for reflection on the whole of reality, but does so from an explicitly local, and therefore vulnerable, standpoint. A process philosopher expects that his or her metaphysical reflections will be continually challenged and overturned, precisely because there is no objective ground from which one could construct a foolproof picture of the world.

Whitehead, like the Mennonites, is very critical of those who allow their own abstractions to blind them to the concrete, though one cannot avoid abstractions altogether.[9] In fact, Mennonite assumptions about the nature of reality mirror several important metaphysical claims of process philosophy—specifically the conception of reality as plural, relational and co-creative. One way to start uncovering some of these metaphysical assumptions is to compare Mennonite educational practices with those of mainline Christian or secular institutions. The differences in educational philosophies often reflect subconscious beliefs about how reality is structured at the most basic level.

In contrast to secular education, which places most emphasis on specialized, isolated knowledge, distinct from any particular religious tradition, Christian schools have generally assumed that education is a process of character formation done in community, and that the virtues one acquires as a part of the educational process are essential to the production of knowledge. This general Christian foundation reflects an ontology of integration or harmony. In it no piece of knowledge can be isolated from another, and no scholarship isolated from the religious tradition that gives it ultimate meaning.

Mennonite institutions are certainly a part of this broad tradition of religious education. But Mennonite education (at its best) is distinct from other forms of Christian education in that it uses the educational process not only to provide the necessary conditions for academic inquiry, but to challenge the methods and assumptions of the discipline itself. This challenge implies a slightly different conception of reality, as a rhythmic movement back and forth between communal integration and the fracturing of that integrated knowledge in the face of its own incompleteness.

Mark Schwehn on Religious Higher Education

To make this point more clearly, it is helpful to consider Mark Schwehn's book, *Exiles from Eden*, which has become a classic in religious higher education circles.[10] As an administrator at Valparaiso University, a school with a proud Lutheran heritage, Mark Schwehn represents one of the most prominent advocates of religious education from a mainline Protestant perspective. *Exiles from Eden* traces the development of modern higher education from the Enlightenment through the early twentieth century. According to Schwehn, modern universities have neglected their responsibility to form the moral character of students, emphasizing instead merely the production and transmission of knowledge. Professors at major public universities would be very suspicious of any attempt to use the classroom as a way of building students' characters.

Though the roots of the problem stretch back at least to the Enlightenment, Schwehn blames one person in particular, namely Max Weber, for the disintegration of academic vocation: When Weber wrote to German scholars about academic work, many still believed that education should be thought of as *Bildung*, or formation of character. Weber attacked the idea that education should provide students with some kind of overarching meaning for their lives; he believed this led to a breakdown of academic discipline and an irrational dependence on the immediate experience of scholars and students.

The ideal scholar, Weber claimed, would set aside any emotion, value, or ethics in his or her pursuit of knowledge. Weberian scholarship is an "impersonal and solitary undertaking" that requires no significant relationships to other people or a community and may even be derailed by such relationships.[11] Its goal is domination of the subject and by extension domination of the self and the world. Weber's conception of scholarship eventually became the norm in Europe and the United States. At most secular universities, it is now assumed that research and teaching should be kept separate from character formation or normative value claims.

From a Christian perspective, the Weberian vision of education is obviously an impoverished vision; we want to be able to talk about education as a more holistic venture. As an alternative, Schwehn proposes that academic truth has to be pursued within communities of scholars and students that consciously promote the character traits necessary for such a pursuit. These academic communities will use different criteria and different vocabularies depending on the discipline—literature or sociology or nursing—but they would have in common the goal of inculcating certain academic virtues in their students.

Schwehn argues that certain traits are required to pursue an academic question, whether one studies history, math or literature. He suggests that the list should include such virtues as humility (recognizing the value of other people's research and interpretation), faith (the capacity to risk our own tightly held beliefs in the pursuit of the truth), self-denial (in the face of better arguments or strong evidence), charity (in our reading of texts) and justice (in our bold identification of error or negligence).[12]

Of course to consider all of these virtues as preconditions for academic work would require us to think about truth not as a purely objective set of facts that any neutral party can discover but as dependent on the communities that cultivate these virtues. Thus Schwehn concludes,

> To ask about the meaning of truth is to raise questions about context, about the boundaries, the vocabulary, and the virtues that collectively define the shape and the substance of a particular community of inquirers whose primary intention is to discover the truth.[13]

It is not that the Enlightenment was completely misdirected; Schwehn realizes, for example, that modern secularism was largely an effort to transcend the religious particularity that sparked devastating wars in seventeenth-century Europe.[14] Therefore, Schwehn argues for an integration of the Enlightenment ideals of rationalism and objectivity with religious value.[15] Stated succinctly, Schwehn's argument is that character formation is necessary to support the kind of rational, civic inquiry that was the ultimate ideal of the Enlightenment. The very institutions that support a democratic society depend on citizens who have the kind of virtues necessary to engage in productive, respectful discourse.

For purposes of this discussion, the important thing to notice is that Schwehn's theory of education presupposes certain basic assumptions about the nature of reality, or in other words, metaphysics. For example, Schwehn believes that truth is primarily about having a common language or set of criteria by which public decisions can be made. In Schwehn's view, this kind of truth can only be discovered in a community capable of having open, rational discourse. This means integrating the insights from all members of the community, integrating the character of each member of the community with his or her knowledge of the academic discipline, and integrating knowledge across disciplinary lines. This kind of education only makes sense if one assumes some kind of connective matrix at the basis of reality that would reward a holistic inquiry.

We can therefore start to talk about Schwehn's ontology, his ideas about the structure of reality. Basically, his educational philosophy depends on the idea that the world is harmonious, uniform, and coherent. It is the Augustinian idea of creation as the unfolding of a transcendent pattern or music[16] or the Lutheran conception of the "communion of being" in which we all participate.[17] In this way of thinking, truth is about finding the connection between things that were previously isolated or separated, in a sort of Hegelian movement toward unification. The goal of religious education, then, is to allow particular communities to transcend their differences and come together to create an orderly, peaceful society.

The Mennonite Difference

In many ways, Schwehn's way of thinking about education might resonate with Mennonite educators. John Howard Yoder's definition of truth in relation to the faith community resembles Schwehn's in relation to the academic community. Yoder says,

> What it means to qualify a statement as "true" in the faith community is not an ontological statement about the status of a proposition. It is an historical judgment about the statement's

compatibility with the life directions and value insights, the narrative memories and the practices, of that community.[18]

For both Yoder and Schwehn, truth is found in a communal activity, one that depends on the specific vocabulary and values of that community.

There is a key difference between the Mennonite and mainline views, however, and it has to do with the Mennonite commitment to nonviolence. Consider Menno Simons' famous quote:

> For true evangelical faith is of such a nature that it cannot lay dormant, but manifests itself in all righteousness and works of love; it dies unto flesh and blood; it destroys all forbidden lusts and desires; it seeks and serves and fears God; it clothes the naked; it feeds the hungry; it comforts the sorrowful; it shelters the destitute; it aids and consoles the sad; it returns good for evil; it serves those that harm it; it prays for those that persecute it.[19]

Menno is summarizing one of the key insights of the early Anabaptist theologians—that truth can only be produced in a context of nonviolence and that a belief or statement delivered violently is false, no matter what the content of that statement is.[20]

Furthermore, nonviolence is defined as a particular kind of response to those who remain on the outside of social acceptability. Logically, this means that, from a Mennonite perspective, truth is defined not just in the internal workings of the community, though that is important, but above all, truth depends on that which is *external* to the community, which challenges the community as an Other.

Mennonite Metaphysics

This claim also has ontological implications. Instead of seeing reality as a single, uniform fabric, it is important for Mennonites to emphasize the discontinuities that allow for the experience of separation and alienation. To love an enemy, for instance, is to recognize that there is an unmistakable difference between oneself and the Other, even if there is a demand to reach out across that boundary. The distance between self/community and the Other is not unbridgeable but is nevertheless a real boundary that limits the communal identity to a particular location.

What we end up with is a picture of reality in which local, multiple sites of integration are in constant flux, responding to the demands made on them by external agents and incorporating these demands into their own identities. Unlike the Hegelian vision of a (more-or-less) linear progress toward integration, the Mennonite ontology would be more similar to Whitehead's process philosophy, which imagines a plurality of dynamic, relational events in a constant rhythm of construction and deconstruction.

Like Schwehn, Mennonites would take issue with the postmodern secular idea of reality as hopelessly fractured and isolated, preferring instead the idea of a relational web. But because a Mennonite perspective defines truth only through the community's successful response to that which is discontinuous with itself, it lacks the potential for coherence that exists in Schwehn's ontology.

In the parable of the sheep and the goats in Matthew 25, which seems to be the main source for Menno's quote about true faith, the king reveals to his subjects that he has been present to them all along in the form of the hungry, thirsty, sick, and incarcerated ones. This story locates sovereignty, or ultimate demand, in those outside of the bounds of "normal" society.

If we apply this to the metaphysical framework just described, then the discontinuities of reality are also the location of the divine. We experience God as the limit or the breakdown of consensus. This is, again, more like Whitehead's metaphysics than Hegel's; for Hegel, God is identified with the world's process of integration or self-actualization; for Whitehead, God is seen as the one who draws events into a novel existence, from outside of their own context. Whitehead's God therefore exists as a constant challenge to the status quo.

The purpose of education is very different when one sees knowledge as produced by an act of love for the enemy or the marginalized. Again, for Schwehn, education is to provide the virtues that are prerequisite for having any kind of academic or civic discourse. Thus education supports the pursuits of history or literature or mathematics; all these disciplines assume the kind of virtues that Christian education provides.

Mennonite education, on the other hand, might see education as a means by which to challenge the academic discourse in whatever discipline one is working. A Mennonite history professor, for instance, will not merely cultivate virtues like patience or charity in her students, though that is necessary, but would teach students to use historical data to question the way that history has been done. How might we need to change the kinds of questions we ask as historians to respond to the demands upon our academic community from those who have been silenced in the past? A Mennonite science teacher might teach students an attitude of awe toward the natural world (as I can imagine Schwehn suggesting)—but also use vocabulary that resists the tendency of scientific discourse toward militaristic metaphors, like the constant "war" between microbes and white blood cells described in biology textbooks.[21] It makes a difference for scientific discourse if we start with the assumption that the enemy or the outsider is a necessary, natural and even, in some sense, divine part of reality.

Truth from a Mennonite Perspective

Given the ontology contained in the words of Menno Simons, what would it mean to pursue truth from a Mennonite perspective? What would it mean to say that true scholarship "feeds the hungry," or "consoles the oppressed," or "seeks that which is lost?" Certainly academic communities cannot shy away from value judgments nor from the task of forming students as holistic, faithful, empathetic individuals. But more than that, educators should spend less time shoring up the existing rules of a discipline and more time asking themselves and their students, What or who does my discipline make invisible? Because if we take seriously the commitment to nonviolence, we encounter God precisely in what has *not* been integrated into our communal identity. And if this transcendent demand is a basic feature of reality, then educators are responsible to prepare students to recognize the fissures and fractures in the consensus of our discipline, our communities and our churches through which God may be briefly visible.

In summary, Mennonite education at its best points toward a distinct way of thinking about reality: the basic structure of things, the relationship between God and the world, and the nature of knowledge and truth. Like Whitehead's "events," we exist as interrelated but distinct components of a constantly changing world. We exist as individuals in community, and our identities are constituted by our relationships with our community and our environment. Inevitably, we seek to incorporate the influences upon us into a coherent whole, and yet that whole is always transcended by the stubborn particularities of our environment; there is always a remainder to our identity.

We might think of God, like Whitehead does, as both the sustainer of our community and as the representative of that troubling remainder. God interacts with the world as the ground of its own creative, constructive process, and as the outsider (or even the enemy) who draws us out into new ways of thinking and being.[22]

In this sense, being explicit about metaphysics would actually heighten the Mennonite awareness of the particularity and incompleteness of any theology—or any discipline for that matter. If reality is not unitextural but made up of a plurality of unassimilable centers of identity, then every identity and every interpretation has a specific history and context, and cannot claim the kind of overpowering rationality that, justifiably, makes Mennonite theologians nervous. At the same time, if reality is essentially interrelated, then we are not left with a naïve relativism where no evaluation can be made between any two perspectives. Rather, truth claims are produced and continually tested in the context of relationships, both within a given community and across the borders of communities. We are compelled to seek coherence even if full coherence is ultimately impossible. More specifically, if God relates to the world as a lure toward the un-integrated, then God has a preferential option for those that fall outside of whatever our society or our community has constructed as normal, sacred, or privileged, in the way that we see Jesus disrupting the norms of his first-century Palestinian context.

In short, I believe that Mennonites have something unique to contribute to the way that Christians think about the world. We should not shy away from the task of constructing coherent and systematic statements about reality, as long as we recognize the provisional nature of such statements, and as long as these statements emerge as organically as possible from our concrete, local realities. Ultimately, the point of metaphysics from a Mennonite perspective is not to come up with a perfectly coherent worldview but to map the ever-shifting limits of our coherence and to encounter the God who dwells at these borders.

Notes

1. J. Denny Weaver, *The Nonviolent God* (Grand Rapids, Mich.: William B. Eerdmans Publishing Co., 2013).

2. "Rather than beginning with foundational, universal first principles, Mennonite theologians will recognize the historical particularity of all forms of reasoning

and will be unembarrassed by our inability to persuade others with different starting points than our own." David C. Cramer, "Mennonite Systematic Theology in Retrospect and Prospect," *The Conrad Grebel Review* 31, no. 3 (Fall 2013): 272.

3. "Both the temptation to start from scratch and the rhetoric of finality can be seen as forms of epistemological violence in the sense that they constitute a retreat from vulnerability. They undercut the possibility of radical reformation, which Yoder has always read as a call to cultivate a fallible stance of openness to the possibility of radical critique at the hands of other interlocutors." Chris K. Huebner, *A Precarious Peace: Yoderian Explorations on Theology, Knowledge, and Identity*, foreword Stanley Hauerwas (Scottdale, Pa.: Herald Press, 2006), 102.

4. For example, Hans Hut says, "[Christ] did not direct the poor man to books, as our uncomprehending scribes do now. Rather, he taught them the gospel, and illustrated it, through their work—to the peasants by their fields, seed, thistles, thorns and rocks." Hans Hut, "On the Mystery of Baptism," in *The Radical Reformation*, ed. Michael G. Baylor (Cambridge: Cambridge University Press, 1991), 157.

5. See John Horsch's criticism of modernism: "The present book was born of the conviction that the modern religious liberalism means the abandonment of the Christian faith. Modernist theology discredits and destroys the foundations of Christianity as Christianity has been known in all ages from the time of its origin. At the same time it discards the true basis for morality. Therefore modernism is the great menace to the Christian Church and to society and the state, though it comes under a religious cloak professing to be a needed improvement on the old faith, and claiming to be called to save the Church from threatening shipwreck." John Horsch, *Modern Religious Liberalism: The Destructiveness and Irrationality of the New Theology* (Scottdale, Pa.: Fundamental Truth Depot, 1921), 3. This foreword does not appear in the 1968 reprint.

6. See Cornelius Wedel: "The *Gemeindekirche* had nothing to do with so-called dogmatic systems. They emphasized much more the earnest study of the Holy Scriptures and the decisive following after Christ in service and benevolent love." Quoted in James C. Juhnke, "Gemeindechristentum and Bible Doctrine: Two Mennonite Visions of the Early Twentieth Century," *Mennonite Quarterly Review* 57, no. 3 (July 1983): 211.

7. I am referring to Robert Friedmann, Chris Huebner, and Scott Holland, respectively. To be precise, Holland comes out of the Brethren tradition but belongs to the broader Anabaptist discussion and has influenced many Mennonite scholars and students.

8. A. James Reimer discusses metaphysics but is more inclined to emphasize commonality with the broader Christian tradition rather than describing any distinctive Mennonite metaphysics.

9. This is Whitehead's "fallacy of misplaced concreteness": "neglecting the degree of abstraction involved when an actual entity is considered merely so far as it exemplifies certain categories of thought." Alfred North Whitehead, *Process and Reality*, Corrected ed. (New York: Free Press, 1978), 7-8.

10. Mark R. Schwehn, *Exiles from Eden: Religion and the Academic Vocation in*

America (New York: Oxford University Press, 1993).

11. Schwehn, *Exiles from Eden*, 15.

12. Schwehn, *Exiles from Eden*, 50-51.

13. Schwehn, *Exiles from Eden*, 37.

14. "Any radical alternative to foundationalism or objectivism will seem to open up the prospect of renewed violence among different communities who would seem to have no rational foundation on the basis of which they might adjudicate the disagreements that might arise among them." Schwehn, *Exiles from Eden*, 31.

15. "I can agree with Stout that, in view of the traumatic religious conflicts that he remembers so well, religion needs Enlightenment. To the extent that my analysis is correct, however, he should agree with me and against Hume that Enlightenment needs religion." Schwehn, *Exiles from Eden*, 54-55.

16. Augustine, *De Musica*.

17. Luther, "The Freedom of a Christian." "Luther endorsed the Augustinian stress on the ontological dependence of creation on the Creator . . . and advocated creation as a continuous process (creation continua). . . . For Augustine, humans existed on account of their participation in the source of being which is God. Luther concurred. . . . Luther's whole reasoning of the presence of goodness in human beings is based on his conviction that the only way such a goodness could indwell in humans was through participation in God's goodness." Jairzinho Lopes Pereira, *Augustine of Hippo and Martin Luther on Original Sin and Justification of the Sinner* (Gottingen: Vandenhoeck & Ruprecht, 2013), 390.

18. John Howard Yoder, *To Hear the Word*, 2nd ed. (Eugene, Ore.: Cascade Books, 2010), 40.

19. Menno Simons, *The Complete Writings of Menno Simons c.1496-1561*, ed. John Christian Wenger, trans. Leonard Verduin, with biography by Harold S. Bender (Scottdale, Pa.: Herald Press, 1956), 307.

20. See Marpeck's letter to the Swiss Brethren in 1547: "Human coercion will destroy all who [support] a human, forcibly imposed faith and all who claim the Word of faith, but who trust and depend upon human protection and power. Moreover, all the actions, of both the old and new [Catholic and Protestant] forcers of faith, are done in the semblance of Christ and His gospel." Here Marpeck is warning against those who claim to be Christian, but use force to support their views. Marpeck believes the use of force invalidates the truth of those claims, even though the content appears to be Christian. Pilgram Marpeck, *The Writings of Pilgram Marpeck*, ed. and trans. William Klassen and Walter Klaassen, Classics of the Reformation, vol. 2 (Scottdale, Pa.: Herald Press, 1978), 448-150.

21. Angela Horn Montel, "Violent Images in Cell Biology," in *Teaching Peace: Nonviolence and the Liberal Arts*, ed. J. Denny Weaver and Gerald Biesecker-Mast (Lanham, Md.: Rowman & Littlefield Publishers, Inc., 2003), 223-234. Many other essays in this volume suggest concrete ways that Mennonite education can challenge dominant academic discourses in various disciplines.

22. "Throughout the perishing occasions of the life of each temporal Creature, the inward source of distaste or of refreshment, the judge arising out of the very na-

ture of things, redeemer or goddess of mischief, is the transformation of Itself, everlasting in the Being of God. In this way, the insistent craving is justified—the insistent craving that zest for existence be refreshed by the ever-present, unfading importance of our immediate actions, which perish and yet live for evermore." Whitehead, *Process and Reality*, 351.

THREE

SALVAGING MENNONITE THEOLOGICAL EDUCATION: IMITATING BLACK FAITH AS IT IMITATES CHRIST

Drew G. I. Hart

Mennonitism and Anabaptism in Tension

Assimilation into White Dominant Culture

Mennonites arrived at Germantown, Pennsylvania, in 1683 to create the first permanent Mennonite community in North America, entering an already ongoing story of oppression and violence that was unfolding all around them.[1] In 1688 some members from this group formally wrote the first petition against slavery in the colonies.[2] This prophetic act would not be repeated again with an equal act in response to slavery in the coming decades and centuries.

Anglo-Saxon Protestant identity was a central marker for belonging and would become one of the central seeds for creating white people of the modern era. Mennonites however, did not exactly accept white identity. Emphasizing German Mennonite identity and their historical lineage, along with Mennonite practices of simplicity, nonconformity, and nonresistance were ways of partly opting out of the full assimilation path.³ Nevertheless, the European background of Mennonite communities provided a measure of acceptance into white society and pulled Mennonites toward an ongoing integration into specifically white—as opposed to German—racial identity.

There is evidence that by the early twentieth century most white Mennonite communities had deeply conformed to the racialized logic of the era. While contemporary white Mennonites have prided themselves on the historical legacy of renouncing the practice of slavery, for generations after that act their communities in fact had not stood up collectively as a faithful counter-witness to the persistent white supremacy that terrorized black people in the United States.

Rarely had white Mennonites intimately identified with the five thousand lynched black men, women, and children during that time.⁴ No ethic of love moved ethnic Mennonites to share black people's burden under white supremacist sieges that routinely bombed black homes and church buildings.⁵ No joining in life together that resisted the racialized and segregated society that treated black people as inferior and forced them to live on the margins in constant fear of white violence.⁶ Not a peep in response to the convict leasing system that emerged after slavery ended, once again finding legally sanctioned ways to coerce hundreds of thousands of black people to labor for white people without pay, under the physical brutality of white overseers. This new form of slavery continued until 1945.⁷

Some notable changes occurred for this Mennonite community in the mid-twentieth century. James and Rowena Lark, an African-American couple, joined the Mennonite church and engaged in a massive church planting effort in black neighborhoods.⁸ In 1943, Harold Bender's "Anabaptist Vision" sparked interest in Anabaptist studies and revived debates around what faithful Mennonite practice actually meant.⁹ In addition, Mennonites had no choice but to notice Martin Luther King Jr.'s message and movement rooted in nonviolence, or Vincent Harding's influential, internal appeals to the Mennonite church, until Harding wearied of the struggle, and left the community because of the frequent apathy and inaction of the church.¹⁰

White Supremacy and German Ethnic Mennonitism

The term *Mennonitism* is often used as an epithet to summarize the problem I have been describing. However, that something called Mennonitism exists is not the problem. The issue is the particular form in which Mennonitism emerged and how it fused German ethnic identity and white Mennonite practice. The problem is defining communal belonging through ethnicity and legacy last names with the result being a racialized system of advantage. Within contemporary images of Mennonitism one might wonder if being born into the right family is valued more than walking in the footsteps of Jesus.

Despite the Mennonite church's increased racial diversity in local communities across the United States, with nearly twenty percent of the Mennonite church now being non-white,[11] there is still a distinct advantage and value attached to the so-called German Mennonite ethnic body. This body quietly reigns supreme in many Mennonite communities and institutions. Yet, the ethnic language merely hides the racialized implications. Said more bluntly, there is a pervasive form of white supremacy within some forms of Mennonitism, which considers bodies with historical and ethnic ties to be at the very top of the social hierarchy of the Mennonite world.

The root of the problem is to be found in our theological ethics. There is a way of being Mennonite that positions itself as superior and from that disposition engages in one-way exchanges. White Mennonites are frequently tempted into a static and fixed servant-savior role in the world. Some of this is nearing idolatry, believing ethnic Mennonitism to be salvific in itself. And theologically it might be true that the church ought to be the community that humbly takes on the presence of Christ in the world.

However, that presence is not a given, and it certainly does not happen when any specific community, with its legacy and bodies, is taken for granted to be equated with the kingdom of God. The very presumption of such an identification is a kind of Christendom impulse rather than the visible manifestation of God's reign, and its consequence is closing off the option of being deeply transformed by others along the way.

Ironically, Mennonites in the twentieth and twenty-first centuries have managed to engage in a devastating theological critique of western Christendom while never taking that same critique to its logical conclusion.[12] That is, they have rarely applied their Christendom critiques to the development of their German Mennonite ethnic identity. There are racialized and theological problems with such an identity that need comprehensive research and deep reflection followed by Christian repentance. Critiquing Christendom while leaving one's own identities untouched is problematic. Traditional white Mennonite critiques of western Christendom frequently fall short of acknowledging that it also delivered and mothered white supremacy into our world.

In forgetting that, Mennonites could frequently speak with a minority slant about Christendom while also assimilating into, and benefitting from, the socially advantaged position of whiteness within the racialized hierarchy of American society. One result of this inclination is that as white Mennonites assimilated further into white society over the years, and began increasing their dialogue partners beyond white Mennonites, the black church and its theologians were typically not pursued as worthy interlocutors.

Discipleship, Hermeneutical Community, Ecclesiology, and Tradition-Based Education

In her book *Anabaptist Ways of Knowing* Sara Wenger Shenk created a table conversation for the Mennonite community to engage more critically in preserving or discarding its traditions and practices. She posed an important question: "How can we draw strength from a particular tradition, a particular story, while cultivating a lively critique of that tradition so as to keep it vital in changing times?"[13]

Among other things, she identified three clusters in the Anabaptist tradition that should influence Mennonite theological education. First was the cluster of *discipleship*. Anabaptists "understood Jesus' teaching in the Sermon on the Mount as well as Paul's ethical admonitions as given and intended to shape Christian conduct."[14] Knowing and discipleship, Shenk noted, are intimately bound together. For her, Hans Denck's famous explication, "No one can truly know (Christ) unless he follow him in life, and no one may follow him unless he has first known him" brings together how discipleship, epistemology, and indwelling the story of Jesus are all inextricably intertwined in Anabaptist ways of knowing.

The second cluster Shenk highlighted was the *hermeneutical community*. Drawing from Stuart Murray, she considered how sixteenth-century Anabaptists interpreted Scripture together, in community. John Roth, however, complicated the idea of simple Anabaptist principles, highlighting the diversity and fragmentation of Anabaptist practice in the sixteenth century. Therefore Shenk argued that

> rather than describing the Anabaptist use of Scripture in fixed, normative hermeneutical principles, we describe them as a series of arguments or debates into which participants were drawn precisely because they agreed on the importance of the issue being debated.[15]

Therefore, hermeneutical practices live in tension within the living Anabaptist tradition and should continue to do so.

Within such tensions, we also navigate a "hermeneutics of obedience" and a "hermeneutic of suspicion." These are both necessary because "communal discernment around Scripture can lead to biblical interpretation which transforms as well as biblical interpretation which justifies the status quo."[16] Therefore Shenk keeps us attentive to our dialogue partners along the way. She explains that "within the interpreting community, the question of who we choose as our primary conversation partners is of critical importance."[17] Choosing dialogue partners carefully while navigating the tension of obedience and suspicion shines light on some initial needs of Mennonite theological education going forward. "The desire to be both a faithful disciple and to continually discern anew what it means to be faithful is the sort of creative tension that can provide a constructive conversation between the tradition and current experience."[18]

Lastly, Shenk turned her attention to *ecclesiology*. Early Anabaptists sought to transform the culture and reform the state church but quickly became disillusioned with this posture. Instead, "The renewal of the church, for the Anabaptists, included a critique of and dissent from any form of 'establishment' Christendom that didn't involve voluntary commitment in defining a visible community."[19] This kind of change meant a renewed communal practice of economics, renunciation of violence, and refusal to take oaths. The church embodies the alternative order of God with an alternative consciousness and ethics.

These practices then, for Sara Wenger Shenk, provide a way of life, and as such, an embodied way of knowing and experiencing our world. Further, her question of who Mennonites are and are not in theological dialogue with is still vital. For the particular conversation in this chapter, an immediate challenge is whether Mennonite education, frequently controlled primarily by and for white Mennonites, either intentionally fosters conversations with the Black Church and its theologians or turns away from such meaningful dialogue. The Black Church certainly has its own traditions and practices that have developed from the underside of western Christendom and white supremacy. Since the Black Church and Mennonites both have a stance outside of Christendom, Mennonites could and should engage with and learn from conversations with the Black Church.

Dialogical Vulnerability and Disciplined Embodiment as Christian Knowing

In *A Precarious Peace,* Chris Huebner explored theology, knowledge, and identity in view of the writings of John Howard Yoder and his mode of dialogue. For Huebner, dialogical vulnerability is the appropriate posture for a Christian, which is the opposite of foundationalist debate and argumentation. Unfortunately, according to Huebner, "all too often the travels of pacifism end up looking more like those of yet another conqueror, proceeding systematically in the pursuit of yet another conqueror, proceeding systematically in the pursuit of more and ever greater control."[20] Nonetheless, he insists that Christian pacifism ought to be offered only as a non-coercive gift and should also be received as a gift. When pacifism seeks to seize control and secure itself, it finds itself enacting a hypocritical mode of life in contrast to its own message of peace.

Being vulnerable before dialogical critique is a necessity for peaceful theological conversation. The opposite of that is monologue, which Huebner contends is an effort to sidestep vulnerability while "articulating one's standpoint as if others do not exist, as if no other relevant participants are in the discussion." This is important. What does it mean to speak and write as Mennonites while not taking seriously the thoughts and perspectives of others? Huebner here calls for a particular theological discourse that refuses to sidestep people that differ and challenge one's own views. He continues, "It is never a question of whether critical and dissenting minority voices exist. Rather, the question is whether one is willing to take those voices seriously." However, being open to dialogical vulnerability and taking those same voices seriously requires hard work. This requires that one remain open "to the possibility of radical critique at the hands of other interlocutors."[21] For this, Huebner encourages the practice of patience. Together, this challenge suggests that Mennonite theological education engage in dialogical vulnerability, refusing to short-circuit theological partners or avoid the messy work that comes with patiently dialoguing with those that offer substantial critiques.

Finally, I want to highlight Huebner's understanding of Christian knowing a bit more. Huebner comprehends Christianity to be "a counter epistemology."[22] He also sees a connection between knowledge and Christian martyrdom. For him, rather than being understood instrumentally as evidence of the commitment to beliefs, or the truthfulness of one's beliefs, or even one's capacity to seize control over the threat of death, Christian martyrdom suggests something else. Dying is actually the embodiment of truth, that is, a life lived vulnerably before God. He explains that this different way of knowing actually "approaches knowledge as an embodied social performance or practice."[23] Knowing and embodiment are deeply intertwined. Christian life calls for "an embodied way of knowing" and "a life of disciplined imitation of Christ."[24]

Before getting to submitting vulnerably to some radical critiques in regard to Mennonite identity, theology, and practice in the United States, Mennonites need to face the reality and devastation of white supremacy. The white Mennonite community has not historically been in any significant ongoing dialogue with African-Americans. However, Huebner's work, when stretched to keep track of black Christian lived experiences, provides new opportunities for Mennonite theological education not only to enter into dialogue with the Black Church and black theology but also to be changed by it.

Mennonites should approach this dialogue but do so thinking about their "tradition dynamically, as an ongoing and constantly changing argument extended through time" rather than "statically, as a kind of deposit, the truth of which is to be protected and secured."[25] This gestures toward a dialogical Anabaptist practice in which black theology has the potential to challenge, hold accountable, and possibly even change the direction of Mennonite theological conversations in the twenty-first century.

The ideals of Anabaptism, peace theology and practices, and the reality of Mennonite assimilation into dominant culture are conflicting tensions. Nonetheless, Anabaptist debates and a truly peaceable theology can guide Mennonite theological education in the right direction, toward a more faithful way. Discipleship to Jesus, debates over communal hermeneutics, an ecclesiological counter-witness, and dialogical vulnerability that remains radically open to critique is necessary for Mennonite theological education.

These ideas are especially vital when the history of western Christendom and white supremacy are both kept in view. These practices and modes of being, according to Shenk and Huebner, help direct us to question who have been excluded as theological dialogue partners in the Mennonite church and whether we are willing to vulnerably take those critiques seriously, with the possibility that radical reformation might truly be necessary. Since Anabaptism is indeed a living conversation and debate, it is not condemned to the same cycle and patterns that its participants have frequently found themselves stuck in. New embodied and dialogical ways of knowing are possible.

Imitating Black Faith as It Imitates Christ

Turning the Subject—M. Shawn Copeland

M. Shawn Copeland, in her book *Enfleshing Freedom*, discussed the "turn to the subject" that happened in the West during the Enlightenment. For Copeland, Christianity's involvement and partnership with domination had devastating consequences for the church in the West. And it is in this shadow that Western society spoke of "the person" and "the human subject." This abstract universal language hid the specific subject that was always implied by these terms: "the white, male, bourgeois European subject."[26]

With the turn to the subject, the "white male bourgeois European" displaced the role of God. In response, Copeland says that the church must renounce this turn to the subject that masks domination practices with universal language. Instead, she calls for "a new anthropological subject."[27] She suggests a very particular body. The bodily experiences of poor women of color are centered, the very oppressed bodies that continue to be overlooked while suffering under the dominating hierarchies of race, class, and gender.

Copeland acknowledges the risk of constituting black women's bodies, in particular, at the center of God's liberating action. However, centralizing oppressed bodies for her is not a game of identity politics.

Instead it is centered in Jesus' own story. She explains that the church responds to societal domination by its "praxial affirmation of the anthropological yes begun in the ministry and sacrificial love of Jesus of Nazareth, whose solidarity with the outcast and poor revealed God's preferential love." Therefore, that "revelation" she proclaims, "directs us to a new anthropological subject of Christian theological reflection—exploited, despised, poor women of color."[28] So, this turning of the subject corresponds with the subjects frequently turned to in Jesus' own ministry.[29]

For Copeland, such a turn guides the church toward the practice of solidarity. Solidarity for her means "the empathetic incarnation of Christian love."[30] This practice of solidarity not only should move us on behalf of "the suffering of the other" but also ought to compel us to "confront and address its oppressive cause and shoulder the other's suffering."[31] Turning the subject (toward the most vulnerable) and the practice of Christian solidarity, then, enacts a "dangerous memory" of the crucified Christ and mystically joins us into the body of Christ visibly in our present society. Put in straightforward Anabaptist vernacular terms, staying attuned to the body of Jesus Christ in the gospel story requires us to centralize the suffering bodies in our society like Jesus himself did. Jesus intimately joined, stood with, loved, and liberated the outcasts, marginalized, and oppressed of his society. Mennonite theological education ought to orient Christians toward embodying that story for our society as well.

The Scholastic Disposition and the Crucified Christ

In his book *Race: A Theological Account*, J. Kameron Carter tackles the theological problem of race. One of the problems with Western theological production, notes Carter, is the way in which it has done "its work in Kantian fashion" or "as an enterprise of the religious elite functioning in the interests of power."[32] Carter then uses the language of Bourdieu, in what he calls "the scholastic disposition." For him, it is the scholar's way of being in the world that is problematic. There is a "forgetting of being" that characterizes the scholastic disposition. Carter suggests that it was "the forgetting of the everyday practices of such people in their real worlds of pain, suffering, poverty, and death."[33] In such forgetfulness, Christianity and Western civilization could be confused and used as interchangeable terms to further ideological projects.

Theological work carried that out. For Carter then, a new mode of being or "a new Christian theological-intellectual practice" is required that emerges from the lived experiences of the very people who have not mattered to scholars engaged in theological production. There is, however, a particular disposition in which theological discourse ought to unfold, and it is at the site of suffering and death. The church must move beyond the pseudo-theological disposition of the scholar and instead enter into the place of suffering "forgotten" by such scholasticism.

The problem of race needs to be addressed as a theological problem of whiteness "that continues to reign as the inner architecture of modern theology" and hence has been a death-dealing discourse of the status quo. How do we escape such a devastating cycle of theological production? Theology, Carter contends, "must do its work in company with and out of the disposition of those facing death, those with the barrel of a shotgun to their backs, for this is the disposition of the crucified Christ, who is the revelation of the triune God."[34] This disposition reveals a Christian orientation in the world and certainly the kind of formative community and places that our practices and theological reflections ought to be shaped in and by.

Carter calls for a new trajectory for twenty-first-century Christian theology. He suggests that theology must learn from "the lived Christian worlds of dark peoples in modernity and how such peoples reclaimed (and in their own ways salvaged) the language of Christianity, and thus Christian theology, from being a discourse of death—their death."[35]

This salvaging of Christian theology invites those locked in the logics and performances of racial hierarchy, including those with a German Mennonite ethnic identity, to take the position of student to those that have reimagined Christian theology from the underside of white supremacy. It is a theological dialogue that seeks to disentangle the reflections and practices of the church of Jesus Christ from denial of its own complicity that brought suffering to many nonwhite people all around the world. In the United States, in particular, it suggests a new disposition alongside of black Christians (and Native Christians) that courageously and creatively aim to follow Jesus faithfully toward pathways out of this nightmare.

Conclusion

This chapter has called for the salvaging of Mennonite theological education so that the living Anabaptist tradition is not merely a dominant cultural practice and discourse. White Mennonites have made many efforts to engage Latin American liberation theologians. Strangely, the same cannot be said in regards to Black and Womanist theologians in the United States. Besides J. Denny Weaver, I have yet to find any ongoing theological engagement by white Mennonite theological educators that takes Black and Womanist theology seriously.[36] The inclination to jump into dialogue with those from another continent while sidestepping black people and their bodily suffering in one's own society is problematic. Such forgetting of black people as potential and fruitful dialogue partners reveals some of the ways that Mennonite theological education has too often been unknowingly trapped in the logics of whiteness.

Sara Wenger Shenk's consideration of Anabaptist practices and Chris Huebner's reflections on dialogical and embodied vulnerability both lead us to the doorstep of the concern at hand. Who are the dialogue partners that are centralized in Mennonite theological education and who are absent? Is Mennonite theological education willing to vulnerably open its discourses up for patient dialogue with Black Church theologians, practitioners, and everyday disciples that seek to follow the way of Jesus, while offering a different vantage point?

This does not mean a non-dialogical acceptance of all Black Church tradition and theology. It does suggest that Mennonite theological education ought to see the diversity and debates within Black theology as a gift to be received and that Christians formed at the bottom of the racial hierarchy offer transformative practices and life-giving perspectives that contribute to breaking out of the logics of white superiority.

Finally, in taking seriously Copeland's turn toward poor women of color and a consideration of Jesus' own expression of love and solidarity, as well as Carter's call for a new social disposition for theological work that reflects the "disposition of the crucified Christ," might it be time for Mennonite theological education to expand its definition of "the way of Jesus"? Might this involve turning toward the very bodies that have been historically oppressed by our society, entering into their spaces of suffering, and learning to see and encounter Jesus from their vantage point? I suggest that such expanded emphases and practices of discipleship, in imitation of black embodied faith, could very well salvage Mennonite theological education in the twenty-first century.

Notes

1. Leonard Gross and Jan Gleysteen, *Colonial Germantown Mennonites*, foreword by John L. Ruth (Telford, Pa.: Cascadia Publishing House, 2007), 19.

2. Gross and Gleysteen, *Colonial Germantown*, 27-29.

3. John D. Roth, *Stories: How Mennonites Came to Be* (Scottdale, Pa.: Herald Press, 2006), 150.

4. James Allen, *Without Sanctuary: Lynching Photography in America* (Santa Fe, N.M.: Twin Palms Publishers, 2000).

5. Gilbreath Edward, *Birmingham Revolution: Martin Luther King Jr.'s Epic Challenge to the Church* (Downers Grove, Ill.: IVP Books, 2013), 22.

6. Tobin Miller Shearer, *Daily Demonstrators: The Civil Rights Movement in Mennonite Homes and Sanctuaries* (Baltimore, Md.: Johns Hopkins University Press, 2010), 6.

7. Douglas A. Blackmon, *Slavery by Another Name: The Re-Enslavement of Black Americans from the Civil War to World War II* (New York: Doubleday, 2008), 53.

8. Roth, *Stories*, 176.

9. Ervin R. Stutzman, *From Nonresistance to Justice: The Transformation of Mennonite Church Peace Rhetoric, 1908-2008* (Scottdale, Pa.: Herald Press, 2011), 91-94, 99-128.

10. Shearer, *Daily Demonstrators*, 98-129.

11. "The Mennonites," *Third Way*, http://thirdway.com/mennonites/ <1 Aug. 2016>.

12. John Howard Yoder, *The Priestly Kingdom: Social Ethics as Gospel* (Notre Dame, Ind.: University of Notre Dame Press, 1984).

13. Sara Wenger Shenk, *Anabaptist Ways of Knowing: A Conversation About Tradition-Based Critical Education* (Telford, Pa.: Cascadia Publishing House, 2003), 17.

14. Shenk, *Anabaptist Ways of Knowing*, 43-44, quote 44.

15. Shenk, *Anabaptist Ways of Knowing*, 50.

16. Shenk, *Anabaptist Ways of Knowing*, 52.

17. Shenk, *Anabaptist Ways of Knowing*, 53.

18. Shenk, *Anabaptist Ways of Knowing*, 54.

19. Shenk, *Anabaptist Ways of Knowing*, 55.

20. Chris K. Huebner, *A Precarious Peace: Yoderian Explorations on Theology, Knowledge, and Identity*, foreword by Stanley Hauerwas (Scottdale, Pa.: Herald Press, 2006), 100.

21. Huebner, *A Precarious Peace*, 102.

22. Huebner, *A Precarious Peace*, 134.

23. Huebner, *A Precarious Peace*, 137.

24. Huebner, *A Precarious Peace*, 143.

25. Huebner, *A Precarious Peace*, 110.

26. M. Shawn Copeland, *Enfleshing Freedom: Body, Race, and Being* (Minneapolis: Fortress Press, 2010), 86.

27. Copeland, *Enfleshing Freedom*, 90.

28. Copeland, *Enfleshing Freedom*, 89.

29. This turning of the subject finds echo in a comment in Chapter 1. J. Denny Weaver also noted how the story of Jesus ought to realign our theological education and focus towards being among oppressed and marginalized peoples because "the story of Jesus brings forth a critique of much of what transpires in United States society." This critique includes "a persistent racism that lurks below the surface" of our society.

30. Copeland, *Enfleshing Freedom*, 93.

31. Copeland, *Enfleshing Freedom*, 94.

32. J. Kameron Carter, *Race: A Theological Account* (New York: Oxford University Press, 2008), 372.

33. Carter, *Race*, 373.

34. Carter, *Race*, 377.

35. Carter, *Race*, 378.

36. J. Denny Weaver, *The Nonviolent Atonement*, 2nd ed., greatly rev. and expanded (Grand Rapids: Willliam B. Eerdmans Publishing Co., 2011); J. Denny Weaver, *The Nonviolent God* (Grand Rapids, Mich.: William B. Eerdmans Publishing Co., 2013); J. Denny Weaver, "Theology in the Mirror of the Martyred and Oppressed: Reflections on the Intersections of Yoder and Cone," in *The Wisdom of the Cross: Essays in Honor of John Howard Yoder*, ed. Stanley Hauerwas, et al. (Grand Rapids: William B. Eerdmans Publishing Company, 1999), 409–29.

FOUR

FROM GOSHEN TO DELANO: TOWARD A RELATIONAL MENNONITE STUDIES

Felipe Hinojosa

In this chapter I propose that Mennonite studies are better served when we take a relational approach that examines Mennonite identity and culture from the outside in rather than the inside out.[1] The significance of a relational approach is symbolized by my title, "From Goshen to Delano." Here the journey west from the Mennonite mecca of Goshen to the center of Mexican American farmworker activism in Delano, California, centers the experiences of Latinas and Latinos and offers us new possibilities for understanding Mennonite racial politics in the 1960s and 1970s. As a way to set up my proposal for relational Mennonite studies, I begin the essay with some personal history that explains my own engagement as a Latino historian with Mennonite history.

When I started the PhD program in History at the University of Houston in 2004, I knew that I wanted to write a dissertation on Latino religious activism and specifically on Latinos in the Mennonite church. My dissertation advisor, who became very supportive of my topic, was initially shocked by the topic: "Latino Mennonites, really?" he responded—"There are Latino Mennonites?"

I was not offended by his shock. I knew right from the beginning that I would have to explain who the Mennonites were and why Latinos would ever join a church that was predominantly white and mostly found in the Midwest or East Coast. In the early 1970s "minorities" in general made up only about 6 percent of the Mennonite church, and the most direct social movement activities during the civil rights era came out of what was then called the (Old) Mennonite Church in places like Indiana and Pennsylvania.[2] So I clearly remember thinking about the choices I had to make about how best to write this history because I believed it had something important to say about the religious and political lives of Latinos in twentieth-century America.

I have since learned that even Mennonite writers who write about the Mennonite experience have to explain Mennonites. Prominent Mennonite writers from Rudy Wiebe to Julia Kasdorf have also had to make the famous "auto-ethnographic announcement," a declaration of identity and an explanation of just whom it is they are writing about. Who are these Mennonites you speak of?[3]

I devoted several pages in my book, *Latino Mennonites: Civil Rights, Faith, and Evangelical Culture*, to explaining who the Mennonites are and why writing about Latino Mennonites matters. I am glad I did this. I have received positive reviews from scholars across the country who knew little about Mennonites and much less that there are Latinos and African-Americans who have been a part of the Mennonite church since at least the 1920s.

Of course, there were advantages to writing the history of Latino Mennonites. First, this was a "Latino" story, not one limited to Mexican Americans and white Mennonites in south Texas. The story included Puerto Ricans from New York City and Puerto Rico, and Mexican Americans from Chicago and Iowa who in 1968 joined African-Americans to form the Minority Ministries Council. In choosing to write a social movement book on the Minority Ministries Council, I quickly learned that this was one of the few interethnic religious movements in the United States. Most other Protestant denominations did have African-American and Latino groups that worked for social justice in the 1960s and 1970s, but few actually worked together like they did in the Mennonite church.

After only a few days of research at the archives at Goshen College, I realized that the prominent narrative in Mennonite studies (that African-Americans and progressive whites were active during the civil rights movement but Latinos were mostly irrelevant) was a fabrication, a piece of fiction and a harmful one that supported the notion of Mexicans and Puerto Ricans as perpetual foreigners and apolitical.

Truth is, Latinos were at the center of these movements in the Mennonite church. They forged interethnic alliances with African-American Mennonites, organized cross-cultural youth conventions and educational programs, worked for better services for migrant farm workers, and moved the church to be more culturally relevant for people of color, all in the 1960s and 1970s.

It was also very clear to me that there were some great stories here: Puerto Rican Mennonites and the Young Lords in New York City, the Lawndale Choir in Chicago, the opportunity to stake claim to the political aspirations of *mujeres evangélicas* (Latina evangelicals), and Mennonite engagement with the United Farm Worker movement in central California. At the height of the civil rights movement, Latinos and Latinas from the Midwest, South Texas, Puerto Rico, and New York City worked to make the Mennonite church a more inclusive place.

I begin with all this because I want to be clear that the political and ecclesiastical work of Latino Mennonites was more than an historical quirk. These movements revealed the creative possibilities and hopes of Latino religious activism in three important ways: 1) Latina/o religious activism was reformist, not revolutionary; 2) it was always gendered; and 3) it created possibilities for interethnic collaborations. It also became very clear that the surge of Latino religious activism started as an effort to diversify the church and later evolved into a movement that found strength in multiethnic collaborations and in its gendered hopes for redefining Mennonite identity. One example of this was the numerous sermons by ministers like Lupe De León, whose Chicano politics and "Jesus made a macho outta me" sermons very directly countered what some saw as a "feminized" church with an apolitical peace theology.[4]

I also learned that what kept Latinas and Latinos engaged and willing to fight for inclusion in a largely white and rural church with a strong peace tradition had everything to do with the relationships, collaborations, and interethnic political movements they forged with African-Americans and progressive Anglos. This commitment was critical because Latinos, and other people of color, saw white Mennonites as a close-knit family that shared similar and familiar last names: Yoder, Miller, Brubaker, Friesen, Wiebe. The Puerto Rican church leader and pastor José Ortiz always used to say—jokingly and from a distance—that Latinos should not enter the debates and fights among white Mennonites. These were *"peleas entre primos"* (fights among the cousins). In other words, this was a family fight, José would say, it has nothing to do with us.[5]

For Latinos looking from the outside in, the vision of white Mennonite culture in the 1960s and 1970s was racialized (Mennonites were white, not ethnic), gendered (women did not wear make-up, the men built barns, the women baked bread), and quiet (most white Mennonites worshipped very quietly). These racialized and gendered perceptions were a reflection of the realities of white Mennonites in the years after World War II as the lure of Americanization and whiteness at home coincided with an increase in global missions.[6] On one hand, the mission field was a place to maintain past ethnic identity; on the other hand, the mission field opened the doors of a white church to the future of a faith tradition slowly embracing its evangelical call.[7]

There was a relational dynamic, spurred on by how white Mennonites saw themselves in relation to other racial and ethnic minority groups. In south Texas and Puerto Rico, for example, white Mennonites carried with them strong beliefs around the deficiency of Mexican and Puerto Rican culture and its need for salvation. Mennonite missionary Amsa Kauffman was often the most vocal about his racist visions of Mexican Americans whom he labeled a "brown race . . . that as a class are more or less ignorant and given to vices, shooting and cutting affairs." In Puerto Rico, Civilian Public Service workers struggled with how to categorize the multiracial complexions of Puerto Ricans. In one report, one CPS worker noted how "[Puerto Rican] physical features are very much like our own . . . except for the negro or Indian influence." Those perceptions were not limited to white Mennonites but part of a larger narrative of racial exclusion that treated Mexican Americans and Puerto Ricans as "foreigners in a domestic sense" and "second class citizens" throughout much of the history of the United States.[8]

For Latino Mennonites, it was exactly this history of racism and economic oppression that moved them, as one pastor confessed to me, "from preaching John 3:16 to shouting Chicano Power!"[9] This was the power of the civil rights movement and a major reason why I decided that the history of Latino Mennonites needed to be written. I wanted to find out how the politics of the Chicano and Puerto Rican civil rights movements shaped the Mennonite church and how Latinos struggled for inclusion into a predominantly white church in the 1960s and 1970s.

Relational Mennonite Studies

The rest of this essay lays out some initial ideas about how we can begin to embrace a relational approach to Mennonite studies. Historian Natalia Molina has written extensively on the benefits of taking a relational approach in Chicana/o history specifically and historical studies in general. Molina suggests that a relational approach "recognizes that race is a mutually constitutive process and thus attends to how, when, where, and to what extent groups intersect. It recognizes that there are limits to examining groups in isolation."[10] Moving from Goshen to Delano, and the metaphorical and literal borders crossed along the way, can help expand Mennonite history specifically and Mennonite studies more broadly in a way that, as historian Luis Alvarez describes it, moves beyond "a kind of silo or vertical model of organization, with each field left to produce knowledge on a particular race or ethnic group without much consideration to how different groups engage one another."[11]

A relational approach moves us to think about how cultural production and consumption, race and sexuality, immigration, and struggles for dignity operate across ethnic, racial, sexual, and regional boundaries. So, what would it mean to deterritorialize Mennonite studies, to move away from its ethnic trappings, and to position it as a field that engages a relational approach to identity, race, sexuality, religious devotion, and evangelicalism? First, that moves us, as Hildi Froese Tiessen argues, "not to abandon identity issues in Mennonite writing altogether but to probe them more vigorously."[12] This takes us toward Mennonite studies from the outside in, a new and fresh perspective that moves us away from the traditional inside-out scholarship far too common in Mennonite studies.

One example of the traditional, inside-out history we need to move away from is the four-volume series, "The Mennonite Experience in America."[13] Well written and meticulously researched, these comprehensive works are emblematic of the inside-out scholarship that is common in Mennonite historical studies. Why is this the case? One explanation is that Mennonite historians rarely engaged non-religious, or non-

Mennonite, archives in their research for each of the volumes included in this set. In a reflection piece written in 1997, Paul Toews explained that in writing these four volumes each historian took "many trips into the archival centers of the Mennonite universe [and] bypassed the bright lights of the nation's metropolitan centers." Toews goes on to note that this four-volume series missed "the National Archives or the Library of Congress in Washington, D.C., the Widener Library at Harvard in Boston, the American Philosophical Society Library in Philadelphia, or the Henry Huntington Library in Los Angeles."[14] What insights might these archives have revealed about how non-Mennonites viewed and interacted with Mennonites?

So how do we do Mennonite studies from the outside in and what might that endeavor look like? One place to start is to rethink how Mennonite scholars approach and write about the civil rights movements of the 1960s and 1970s. Much of the Mennonite literature on this topic perpetuates the simplistic idea that white Mennonites were progressives on questions of race, social movements, and protest. Often this means that the complexities—and anxieties—that many white Mennonites had about the movements and social protest in general are left out of the narratives. We need a more complicated portrayal of how this moment transformed Mennonite identities, politics, and people's everyday lives.

I begin with a case study that chronicles the story of Mennonite engagement with the Farm Worker movement in central California in the 1970s. I use that case study as a spring board to ask a much broader question about how understanding Mennonite involvement in the Farm Worker movement—how going from Goshen to Delano—can move us toward a relational approach to Mennonite studies. How can we expand the contours, the geographies, and the characters of Mennonite history? How can we conceptualize Mennonite studies not in isolation (whether in Goshen or Winnipeg) but in relation to other racial and ethnic groups? How can we engage in a scholarship that crosses borders and is not afraid to move beyond identity even as it continues to chase after it? As the literary critic and writer Hildi Froese Tiessen argued, "Ah, how to both embrace certain treasured aspects of Mennonite identity and escape its imperatives at the same time?"[15]

From Goshen to Delano

Goshen, Indiana, located in the northern part of Indiana near the Michigan border, is familiar to most Mennonites. It is home to a Mennonite liberal arts college, Goshen College, and has a large number of Mennonites who have lived in the area for generations. Delano, of course, is the small town in central California—in the San Joaquin Valley—where César Chávez and Dolores Huerta started the National Farm Worker Association in 1962 and where in 1965 they joined striking Filipino farmworkers in what became the most successful agricultural strike and boycott in U.S. history.

When César Chávez began visiting farm workers, literally going door to door in towns across the San Joaquin Valley, he worked to forge relationships with families and convince them that their working conditions could indeed change. With no labor organizing or collective bargaining rights, farm workers had little faith in the possibility of change. In the fields where they worked, they lacked drinking water, restroom facilities, lunch or rest breaks. To make matters worse, their jobs did not fall under minimum wage laws or qualify for unemployment insurance. With little attention and their rights severely limited, organizing farm workers was a tremendous gamble. The farm worker movement, or "La Causa" as it was also known, captured the imagination of people across the country and helped cement César Chávez as a national civil rights leader.

Jocele T. Meyer, a Mennonite from Cleveland, Ohio, was one such person who was passionate about the movement. In 1973 Meyer, a member of the Women's Missionary and Service Commission (WMSC), a Mennonite women's organization, was excited about the possibilities of supporting the work of the National Farm Worker Ministry (NFWM). Her midweek Bible study group at Lee Heights Mennonite Church in Cleveland had been discussing the plight of farm workers. Along with other Mennonite women, she subscribed to the NFWM mailing list and related publications that covered farm worker issues from "Church Women United."

In December 1973 the NFWM met in Cleveland to garner support, speak to the issues of farm workers in the Midwest, and to boycott the local Fisher-Fazio supermarkets, northeastern Ohio's largest grocery chain. At the request of one of the Minority Ministries Council's leaders, Lupe De León, Meyer was in Cleveland to represent the WMSC and help support the farm worker cause. But when Meyer learned that part of the meeting involved picketing and leafleting she became nervous. She was familiar with the boycott of Fisher-Fazio and had stopped shopping in their stores, even though "they have some of the best specials in the city." She was learning to avoid non-UFW head lettuce and grapes but still struggled and admitted that she "unthinkingly ate a lettuce salad at a restaurant last week."

Picketing was not easy. "Had this been a supermarket in my neighborhood," Meyer admitted, "I am not sure I would have joined them." But she stood there, passed out leaflets, and spoke to people as they entered the grocery store. Knowing that Mennonites have shied away from union participation, she nonetheless believed that "the plight of these workers who supply most of the fresh fruits and vegetables we buy at the super market is something we dare not be blind to."

Meyer's decision to picket one of Ohio's largest grocery store chains was not an easy one. Aside from her own anxieties, she was also aware that throughout much of their history Mennonites balked at union participation. In fact, for some Mennonites, as historian Janis Thiessen reminds us, "[k]illing someone as a soldier in wartime was morally equivalent to walking a picket line in peacetime."[16] That seems like an extreme perspective, but viewing it in this context along with understanding Meyer's story and others like hers provides us with a different angle. It actually puts into perspective why there might have been such unease about César Chávez and the farmworker movement. For Mennonites, especially historian and ethicist Guy F. Hershberger (or "Mr. Peace" as some Latinos called him), the union tactics of César Chávez and the UFW were too violent.

Among the most vocal anti-UFW voices in Mennonite churches in California were the small but wealthy segment of growers from multiple denominational bodies—the Mennonite Brethren, General Conference, and (Old) Mennonite Church—all of whom became entangled in a struggle and a movement that, frankly, they barely understood. These tense and contested interactions with Filipino and Mexican farmworkers positioned the once rural, ethnic, and quiet Mennonites as part and parcel of a white and racist grower segment in the San Joaquin Valley in the 1960s and 1970s.[17]

In 1974 denominational leaders joined members of the Peace Section of MCC in a series of meetings with Mennonite growers in central

California, most of whom were Mennonite Brethren or General Conference Mennonites. The meetings were part of a process to appease the fears of Mennonite growers who believed that their respective church bodies were sympathetic to the UFW cause.

The group that arrived was welcomed in California only after MCC stated that it did not support Chávez or the UFW. MCC accepted this stipulation from the Mennonite growers. One of the first persons they met with was Alvin Peters, who in the early 1970s was at the center of the farm worker debate within the Mennonite church. When Peters extended an invitation to church leaders he did so assuming that Mennonites on the East coast did not understand the dynamics of farm labor disputes in California. He also feared that growers were being demonized by sympathetic Mennonites who sided with Chávez, which is why Peters thrived on sharing the perspective of the growers in central California. Another vocal Mennonite grower, Ray Ewy, also complained that Mexican American farm workers "are violent... [and] carry knives...." He believed the UFW flags had razor blades in them where they were attached to the pole. Ewy went on to say that 'the Mexicans should be able to laugh at themselves like the Japs did about their internment.'"

In the end, the MCC report mostly sympathized with the growers. MCC leaders stood by grower claims that farm worker wages were some of the highest in the nation, and they left unchallenged the claim that poverty among farm workers was more the "result of mismanaging money or unwillingness to work when work is available" than low pay.

Mennonite growers painted a picture of near-perfect relationships with their workers, who they claimed were "generally satisfied... [and] would leave if the farmer would join the UFW." Another Mennonite grower, Richard Hofer, did not understand why activists were clamoring for better housing since "that kind of people do not want nice houses. They're not like us." The "us" is important here because the "us" is not the ethnic Mennonite community but the capitalist class shaped by the white supremacy that thrived in central California.

Mennonite growers were also unanimous in their belief that the church should not side with the UFW and that it "should rather preach the gospel." As a result MCC leaders chose to take a cowardly position as they worried that siding with Chávez and the UFW would alienate wealthy Mennonite growers whose financial donations at the annual MCC Relief Sale fundraiser helped raise thousands of dollars for the work of the MCC. The conflicts raised by the farm worker movement reveal the complex responses—from Meyer to Mr. Peace (Hershberger)—of white Mennonites and the ways in which their political choices varied.

These cultural exchanges suggest that Mennonite identity is deeply shaped by how Mennonites have historically related to other racialized groups and how they have engaged political struggles across the country and the world. Goshen to Delano is a move West, but it also calls us back. Back to the American Midwest—to the Canadian Prairies—where it inspires us to reimagine Mennonite histories and pushes us to look at Mennonite studies from the outside in.

From the activism of people like Jocele T. Meyer and the work of Latinas and Latinos in the Minority Ministries Council in the 1970s, we learn that Mennonite identity and Mennonite activism have never been singular, never one dimensional, never just in the Midwest, never just in the U.S. Mennonite identity is a plurality.

What does this mean? Well, it means we should write about pacifism in relation to Mennonites who have served in the military. It means that when we write about the ethnic Mennonite community, we should also write about whiteness, about racism, and about the workings of hetero-normative patriarchy. It means that we should not just write about progressive and liberal politics within the Mennonite church but also about conservative movements and ideologies.

These are not easy transitions, not easy conversations, but necessary to better understand how power is choreographed in the Mennonite world and how grassroots movements of resistance have worked to upend power relations. Not as a way to romanticize interethnic coalitions but to be honest about the moments of racial conflict, sexism, and homophobia. It is not only about finding commonality but about revealing the moments of disjuncture, the moments of conflict amid supposed cooperation.

Engaging in this work also reveals that it is virtually impossible to capture the full complexity of the Mennonite experience without accounting for how white Mennonites have enagaged African-American, Latino, Indigenous, Asian American, and immigrant Mennonites. We begin to realize, as Luis Alvarez reminds us that

> culture is not a unified system of shared meaning, but a system of multi-vocal, contested, and complex symbols in constant negoti-

ation between various groups, and that the study of race and ethnicity is best understood by using comparative and interdisciplinary methods.[18]

While stories of activism inspire us—to serve with MCC, to do community work—they should also inspire us to transform Mennonite higher education and to craft new models, new kinds of social relations, and to reenvision Mennonite studies. To do so means that we grapple with how to make our Mennonite colleges and universities more reflective of the changing demographics and relevant for a twenty-first century student body that is less likely to be Mennonite. Doing this is more than simply about following demographic trends.

This is also about expanding how we see ourselves as communities of faith that represent multiple formulations and expressions of Mennonite identity. We do this by reimagining our sense of place—from South Texas to Kansas to New York City—where a new Anabaptism is being born, where it has thrived as a grassroots movement. Unrecognizable to some, this is a grassroots Anabaptism that includes expressions of Pentecostalism and evangelicalism and is political, radical, revolutionary, and reformist all at the same time. The quest is to find those stories that remain hidden from view, stories that highlight our struggles, our fights, our social movements, the changing fashions, and the artistic expressions that have remained clouded by the false rumor that Mennonites have always been the "quiet in the land."

Notes

1. This chapter is Felipe Hinojosa's keynote address from the Bluffton conference, printed here with revisions to fit the book format. It was previously published in *Mennonite Quarterly Review* with permission of author, editor, and Cascadia Publishing House.

2. The two largest Mennonite denominations, the (Old) Mennonite Church and the General Conference Mennonite Church, which are referenced in this essay, began a merger process in the 1990s, with the new denomination called Mennonite Church USA. The new denomination has had a complicated history thus far as old loyalties remain strong among the older generation of Mennonites. The question of LGBT inclusion has also loomed large. In 2015 Mennonite Church USA and its area conferences began a prolonged series of discussions and changes around issues of LGBT inclusion, of which the outcome will not be known for a number of years.

3. Julia Spicher Kasdorf, "The Autoethnographic Announcement and the Story," in *After Identity: Mennonite Writing in North America*, ed. Robert Zacharias (Univer-

sity Park, Pa.: Penn State University Press, 2015), 21-36.

4. Felipe Hinojosa, *Latino Mennonites: Civil Rights, Faith and Evangelical Culture* (Baltimore, Md.: Johns Hopkins University Press, 2014), 98-99; see also Beth E. Graybill, "'Finding My Place as a Lady Missionary': Mennonite Women Missionaries to Puerto Rico, 1945–1960," *Journal of Mennonite Studies* 17 (1999): 152–73.

5. Interview with José Ortiz, interviewed by Felipe Hinojosa, Goshen, Indiana, April 2007.

6. Tobin Miller Shearer, "Conflicting Identities: White Racial Formation Among Mennonites, 1960-1985," *Identities* 19, no. 3 (2012): 268-284; Philipp Gollner, "How Mennonites Became White: Religious Activism Cultural Power, and the Limits of Race," in *Good White Christians:How Immigrants Shaped Race, Changed America—and Lost Their Flavor*, PhD diss., Philip Collner (University of Notre Dame, 2016).

7. For more on the relationship between evangelicalism and Anabaptism, see Jared S. Burkholder and David C. Cramer, eds., *The Activist Impulse: Essays on the Intersection of Evangelicalism and Anabaptism* (Eugene, Ore.: Pickwick Publications, 2012).

8. Hinojosa, *Latino Mennonites*, 64-65.

9. Lupe De León, interview by author, Mathis, Tex., June 2007.

10. Natalia Molina, *How Race is Made in America: Immigrants, Citizenship, and the Historical Power of Racial Scxripts* (Oakland, Calif.: University of California Press, 2013), 3.

11. Luis Alvarez, "From Zoot Suits to Hip Hop: Towards a Relational Chicana/o Studies," *Latino Studies* 5, no. 1 (2007): 56.

12. Hildi Froese Tiessen, "After Identity: Liberating the Mennonite Literary Text," in *After Identity*, 212.

13. For the four volume series, see Richard K. MacMaster, *Land, Piety, and Peoplehood: The Establishment of Mennonite Communities in America, 1683-1790*, Mennonite Experience in America, vol. 1 (Scottdale, Pa.: Herald Press, 1984); Theron F. Schlabach, *Peace, Faith, Nation: Mennonites and Amish in Nineteenth-Century America*, The Mennonite Experience in America, vol. 2 (Scottdale, Pa.: Herald, 1988); James C. Juhnke, *Vision, Doctrine, War: Mennonite Identity and Organization in America 1890-1930*, Mennonite Experience in America, vol. 3 (Scottdale, Pa.: Herald Press, 1989); Paul Toews, *Mennonites in American Society, 1930–1970: Modernity and the Persistence of Religious Community*, The Mennonite Experience in America, vol. 4 (Scottdale, Pa.: Herald Press, 1996).

14. Paul Toews, "The Quest for the Mennonite Holy Grail: Reflections on 'The Mennonite Experience in America' Project," *Direction* 26, no. 1 (Spring 1997): 43.

15. Tiessen, "After Identity," 216.

16. Janis Thiessen, "Communism and Labor Unions: The Changing Perspective of Mennonites in Canada and the United States," *Direction* 38, no. 1 (Spring 2009): 23.

17. For more on whiteness and Mennonites, see Shearer, "Conflicting Identities".

18. Alvarez, "From Zoot Suits to Hip Hop," 69.

CHAPTER FIVE

MENNONITE EDUCATION, PLURALISM, AND THE DIALOGICAL NATURE OF TRUTH

Benjamin Bixler

Introduction

In coming years, to play a vital role in both church and wider society Mennonite education will need to learn to live and witness in an increasingly pluralistic context, whether in society or Mennonite schools. Key for this task is accepting the dialogical nature of truth. In this chapter, I argue for an Anabaptist-Mennonite view of education centered on understanding the dialogical nature of truth and advocating for including different perspectives in shaping the future of Mennonite education. For this discussion, the theology of David Tracy and the theory of Mikhail Bakhtin will provide important components in understanding dialogue as key to creating a Mennonite educational experience that is truly transformative for all students, whether Mennonite or not.

The discussion will apply particularly to higher education—the Mennonite colleges, universities, and seminaries that are part of Mennonite Education Agency. It could also be applied in high school settings, but with necessarily different practical applications.

In speaking of a "pluralistic context," I am describing the plurality of ideas, cultural traditions, ethnicities, and religions that are present in our American society, and the tolerance that exists for that variety. The concept of a "melting pot" has long been the metaphor used in talking about American assimilationist ideals, where "the melting pot exerts pressure on any entity—including ethnic religious traditions like Mennonites—to give up something of its particularity to join America."[1] However, our American context has by and large become much more pluralistic in the recent past, and today the particular and unique experiences of individuals and minority groups have become valid expressions of what it means to be an American. Institutions of higher education, even more so than the broader culture, have moved away from a melting pot ideal and toward encouraging and valuing the perspectives contributed by unique experiences.

Mennonite higher education institutions are no exception and are much more open to new ideas than they have been historically, now reflecting a wide variety of ethnic/cultural perspectives and even religious perspectives. It also appears that Mennonite education reflects this acceptance of pluralism even more so than the historic Mennonite communities from which many of their Mennonite students come. As such, Mennonite educational institutions represent a hopeful witness of how to listen carefully and value the experiences of those who are different. This witness can serve as an antidote to a concerted backlash to pluralism coming from some segments of American culture.

In the conservative corners from which many Mennonite students emerge, the response to pluralism has not been a call to return to the melting pot but rather an outright hostility to those who are different. This can be clearly seen in the 2016 political process in which Republican Party candidates ran on platforms that capitalized on the racist and xenophobic fears of many Americans.[2] In this call for diversity of perspectives in Mennonite education and for understanding the dialogical nature of truth, I am expanding the introduction to pluralism and dialogue sketched in the Introduction to Part One.

Education as Transformation

Mennonite education has varied in its approach to wider culture and to the cultural shift toward pluralism. Through the twentieth-century, Mennonite education has wrestled with the question of the purpose of education.³ And as this book was being edited, a new round was precipitated by actions of Eastern Mennonite University and Goshen College and then Bluffton University to change hiring practices to include persons in committed, same-sex relationships. These actions set off a debate concerning their membership standing in the Council of Christian Colleges and Universities (CCCU) and led to the decision of all three institutions voluntarily to withdraw their memberships.

This debate about the membership of Mennonite schools in the CCCU poses a central question about the role of higher education in America in general and for Mennonite education in particular. Does education preserve traditional understandings? Or does it rethink, challenge, and adapt those understandings through exposure to new ideas?

A little historical background provides some context for answering this question. When Mennonites first entered higher education, the answer to the question was clear. John Roth characterized the impetus for Mennonite education as "largely a defensive means for preserving a sociological and theological birthright—with the overwhelming majority of students, teachers, and administrators rooted in local Mennonite congregations."⁴ Thus Mennonite education began as a way to resist (at least some aspects of) the melting pot, cultural assimilation tendencies in American culture.

This stance of defending Mennonite identity against the broader culture softened over the years. "Today," Roth writes, "these schools embrace a broader mission . . . nurturing relationships with people beyond the traditional boundaries of the Mennonite community."⁵ Roth argues that "an Anabaptist-Mennonite identity at its best is genuinely missional and eager to welcome, embrace, and learn from all students even if they do not share all the same basic assumptions and convictions expressed in the school's mission statement."⁶ This welcoming of students who are not Mennonite requires new models of education since this new-found diversity, "requires greater sensitivity and respect for alternative, even oppositional perspectives"⁷ as well as "genuine openness to the theological and cultural diversity that students bring with them."⁸ Roth briefly mentions that "constructive conversations [and] structured dialogue"⁹ are happening but does not fully explore the implications of what it means to be in dialogue with others who hold oppositional perspectives.

I believe that true transformation occurs only when we engage in dialogue with those who are different from ourselves and confront ideas that challenge our assumptions. To understand what openness in dialogue in Mennonite education might mean, I draw on perspectives from David Tracy and Mikhail Bakhtin.

David Tracy and Mikhail Bakhtin[10]

Theologian David Tracy[11] envisions truly transformational dialogue when he proposes a theology of critical correlation, which leads to a mutually beneficial dialogue that risks everything. Tracy seeks to move beyond the work of Paul Tillich, who argued for a correlational method by which Christian understandings were able to provide answers for questions posed from outside Christianity. In Tracy's critical correlation, however, the questions and answers can come from either side of the equation:

> The fact is that Tillich's method does not call for a critical correlation of the results of one's investigations of the "situation" and the "message." Rather, his method affirms the need for a correlation of the "questions" expressed in the "situation" with the "answers" provided by the Christian "message.". . . . If the "situation" is to be taken with full seriousness, then its answers to its own questions must also be investigated critically. Tillich's method cannot really allow this. . . . Tillich's method does not actually correlate: it juxtaposes questions from the "situation" with answers from the "message."[12]

Tracy envisions a two-way conversation, mutually beneficial dialogue allowing Christians to engage with those who hold different beliefs. This dialogue requires that participants claim their religious beliefs and then to be willing to enter into genuine dialogue:

> For my part, I cannot enter an interreligious dialogue as other than a Christian. Even my willingness to enter for me, is a result of a two-fold commitment: a faith commitment to love of God and neighbor—the heart of Christianity in that command and empowerment of the God decisively manifested in Jesus Christ; and an ethical commitment to these honorable (Western) meanings of what genuine dialogue is (from Plato to Gadamer).[13]

Claiming Christian self-identity is a critical first step in the process, but then an equally important step is to be willing to participate in dialogue. Tracy believes that "if genuine dialogue is to occur, we must be willing to put everything at risk."[14] Thus Mennonite education must be thoroughly grounded in an Anabaptist understanding of the Christian faith, and yet also be willing to take risks in engaging in dialogue with those who may challenge those Anabaptist understandings. This is what it means to risk everything, and only in this way can genuine transformative dialogue take place.

Another perspective on dialogue comes from Russian literary theorist Mikhail Bakhtin, who argued for the dialogical nature of truth. For Bakhtin, this dialogical nature can most clearly be seen in literature, from which he developed his understanding of polyphony as "a plurality of independent and unmerged voices and consciousnesses."[15] For Bakhtin, polyphony was most clearly seen in the novels of Dostoevsky, where "a plurality of consciousnesses, with equal rights and each with its own world, combine but are not merged."[16] Bakhtin saw that when an idea was placed in dialogue it became stronger. In the novel *The Brother's Karamazov*, "[Raskolnikov's idea] enters into dialogic contact with another very strong and integral life-position, Sonya's, and thus reveals new facets and possibilities inherent in it."[17] In embracing Bakhtin's understanding of dialogical truth, Mennonite education can engage with other "strong and integral life positions," realize "new facets and possibilities" in itself, and explore new depths of meaning amid conversation with those who hold different beliefs.

Bakhtin's dialogical truth has been applied to the field of biblical studies, which should come as no surprise, given that the various books of the Bible were written in such disparate contexts, in different locations, and over a vast range of time. In particular, the Hebrew Scripture (Old Testament) dialogues with itself on how the Israelites should treat foreigners—according to Ezra and Nehemiah, foreign persons should be excluded, while the books of Ruth and Jonah advocate for the inclusion of those outside the ethnic boundaries of Israel.[18] Carol Newsom, an Old Testament scholar, sees the book of Job as a dialogical work, and offers insights not just for how to read the text of Job but also for how to engage with persons and ideas different from our own perspectives:

> As Bakhtin rightly insisted, in a polyphonic composition the author (and one might add, the reader) does not give up holding

passionately to claims of truth. But such positions are held in humility, as one engages in the discipline of seeing how one's position appears from the perspective of another, listening to the objections that one must answer, seeing what one's own position hides from itself, and being open to the possibility of modification in light of dialogical engagement.[19]

This process of engaging, listening, seeing, and being open to change are essential to encountering new ideas in a text and also to encountering new people. Newsom seems to be laying out a way forward in our theological disagreements as much as she is speaking about how to read a text. This openness to the possibility of modification necessarily precedes transformation, and that transformation takes place when engaging with those who are different. Newsom recognizes the value of other perspectives when she states, "the only conclusion to a study of the dialogical structure of Job can be the advice to go and reread the book in the company of others who will contest your own reading."[20]

This suggestion to read *in the company of others who will contest your own reading* envisions how to conduct education and scholarship in Mennonite education. Felipe Hinojosa, in his keynote presentation, made the case for "relational Mennonite studies" where we study Mennonite faith "from the outside in."[21] His suggestion parallels what I am advocating when I call for dialogue with "the other"—persons who have different life experiences or who see the world in new ways—as guided by critical race theory, post-colonial theory, queer theory, trauma theory, and many others.

Returning to Bakhtin's theory, it is also helpful to name the dangers of a lack of dialogic understandings, which is understood as monologic construction. These monological constructions are "a falsification of the truly complex and ultimately unexplainable dialogical character of human discourse and reality." These monological statements are necessary at times (like in presenting a paper at a conference), but one must understand they are always "provisional monologizations."[22] When these monologizations are understood to be truthful for all time, rather than provisional, there is great danger. Scott Holland has observed that since "Bakhtin argued that all existence is dialogical [it is] always in danger of being monologized by authoritarian political, moral, or religious discourses and interpretations."[23]

The Dangers of Monolingual Practice

So, what happens when aspects of Mennonite education are monologized? What does it look like when Mennonite education fails to listen to a range of voices and perspectives and dwells in monological identity for too long? As one example, it is helpful to examine the question of the racial diversity of faculty at Mennonite schools. John Roth names systemic discrimination as a concern in his book but does not expand on this.[24]

In reflecting on my sources for this presentation, all of the sources that I rely on are white. This is a fault largely of my own making but also an intentional reflection of my Mennonite education and the history of the Mennonite academy. My sources represent the limited range of exposure during my time spent in Mennonite education as well the narrow range of those writing about Mennonite education. I've been shaped in a particular way by my eighteen years in Mennonite education, where I have had only two teachers or professors of color while a student and no colleagues while a teacher.

Willie James Jennings recently wrote about the principality of whiteness in higher education, naming the need to listen: "We need Christian intellectuals who will listen to their sisters and brothers who live beyond the vale of whiteness and allow themselves to be changed through the listening." This ability to "allow themselves to be changed through the listening" is what Bakhtin and Tracy point toward in naming how true dialogue happens. In Jennings's argument, the dangers of not being changed are real: we fail to recognize the ways in which higher education is complicit in the ongoing oppression of persons:

> We who work and live in the academy are yet to face our spiritual bondage in this regard. The history of Christian institutions of higher education in this country is not simply the history of Christian striving. . . . It is also the story of racial assimilation and of a reality of formation that constantly reestablishes whiteness. Until Christian educational endeavors in this country face this legacy and its ongoing influence on what we imagine an educated person to look and sound like, we will constantly confuse racial assimilation with Christian formation.[25]

Those of us in the dominant white power structures of Mennonite education must come to recognize the dangers of not allowing others to enter into the conversation. The issue is not just about representing the diversity that exists in our communities and in the broader Mennonite church. It is also an issue of how we are forming the next generation of Mennonites to understand themselves.

There are hopeful glimpses in Mennonite education; Mennonite Education Agency has participated in Hope for the Future,[26] EMU and Goshen reported record numbers of diversity in their fall enrollment, and J Denny Weaver has engaged black and womanist theology in his academic work.[27] Yet it seems telling that when John Roth speaks of diversity in Mennonite education, he speaks of the "theological and cultural diversity that *students bring with them*."[28] Diversity is coming through student enrollment numbers (often as a mean of financial stimulus), not as intentional shaping of faculty and administration.

Mennonite education could be more intentional in fostering diverse perspectives entering the classroom through course content, the instructor, or providing diverse administrative leaders. We must take seriously the call of Jennings to overcome this legacy of whiteness in Mennonite education. This issue serves as an example to better understand the value of the dialogical nature of truth, and there are other ways that monologization has entered Mennonite education. My hope is that an awareness of the value of dialogue will allow Mennonite education to resist the monologizations that limit the effectiveness of these schools.

A Practical Application: Mennonite Schools, LGBT Acceptance, and the CCCU

The initial tension around the question of hiring faculty in committed, same-sex relationships and the eventual withdrawal of the three Mennonite schools from the CCCU poses a very practical example of the question of dialogue (or lack of it) between opposing views.

First, I believe Mennonite schools would benefit from unapologetically naming their Anabaptist identities. Shirley Showalter, former president of Goshen College, claims that "the best contribution Goshen College can make to American higher education is to be Mennonite to the core."[29] A similar sentiment was expressed during my time as a teacher at Eastern Mennonite School. In response to a Mennonite Education Agency leadership conference, we were challenged with the words of Isaiah 54:2: "Enlarge the place of your tents, stretch your curtain wide, do not hold back; lengthen your cords, strengthen your stakes." Strengthening stakes is a way to strongly affirm and claim Anabaptist values and perspectives, while stretching the curtains welcomes all to participate in that Anabaptist experience.

In specific reference to the controversy in the CCCU over inclusion of same-sex marriage in the hiring practices at Mennonite schools, the Anabaptist affirmations of same-sex marriage were not arrived at lightly, as Jared Burkholder, professor of history at Grace College, recognized: "Anabaptist notions of justice flow from a peace ethic forged through generations of constant dialogue, reflection, and hard choices . . . the result of concerted ethical dialogue, biblical reflection, and a tenacious commitment to a robust heritage of peacemaking."[30] As Mennonite educational institutions claim these notions of justice as well as other Anabaptist convictions, they must do so rooted in their Anabaptist faith convictions.

Second, Mennonite education must resist being forced into monologic understandings that are not provisional. Dialogue requires an openness to transformation. In their broader associations with other institutions, Mennonite educational institutions can reflect a commitment to dialogue by being continually open to transformation. When conformity is the goal of diverse relationships, those relationships may no longer serve their purpose. In reflecting on the origins of the CCCU, Myron Augsburger notes,

> As to the CCCU, which I helped to develop in its origin and later served, we had a stance of evangelical faith with a primary commitment to bring a Christian perspective to education. But this was with the diversity of the many denominations represented. In fairness, we did not develop a confessional statement but respected the role of each school. There was unity with diversity, no one position dominated the other, each was responsible to be faithful to the Lord and to his Word, as they interpreted the faith.[31]

As the CCCU pushes for conformity of beliefs, rather than continuing to allow for diversity within denominational understandings, then that affiliation might no longer serve the needs of Mennonite education seeking dialogue.[32] As Showalter observes: "True diversity in the academy does not dictate uniformity. It gathers up the many models, asking each to be as true to its tradition as possible while also engaging other voices both inside and outside its community."[33] In this instance, out of respect for the desire for uniformity in the CCCU, the Mennonite member institutions withdrew rather than putting the remaining CCCU members in the position of needing to discipline or expel the Mennonites. On the other hand, by withdrawing, the Mennonite institutions have been pursuing a goal of dialogue within academia. The CCCU has seemed to be pushing for uniformity, which is not the goal of the Mennonite academic institutions.

I believe education functions best when it listens to progressive/liberal voices as well as conservative/fundamentalist voices. Only when both of these competing voices are held in tension is there a possibility for dialogue. This dialogue is difficult, and I do not have a good answer for how it can happen. As someone who attends a Lancaster Mennonite Conference (LMC) church and personally wants to remain a part of Mennonite Church USA, I struggle with how to remain in dialogue among oppositional perspectives. I recognize that these claims are in tension with one another, and that holding them in tension is not comfortable or even intellectually possible.

In participating in LMC conversations over leaving MC USA, it was clear that being linked with MC USA was draining participants' energy for local work, due to a concern over allowing others in the denomination to continue in what LMC understands to be sin. However, if those from LMC and other conferences who are on the more conservative end of the theological spectrum leave the church, those voices become silent in the dialogue; with no oppositional dialogue partners, the middle position shifts in a more progressive direction.

Yet I want to hold out hope that even as both sides hold to their firm convictions, somehow there can be an understanding that truth lies in the process of dialogue between those two different perspectives. Perhaps with boundary maintenance removed as an issue for LMC, constructive dialogue can now emerge.

In the end, I am also left with many questions to which I do not have answers. In the spirit of resisting monological truth claims, I'd like to close with these questions in the hope of this being the start of a dialogue rather than end of a monologue:
- Is there a danger of our educational institutions becoming echo chambers, where we only ever hear from similar voices? When we

share more in common with progressives from other denominations (or even other faiths) than we do with conservatives of our own denomination, from where do those oppositional voices required for dialogue come?
- How do we continue to be in relationship with those who do not want dialogue and want to end conversations in the interest of monologic truth statements? The challenge is to continue to be in relationship with those seeking to be true to their own understandings of what it means to be faithful.
- Can we have better dialogue when the covenant aspects of relationship/affiliation are removed? When boundary maintenance is no longer a primary concern, does dialogue become easier? If so, what is the role of mutual accountability in the relationship?

Notes

1. J. Denny Weaver, *Anabaptist Theology in Face of Postmodernity: A Proposal for the Third Millennium*, foreword by Glen Stassen, The C. Henry Smith Series, vol. 2 (Telford, Pa.: Pandora Press U.S., copublished with Herald Press, 2000), 37-38. In this book, Weaver writes of "the resistance to multiculturalism in the United States." This resistance remains today, but has taken the form of reaction to the gains made by those advocating multiculturalism and pluralism.

2. The Republican nomination and election of Donald Trump revealed that a significant portion of the American public supports these ideas. Senator Elizabeth Warren stated that "Trump has built his campaign on racism, sexism, and xenophobia." (https://www.facebook.com/ElizabethWarren/posts/10153739034223687 <5 May 2016>.

3. Rodney J Sawatsky argues that a church-world duality informs Mennonite education, at least implicitly. "Using H. Richard Niebuhr's categories, if 'Christ against culture' characterizes the more radical dualism of the old order, especially from the 1960s onward, a 'transformation of culture' approach became increasingly operative in the colleges as service, peace, and justice emphases became central." Rodney J. Sawatsky, "What Can the Mennonite Tradition Contribute to Christian Higher Education?" in *Models for Christian Higher Education: Strategies for Success in the Twenty-First Century*, ed. Richard T. Hughes and William B. Adrian (Grand Rapids, Mich.: William B. Eerdmans Publishing Co., 1997), 195-196.

4. John D. Roth, *Teaching That Transforms: Why Anabaptist-Mennonite Education Matters* (Scottdale, Pa.: Herald Press, 2011), 20.

5. Roth, *Teaching That Transforms*, 20-21.

6. Roth, *Teaching That Transforms*, 202.

7. Roth, *Teaching That Transforms*, 203.

8. Roth, *Teaching That Transforms*, 206.

9. Roth, *Teaching That Transforms*, 206.

10. Since my introduction to David Tracy and Mikhail Bakhtin came through Anabaptist theologian Scott Holland, they seem to be fitting partners for Mennonite education. See Scott Holland, "How Do Stories Save Us? Two Contemporary Theological Responses," *Conrad Grebel Review* 12, no. 2 (Spring 1994): 131-153.

11. I deal more fully with David Tracy's theology in my master's thesis. See Benjamin Bixler, "Prophetic Challenges in Dialogue with Popular Culture," unpublished master's thesis (Harrisonburg, Va.: Eastern Mennonite Seminary, 2013), 22-37.

12. David Tracy, *Blessed Rage for Order: The New Pluralism in Theology* (New York: Seabury Press, 1975), 46.

13. David Tracy, *Dialogue with the Other: The Inter-Religious Dialogue* (Grand Rapids, Mich.: William B. Eerdmans Publishing Co., 1991), 95.

14. Tracy, *Dialogue with the Other*, 95. While Tracy has in mind inter-religious dialogue, I believe that this understanding of dialogue also applies to dialogue among Christians. While Christians do have the same reference point (Jesus or the Bible), their understanding of what Jesus or the Bible represents can often be radically different (as an example, many Christians understand their Christian faith as compatible with war and violence, while others, including Anabaptists, do not). Despite these differences, dialogue is the only way to truly come to understand the position of another, even another Christian with whom I might disagree profoundly.

15. Mikhail Bakhtin, *Problems of Dostoevsky's Poetics*, ed. Caryl Emerson, Theory and History of Literature, vol. 8 (Minneapolis: University of Minnesota Press, 1984), 6.

16. Bakhtin, *Problems of Dostoevsky's Poetics*, 6.

17. Bakhtin, *Problems of Dostoevsky's Poetics*, 89.

18. J. Denny Weaver described a conversation in the Old Testament abut the violence and nonviolence of God. See his *The Nonviolent God* (Grand Rapids, Mich.: William B. Eerdmans Publishing Co., 2013), 89-150, and Chapter 7 in this volume.

19. Carol A. Newsom, *The Book of Job: A Contest of Moral Imaginations* (Oxford; New York: Oxford University Press, 2003), 262.

20. Newsom, *The Book of Job*, 264.

21. See Chapter 4 in this volume.

22. Dennis T. Olson, "Biblical Theology as Provisional Monologization: A Dialogue with Childs, Brueggemann and Bakhtin," *Biblical Interpretation* 6, no. 2 (April 1998): 174.

23. Holland, "How Do Stories Save Us?" 151-152.

24. Roth, *Teaching That Transforms*, 209.

25. Willie James Jennings, "The Fuller Difference: To Be a Christian Intellectual," *Fuller Magazine*, https://fullerstudio.fuller.edu/the-fuller-difference-to-be-a-christian-intellectual/ <24 Sept. 2015>.

26. Mennonite Church USA, "Hope for the Future," http://mennoniteusa.org/what-we-do/undoing-racism/hope-for-the-future/ <25 Jan. 2016>. Hope for the Future is a project of Mennonite Church USA with a goal to "bring together leaders

of color from across the church, sometimes with white allies, to explore the ways that power, privilege and racism function in our denomination." Mennonite Education Agency has been active in this work. Mennonite Education Agency, "Hope for the Future," http://www.mennoniteeducation.org/OurWork/Pages/Hope-for-the-Future.aspx <25 Jan. 2016>.

27. See J. Denny Weaver, "Theology in the Mirror of the Martyred and Oppressed: Reflections on the Intersections of Yoder and Cone," in *The Wisdom of the Cross: Essays in Honor of John Howard Yoder*, ed. Stanley Hauerwas, et al. (Grand Rapids, Mich.: William B. Eerdmans Publishing Co., 1999), 409-29; J. Denny Weaver, *The Nonviolent Atonement*, 2nd ed., greatly rev. and expanded (Grand Rapids: William B. Eerdmans Publishing Co., 2011), chs. 4, 6.

28. Roth, *Teaching That Transforms*, 203, emphasis added.

29. Shirley Hershey Showalter, "Deep Calls to Deep: Spirituality and Diversity at Goshen College," in *Education as Transformation: Religious Pluralism, Spirituality and a New Vision for Higher Education in America*, ed. Victor Kazanjian and Peter Laurence (New York: Peter Lang, 2000), 203. I find it encouraging that Showalter asserts that "Increasingly, to do so [to be Mennonite] is multicultural. It certainly does not mean being exclusively Swiss-German American in ethnicity."

30. Jared S. Burkholder, "How Peacemaking Helps Frame the Context of Anabaptism, Sexuality, and Higher Education," blog entry, https://pietistschoolman.com/2015/10/06/how-peacemaking-helps-frame-the-context-of-anabaptism-sexuality-and-higher-education/ <15 Oct. 2015>.

31. Myron Augsburger, "Unity with Diversity in CCCU," *Mennonite World Review*, 29 September 2015, http://mennoworld.org/2015/09/29/the-world-together/unity-with-diversity-in-cccu/ <15 Oct. 2015>.

32. The tension between the broader evangelical community and Anabaptists has been summarized well in Devin Manzullo-Thomas, "Mennonites, Evangelicals, and the Sexuality Debate in Christian Higher Ed," blog entry, https://pietistschoolman.com/2015/08/12/mennonites-evangelicals-and-the-sexuality-debate-in-christian-higher-ed-devin-manzullo-thomas/ <12 Oct. 2015>.

33. Showalter, "Deep Calls to Deep," 203.

Part Two
The Bible

Part Two: The Bible

Reformers in the sixteenth century appealed to the Bible as an authority over against the authority of the pope. Anabaptists appealed to the Bible repeatedly in their renewal efforts. Ever since the sixteenth century the Bible has played a central role in the varied Protestant traditions, and eventually for Catholics as well. Mennonites have most definitely identified themselves as a biblical people. Teaching the Bible should be central to education for Mennonites.

What was not recognized in the sixteenth century was that although all reforming groups appealed to the Bible, they were reading and using the Bible differently. An appeal to the Scripture did not resolve their differences. In the twenty-first century, the Bible remains important for all Christians. While there is still no consensus on how to read the Bible, we are better prepared now to understand differences than Christians were in the sixteenth century. Today we can at least observe the perspective that an individual or a group brings to the Bible.

For the book in hand, the Bible is used and discussed in what might be variously called an Anabaptist perspective or a Mennonite perspective or a peace church perspective. When we understand the term, it can also be called reading from a marginal perspective.

One dimension of an Anabaptist or Mennonite reading of the Bible is the assumption that it serves as the primary norm for faith and practice. The assumption is that faithful Christians obey commands found in the Bible and follow the example of Jesus as it is presented in the Bible. For the peace church, perhaps the most important mark of obedience to biblical teaching would be to follow Jesus' example of refusing to use violence, and his injunctions in the Sermon on the Mount, when he said "love your enemies," and "resist not evil." Following this example and these sayings meant a rejection of violence and a commitment to pacifism by many Mennonites, Brethren and Quakers, who became know as Peace Churches.

The majority of Christians have not interpreted the Bible in a way that made pacifism the norm for Christian behavior or the symbol of obedience to the example of Jesus. In this context, the pacifist reading of the Bible is a reading from the margins of the broad Christian tradition. In this case, margin clearly does not mean unimportant. On the contrary. It is this marginal reading that has given the Anabaptist, Mennonite tradition its most well known identity.

But another marginal reading challenges the majority Anabaptist, Mennonite tradition. The dominant Christian tradition has been largely silent on the evil of racism. The dominant Christian traditions of Europe supported the colonial enterprise around the world, with its subjugation of people of color. Even when slavery was finally done away with in North America in the nineteenth century, the majority theology was largely silent on questions of slavery and white supremacy. It appears that on this issue, the majority of Mennonite theology was aligned with the silent American majority. It was voices from the Mennonite margins, as illustrated by the essays in Part One by Drew Hart and Felipe Hinojosa, that make visible this characteristic of the Mennonite majority.

Recently a pacifist perspective on the Bible has provoked another discussion. It stems from the belief, clearly articulated in the first chapter of this book, that God is revealed in the person and life of Jesus. The logical spin off, which has become a topic of discussion among Anabaptists in only the last two decades, is that since Jesus rejected violence and since Jesus revealed God and the reign of God, then God should also be understood in nonviolent terms and images. In the history of Christian doctrine, that conclusion is very much a conclusion from the peace church margin of the Christian tradition. That conclusion calls for rethinking a great deal of traditional theology, particularly the understandings of atonement and the character of God.[1]

The idea of a nonviolent God calls immediately for dealing with the accounts of great violence in the Old Testament and the God who exercises or sanctions that violence. Part Two presents several different ways to read the Bible from the Anabaptist, Mennonite margin. The first two deal, at least in part, with the idea of divine violence viewed from a pacifist perspective. Laura Brenneman is concerned that we take the whole

Bible seriously, which means paying particular attention to its marginal voices. She is also cognizant that when the Bible is read from a pacifist perspective, the stories of war, violence, and war heroes in the Old Testament pose a particular problem. Her solution is to approach the Bible as a choir with multiple voices, all of which are important, but with a particular concern to hear marginal voices. She opens her chapter with a description of sixteenth-century Anabaptist principles of biblical interpretation and then asks how seeing the canon as a choir would fit with those principles.

The chapter by J. Denny Weaver poses a different approach to a marginal reading from a pacifist perspective. The chapter suggests another way to deal with the violence of the Old Testament while keeping the entire Bible in view. Weaver identifies a strand of nonviolent actions with divine blessing throughout the Old Testament, which is in "conversation" with the images of the God who sanctions violence. Resolution to this conversation comes when one sees that Jesus, who is a continuation of the story of the Israelites, is a bearer of the nonviolent side of the conversation. Thus the God revealed in the story of Jesus is a nonviolent God, who is best represented by the nonviolent tradition in the Old Testament.

But the Bible itself has margins, namely what is called the Apocrypha, the ancient writings that were included in the Greek translation of the Old Testament but not the Hebrew Bible. These writings appear in some collections of the canon but not others, with their inclusion debated as far back as the earliest Christian centuries. This history makes these writings marginal to the parts of the canon on which all traditions agree. In the third chapter of Part One, Jackie Wyse-Rhodes invites us to join the discussion about the Apocrypha, and provides reasons why reading the Apocrypha contributes significantly to our understanding of the entire canon. An Afterword then demonstrates how early Anabaptists used the Apocrypha as Scripture.

Note

1. For a book-length discussion of the nonviolence of God that is derived from a nonviolent atonement image, see J. Denny Weaver, *The Nonviolent God* (Grand Rapids, Mich.: William B. Eerdmans Publishing Co., 2013).

CHAPTER SIX

BIBLICAL INTERPRETATION IN AN ANABAPTIST PERSPECTIVE: CANON AS CHOIR

Laura L. Brenneman

Although the Bible is by far the best source to Jesus Christ from whom Christians take their name, there has never been a consensus on how to interpret the diverse kinds of literature in the Bible. In this chapter, I will discuss Anabaptist ways of reading the Bible—the principles of both early Anabaptists as well as practices of contemporary Mennonite biblical interpretation. Then with those ideas in mind, I will make a proposal for an additional interpretive principle that is in concert both with good practices in biblical studies and with Anabaptist values. In this essay, I suggest an image of the canon as a choir as a way of understanding the diverse voices in Scripture.

Principles of Anabaptist Biblical Interpretation: Traditional Views

In *Biblical Interpretation in the Anabaptist Tradition*, Stuart Murray observes that although Anabaptists were separated geographically, did not have much leisure time for developing systematic theologies, experienced persecution, and took different stances depending on which opponents they were facing, their opponents did see them as generally adhering to several common principles:

1) The Bible is self-interpreting (*scriptura sui ipsius interpres*)
2) Interpretation is Christocentric.
3) The two testaments have different weight.
4) The Spirit and the Word are both important. In fact, Anabaptists were accused of both literalism and spiritualism.

5) Anabaptists had a congregational hermeneutics: they encouraged every person to interpret and then to check interpretations in community. This practice may be the Anabaptists' most radical contribution.

6) Anabaptists had a hermeneutics of obedience. That is, serving Christ, often called discipleship, is the most important lesson of Scripture. As such, all interpretation has ethical implications and has to be applied.[1]

In an essay from the 1980s, Walter Klaassen identifies presuppositions and principles of early Anabaptist biblical interpretation similar to Murray's description.[2] The hermeneutical principles of Christocentrism, the primacy of New Testament over Old Testament, the understanding that the Bible illuminates itself, and appeal to both letter and Spirit were, in turn, built on the presuppositions that

- Scripture not only witnesses to Christ's salvation, but also provides specific directions to individuals and communities of believers.
- Scripture is the word of God and will be illumined by God's Spirit.
- There is a close association between understanding Scripture and obedience.
- Although the Bible is the chief medium of God's word, God's Word is also broader than the Bible.

Finally, Klaassen shows that these presuppositions and principles were borne out in practices of Anabaptist communities. They limited reliance on scholarly input while subjecting interpretation to communal discernment, and they saw a strong connection between discipleship and knowledge.

Observations in a 1977 statement adopted by the Mennonite General Assembly recall the earlier Anabaptist emphases.[3] The statement notes that in contemporary Mennonite biblical interpretation there is still an emphasis on a close reading of Scripture and its plain sense but with aid from scholarship; the presence of the interpretive community;

more weight on the New Testament as fulfillment of prophecy than Old Testament; a Christocentric interpretation; the Spirit-empowered interpretation of Scripture (but not Spirit alone); and obedient response. Moreover, the statement noted that Mennonites still tend to be skeptical of scholarly criticisms along with acknowledgment of the usefulness of some scholarship. There is a wariness of the influence of the wider culture, of the individualism of contemporary society and its reliance on reason, and of national allegiances. In terms of practice, the Mennonite General Assembly observes, "The Bible is to be interpreted within the context of the believing, obedient community, as that community seeks to communicate its message to the world."[4]

Is Canon Within a Canon a "Necessary" Conclusion?

One of the critiques (past and present) of Anabaptist biblical interpretation is that in its commitment to Christocentrism it functions with a canon within the canon. When I was pursuing my PhD in England, my supervisor, an Anglican priest and a professor, argued to one of his undergraduate classes that Mennonites' commitment to pacifism is an example of making a canon within a canon. That is so, he said, since the only basis within Scripture for pacifism is in the Sermon on the Mount. As another example, I have observed Mennonite theologians who do not make much use of the Old Testament nor seem to know it well.

As a biblical scholar, selective uses of the Bible troubles me greatly. And while I believe that my PhD supervisor's understanding of Mennonite theology is flawed, indeed one of the easiest texts to use in demonstrating a peace ethic and the importance of love of neighbor is the Sermon on the Mount, and I find many Mennonites relying primarily on that text to demonstrate pacifism. Perhaps that's not a bad thing. However, I do not think that this reliance on one text is fully congruent with traditional Anabaptist principles of interpretation. Rather, perhaps the better way is to consider the canon as a model of community, akin to the Anabaptist principle of a community hermeneutic.

What do I mean by this? To illustrate, let's take three biblical figures, Joshua, Jonah, and Jesus. From an Anabaptist Christocentric perspective, it may seem axiomatic that Jesus has the final word. But let's pause for a few minutes. What if that conclusion sets up a competitive dynamic that is out of place in biblical interpretation? If we set aside the need to choose among voices, the scene changes. Instead of having only a soloist, we have a choir, where not every voice will sound the same or have the same part, but the diversity is rich and enriches the audience. So, what part does each of these voices have?

Joshua is the commander, the warrior, the purifier, which is true to the text but partial. Joshua is also portrayed as the perfect disciple. He follows the Lord's will as an instrument of warfare and sacrament, a role visible in requiring the circumcision of the men of fighting age before battle (Josh. 5). Joshua's warring is not a *realistic* picture of warfare but an *idealistic* picture of how to behave before the holy God.

Moreover, although Joshua's wars are portrayed as total and successful in the first part of the book, we find as the book goes on that the so-called conquest is partial (as in Josh. 13:1; 15:63), and the interests of the storyteller are less about military conquest and more about purity and obedience of the people of God. This emphasis appears clearly in the stories of Achan and Jericho (Josh. 6 and 7). Joshua's voice in the choir is loud and strong. There are many representatives in the choir of the people of God that trumpet covenant obedience and reward for this obedience as well as the necessity of purity to maintain covenant obedience. Although it is a strong voice, it is not the only voice in the choir of canon.

Against his best efforts to be an unfaithful disciple, Jonah is a successful prophet of God. Unwillingly he is compelled to go to the enemy, and in preaching God's righteous punishment, he ushers in God's mercy. He loathes that result but had suspected it would go this way (see Jonah 4:1-3). Jonah's will is not to do God's will, but God's will wins out anyway.

This Old Testament book is about the unstoppable nature of God's mercy, which appears in the response of the people and animals of Nineveh (3:6-10). Jonah is a quieter voice in our choir, but it is not subtle. It is the eccentric voice. It is often inconvenient, even to the one who bears it. Jonah would have preferred a different part; Jonah tried to get a different part, but the one he received was inescapable and impossible to ignore. Whereas Joshua's strong and sure voice did not achieve the sweeping conquest of the land, Jonah's thin and reluctant voice was utterly compelling.

And what of Jesus? His vocal range is incredible, from the weak cry of a newborn to thunderous command of the stormy sea and rage at the profiteers in the temple to heart-to-heart talks with those at the margins of society—tax collectors, children, women who came to learn at his feet, those needing healing, and sinners. In Jesus, we not only have portraits of divinity, we see the fullness of humanity. In learning about and listening to Jesus, we see the full partnership between God and humanity.

Like Jesus, the canon shows us the partnership between God and humanity. Humans, in relationship with God, produced the works of the Bible. These humans were inspired by God and trusted by God, yet remained fully human. And the work itself, as a fully human expression of fully divine inspiration, is, I suggest, a picture of community. Despite the fact that most of the authors, editors, or preservers of the biblical traditions never knew each other, their work resides together in the bound edition that we hold in our hands. They are here together, in this volume, like a choir, with many voices, some stronger and more attention-grabbing, others quieter, shier, and some perhaps not as easy to listen to. The voices beckon us, to be heard, in our fully human, yet fully divinely commissioned communities.

We, then, are part of the incarnational reading of the text. Joshua, Jonah, and Jesus sing out to us and we must listen well and join in. We sing, too. And because our choir is so similar to the canonical choir, we must listen not only to the dominant voices, but to the weaker, not-as-well represented, or shier voices. This is where our songs combine, in our fully human expressions of our experiences with the living God.

Anabaptist Interpretation and Canon as Choir

How might this model of canon as choir connect with traditional Anabaptist principles of biblical interpretation identified above?

1) *The Bible is self-interpreting (scriptura sui ipsius interpres):* in the model of the canon as a choir, knowing the Bible well, that is, "listening to it," aids in interpreting it well. This is not a claim, however, that every note and every voice in the canon will sound exactly the same. Canon as choir requires a deeper listening and, sometimes, additional perspectives from our own communities to notice all that is necessary for good interpretation. Thus a congregational hermeneutic is part of the Bible's self-interpretation.

2) *Christocentrisc interpretation:* the canon as choir, which looks at it as a fully human and fully divine project, puts the incarnate Christ at the

center. This does not mean that we see Jesus present in every text. However, the divine-human partnership of the canon can call us into fuller humanity—just as Christ calls us into a fuller humanity—as well as a deeper relationship with the divine. This divine-human partnership is also called covenant and it is found throughout the biblical canon.

3) *The two testaments have different weight:* in the model of canon as choir, there might still be more weight put on the New Testament, following our Anabaptist spiritual ancestors. However, my point in using the examples of Joshua, Jonah, and Jesus is to say that better knowledge of the Bible coupled with the approach of paying attention to quiet voices in the text shows that the Old Testament traditions offer a lot more than many Anabaptists realize. They show God's purposes just as the New Testament does.

4) *Congregational hermeneutics:* the canon as choir places the canon in the congregational hermeneutic, where little-honored texts are brought into the fold to be added to our interpretations. Then, as we grow more attentive in listening to these voices, we can be shaped and changed by them to become better listeners to the marginalized people around us.

5) *Hermeneutics of obedience:* discipleship means following the voice of Jesus, which is multi-vocal and multi-faceted. Jesus' voice is echoed throughout the canon. This voice, though, is not based on the idea of Jesus' pre-existence but on his full humanity. Thus the humanness of the text is in concert with the full humanness of Jesus, who (in paraphrase of Heb. 4:15) is able to sympathize with us because he has experienced the same weaknesses. Thus, our discipleship will have an incredible range, be multi-faceted, and perhaps look more like Jesus.

Adding a Seventh Anabaptist Interpretive Principle?

Since I am part of the interpreting community, it is appropriate for me, in good Anabaptist style, to suggest something for consideration to the interpreting community. I would like to add a seventh interpretative principle to the six principles given above. This seventh is, I believe, inherent in the other six. My suggestion concerns marginal voices. Since marginal voices round out a choir but are less dominant and harder to hear, I suggest that we must pay greater attention to them. Thus, I think that privileging marginal voices should be added as a principle of Anabaptist hermeneutics. This principle will impact not just biblical interpretation, but also how we listen to each other and discern how we act as a community

Do We Still Adhere to the Traditional Anabaptist Principles?

I hope this chapter opens up conversation, perhaps along the following lines. Consider the traditional Anabaptist principles of biblical interpretation laid out here and how your community makes use of them. Further, reflect on the portrayal of the biblical canon as a choir of voices as a way to show that although some voices are louder than others, all of them are necessary for the church community today; similarly, since there are quieter voices, it is important to listen more carefully and attentively for them. Our church communities are like the canon, where it makes sense to privilege and listen more closely to the non-dominant voices. Should giving special attention to the quieter voices—as I have proposed—become a constitutive Anabaptist principle of interpretation?

Finally, identify which principles of interpretation are important to you and your church community. Consider whether there are others to add to the ones already identified in this essay.

Thus in a spirit of conversation, I conclude:

- Do you think there are some original principles of Anabaptist interpretation that are more important than others? Which ones and why?
- Are there principles that are missing from the list of traditional values? What might be good additions?

Notes

1. Stuart Murray, *Biblical Interpretation in the Anabaptist Tradition*, Studies in the Believers Church Tradition (Kitchener, Ont.: Pandora Press, 2000), 211-215.

2. For the following, see Walter Klaassen, "Anabaptist Hermeneutics: Presuppositions, Principles and Practice," in *Essays on Biblical Interpretation: Anabaptist-Mennonite Perspectives*, ed. Willard Swartley, Text-Reader Series (Elkhart, Ind.: Institute of Mennonite Studies, 1984), 5-10.

3. Mennonite Church General Assembly, "Biblical Interpretation in the Life of the Church," adopted June 18-24, 1977, Estes Park, Col., Appendix I in *Slavery,*

Sabbath, War and Women: Case Issues in Biblical Interpretation, Willard M. Swartley (Scottdale, Pa.: Herald Press, 1983), 235-249.

4. Mennonite Church General Assembly, "Interpretation in the Life of the Church," 248.

CHAPTER SEVEN

DIVINE VIOLENCE
AND THE OLD TESTAMENT

J. Denny Weaver

When the argument is presented for a nonviolent God, one of the most obvious and most frequent problems raised concerns the Old Testament.[1] The violence in the Old Testament and the violence attributed to God described in the Old Testament are well known.

How does this biblical presentation of divine violence relate to the belief that the God revealed in Jesus is a nonviolent God? How do we reconcile the divinely sanctioned violence by God's people in the Old Testament with Jesus' teaching and modeling of nonviolent confrontation for his followers?

These are indeed serious questions. To face the problem squarely, the first section of this chapter presents a sample of instances of violence enacted or blessed by God selected from throughout the Old Testament.

In its dealing with the Old Testament, this chapter demonstrates an approach to biblical interpretation that understands the story of Jesus as a continuation of the Old Testament and that considers the entire Old Testament to be an integral part of the canon for Christians.

A Violent God

The well-known story of the *Great Flood* in Genesis 6-8, modeled in children's toys with boat and cute animals, pictures almost unimaginable divine violence. The wickedness of people made God so angry that God produced the flood that covered the entire earth and killed every living thing, except for Noah and his family and the animals Noah had collected on the ark. This story of the destruction of almost all living beings on earth, both human and animal, features virtually unfathomable violence carried out by God.

When the Children of Israel, who were slaves in Egypt, escaped in the exodus, Moses assisted God in using water to kill the pursuing Egyptian army. Again, God was directly responsible for killing a great number of people.

In the book of Deuteronomy, many violations of the *law code* are punishable with the death penalty. Deeds or conditions worthy of the death penalty encompass anyone (including family members) who tempts someone to worship a god other than Israel's God (13:1-11; also 17:2-7), a rebellious son (21:18-21), a bride discovered not to be a virgin, and a couple discovered in adultery (22:13-22).

Stories of the *conquest of Palestine* report that God frequently commanded the Israelites to carry out great violence. As reported in Joshua 1-12, the conquest was very bloody and violent. One example is the conquest of Jericho. Children in Sunday school classes enjoy marching around a pretend city and having the walls fall down. Not usually acted out by the children is what followed the collapse of the walls—the Israelites stormed into the city and massacred every living person, and every living thing of value, "men and women, young and old, oxen, sheep, and donkeys" (Josh. 6:21).

When Achan kept some of the booty from Jericho and hid it in his tent, God punished the Israelites by having them defeated in their attack on the city of Ai. When the investigation uncovered the loot in Achan's tent, he and his whole family were stoned and their possessions burned. With that punishment carried out, the next attack on Ai succeeded. With God's approval, on that day all the men and women of Ai, twelve thousand people, were slaughtered (Josh. 7:1-8:29).

A story in the book of Judges reports killing with graphic details. Judges 4 recounts the story of prophetess and judge Deborah, who sent Barak against an army led by Sisera under King Jabin. God threw Sisera's army into panic, and Barak's army massacred all of them. Sisera fled on foot and came to the tent of Jael. She welcomed a weary Sisera into her tent, covered him with a rug, and gave him milk to drink. When he fell asleep, Jael took a hammer and drove a tent peg through Sisera's temple, nailing his head to the ground. When Barak arrived, Jael showed him her handiwork. God receives credit for the massacre of King Jabin's army as well as Jael's action as the story concludes, "So on that day God subdued King Jabin of Canaan before the Israelites" (Judg. 4:23).

Divinely sanctioned massacres seemed almost routine for the *kings of Israel*. The judge Samuel passed along a charge to Saul, the first king of the Israelites, to punish the Amalekites with destruction because they opposed the Israelites. "Kill both man and woman, child and infant, ox and sheep, camel and donkey" (1 Sam. 15:3). Saul did a lot of killing but spared King Agag and the best of the livestock. This sparing so angered God that God withdrew the kingship from Saul and gave it to David.

The exploits of David begin in 1 Samuel 16 and occupy the remaining nine chapters of 1 Samuel, all of 2 Samuel and the first two chapters of 1 Kings. Second Samuel 7 recounts the promise made by God that a son of David would build a permanent place of worship and God promises, "Your house and your kingdom shall be sure forever before me; your throne shall be established forever" (7:16). The chapter following summarizes wars fought by David. He defeated Philistines and Moabites. He took 1,700 horsemen and 20,000 foot soldiers from King Hadadezer of Zobah, and then David killed 22,000 Arameans who came to help King Hadadezer. And upon return from these battles, he killed 18,000 Edomites. This section of text concludes, "And the Lord gave victory to David wherever he went" (2 Sam. 8:14).

God also punished David. Late in his rule, David commissioned a census of Israel's population. This census displeased God. As punishment, David was given the choice of three years of famine in Israel, three months of devastation from enemies, or three days of pestilence in Israel. On David's choice, God sent the plague, and 70,000 people died (2 Sam. 24:15). Thus the story of David contains both God's blessing on killing and death caused by God as punishment.

Writings of the Prophets frequently refer to violence as punishment worked or sanctioned by God. One example comes from the writings of Isaiah, who was active for some forty years at the end of the eighth century BCE. A complete cycle of this divine punishment occurs in Isaiah

10:5-19, as the punisher becomes the punished. In verses 5-11, the prophet gives voice to God, who is sending Assyria, "the rod of my anger ... against a godless nation," namely Israel. But in verses 12-19, Assyria in turn also falls under divine judgment because of "the arrogant boasting of the king of Assyria and his haughty pride." Thus God vaunts himself, claiming "by the strength of my hand I have done it," when it was actually God's doing. Then the divine punishment falls on Assyria. Thus "the Sovereign, the Lord of hosts, will send wasting sickness among his stout warriors" (10:16).

Almost a century later, in 612 BCE, Nineveh, the capital city of Assyria fell to invaders. The prophet Nahum gives voice to God, who takes credit for the destruction of the ones who plagued Israel. "A jealous and avenging God is the Lord, the Lord is avenging and wrathful; the Lord takes vengeance on his adversaries and rages against his enemies" (Nah. 1:2).

Many Psalms, the worship music and the poetry of Israel, also appear to portray this powerful and vengeful God. Psalms call the people to praise or bow in awe before the majestic creator God, the God of Israel. This God controls all things. This control covers the forces of nature, when the Israelites escaped from Egypt in the exodus (for example, Psalms 78:11-16, 43-48). It also covers the fortunes of nations, where God expresses anger and wrath, whether against a disobedient Israel (Ps. 106:40-41), or the enemies of Israel (135:10-12).

This sample of vignettes from across the Old Testament could be expanded greatly. They all picture a God who uses violence as punishment and judgment. At times God exercised the violence directly, as in the stories of the great flood and the exodus. Other times it is Israel's leader or Israel's army who follow instructions from God to carry out the violence. And on occasion, when Israel needs punishing, it is the enemies of Israel who are directed to carry out God's violent punishment. The divine violence falls on those who disobey and oppose the will of God, whether Israel or Israel's enemies. Being God's chosen people means not only blessing; it also carries responsibility with punishment for failure to obey.

If these writings of violence and vengeance by the God of Israel were all that we knew, it would be obvious that Israel's God was a violent God. But these images of divine violence are by no means the only image of God present in the Old Testament.

The Old Testament has other images of divine working and other kinds of obedience to God as well. Picturing these additional images will bring out the fact that the Old Testament does not present a uniform picture of God. In fact, it actually poses a conversation about the character and identity of God that readers of the Bible today can and must join.

A Nonviolent God

Consider the two *creation narratives* in Genesis 1 and 2. In the first of these narratives, God creates with the Word, by speaking. There is the familiar sequence of six creative days: day 1, light and darkness; day 2, the dome to separate the waters above from waters below; day 3, the emergence of dry land with vegetation; day 4, the sun, moon and stars; day 5, swimming and flying creatures; day 6, wild, tame, and crawling animals, and male and female human beings. The seventh day was a day of rest.

The narrative of Genesis 2 has a different mode of creation and a different order for the appearance of living things. This account pictures God in the image of a sculptor or potter. All creation occurs in one day, with God kneeling on the ground, fashioning living beings out of clay. God fashioned the male human, a garden for him to inhabit, then animals, and finally the female human. And the man recognized the woman as like him and declared her "bone of my bones and flesh of my flesh."[2]

The two creation narratives open many rich and fruitful theological discussions. The theological point of most concern for present purposes, namely the nonviolence of God, appears clearly when these biblical stories are compared with another creation account from about the same period. This account appears in the Enuma Elish, an ancient Babylonian saga inscribed on clay tablets at about the same time as biblical Abraham would have lived.

The account of creation in Enuma Elish appears in the middle of a long-running saga about the lives and adventures of the gods. In this saga, young gods prodded the female god Tiamat to rebel against the head god, Marduk. Tiamat and Marduk fought. When Timat opened her mouth to engulf Marduk, he blew the wind into her so that she expanded like a huge balloon. He then shot and killed her with an arrow.

With Tiamat vanquished, Marduk took his sword and sliced the round body of Timat in two, like a shell fish. He lifted the upper half up and formed the dome of the sky. He then created stations in this great dome of the sky for various deities—the sun for the day time and moon and stars for the night. Next, Marduk conducted an investigation to discover who had put Timat up to the rebellion. Kingu was revealed as the guilty party. As his punishment, Kingu was killed and his blood was used to make human kind, called "a savage," whose purpose was to serve the gods while they took their leisure.

Both similarities and differences of Genesis 1-2 and Enuma Elish are instructive. The two biblical accounts and Enuma Elish share a common world view, namely a flat earth with a dome over it which contains the heavenly bodies. They have the same misunderstanding of how the cosmos actually works—day and night existing independent of sun, moon and stars, which are entities placed into light and darkness. Genesis 1 and Enuma Elish have the same order of creation as far as the latter's details go—light and darkness existing before the heavenly bodies, plants growing without benefit of sunlight. I note in passing that the effort to reconcile the Bible's accounts with science also validates the "scientific orientation" of Enuma Elish, which few writers would want to do.

It is the differences between the two Genesis accounts and Enuma Elish that make visible the orientation of the Bible's accounts. In Genesis, human beings are declared "very good," or are "made in the image of God" and pictured as the culmination of creation or that for which everything else was made. Such descriptions pose a marked contrast to Enuma Elish's designation of humans as "savages."

Further, whether the creative image is that of a spoken word or the hands of a sculptor, the Genesis accounts display divine purpose and order. Compare these statements of design with the spontaneity and randomness of developments emerging out of chaos in Enuma Elish—the heavens and earth are fabricated from the dead body of a rebellious god, and human beings occur as savage servants in the aftermath of identifying the instigator of the rebellion.

Finally, note again how violent the story is in the Enuma Elish—killing a god and dismembering the body, which then becomes building material for the cosmos, and killing another god whose blood becomes the material from which human beings are made. In light of that violence and blood, it should jump out that the God of the Genesis accounts creates without violence. The Bible pictures creation as a product of divine intention and entirely without violence. The Bible begins with images of a nonviolent God.

But this nonviolent God who lovingly created human beings is the same God pictured in Genesis 6-8 as being angry enough to kill all living creatures except for Noah and his family. The story of the *great flood* concludes, however, with God's promise never again to destroy every living creature, and a promise that the seasons will continue, "summer and winter, day and night, shall not cease" (Gen. 8:22).[3]

The promise that the seasons and day and night will continue without end confirms the affirmation about the order and purpose of creation from Genesis 1 and 2. There is continuity of the understanding of God from the creation stories to the flood account, a continuity of a desire for order and purpose.

Another kind of theological continuity also surfaces in the account of the flood. Although the account in Genesis does not use the term *repent*, that God promised never again to destroy every living thing implies that God repented of the destruction caused by the flood. Repentance, accompanied by a promise not to do it again, reflects the idea of a God who does not resort to violence, or at least no longer resorts to violence.

Some readers may be surprised to read that God could "repent," that God could change God's mind. In fact, that God could repent or change God's mind is a departure from the traditional idea of a God who was and is always the same.[4] To defend this idea of an unchanging God, it is claimed, God must be responsible for all the violence depicted in the Bible, including the vengeance of a flood to destroy all living things and the massacres just described. However, the Bible has another picture of God as well, a nonviolent picture. A God who can repent is consistent with that God. It is also consistent with the story of Jesus' encounter with the Syrophoenician woman, in which her pleas lead Jesus to change his mind (Matt. 15:21-28; Mark 7:24-30).

It is the loving God of creation and the God who repented of destroying all living things that is the God of the *Patriarchs*. This God called Abraham and promised to give him land in a new location and to "make of [him] a great nation," and through this nation "all the families of the earth shall be blessed" (Gen. 12:2-3).

Establishing Abraham as the father of a nation with future blessing sets up the story line for the rest of the Bible. How Abraham and his descendents understood this calling and attempted to carry it out establishes the plot for the ongoing narrative of the Bible. Will the descendents live up to their side of the covenant, and how will God respond when they fail? Understandings in Israel differed on how to live in this story that began with Abraham and about the character of the God of the story. Above we saw parts of the story that assumed a violent God was directing Israel. Now this section points to a different understanding of the God of this plot that began with the call of Abraham.

Abraham and his nephew Lot lived near each other in south central Palestine. Each grew wealthy with great herds of livestock. With the large herds, the land could not support both and their herders quarrelled. But rather than fighting over the land, Abraham proposed that they separate. He gave Lot the choice of land and they parted amicably.

Isaac, son of Abraham, also possessed large herds and a large household. He lived in the region of Gerar in the south of Palestine in a region ruled by King Abimelech of the Philistines. Abimelech's people became jealous of Isaac' success and stopped up his wells. Rather than fighting, Isaac moved and dug new wells. This same scenario played out two more times, and after the third move and the digging of new wells, Isaac was left in peace.

These two stories of Abraham and Isaac display nonviolent responses to conflict. One can interpret these stories to say that when there is faith in God's promise of land, then God's followers do not need to fight for it.

One need not place the blame on God for drowning the entire Egyptian army in the exodus. People are responsible for the problems that they bring on themselves. The mobile Egyptian army, driving heavy chariots, ventured out into sands in which the wheels bogged down while foot traffic could pass easily over the sand. In pursuing the escaping slaves, the army put itself in a vulnerable position. Whether tides or winds pushed the water back, when it returned the Egyptians were caught where they should not have been and were drowned. Rather than saying that God drowned the army, it is possible to conclude that the army suffered destruction that it brought on itself.

The first 12 chapters of Joshua present the *conquest of Palestine* as an accomplished fact, carried out by bloody conquest. However, the book of Joshua also lays out a quite different version of the occupation of Palestine by the Israelites. Immediately after the first twelve chapters describe a supposedly complete picture of the conquest, chapter 13:1 says that Joshua was "old and advanced in years," and "very much of the land still remains to be possessed."

The remainder of the book describes a pattern of settlement that differed greatly from the account in the first twelve chapters. In this second version, individual tribes moved in independently of others, and settlement often occurred by osmosis and integration into the existing society. There were of course, some military operations. But these other accounts of settlement by moving in and settling and of incomplete settlement indicate that the description of military success attributed to God was actually a stylized recitation rather than a historical account. Thus the book of Joshua clearly holds open the possibility of another, nonviolent understanding of God and the way God's people settled the land and confronted their enemies.

An example with minimal violence in the time of *Judges* comes from a story of Gideon in Judges 7. When a huge army of Midianites threatened the Israelites, Gideon sent out a call and roused an army. However, God sent the message that Gideon had too many men. He allowed all those who were frightened to return home. Twenty-two thousand left and ten thousand remained. God told Gideon that it was still too many—when victory came people would credit the size of the army rather than God. Gideon then brought his army down to the water to drink. Those who put down their weapons and put their faces in the water Gideon sent to one side, and to the other side he directed the three hundred who scooped water and lapped it out of one hand. He kept the three hundred and sent the remainder home.

For equipment when they faced the Midianites, Gideon instructed each of the three hundred men to carry a trumpet and a torch hidden inside a pitcher. In clusters of one hundred, they positioned themselves around the camp of the Midianites. At Gideon's signal, they all broke their pitchers at once and began blowing on their trumpets and shouting, "A sword for the Lord and for Gideon!" Seeing the sudden burst of light and hearing the noise, the startled Midianites panicked. Thinking that they were surrounded by a huge army, they started running and hacking at each other. Gideon's three hundred men chased after them. Two captains were captured and killed, but there was no slaughter.

This story from Gideon is a victory through a ruse and creative imagination. It is an example of nonviolent resistance, carried out via commands from God with virtually no killing by the Israelites. That Gideon later engaged in military activity and violence does not detract from this particular story as an example of active nonviolent resistance.

Although God's blessing was claimed on the wars of *King David*, his wars did not go entirely without censure. David had planned to build a great temple in Jerusalem. However, he reported that God told him, "You shall not build a house for my name, for you are a warrior and have shed blood" (1 Chron. 28:3). Solomon, David's son and future king, was the one to build the temple, even though Solomon kept a standing army and was a harsh taskmaster. Having him build the temple is a censure of David's violence and an interpretation that fits with the idea of a nonviolent God.

Chapter 6 of 2 Kings features a story of the *Prophet Elisha* who repelled an invasion with another ruse and food. With God's help, Elisha had several times warned the Israelite king of ambushes set up by the king of Aram. Finally, totally frustrated with Elisha, the king sent an army to capture him. But when this invasion force arrived at the house of Elisha, at Elisha's prayer their eyes were blinded so that they did not recognize him. Elisha offered to lead them to the man they sought. He led them into Samaria, where they were surrounded by the army of the Israelite king, who wanted to massacre the invading Arameans. But instead of a massacre, Elisha instructed the king to prepare food for the Arameans. After they had eaten, the story concludes, "And the Arameans no longer came raiding into the land of Israel." This turning away of an enemy with the help of God and a ruse, followed by kindness, most definitely constitutes an example of active nonviolence.

Alongside the violence of God in writings of *prophets and psalms*, the Suffering Servant poems from the second section of Isaiah (in particular Is. 42:1-4; 49:1-6; 50:4-9; 52:13-53:12) present a much different image of God along with the idea of being willing to suffer for others. We do not need to determine the identity of the Servant to see that the God of the Servant is a God who works through patient suffering, that is, a nonviolent God. The God of the Servant stands in marked contrast to the violent God who perpetrates and sanctions massacres of thousands.

Nineveh has a central location in the book of Jonah, but Jonah's conclusion differs greatly from that of Nahum. In the well-known story,

Jonah fled from the call to preach to pagan Nineveh. Consequently, he spent three days in the belly of the large fish. After being returned to land, Jonah did preach to Nineveh but was angry when God relented (God's mind changed!) and God spared the city. When Jonah declared himself angry enough to die, God chastised him for caring more about a bush than for the hundred and twenty-thousand children in the city (Jonah 4:10-11).

The book of *Jonah* is a parable that interprets Israel's history. Jonah represents unfaithful Israel punished by captivity in Babylon (the great fish or whale) and then returned to Palestine (spit up on the shore) for another opportunity. Despite their repeated disobedience—symbolized by Jonah's flight and then his continuing anger—God remains faithful to Israel as a merciful God, but a God who also shows mercy even to the enemies of Israel, represented by the city of Nineveh. Thus the parable actually shows that God cares not just for the Israelites but for all people. Because of the contrast of attitudes toward Nineveh in Nahum and Jonah, some commentators have suggested that the writer of Jonah intended to provide the image of a merciful God as a counter to the image of the vengeful God of Nahum.[5] Thus the book of Jonah can be listed among the images of a nonviolent God.

The monarchy in Israel came to an end some six centuries before Jesus, when the king and other leaders and numbers of people were taken to Babylon as captives. After more than four centuries of rule by kings, *in exile*, they had no ruler of their own, no political establishment, no monarch. In a sense, it was a return to the conditions before rule by the dynasty of King David.

The prophet *Jeremiah*, who was living in a Jerusalem now controlled by the invaders, wrote a letter to these exiles in Babylon. His letter gave them advice stated as a message from the God of Israel. Jeremiah told them to stop pining after that life in Jerusalem. They should maintain their identity as God's people in this new land but settle down, raise families, learn trades, and "seek the welfare of the city where I [the God of Israel] have sent you into exile, and pray to the Lord on its behalf, for in its welfare you will find your welfare" (Jer. 29:7).

In other words, living as God's people Israel did not depend on having their hands on the means of political control, but the people would find meaning through working for the society in which they now lived. Nothing about living as God's people depended on having a king or control of government or their own army. As God's people, they could learn to speak the language and develop vocational skills that would benefit the society where they now lived.

Stories in the book of *Daniel* illustrate this witness. The first chapter of Daniel tells of Daniel, Hananiah, Mishael, and Azariah, renamed Belteshazzar, Shadrach, Meshach, and Abednego by the palace master. They were among the captives brought in for education that would enable them to enter the king's service. The young men were willing to learn the local language and a useful skill, but to assert their distinct identity, they rejected the royal food and wine and asked for a diet of vegetables and water. In other words, the young exiles maintained their own cultural and religious identity as Hebrews who worshipped the God of Israel rather than the gods of Babylon, even as they learned skills that would benefit Babylon's society. In contemporary language, we can say that maintaining a distinct identity was a matter of nonviolent cultural resistance. Since they thrived on their own kind of food, they were allowed to continue with it as they worked for the king.

Daniel 3 tells another story of Shadrach, Meshach, and Abednego. Daniel got them appointed to be civil servants with responsibilities for the province of Babylon. After the three refused to worship the gods of King Nebuchadnezzar and the golden statue that he had set up, they were bound and thrown into a furnace. But when the three were not harmed in the fire, the king acknowledged the God of Israel and gave them a promotion. This story is another example of nonviolent, cultural resistance. These stories portray ways the Hebrews maintained their own religious and cultural identity, which combined witness to the God of Israel with work for the good of Babylon. The familiar story of Daniel and the den of lions in the sixth chapter has a similar outcome and meaning.

These stories from the book of Daniel illustrate and put a theological blessing on and encouraged the cultural resistance of the Hebrew captives. They maintained their identity as worshipers of Yahweh in a society where they had no control of political authority but nonetheless worked for the blessing of the culture in which they were captives. Their witness required courage and could be confrontational. Today we would call it nonviolent social protest or social resistance.

The Conversation

This sample of stories and texts about God and obeying God selected from across the Old Testament demonstrates that there are images of God that pose a counter-weight to the well-known violent images. Many of the stories just cited are well-known individually. What may seem new is the idea of connecting them to show that together they do present a different image of God than that of the God who exercises great violence in judgment and punishment. Rather than present a uniform picture of God, the Old Testament offers a conversation—even a debate—about the character of God.

If our knowledge of God were limited to the Old Testament, it would not be possible to determine the character of God by putting a finger, whether an actual or figurative finger, on a particular story and then repeating it loudly. For any story or text thus recited, a text could be cited from the other side of the debate. But we are not left with the equal-sided shouting match pictured in this section and the previous one. A resolution to this debate occurs in the New Testament.

A Resolution[6]

In Chapter 1 of this volume, we saw the story of Jesus, the Messiah. He was a continuation of the story of the Israelites from the Old Testament, and those people who accepted Jesus as the Messiah (who came to be called Christians) are one continuation of the people of God who trace their origin to Abraham.[7] Both sides of the conversation about the character of God in the Old Testament claimed to speak for God and to be living as the people of God. But the story of Jesus most obviously aligns itself with one side of the conversation about God.

The story of Jesus, who rejected violence, finds its roots in the images of the nonviolent God and the nonviolent responses to conflict. There were the images of creation without violence and the willingness of the Patriarchs not to fight for land. When the people trusted God, there was salvation from enemies without violence or with minimal violence. Jesus' teaching about sharing wealth and living generously with wealth, about dealing with an oppressive economic system by walking naked, or about going the second mile to embarrass a solder of the occupation all assume that the people of God are able to act without a king or central authority to validate or enforce their actions.

In other words, Jesus is carrying forward the situation that had been the case at least since Jeremiah's letter to the exiles in Babylon, when he told them how to live as the people of God when they no longer controlled the government. Stories in the book of Daniel provided some illustrations.

A century and a half later, Jesus was continuing that tradition, teaching how the people of God can and should live without controlling the reins of political power. Without needing a king or emperor, they could be a living witness to the orientation and values of the reign of God: sharing wealth, confronting discrimination against ethnic and racial groups, opposing second-class status for women, demonstrating nonviolent approaches to conflict, and more.

And with reference to the character of God, if we believe that God is revealed in Jesus, then the clear conclusion is that God is nonviolent. A nonviolent Jesus reveals a nonviolent God, a God visible already in the Old Testament when we have eyes to willing to find that God.

This way of understanding the Old Testament sketched here makes it integral to the story of Jesus. Seeing the sides of the conversation adds greatly to our understanding of the significance of Jesus' way of revealing the reign of God and of his teaching and modeling of a way for his disciples to live. Seeing Jesus as carrying forward the story of the Old Testament does not mean that Jesus or the New Testament supersedes or renders less significant the Old Testament, as I was taught in the church of my youth. The approach sketched here considers the Old Testament to be integral to the Christian canon.

Further, the approach here is anything but a picking and choosing of the parts of the Old Testament that I happen to like. It is precisely because it contains the problematic parts that we can see that a genuine conversation is going on, and it is this conversation that points to the significance of Jesus.[8] Notice that this approach allows the problematic texts to stand as written. There is no effort, as some have done, to soften the violent texts or divine commands to massacre by arguing that the emphasis is not on killing but on obedience to God, an obedience that we can then follow. Rather, the approach outlined here allows these texts to stand as what they appear to be: texts that claim divine sanction of massacres. But even as these texts stand with their stark blessing of violence, the Bible as a whole text points to the nonviolent character of God and the reign of God.

Notes

1. The discussion in this chapter draws on material from Chapters 10-12 of my book, *God Without Violence: Following a Nonviolent God in a Violent World* (Eugene, Ore.: Cascade Books, 2016).

2. Reading these stories as scientific accounts presents a number of well-known difficulties, beginning with the order of events in Genesis 1. These problems include the cosmology of a flat earth with a dome over it, the existence of alternating light and dark as day and night without benefit of sun and the rotation of the earth. Plants appear on day three and produce seeds and fruit, and are thus engaging in photosynthesis which requires sunlight that does not appear until day four.

Compound those difficulties with the fact that the order of events in Genesis 1 differs significantly from that in Genesis 2. In the first story, human beings both male and female are created last, on a teeming earth and as the culmination of creation. In contrast, the second story features the male human created first, followed by plants and animals and finally a female human. Much ink has been spilled trying to reconcile these creation accounts with science. That impossible task should be abandoned, not only because it is impossible but also because these are not scientific stories and are not intended to correspond to the science known in the twenty-first century. In Chapter 20 of the volume in hand, Angela Horn Montel gives suggestions for teaching contemporary science to skeptical students who see Genesis as science.

3. As was true for the Genesis accounts of creation, this story of the great flood cannot be historically or scientifically true. The problems are many—contradictions between the accounts (one pair versus seven pairs of clean animals, different lengths of time rain fell, and more), the absence of archeological evidence to collaborate a worldwide event, the location of enough water to cover the entire earth, the impossibility of collecting animals from innumerable habitats from around the world and loading them on a small ark with sufficient food for the duration, Noah's family handling the feeding and cleaning of all those animals, and more. But as was true for the two creation accounts, no need exists to explain this narrative in accord with twenty-first century knowledge of science and archeology. It is rather a theological account, with an important affirmation about the character of God.

4. For development of the idea that God can change God's mind, see John Sanders, *The God Who Risks: A Theology of Providence* (Downers Grove, Ill.: InterVarsity Press, 1998).

5. For the contrast of Nahum and Jonah see Klaas Spronk, *Nahum*, Historical Commentary on the Old Testament (Kampen, The Netherlands: Kok Pharos Publishing House, 1997), 8-10, 16; and Peter Machinist, "Nahum," in *The Harper Collins Bible Commentary*, rev. ed., James L. Mays (New York: HarperCollins, 2000), 665.

6. On reconciling violence and nonviolence in the biblical writings, I refer to Eric A. Seibert, *Disturbing Divine Behavior: Troubling Old Testament Images of God* (Minneapolis: Fortress Press, 2009), John Dominic Crossan, *God and Empire: Jesus*

Against Rome, Then and Now (New York: HarperCollins, 2007), and Jack Nelson-Pallmeyer, *Jesus Against Christianity: Reclaiming the Missing Jesus* (Harrisburg, Pa.: Trinity Press International, 2001).

7. That is, people who did not recognize Jesus as Messiah are also a continuation of the story of the Israelites from the Old Testament. Today they are the several streams of Judaism. People who did and did not accept Jesus as Messiah worshiped together for a number of centuries without this disagreement being one that resulted in mutual rejection. Scholars from either side have never reached a consensus on when this division became permanent.

In this light, Christians and Jews today could still be having the debate about whether the Messianic age began with Jesus. Rather than seeing themselves in mutually exclusive traditions, they should learn to see themselves as members of the same family, who have an ongoing disagreement about Jesus. For extensive discussion of this understanding of the relationship of Christians and Jews, see John Howard Yoder, *The Jewish-Christian Schism Revisited*, ed. Michael G. Cartwright and Peter Ochs (Grand Rapids, Mich.: William B. Eerdmans Publishing Co., 2003), and Daniel Boyarin, *Border Lines: The Partition of Judaeo-Christianity* (Philadelphia: University of Pennsylvania Press, 2004).

8. Chapter 8, by Jackie Wyse-Rhodes, expands this conversation to include the Apocrypha, when it points to the pacifist orientation of Daniel that is made visible in comparison with the Apocrypha's books of the Maccabees, which were written close to the time of Daniel.

CHAPTER EIGHT

READING THE APOCRYPHA

Jackie Wyse-Rhodes

When compared with sixteenth-century Anabaptists, Mennonite readers of the Bible today are quite unfamiliar with the Apocrypha. This chapter offers seven reasons why Mennonites should read the Apocrypha and also the Pseudepigrapha—and why these less frequently canonized books should be taught in Mennonite settings.

The Apocrypha generally includes the following books: Tobit, Judith, Sirach, Baruch, the Wisdom of Solomon, 1 and 2 Maccabees, and the additions to Esther and Daniel. The Eastern Orthodox canons contain even more books, like 2 Esdras, 3 Maccabees, and Psalm 151. The Pseudepigrapha is a category without definite boundaries, since it consists of early Jewish and Christian literature that was (almost) never canonized, and so the list of books it comprises is malleable based upon one's point of view. From the Pseudepigrapha, I will be considering only the book of 1 Enoch, which was canonized in just one tradition, that of the Ethiopian Orthodox church, and which is quoted in the New Testament book of Jude.

First: a question of definitions. Besides simply listing the books it contains, in what other ways can we talk about the Apocrypha? We might say that the Apocrypha is a set of books that are included in Catholic and Eastern Orthodox biblical canons but excluded from

Protestant canons. This is an accurate and contemporary answer which casts these disputed books of the Bible in Reformation terms. However, a more fruitful way to answer this question is as follows: The Apocrypha is a group of books that are included in the Septuagint, an ancient Greek translation of Jewish scriptures. By framing the Apocrypha in this way, one situates these books within their ancient literary pre-Christian contexts. Though the canonicity of the Apocrypha was debated during the Reformation, such conversations have their origins in early Judaism. The Hebrew Bible was translated into Greek multiple times, and the version we call the Septuagint emerged gradually, starting in about the third century BCE. The oldest extant Septuagint manuscripts were found among the Dead Sea Scrolls at Khirbet Qumran, which means that our manuscript evidence for the Septuagint reaches back in time equally as far as our manuscript evidence for the Hebrew Bible. The Septuagint is an early and reliable textual witness, and the Septuagint includes the Apocrypha.

Therefore, when we consider the question of why Mennonites should read the Apocrypha, we are joining a conversation as old as the Bible itself. The early church fathers exhibited disparate opinions on the status of the Apocrypha—but then again, they also disagreed about whether or not to canonize now-familiar biblical books like Revelation. The early Jewish community did not include the Apocrypha in the Hebrew Bible, and this may have been at least partly a reaction to the popularity of the Septuagint among Christians. Though Jewish in origin, and read by communities of Jews for centuries, in the late first and second centuries, the Septuagint (and with it, the Apocrypha) came to be associated with the Christian movement, and this version of the Bible subsequently fell out of favor in Jewish circles which sought to differentiate themselves as Torah-centered communities. Another reason that first-century Jews may have found the Septuagint suspect is the fact that it was written in Greek rather than Hebrew or Aramaic.

I suggest that we would do well to join this old conversation about Scripture. Why should Mennonites, or other Protestants for that matter, read the Apocrypha? Here are seven reasons I find compelling.

(1) As I just explained, early Jewish and Christian communities were writing and reading the Apocrypha. When we open the Apocrypha, we encounter literature that was familiar to the earliest biblical readers and writers. One of the biggest challenges in reading the Bible

today is figuring out how to enter the ancient imaginations of its early interpreters, despite the "ugly broad ditch"[1] that separates us from the text, a ditch filled with thousands of years of cultural assumptions and language barriers. Simply put, our view of the past is often obscured.

How do we know the early Jews and Christians were reading "non-canonical" books? I offer just one piece of evidence among many: the New Testament tells us so. The book of Jude consists of one chapter, twenty-four verses long, encouraging readers to keep the faith and maintain moral purity. The letter offers positive and negative examples from the Jewish Scriptures (what Christians call the Old Testament), as we might expect. Jude then goes on to quote an unidentified source about Moses as well as the pseudepigraphic book of 1 Enoch.

> But when the archangel Michael contended with the devil and disputed about the body of Moses, he did not dare to bring a condemnation of slander against him, but said, "The Lord rebuke you!" But these people slander whatever they do not understand, and they are destroyed by those things that, like irrational animals, they know by instinct. Woe to them! For they go the way of Cain, and abandon themselves to Balaam's error for the sake of gain, and perish in Korah's rebellion. . . . It was also about these that Enoch, in the seventh generation from Adam, prophesied, saying, "See, the Lord is coming with ten thousands of his holy ones, to execute judgment on all, and to convict everyone of all the deeds of ungodliness that they have committed in such an ungodly way, and of all the harsh things that ungodly sinners have spoken against him." (Jude 9-10, 14-15 NRSV, quoting 1 Enoch 1:9)

When the book of Jude was written, only the Torah and some of the Prophets had stabilized into anything resembling a canon. Because of this, it would be anachronistic to argue that the author of Jude was drawing from a "canon" which included 1 Enoch, because the idea of a closed canon did not yet exist. However, one can say with confidence that the author of Jude quoted 1 Enoch in a manner parallel to his usage of texts that were already considered authoritative by early Jewish and Christian communities. All of these sources were considered trustworthy and revelatory by the author of the book of Jude, a book that Christians, in turn, consider trustworthy and revelatory today.

(2) Reading the Apocrypha helps us interpret the rest of the canon accurately. For example, 2 Peter 3 depicts the end of the earth in fire. For modern readers, the book's rhetoric exemplifies apocalyptic and eschatological language:

> But the day of the Lord will come like a thief, and then the heavens will pass away with a loud noise, and the elements will be dissolved with fire, and the earth and everything that is done on it will be disclosed (2 Pet. 3:10, NRSV).

Second Peter's view of the end comprises destruction of the created order. Within the New Testament, this stark image is balanced by the book of Revelation's more hopeful view of the restoration of the cosmos through the creation of a new heavens and a new earth (Rev. 21). However, if one reads 2 Peter alongside the Pseudepigrapha, it becomes apparent that 2 Peter's depiction of the end of days is not only in tension with that of Revelation; it is a minority report. Other apocalypses, most of them never canonized, tell a different story—a story of judgment, to be sure, but one that is followed by the restoration of the earth to its intended pristine glory.

In these apocalyptic books, there is little division between the spiritual and the physical realms. This is demonstrated most clearly in 1 Enoch, in which the biblical figure of Enoch is taken on a tour of the heavenly realm, and much of what he sees there has to do with the workings of nature. Enoch sees the sources of the waters and the winds, as well as the storehouses for rain, snow, and hail and the angels who release them at their proper times. Enoch sees the four corners of the earth, even the ends of the earth—and all of these natural and earthly elements are located somewhere in the heavenly realm. In the early Jewish imagination, heaven and earth are inextricably linked. In the eschaton, it would make no more sense for the earth to be destroyed than it would for the heavens to go up in smoke along with it.[2]

(3) Reading the Apocrypha makes our study of the Bible historically responsible. Without the Apocrypha, we skip from the latest text of the Hebrew Bible, Daniel, to the earliest text of the New Testament, 1 Thessalonians, without thought or regard for the two centuries of history, politics, and religious change that separate them.

The second half of Daniel, which consists of apocalyptic vision reports, can be dated confidently to 167-164 BCE, a remarkably precise three-year span. Daniel's famous vision of monstrous beasts emerging from the sea symbolizes the rise and fall of empires, the fourth of which is Greece. In a disturbing and bizarre image, Daniel describes this final beast:

> After this I saw in the visions by night a fourth beast, terrifying and dreadful and exceedingly strong. It had great iron teeth and was devouring, breaking in pieces, and stamping what was left with its feet. It was different from all the beasts that preceded it, and it had ten horns. I was considering the horns, when another horn appeared, a little one coming up among them; to make room for it, three of the earlier horns were plucked up by the roots. There were eyes like human eyes in this horn, and a mouth speaking arrogantly. (Dan. 7:7-8, NRSV)

This creepy little horn with eyes and an arrogant mouth symbolizes the Greek ruler Antiochus IV Epiphanes, who was working to outlaw Jewish practices between 167 and 164, going so far as to desecrate the Jewish temple in Jerusalem, possibly by setting up monuments to Greek deities inside. Antiochus symbolizes the empire with which the writers of Daniel are struggling, but in the end the book forbids active or violent resistance to this empire. In Daniel, the struggling believers are instructed to watch and wait. There will come a day when "those who are wise shall shine like the brightness of the sky, and those who lead many to righteousness, like the stars forever and ever" (Dan. 12:23)—but that day will come in God's time, and cannot be brought about by human action.

For Mennonite sensibilities, this rings true. But such a pacifist perspective was not universally embraced among the Jews of the time, and we will only realize this if we pay attention to sources like 1 Maccabees, in which fighting (once even on the Sabbath) is condoned, as well as the Animal Apocalypse of 1 Enoch 85-90, in which sheep (symbolizing the Jews) are given swords to slay the beasts (the Greeks) who pursue them. Reading the Apocrypha and Pseudepigrapha in this case helps us consider Daniel in its proper context and to imagine the ancient debate about how to respond best to the evils of empire while remaining faithful to God—a question just as relevant today.

(4) The early Anabaptists were still reading the Apocrypha. Early Anabaptist writers used the Apocrypha as a source of teaching and instruction in exactly the same way that they used biblical writings. To ex-

pand upon this point, I am grateful to J. Denny Weaver for writing a survey of Anabaptist use of the Apocrypha as an Afterword to this essay.

(5) Some Anabaptists still read the Apocrypha today. In fact, the Apocrypha is generally included in German Bibles used by the Amish, and the story of Tobit is traditionally recited at Amish weddings, introduced with words like the following:

> So one turns to the book of Tobit. Although it is an apocryphal book and is not counted among the books of Holy Scripture, it nevertheless gives a beautiful teaching, strengthens the pious and God-fearing ones in the faith, especially in regard to marriage, and leads through all trial and tribulation to the hope that God finally will bring things to a conclusion with joy. So one begins in the book of Tobit...."[3]

(6) The majority of Christians in the world today still read the Apocrypha. As Mennonites, sometimes we forget that only 37 percent of the world's Christians are Protestant.[4] Therefore, reading the Apocrypha is an act of ecumenical goodwill and solidarity that will increase our ability to understand and commune with the larger body of Christ.

(7) Mennonites should read the Apocrypha because it would bring our practice of Bible reading in line with our (desired) practice of theology and ethics. Anabaptists endeavor to follow Christ in all aspects of life, to seek peace in all spheres of life, and to advocate for marginalized voices. Too often, we restrict our Bible reading to those parts of the canon that most explicitly seem to support our convictions—namely, the Prophets and the Gospels. But just as the world is full of both beauty and horror, and just as our lives can be simultaneously tragic and joyous, the texts we call Scripture contain great complexities. It does us no good to deny the problematic parts of our world, and it does us no good to ignore Scriptures that make us uncomfortable.

Reading *all* of the early Jewish and Christian literature that is available to us today will bring us into contact with voices from the past which have been silenced—voices which, knowingly or unknowingly, we have silenced by ignoring them. When we read the Bible, if we also seek to *be read by* the Bible—if reading Scripture is a dialogical act, a conversation with those who can no longer speak for themselves—then we desperately need the expansiveness and diversity offered by the Apocrypha and Pseudepigrapha.

To be sure, a greater variety of viewpoints will not simplify the way we tell the Christian story. It will probably challenge our revered mental images of whom the early Christians might have been and what they may have believed. But casting such a wide literary and scriptural net will also open our ears to what Laura Brenneman calls the choir of the canon (see Chapter 6). The Apocrypha and Pseudepigrapha are ready and waiting to fill out that choir in both harmonious and discordant ways, and in so doing, these marginalized voices will make the music richer.

Afterword: Anabaptist Use of the Apocrypha
By J. Denny Weaver

Many references to the Apocrypha are found in writings across the major Anabaptist traditions. The examples come from easily accessible sources, and this survey is by no means exhaustive.

In addition to Ecclesiastes and Proverbs, Menno Simons cites Sirach, also known as Ecclesiasticus or Ben Sira, when speaking of "the fear of the Lord" as the beginning of wisdom. He refers to Sirach when he counsels forgiveness and argues against seeking vengeance.[5] In fact, Sirach comes up frequently in Menno's writings, such as in his "Reply to Gellius Faber":

> Wherever the law is preached rightly and taken to heart so that it reveals its nature and power, there we find a broken spirit, a penitent, humble heart, and a conscience which trembles before the Word of its God, which checks and drives out sin, as Sirach says.[6]

Menno also quotes from 2 Esdras and Tobit.

Among Dutch Anabaptists, 2 Esdras 5:1-7 played an important role in the eschatological thinking of Melchoir Hofmann.[7] Menno's colleague Dirk Philips made frequent reference to the Apocrypha. The Scripture index to his collected writings covers more than a page and lists texts he cited from eleven different books of the Apocrypha. One example is Dirk's use of Wisdom of Solomon 2:23 and Ecclesiasticus [Sirach] 17.3 along with Genesis 1:26 and 5:1, and James 3:9 to state that human beings were created in the image of God.[8] David Joris, a member of another faction of Dutch Anabaptists, quotes from five apocryphal books.

The Froschauer Bible, which Swiss Anabaptists used, contains the Apocrypha. The letter by Conrad Grebel and his friends to Thomas Müntzer quotes the Apocrypha. Grebel included the twelfth chapter of Wisdom of Solomon in a list of Scripture texts that supported their belief that "all children who have not attained the knowledge to discern between good and evil and have not eaten of the tree of knowledge are surely saved through the suffering of Christ, the new Adam."[9]

Balthasar Hubmaier made a significant use of the Apocrypha in his defense of free will. In his second tract on freedom of the will, he bases a two-page section on Ecclesiasticus 15, which says that the Lord placed the first humans in the garden with "free choice" (Sirach 15:14).[10]

In one of two long citations from 4 Esdras (2 Esdras in modern numbering) in his letter from prison to his congregation at Horb, Michael Sattler uses that writer's words to encourage his congregation to be faithful to the end of the world. "Await your Shepherd, for He will give you the rest of eternity, for He is near, who will come at the end of the world; be ready for the recompense of the kingdom!"[11]

The South German and Moravian Anabaptists also made liberal use of the Apocrypha. In one passage, Hans Denck cited Ecclesiasticus [Sirach] 27 along with Psalm 7 in an admonition to avoid "all selfish pursuits of this carnal life," and not to throw life away "as chaff to the wind." A bit later, he listed chapters 11 and 12 of Wisdom of Solomon along with biblical texts to say that God "gives everyone reason, grace and power to be transformed."[12] Pilgram Marpeck cited Judith 10:1-5 in a passage where he was emphasizing that it is not external appearances but the fruit of actions that determines their rightness. Judith had adorned herself "sumptuously," which could have been judged as "arrogance." However, since she used her appearance to gain entrance to the private chamber of Holophernes, the commanding general of Nebuchadnezzar's army, where she deceived and then beheaded him, the defeat of this enemy of Israel displays the rightness of her sumptuous appearance.[13]

Hutterite leader Peter Walpot used Sirach 13 [Ecclesiasticus] as the basis for the admonition that before surrendering goods to the community, one should be firmly grounded in the truth, lest later one wish to have the goods returned.[14] Peter Rideman referred to Wisdom of Solomon 13:1-3 and 15:14-19 in discussing the error of those who appropriate the material parts of God's creation for themselves rather than recognizing that all of God's creation is to be held communally.

In another context, Riedemann included texts from 1 Maccabees 2, 3, 4, 5, and 6 in a long list of Scriptures that show God's calling for revenge before it was abolished with the coming of Christ.[15] References to the Apocrypha are scattered throughout *The Chronicle of the Hutterian Brethren*. A section dealing with the second Great Persecution notes that "the prophet spoke the truth" when writing that there would be violent attacks on those that fear the Lord. This prophet was Ezra, quoted from 2 Esdras 16:70-75, followed by words of comfort quoted from Wisdom of Solomon 5:15-16. And the *Chronicle* writer can praise "the virtuous, praiseworthy Judith,"[16] mentioned above for Marpeck.

Last to be mentioned is the *Martyrs Mirror*, in which multiple citations appear from the Apocrypha. For example, Anneken Jans quoted 2 Esdras 7:6-9 in the letter she left to her son Isaiah before her martyrdom. In urging her son to follow the narrow but dangerous way of Christ, she used this text which described a city full of good things built on a plain but approached only along a narrow path with fire on one side and deep water on the other. A man can never receive this city as an inheritance, Anneken said, "if he never shall pass the danger set before" the city.[17]

In these examples, early Anabaptist writers cited texts from the Apocrypha alongside texts from what today is considered canonical Scripture. No distinction was made between the two. For these writers, the Apocrypha was Scripture.[18]

Notes

1. This term for the distance between the Bible and its modern interpreter was first coined by Gottwald Ephraim Lessing, an eighteenth-century German philosopher.

2. One exception that proves the rule is found in 4 Ezra 7:39-44, which claims that at the final judgment, the sun, moon, stars, clouds, lightning, wind, water and air will actually cease to exist. The temporal aspects of the natural world will also disappear—including darkness, evening, morning, summer, spring, harvest—as will meteorological ones: heat, frost, cold, hail, rain, and dew. In this case, when the earth is destroyed, the heavens disappear along with it. Later in 4 Ezra, both are restored in a consummate act of re-creation.

3. Harold S. Bender and Nanne van der Zijpp, "Apocrypha," *Global Anabaptist Mennonite Encyclopedia Online* (1953), http://gameo.org/index.php?title=Apocrypha&oldid=119941 <27 June 2016>.

4. "Global Christianity—a Report on the Size and Distribution of the World's Christian Popoulation," *Pew Research Center*, 19 December 2011, http://www.pew-

forum.org/2011/12/19/global-christianity-exec/ <28 June 2016>.

5. Menno Simons, *The Complete Writings of Menno Simons c.1496-1561*, ed. John Christian Wenger, trans. Leonard Verduin, with biography by Harold S. Bender (Scottdale, Pa.: Herald Press, 1956), 949, 951, 1033.

6. Menno Simons, *Complete Writings*, 717-718.

7. George Huntston Williams and Angel M. Mergal, eds., *Spiritual and Anabaptist Writers: Documents Ilustrative of the Radical Reformation*, The Library of Christian Classics, vol. 25 (Philadelphia: The Westminster Press, 1957), 189n15.

8. Cornelius J. Dyck, William E. Keeney, and Alvin J. Beachy, trans. and eds., *The Writings of Dirk Philips 1504-1568*, Classics of the Radical Reformation, vol. 6 (Scottdale, Pa.: Herald Press, 1992), 294.

9. Leland Harder, ed., *The Sources of Swiss Anabaptism: The Grebel Letters and Related Documents*, Classics of the Radical Reformation, vol. 4 (Scottdale, Pa.: Herald Press, 1985), 290.

10. Balthasar Hubmaier, *Balthasar Hubmaier: Theologian of Anabaptism*, trans. and ed. H. Wayne Pipkin and John H. Yoder, Classics of the Reformation, vol. 5 (Scottdale, Pa.: Herald Press, 1989), 453-55.

11. John H[oward] Yoder, trans. and ed., *The Legacy of Michael Sattler*, Classics of the Radical Reformation, vol. 1 (Scottdale, Pa.: Herald Press, 1973), 56, 62, quote from 2 Esdras 2:34-35, 62.

12. Daniel Liechty, ed. and trans., *Early Anabaptist Spirituality: Selected Writings*, preface by Hans J. Hillerbrand, Classics of Western Spirituality (Mahwah, N.J.: Paulist Press, 1994), 122-123.

13. Pilgram Marpeck, *The Writings of Pilgram Marpeck*, ed. and trans. William Klassen and Walter Klaassen, Classics of the Reformation, vol. 2 (Scottdale, Pa.: Herald Press, 1978), 348.

14. Liechty, *Early Anabaptist Spirituality*, 188-189.

15. Peter Riedemann, *Peter Riedemann's Hutterite Confession of Faith*, John J. Friesen, Classics of the Radical Reformation (Scottdale, Pa.: Herald Press, 1999), 119-120, 221-222.

16. *The Chronicle of the Hutterian Brethren*, vol. 1, ed. and trans. Hutterian Brethren (Rifton, N.Y.: Plough Publishing House, 1987), 312, 756.

17. Thieleman J. van Braght, ed., *The Bloody Theater or Martyrs Mirror, Compiled from Various Authentic Chronicles, Memorials, and Testimonies*, trans. Joseph F. Sohm (Scottdale, Pa.: Herald Press, 1987), 453.

18. For a recent article that supports this conclusion, see Jonathan Seiling, "Solae (Quae?) Scripturae: Anabaptists and the Apocrypha," *The Mennonite Quarterly Review* 80, no. 1 (January 2006): 5-34.

Part Three
Ecclesiology

Part Three: Ecclesiology

Anabaptist Mennonites have long emphasized the church as a community. The followers of Jesus form an integrated and interwoven community. They are more than individual souls saved by Jesus who just happen to find themselves in proximity at Sunday worship. Their relationships to each other are important and integral to the community.

To use a sports analogy, the relationship of members of the church as community are like those of a baseball team rather than a track team. It is called a track team, but the performance of one athlete does not impact another's effort—the pole vaulter who clears no height does not impact the runner entered in the mile race—though the individual events in track do contribute to the team's overall score. In contrast, when the shortstop throws wildly to first base, the entire baseball team is impacted. The church gathered around Jesus has that kind of interconnected relationship, in which there is mutual support and mutual accountability among members.

The church as community gathered around Jesus is the earthly extension of the mission of Jesus to make visible the reign of God on earth. Jesus called men and women into his circle and gave them the mission to witness to the reign of God. That is what the church does when it incorporates new people into its body. Baptism is the ritual of becoming a part of the community. The service of the Lord's Supper emphasizes mutual support and sharing of food and earthly possessions. Singing in worship blends individual voices into a whole. Members of the community participate in worship by reading Scripture, taking up the offering, teaching in Sunday school, or taking a turn to preach. The church has programs of service in the community, and individual members participate in many avenues of community service out of their sense of Christian witness. Together all of these things contribute to the fact that the church as community continues the mission of Jesus to make present the reign of God on earth. Mennonite theology has made much of the existence of the church as the community that continues Jesus' mission and witnesses to the presence of the reign of God today.

However, the chapters of this section are not one more exposition of the church as community. The church that continues the mission of Jesus does not do so perfectly. The church has flaws. The chapters in this section recognize these flaws, as they deal with problem areas or neglected areas in understanding the community that is the church. Sarah Bixler's chapter addresses an issue that has received little attention in the discussion of the church as community, namely the development of the individual self in this community. Her analysis deals with both psychological and theological dimensions of the self in community, particularly for adolescents within Mennonite education. She concludes that Mennonite education represents a community that is well positioned to facilitate the realization of the God-given self in spiritual transformation.

Mennonites have never been particularly adept at dealing with conflict in the community. The conflict of the last number of years has produced ongoing discussions and parting of ways around the seemingly intractable issues of LGBTQ inclusion, whether they can serve as church leaders and participate in the covenant of marriage. Hannah Heinzekehr's chapter deals with the ironic fact that the peace church cannot settle its own conflict. She concludes with a suggestion for the future of Mennonite education.

Gerald Mast discusses another dimension of problems within. Where much of Mennonites' previous theological discussion of the nature of the church has emphasized its capacity to witness to the reign of God, the implication is that the witnessing church poses a shining example. Mast's chapter emphasizes the failures of the church as community, but puts that condition of failure in a positive light. At church, students will observe the failures of the church and its ongoing conflicts, and come to terms with their own failures and limitations, which in turn creates the context in which to experience and receive the gift of what God is doing in the world through a flawed vessel. The church can thus become a laboratory in which students learn what it means to engage the world hopefully amidst disappointment and failure.

Leadership of the church as community can be problematic. Much has been made theologically of the communal character of authority in the church. Often the pastor as "servant-leader" has been used as the symbol of that communal leadership. However, Malinda Berry's chapter points out that Mennonites have rarely dealt with the actual meaning of servant leadership, and concludes with how it should function in conjunction with the priesthood of all believers.

CHAPTER NINE

MAKING PEACE WITH OURSELVES: MENNONITE PEACE EDUCATION AND INTRACHURCH CONFLICT

Hannah E. Heinzekehr

During my junior year in college at Bluffton University, I spent many hours downstairs in the Musselman Library perusing copies of *Sword and Trumpet*, the long-running quarterly Mennonite periodical begun in 1929 by Bishop George R. Brunk, in collaboration with Virginia Conference of the (Old) Mennonite Church. Upon its founding, the purpose of *Sword and Trumpet* was described as "Devoted to the Defense of a Full Gospel, With Especial Emphasis upon Neglected Truths, and to an Active Opposition of the Various Forms of Error that Contribute to the Religious Drift of the Times."

Although the *Sword and Trumpet* is still being printed today, I spent most of my time perusing volumes from its inception and through the 1950s. And although I found much of this reading fascinating, I was not in the library leafing through *Sword and Trumpet* of my own accord. As Professor J. Denny Weaver's student research assistant, I had been sent to the library to track all the appearances of two-kingdom theology: theology that made a distinction between the not-yet-but-coming soon Kingdom of God and the inherently fallen and sinful kingdom of the world. In those early days (and perhaps still) the writers featured in

Sword and Trumpet planted themselves firmly in the eschatological lineage of early Anabaptists like the martyrs or the writers of the 1527 Schleitheim Confession who stated,

> From all this we should learn that everything which has not been united with our God in Christ is nothing but an abomination which we should shun. By this are meant all popish and repopish works and idolatry, gatherings, church attendance, winehouses, guarantees and commitments of unbelief, and other things of the kind, which the world regards highly, and yet which are carnal or flatly counter to the command of God, after the pattern of all the iniquity which is in the world. From all this we shall be separated and have no part with such.[1]

At the time, as a twenty-two-year-old college student studying theology, I felt in touch with the pulse of the Mennonite church. I remember feeling grateful that we had moved on from this worldview, which abandoned the world to its devices while striving for some "heaven light years away," as the words to the hymn, "Here in this place," aptly describe.

However, since then, I have come to believe that the roots of this particular ecclesiogical framework are more deep-seated than I realized. I have come to realize that the kingdom of the world is also present within the church, and perhaps nowhere is this more in evidence than when we look at the history of Mennonite intrachurch conflict management and (often) conflict avoidance. I would argue that a theological framework that sets up a dichotomy between the kingdom of heaven (the church) and the kingdom of earth (the world) automatically disadvantages the ability to address intrachurch disagreements.

To equip the next generation of Mennonite (and other denominational) leaders in an increasingly polarized society and church, Mennonite education could and should continue to evolve and advance its peacemaking curriculum. Included should be skills for nonviolent communication and relating to "the other" who occupies the spaces nearest to us, including within our churches.

This lack of skill for addressing conflict within the church is particularly ironic given the Mennonite status as giants of sorts in the international restorative justice and peacebuilding communities. Mennonites Lisa Schirch and John Paul Lederach travel internationally, helping to diffuse tensions and set up just peacebuilding processes and have taught peacemakers that include the likes of Liberian peace activist Leymah Gbowee, the 2011 Nobel Peace Prize winner. Howard Zehr's 1990 book, *Changing Lenses*,[2] is considered to be one of the texts that helped to pioneer the movement for restorative justice in the American criminal justice system. And the peace, justice, and conflict studies major at Goshen College made it onto a Buzzfeed list. That content-aggregator site named the major one of the "13 Unexpected College Majors That Can Lead to Incredible Careers."[3] Clearly, Mennonite peace education has been one of our most high profile and influential programs.

However, despite this stellar international peacemaking track record, Mennonites themselves still fall prey to the Protestant quagmire of heated intrachurch conflicts that result in the splintering and shrinking of their denominations. Despite years of teaching conflict transformation at Mennonite institutions of higher education, Mennonites seem most interested in working to solve conflicts beyond themselves while locked in intractable disagreements within their own communities.

Current conversations within Mennonite Church USA and Mennonite Church Canada regarding the inclusion of lesbian, gay, bisexual, transgender and queer (LGBTQ) individuals in the life and leadership of the church have led the church to yet another crossroads. As of this writing (with more developments likely by publication), in the six months since this essay was originally presented, two regional Mennonite conferences, Lancaster and Franklin, have announced decisions to leave Mennonite Church USA, citing concerns about polity, hermeneutics and movements toward greater acceptance of LGBTQ individuals. And as Rachel Waltner Goossen's in-depth look at the many failed attempts to address Mennonite theologian John Howard Yoder's sexual abuse illustrates profoundly, within the church, we are often unwilling or unable to name and adequately address our own abuses of power and privilege.[4] Although peace education seems to have taken deep root among stereotypically progressive individuals who would eschew the term, Mennonite peace education, by and large, has had a missional slant, training peacemakers to deal with conflicts beyond the denomination and congregation.

This juncture is where the return to two-kingdom theology is lodged. Perhaps the reason for our inability to make peace with each other is that the majority of our education in conflict transformation is pointed primarily outwards at a so-called "broken world" in need of healing rather than inward at our own sinful communities. In an essay reflecting on John Howard Yoder, Gerald Mast explores the ways that Yoder's sexual violence continued in part due to the inability to address sin within the church. Mast says,

> We might ask why processes of this nature [discipline and accountability] have been such a challenge for the church. Perhaps one reason for the difficulty is the shame associated with sin in a community where sin is seen as conquered or seldom discussed any longer.[5]

Although arguably sin is an inherent part of the human condition—"all have sinned and fall short of the glory of God" (Rom. 3:23)—Mennonites have tended to focus on their role as a contrast community that does not belong to or emulate the ways of the world (John 17:16). As Mast describes it, to acknowledge fallenness within the church would to be acknowledge our inability to conquer sin.

Over the course of the nearly ten years that I have spent working in Mennonite denominational agencies and institutions, I have seen this pattern of denial about "internal faults" reenacted again and again. There is significant overlap between Mennonite educational institutions and denominational leaders. In fact, according to the most recent People in the Pew study, while now ten years old, attending a Mennonite college was the highest indicator of whether a person would stay involved in the church, and a high percentage of denominational leaders were products of Mennonite education at some point in their educational careers. This means they have likely encountered teaching focused on restorative justice, peacebuilding and conflict management.

Despite this widespread training, it seems hardest for us to "first take the log out of [our] own eye" before pointing at our neighbors. Most of our intrachurch conflicts in the last fifty years have stemmed from disagreements over who can participate in church and how, with discussions circling around race, gender, and divorce, to name a few topics.

As Felipe Hinojosa says in his chapter in this book, to understand who we are and how we operate, we must look at the disjunctures or the moments in our history where things have not gone well. It would seem that Mennonites, especially white Mennonites (myself included), have struggled to come to terms with their own power and privilege and, frankly, with power in general. In 2014, Gordon Houser, editor of *The Mennonite* magazine, launched a heated online debate when he proposed the creation of a list of the "most influential Mennonites," modeled on *Time* magazine's annual list of influential people. While many people sent Houser submissions, others took to Facebook, Twitter and blogs to decry this practice as inherently unbiblical and un-Christ-like.

This phenomenon was fascinating to me, since, whether we acknowledge it or not, influence and power are in operation in our denomination. Houser himself predicted this reaction. In his original call for names, he wrote,

> I already hear the objections. In our bones, we [Mennonites] resist focusing on individuals or lifting some up as more important than others. But we're discussing influence. Do we deny that some people in our midst have influence? What might we learn by naming them or at least debating who they might be? Is there some value to talking about influence?[6]

So where does this discomfort with conceptions of power and privilege come from? In his forthcoming dissertation, Philipp Gollner is beginning to explore the idea of the Mennonite transition from a distinct ethnic group to assimilation in the United States, similar to the Irish or Jewish populations, who transitioned toward white identity as part of their assimilation into United States society. Add to this a history for most European Mennonites that includes fleeing from persecution by other Christians, persecution that has been well-documented in volumes like the *Martyrs Mirror*, and all the trappings are there for a victim complex. Andre Gingerich Stoner, Mennonite Church USA director for holistic witness, writes,

> A victim mentality can lead to a quietism that hampers our witness and to a strange combination of self-righteousness and low self-esteem. . . .This sense of being a victim seems especially incongruous in our American context, where many of us have become affluent and carry white privilege and power. Despite the evidence, because of the martyr legacy we may still feel like victims. This mentality makes it hard for white Mennonites to be honest about the power and privilege we have, an important step in confronting the racism within us, our church and our culture.[7]

In fact, Drew Hart writes,

> Those that practice and identify with Anabaptism in the twenty-first century in America tend to be white, privileged and undeniably situated in dominant culture. If societies—as living mechanisms, inherently having systems of advantage and disadvantage—manage those who participate in them, then it would seem that American Anabaptists are increasingly not only benefitting from societal advantages, but are blind to them altogether.[8]

Hart's comments give reality to a similar remark in the first chapter of this book.

So what happens when a group that, in fact, carries power and privilege in society is predisposed to see itself as marginalized? One symptom is supposedly "flat" institutional structures and processes, which often mask where and how power is operating. Calvin Redekop notes that Anabaptist-Mennonites have, in general, wanted to limit the use of power only to what is necessary for the common good. He notes that Anabaptists rejected the structures and ways of wielding power that were common to the Roman Catholic Church, especially by focusing on a voluntary entry into the church through adult baptism and a congregational ecclesiology that limited any one individual's reach. However, today we do have national denominational structures, and part of the tension that exists in our structures is a desire to do something together more broadly while also respecting the autonomy of area conferences and individual congregations.

As part of her master's project, Alyssa Bennett Smith, a recently convinced Mennonite, spent a year reading through Mennonite Church USA polity and practice documents, with the goal of creating a resource that would help interpret to "people in the pew" the ways of navigating denominational structure. What prompted the project for Bennett Smith was an experience sitting in a meeting with area conference and denominational leaders at Western District Conference in Kansas and realizing, she writes, "that very few people knew exactly how these [denominational] documents [like the *Confession of Faith* or Membership Guidelines] factor into our lives as members of Mennonite Church USA because on a day-to-day basis, they simply don't," along with a general sense that there was confusion and disagreement over the processes that polity documents actually implied.[9]

Indeed, as someone who has spent probably more time over the course of the past two years with the Mennonite Church USA bylaws than the average churchgoer, I can say clearly that there are points and processes in our bylaws that are vague and leave implications open to the interpreter. Over the course of 2014 and 2015, as they sought to respond to the decisions by area conferences to begin licensing LGBTQ individuals, the Executive Board of Mennonite Church USA had many conversations about the nature of its authoritative role. While using the same bylaws, board members have come to very different conclusions about their responsibility (or not) to take action in each of these situations.

One of the biggest challenges of our current Mennonite structure and processes, which include many different committees and task forces and boards, is that they are a mashup of communal and hierarchical practices and they are convoluted. The structures themselves can become inherently conflict avoidant. And within that, they divorce any one individual within the system from feeling like he or she holds power or the ability to make a change.

I have felt this conflict avoidance within myself as a denominational staff person. For example, when people came asking me to intervene in conflict or to advocate against a certain injustice, my first reaction was often, "But what can I do about that? That's the executive director's job. Or the board's job." In our system, it is easy to avoid taking responsibility for conflicts or working to undo them. Because we have tried to set up webs of committees or groups that, at their best, provide checks and balances and allow many voices to be heard, there is often confusion about how or where decision-making should be lodged. And because we are unclear (perhaps sometimes intentionally) about where power actually lies in our systems, they can easily become loaded with traps or hurdles which prevent newcomers from navigating them successfully. Obviously this particular topic could take up an entire paper.

So what is the role of Mennonite education in looking both outward and inward? What is the role of educational institutions in calling denominational leaders, like myself, to be better at not avoiding conflict; better at naming injustice when it exists; and better at putting in place transparent, bridge-building processes that draw on what we know and have learned about conflict transformation and active nonviolence (not nonresistance)? What is the role of Mennonite education in being intentional about seeing church or nonprofit administration as a viable (and much-needed) career path and actively equipping individuals for this work?

We need to shift the focus of our peace education from the idea that we are equipping an individual with skills to go out and serve as experts or conflict mediators "beyond themselves" or their local communities, to an understanding that we are offering students skills for living and solving conflicts in their own context as well as for navigating the world. The Mennonite Church USA "Vision: Healing and Hope" statement says, "God calls us to be followers of Jesus Christ, and, by the power of the Holy Spirit, to grow as communities of grace, joy and peace, so that God's healing and hope flow through us to the world." This vision statement does not start with a movement to the world but first calls the church to cultivate an awareness of the Holy Spirit and to work alongside it to make sure that our own communities bear the marks of grace, joy and peace. In fact, the integrity of our outward witness will depend on it.

What would it look like to educate people and remind them that no one is exempt from conflict, including our own church and church communities? While part of our role is helping other individuals and groups to navigate this terrain, it is also our responsibility to create healthier patterns and conversations in the communities with which we are most intimately involved. How do we equip people to navigate in a context where narratives will not be uniform and linear but multiple and varied? And how can we continue to weave anti-oppression work and meaningful relational encounters with each other and those who are "other' to us into the very fabric of our education?

On a denominational level, this will mean fundamentally remembering that the church is not exempt from the pitfalls of the world. The sin we seek to avoid cannot be avoided. It is here among us. And rather than trying to erase or bury or deny the marks of that brokenness, our work should be to name it and struggle against its reoccurrence.

We are all part of one messy kin-dom; wounded healers who are also empowered to continue working as midwives of justice, helping to birth God's Spirit into our communities and the world in new, restorative ways. What will it look like to train leaders who are willing and equipped to step into this fray? There are no easy answers, but my hope is that the question is clearly on the table as Mennonite education moves forward.

Notes

1. John H[oward] Yoder, trans. and ed., *The Legacy of Michael Sattler*, Classics of the Radical Reformation, vol. 1 (Scottdale, Pa.: Herald Press, 1973), 38.

2. Howard Zehr, *Changing Lenses: A New Focus for Crime and Justice*, 3rd ed., A Christian Peace Shelf Selection (Scottdale, Pa.: Herald Press, 2005).

3. https://www.buzzfeed.com/discoverstudentloans/unexpected-college-majors?b=1&utm_term=.snG5OyW03#.wqOojJ62v <9 May 2016>.

4. Rachel Waltner Goossen, "'Defanging the Beast': Mennonite Responses to John Howard Yoder's Sexual Abuse," *The Mennonite Quarterly Review* 89, no. 1 (January 2015): 7-80.

5. Gerald J. Mast, "Sin and Failure in Anabaptist Theology," in *John Howard Yoder: Radical Theologian*, ed. J. Denny Weaver, foreword by Marva J. Dawn, afterword by Lisa Schirch (Eugene, Ore.: Cascade Books, 2014), 358.

6. Gordon Houser, "The Top 10 Most Influential Mennonites," *The Mennonite*, June 2014, 53.

7. Andre Gingerich Stoner, "Our Victim Mentality," *Mennonite World Review*, 28 May 2012, 5.

8. Drew G. I. Hart, "Anablacktivism: Following Jesus the Liberator and Peacemaker in the 21st Century," in *A Living Alternative: Anabaptist Christianity in a Post-Christendom World*, ed. Joanna Harader and A. O. Green (Garden City, New York: Etelloc Publishing, 2014), 204.

9. Alyssa Bennett-Smith, "Grace at the Table" (25 June 2016), http://mennoniteusa.org/menno-snapshots/grace-at-the-table/ <13 July 2016>. The master's thesis is Alyssa Bennett Smith, *Grace at the Table: A Resource for Understanding the Polity of Mennonite Church USA,* http://mennoniteusa.org/wp-content/uploads/2015/06/Grace-at-the-Table.pdf <13 July 2016>.

TEN

THINKING OF MYSELF AS YOUR SERVANT IS A BAD IDEA: MENNONITE EDUCATION AND THE PROBLEM OF THE SERVANT LEADERSHIP PARADIGM

Malinda Elizabeth Berry

Introduction

You do not have to spend much time on the campus of a Mennonite Church USA-affiliated school before you hear the words "servant leadership." Indeed, the term *servant leader* has been a buzz phrase in Mennonite institutions and schools for several decades. Yet while Robert K. Greenleaf's (1904-1990) writings gave rise to the term, Mennonites' organizational and institutional use of servant leadership shows only modest interaction with his work, such that servant leadership often reflects our own preconceived understanding of what servant leadership must mean, which at its worst is intellectually dishonest.[1]

Another problem crops up when our reliance on servant leadership in Anabaptist-Mennonite pedagogy and curricula fails to include robust engagement with either Greenleaf's theories or the thought leaders who have taken up the mantle of his work: We fall prey to an intellectual pragmatism by assuming stances, using ideas, and employing language that advance our arguments unaware of the cultural and philosophical commitments that give rise to particular ideas. Neither of these tendencies serve us well theologically, sociologically, or psychologically.

To have integrity, we Mennonite students, teachers, administrators, pastors, and congregants would do well to affirm and practice the pillars of servant leadership embedded in a contemporary articulation of the priesthood of all believers. Such a commitment could help us avoid the pitfalls of practicing anemic, misappropriated servant leadership, an evaluation we can make when we actually engage literature from the Robert K. Greenleaf Center for Servant Leadership.

Stated another way, the problem that I am identifying and addressing is the gap between our espoused commitment to servant leadership and the lack of evidence that we adhere to its basic principles in our denominationally affiliated organizations and institutions. The chapter begins with a description of the issues Robert Greenleaf was addressing and how he understood the concept of servant leadership. Then I will offer an account of Mennonite misappropriations of servant leadership. Finally, and most importantly, I will sketch the healthy function of a servant leader in the context of a contemporary, Anabaptist articulation of the priesthood of all believers.

Robert K. Greenleaf and Servant Leadership

In 1970, Greenleaf, retired American Telephone and Telegraph (AT&T) corporate manager and convinced Quaker, published an essay intended to respond to two societal challenges. The first challenge had been issued four decades earlier by his sociology professor:

> There is a new problem in our country. We are becoming a nation that is dominated by large institutions—churches, businesses, governments, labor unions, universities—and these big institutions are not serving us well. . . . Nothing of substance will happen unless there are people inside these institutions who are able to (and want to) lead them into better performance for the public good. Some of you ought to make careers inside those big institutions and become a force for good—from the inside.[2]

The second challenge came from Greenleaf's own reaction and response to the student movements of the 1960s. He saw "distinguished institutions show their fragility and crumble." He was searching "for an understanding of what happened to them," and seeking "to help heal their wounds."[3] Greenleaf gave his topic the name, servant leadership.

Although he coined the term, Greenleaf was always clear that servant leadership was his way of drawing together two seemingly opposing roles that have been pillars of Western societies: servant and leader. As Greenleaf advocates James Sipe and Don Frick explain, while "the notion of leading by serving has been around for several millennia in the teachings of every major religious tradition," Greenleaf's innovation was "to describe [leading by serving] as a personal journey and a management strategy, for both the public realm and the private sector."[4] So, at the most basic level, servant leadership is a management strategy.

It does not take long, when paging through Greenleaf's classic *Servant Leadership: A Journey into the Nature of Legitimate Power and Greatness*, to discover that servant leadership is also a philosophy that, in the subtitle phrase, takes adherents on a personal journey. Don Frick, Greenleaf's biographer, argues that Greenleaf's journye involved three interwoven identities: servant, seeker, and leader. Each identity had a definition and function in Greenleaf's servant leadership philosophy. First,

> a servant is not a "service provider," a martyr or a slave, but one who consciously nurtures the mature growth of self, other people, institutions, and communities. This is done in response to the deepest guidance of spirit, not for personal grandiosity. Servanthood is a function of motive, identity and right action.

Second, "a true seeker is open to experience from all quarters and follows a path without always knowing the destination." Third,

> an authentic leader is one who chooses to serve, and serves first, and then chooses to lead. This kind of leader—a servant-leader—employs reflection, listening, persuasion, foresight, and [political acumen] to act ethically and "go out ahead and show the way." A servant-leader may operate quietly or publicly, but his or her title—President or CEO—is not the point. The janitor of a school may be a more powerful servant-leader to students than the principal.[5]

In *Servant Leadership*, Greenleaf enumerates a variety of sites (i.e., executive leadership, boards of trustees, small businesses, liberal arts curricula, contemporary prophets/seekers, etc.) in which he believes his strategy and philosophy can alleviate challenges to leadership in the post-1960s, "anti-leader" age. While the sites explored in Greenleaf's writings begin with the individual who serves first and leads second, he focuses his essays on three types of institutions—churches, universities, and businesses—because he believes they are the most influential in (re)building a good society.

In the case of the United States, Greenleaf sees a good society that has fallen apart and holds that

> if a better society is to be built, one that is more just and more loving, one that provides greater creative opportunity for its people, then the most open course is to raise both the capacity to serve and the very performance as servant of existing major institutions by new regenerative forces operating within them.[6]

If we listen, we can hear Greenleaf's Quakerism asserting itself in his vision of a twentieth-century peaceable kingdom.

But what is the substantive content and "how-to" of this vision where a society's institutions are serving the people and these institutions are being led by people who are servants?

Admittedly, Sipe and Frick write, "Greenleaf did not provide a universal checklist or a formula for becoming a Servant-Leader. He wanted each person and organization to apply the principles and values in ways that made sense to them."[7] At the same time, he did describe three concerns the servant leadership paradigm's content is meant to address:

1. for people who focus their attention on social problems by analyzing them as products of systems, ideologies, and movements, servant leadership offers a reframing of these dynamics to help us discover the power individuals can have as change-agents within these systems;

2. for everyday people who tend toward serving and to "deny wholeness and creative fulfillment," servant leadership calls them to risk their own significance by stepping into more formal roles of leadership;

3. for cultures that believe leaders are born not made, servant leadership challenges the two-part assumption that a) leadership education is only for those natural-born leaders and b) the best leaders are those who have received the "right" education.[8]

From this conceptual location, Sipe and Frick have sought to "operationalize" Greenleaf's basic teachings beginning with his belief that servant leadership is a teachable and measurable skill set.

In its operationalized form based on Greenleaf's writings and teachings, servant leadership has seven pillars embedded in Sipe and Frick's definition of servant-leaders as "a person of character who puts people first. He or she is a skilled communicator, a compassionate collaborator who has foresight, is a systems thinker, and leads with moral authority."[9]

Sipe and Frick note the resonance between Divine Wisdom who has built her house with seven hewn pillars (Prov. 9:1) and the seven "qualities of character" that make a leader a servant-leader; this resonance suggests to me that wisdom is the primary virtue of Greenleaf's paradigm. "The Seven Pillars are mounted on a solid foundation of organizational culture and strategy," Sipe and Frick explain. "Together, they support and sustain the organization's employees, its customers, clients and stakeholders, and ultimately, the larger community."

Furthermore, servant leadership views these components (the organization, its culture, strategy, servant-leaders, employees, customers, and community) as an inverted pyramid of sorts, "honoring Greenleaf's notion that the authoritarian, top-down model of organizational leadership is upended with a Servant-Leader at the helm" because "Greenleaf believed that the designated leaders in an organization—who are smaller in number—should support and serve the greater numbers—those who are 'doing the work.'"[10]

Each of servant leadership's pillars is comprised of three leadership traits or competencies. The collection of skills serves two purposes. First they create the profile of effective servant-leaders because "whenever any traits are present in adequate measure, and as they accumulate, they serve to enrich and fortify the Servant-Leader and those who surround him or her." And second, the skills can make up the evaluation rubric to assess servant-leaders' performance in their roles.[11]

To summarize, when we look to literature about servant leadership developed by Greenleaf and carried on through the work of people affiliated with the Greenleaf Center, we see that it is a Quaker-influenced utilitarian management strategy that considers the most effective leaders to be those who serve first and lead second. In its indigenous societal context of the United States, servant leadership is also an existentialist-oriented philosophical stance toward the anti-establishment politics of the 1960s that left many people cynical about legitimate power.

Because servant leadership rejects the maxim "leaders are born, not made," it is also an approach to leadership education and organizational ethics that stands in stark contrast to corporate and organizational cultures

> that practice a modern form of Darwinian capitalism . . . [populated by] adrenaline-driven workers who must stay wired to challenges of the global economy . . . [and] disciples of the latest theories of leadership that use war, sports, and machines as their underlying metaphors.[12]

Thus we can also see that servant leadership is a strategy and philosophy oriented toward the social good. It holds that our society is healthier when we focus on human growth and development in communal terms rather than hierarchical ones.

We can also begin to describe servant leadership in negative terms; that is, to say what it is not. Here are three negative observations. First, service and servanthood, as defined within the servant leadership paradigm, are not borne of self-abnegating self-sacrifice which are the hallmarks of most definitions of Christian service. Greenleaf paints a picture of service as a description of work that involves helping others accomplish a task while simultaneously being enriched and transformed by that interaction and relationship.

Second, the Greenleaf tradition of servant leadership is neither hierarchical nor egalitarian, a point that I will return to in more detail below.

Third, servant leadership is also not, strictly speaking, a religious-based concept. For example, where most types of Christian ethics begin by making Jesus Christ normative for ethics, servant leadership makes the servant-leader normative for organizational ethics. This makes it possible to combine the two types of ethics so that Jesus Christ becomes the normative and prototypical servant-leader, but it is also possible to practice the ethics of servant leadership without any normative theological principle.

These three negative summary statements are critical. That is because here is where there is greatest slippage in Mennonite appropriations of servant leadership.

Greenleaf's Theological Presuppositions

While servant leadership is not invested in advancing a particular set of religious norms, Greenleaf did operate and develop servant leadership within a set of theological and ethical commitments based in the Historical Peace Church tradition. Sipe writes, "A book could be written on the influence of Quaker thought and practice on Robert Greenleaf's corporate work and servant writings," and it is curious that one has not yet been penned.[13] As a convinced Quaker, Greenleaf found a great deal of inspiration in the lives of early Quakers (sometimes called "Seekers") like George Fox and John Woolman. As their ideas developed into contemporary Meetings, especially of the unprogrammed type, Greenleaf found important spiritual ideas and theological commitments that served as practices that he could translate into meaningful managerial strategies:

> In the Quaker practice of consensus, Greenleaf found a proven way of making decisions that honored all voices and used some of his favorite strategies: silence, listening, and a reliance on spirit as expressed through individual insight. He also learned about the critical role of the [congregational] chair—called the Clerk [of the Meeting] by Quakers—who makes consensus work. A Clerk is a situational leader, no better or worse than anyone else. He or she is a primus inter pares—a first among equals—not a final arbiter.[14]

What begins to come to the foreground are the connections between the neither-hierarchical-nor-egalitarian quality of servant leadership and Greenleaf's particular Christian commitments that helped him conceive of the servant-leader. It seems curious that the roots of servant leadership in a theological tradition that shares kinship with Anabaptism has not been a significant part of the rationale used by Mennonites to advocate for its place in our organizational and leadership culture.

It is difficult to identify the precise moment in which language of servant leadership entered Mennonite organizational consciousness.[15] I suspect that we became aware of this philosophy through managerial/administrative channels rather than scholarly ones, given Greenleaf student and advocate Larry Spears' account of the growing impact of servant leadership across organizational and institutional sectors—beginning with for-profit industries and trustee education and only later experiential and leadership education programs in schools.[16]

Mennonite Misappropriation of Servant Leadership

Being pragmatic, we Mennonites, having been introduced to servant leadership as a leadership strategy and, because of our well-documented commitment to service, have taken Greenleaf's terminology and combined it with our communal narratives about faithful discipleship to the community to produce a pattern of misappropriation of servant leadership.[17] These misappropriations take two forms, both of which impoverish and distort Greenleaf's philosophy and can set us up for organizational failures that make servant leadership look like the problem.

I identify the first type of misappropriation as a problem of Mennonite conventional wisdom. Here I am thinking of the idea that regards terms like servant-leader and servant leadership simply as descriptions of cultural norms that have guided Mennonite leaders' sometimes quiet, sometimes charismatic approaches to building organizations and institutions. It is reflected in the sentiment I have heard any number of times that we should be suspicious of anyone who openly seeks a leadership role. The idea is that the best leaders are those who are most reluctant. The immediate judgment of the terminology's usefulness is as a label for something we think we already know, namely that that servant-leaders would rather be serving than leading, and this reluctance becomes a sign of trustworthiness. Another aspect of this distortion is in recognizing servant-leaders in retrospect rather than intentionally training people to be servant-leaders according to servant leadership's pillars and characteristics.

The second type of misappropriation is a problem of hermeneutics. Rather than studying Greenleaf's writings to understand servant leadership, we allow our traditional biblicism to treat knowledge of Jesus through the New Testament as the basis of servant leadership. This misstep is compounded by looking to other biblical and religious role models for qualities of servant-leaders that conform to the classic Mennonite definition of service without referencing leadership: "living for others rather than self."[18] While these icons may indeed be examples of servant-leaders in the Greenleaf sense, our hermeneutics focus on their Christ-likeness and ways their lives manifest virtues like self-sacrifice, humility, kindness, faithfulness, and peaceable pursuit God's justice.

Within this hermeneutical framework, we do not hail Jesus as a servant-leader (let alone leader); we hail him as a servant, period. This second misappropriation reifies the anti-leader bias that lauds reluctant leaders. It also includes a safe, comfortable, and romanticized portrait of Jesus, which avoids dealing with images such as the angry Jesus, the Jesus who confronted the powers, or the revolutionary Jesus who is turning the world upside-down.

Rather than turning the anti-leader backlash against the idea of servant-leadership, I am suggesting that we apply what Greenleaf actually meant with the concept. As the subtitle of Greenleaf's book puts it, servant leadership, is "a journey into the nature of legitimate power and greatness." He argues that servant-leading institutions are not run by a "single chief" but have an optimal balance of people with "operating talent" (administrators who focus on day-to-day tasks) and those with "conceptual talent" (leaders who go out ahead and show the way). Noting that these talents are not mutually exclusive, Greenleaf writes,

> Both of these talents, in balance and rightly placed, are required for sustained high level performance in any large institution. By optimal balance between the two is meant a relationship in which both conceptualizer and operator understand, respect, and depend on one another, and in which neither dominates the other. In a large institution the council of equals with a primus inter pares serves best when it is predominately conceptual. Whoever in the council has the greatest team-building ability should be primus, even though someone else may have a higher-sounding formal title.[19]

In many ways, Greenleaf's words speak directly to our (collective and individual) ambivalence about exercising power and enacting authority both nonviolently and without undermining our ourselves. To have integrity, we must acknowledge that we do not practice servant leadership to this degree.

While I no longer want to get rid of servant-leader language as I once did, I do want to separate it from the anti-leader bias that can lead to unhealthy and even toxic educational and organizational patterns. Such culture can reward passive-aggressive behaviors and habits enacted by both administrators and employees. We create a climate where we are unable to hold together "servant" and "leader," trapping ourselves in a pit of self-abnegating servanthood of loving neighbor more than self and helping out of resentful obligation rather than commitment to shalom.

Together these patterns contribute to an ethos where many Mennonites agree: we need good leaders. But there is very little agreement about how we find, nurture, and benefit from quality leadership. I suggest that Greenleaf can help us to address this need, in combination with another phrase that Mennonites have used without real clarity about its meaning. This phrase is *priesthood of all believers*.

Priesthood of All Believers: A Servant-Leader in Every Chair

Too Many Cooks, Not Enough Priests

Mennonites are sometimes—perhaps often—unaware that the priesthood of all believers was not a uniquely Anabaptist innovation of the Protestant Reformation. There are various ways to understand the basic concept based on 1 Peter 2:9 and found throughout the Christian church. For the Protestant reformers, ranging from Martin Luther and Menno Simons to John Calvin and John Wesley, this idea that all Christians, through baptism and Jesus Christ's invitation, have some share in priestly work rejects the separation of the Christian community into the ordained, priestly class and the laity. Depending on our theological accent, the idea of a universal priesthood can lead to the elevation of all Christians to lives of holiness, the embrace of everyone's ordinariness (including ordained leaders), or a combination of the two so that there is still particular authority afforded to ordained leaders that laypeople do not have to celebrate rituals, sacraments, and/or ordinances.

Figuratively speaking, Mennonite historical, biblical, and theological reflection on these issues has been all over the map. The entry on this topic in the *Mennonite Encyclopedia* explains that among twentieth-century Mennonites, the priesthood of all believers signals for some "that every Christian is a minister" and for others "a process of making decisions in the church." It can also refer to "the believer's access to God without the mediation of a priest and to being a channel of grace for other Christians." It can represent "the Radical Reformation's rejection of dividing the church into clergy and laity."[20] Pragmatically speaking, priesthood of believers language provides an easy way to explain our actions, whether talking about ecclesiology, denominational organization, spirituality, or leadership education.

In this century, our invocation of the priesthood of all believers is often a reference to congregational leadership models that use some combination of decentralized authority—no formal pastor(s) or a part-time solo pastor, and heavy reliance on lay leadership, sometimes by design, sometimes by happenstance. When it occurs by happenstance, it seems like a rather weak understanding of a universal priesthood. Consider Harold Bender's description of this shared priesthood:

> It means not only that no priest is necessary as a mediator between the human individual and God, so that every [person] has free access to God by repentance and faith in Christ, but also that all believers have a priestly office to perform for each other in that, in Christ, each can be a channel of God's grace to [the other] and indeed has a responsibility to be such.[21]

When we read Bender with a robust understanding of servant leadership, we start to see in the priesthood of all believers what Greenleaf articulated in his late twentieth-century take on a sixteenth-century idea. As he considers the role of the church in our society in both his original essay and in a subsequent essay almost thirty years later, Greenleaf describes what he calls "the growing-edge church." This vision of church sees in itself a renewed institution that has "become a significant nurturing force, conceptualizer of a serving mission, value shaper, and moral sustainer of leaders everywhere."[22]

As he laments the absence of any actual growing-edge churches, Greenleaf wonders: are the criteria unrealistic? Is there a lack of desire to be part of this kind of theological renewal? Or is it a case of needing to move obstacles? Answering the last question with a "yes," Greenleaf chides denominations and congregations for their readiness to hire consultants and fall prey to gimmicks that ultimately do not help faith communities to promote healing in the face of alienation. More than that, he continues, institutions, especially religious ones, rather than bowing to trends, need to accept the difficult task of "nurturing seekers" and serving humanity by helping us rebind ourselves to the cosmos.[23]

How can this happen? By learning from what did not work for Martin Luther and George Fox as they rejected clericalism. In Greenleaf's reckoning, Luther failed to reconcile a sense of radical equality with ordained pastors; Quakers succeeded in achieving equality by becoming pastorless but, early on, had difficulty keeping their movement vibrant.

> The first task of the growing edge church is to learn what neither Luther nor Fox knew: how to build a society of equals in which there is strong lay leadership in a trustee board with a [chairperson] functioning as primus inter pares, and with the pastor functioning as primus inter pares for the many who do the work of the church. Having accomplished this, the second task is to make of the church a powerful force to build leadership strength in those persons who have the opportunity to lead in other institutions, and give them constant support.[24]

In other words, the radicality of Greenleaf's philosophy is not only inspired by the priesthood of all believers, it requires one—congregational and denominational organization so deeply owned and taken responsibility for by church folk that our bureaucratic politics originate from our leaders serving us. These politics are neither internal to the "higher ups" and the structures they work in nor are they an intractable conflict caused by confusion about who is serving whom. Furthermore, accountability is multivalent. A college president, for example, is responsible to her administrative cabinet and her board of directors are responsible to her and she to them, but her pastor is also accountable to her. In the servant leadership priesthood of all believers, accountability is circular, not triangular.

To play on a well-known phrase, while there can be too many cooks in the kitchen, there can never be too many priests in the church. When we say that all Christians are called to think of themselves as priests, that means that we expect each other, among other things, to a) seek holiness, b) tend to our emotional and psychological health, c) strive toward spiritual maturity, d) nurture the life of the mind, e) act with compassion, and f) wrestle with God. The church, indeed the world, can never have too many people doing this kind of work. Jesus' parable about the Good Samaritan can be interpreted in many ways. For this essay, I invoke this story to notice that the Samaritan man acted as a priest to the injured man. When we love ourselves we are able to set our egos aside and come to the aid of a stranger and thereby love that person as we love ourselves. By showing compassion to the other, the Samaritan demonstrated that he loved himself. This is part of the journey toward legitimate power and greatness.

Leaders in Every Chair: The Circle Way

Because Greenleaf did not provide a blueprint for the practice of servant leadership, it is up to us to develop the plans for implementation ourselves. For Mennonite practice of servant leadership, I advocate a particular form of circle process known as PeerSpirit Circling and the circle way. Circle process (sometimes simply "circle") is a genre of process that has a variety of applications. Kay Pranis's description of circle helps to explain circle's appeal as a tool for seeking shalom. "Our ancestors gathered around a fire in a circle," Pranis reports. "Families gather around the kitchen table in a circle. Now, we are learning to gather in a circle as community to solve problems, support one another, and connect to one another."

Pranis trains others to lead Peacemaking Circles designed for neighborhoods interested in restorative justice, schools wanting to address behavioral problems in non-retributive ways, work places where employees want to transform conflicts, and social service organizations that share a vision for creating organic support systems.[25]

Diversity circles are an application to bring racially and ethnically diverse groups of people together to reflect on the systemic impact of racism in interpersonal ways.[26]

Circles assume that some issues are best addressed by gathering a community in the shape of a circle to invite participation that assumes a) there is wisdom available to the group that we cannot access on our own and b) the quality of our speaking and listening are deepened when we have structure and agreements in place.

The application of circle process by PeerSpirit's approach or circle way employs features common to most circles but adds some innovations that appeal to me particularly as a Mennonite peace theologian. These innovations include understanding circle process as a blended archetype, forming circles around a center, rotating leadership, and the principle that there is "a leader in every chair."

Christina Baldwin and Ann Linnea, theorists and practitioners who developed the circle way, introduce two shapes that symbolize contrasting paradigms or archetypes of group process: the circle for collaboration and the triangle for hierarchy. Circle's egalitarianism and its collaboration are part of its draw. Triangle, with its hierarchical archetypal energy, "is useful for passing on information, giving directions, establishing chains of command, developing armies, developing workforces, organizing data, programming computer software, and mass-producing goods." However, the linear virtues of the triangle fail to connect us to the reality of interdependence. This is why Baldwin and Linnea suggest that a problem with "the world today is to think about the triangle . . . as having overtaken its partnership with the circle."[27]

Unlike most forms of circle process, the circle way is structured to keep the circle and the triangle together:

> In symbolism, the circle and triangle are often found together. . . . The partnership of archetypes is the willingness to combine the best attributes of both social structures and to know when to call on each of their strengths and to experience their balance.[28]

The circle way seeks a rebalanced partnership. Baldwin and Linnea explain:

> The circle way is a practice of reestablishing social partnerships and creating a world in which the best of collaboration informs and inspires the best of hierarchical leadership. The chief needs a council that brings the voices of the village to his or her ear. The president needs a cabinet. The coach needs a team. The teacher needs students. The elders need children. And the meetings need to change.[29]

The circle way's partnership of circular and triangular forms is precisely the same move servant leadership makes. In both modes, there is a commitment to make sure that no one is powerless.[30]

Baldwin and Linnea characterize the circle's center—a visual focal point in the middle of the circle created by a candle, a vase of flowers, objects representing each person on the rim—as transpersonal space. Because it is "a place that belongs to everyone and to no one," the center helps us unlearn habits of conversation that can treat circles as spaces waiting to be filled with interpersonal stuff.[31]

The circle way begins with some basic agreements that help building consensus as well as identify as a triangle of leadership that is part of the circle. Baldwin and Linnea argue that "the use of agreements allows all members to have a free and profound exchange, to respect a diversity of views, and to share responsibility for the well-being and direction of the group."[32]

By identifying a trio of leaders, the circle way creates an expectation of collaboration from the planning process through to the conclusion of the circle. The host prepares the physical space for a conversation and helps to determine the conversation's scope or intention. The guardian gives special attention to keeping the group aware of its shared intention, the scribe records the group's process and any unresolved questions.

When the circle and the triangle work in harmony, meetings become an opportunity for conversations that actually matter both because they are significant to those who show up and because they help to move work forward. This mattering requires what Baldwin and Linnea describe as the presence of a leader in every chair.[33]

Conclusion

Both servant leadership and the circle are philosophies and methodologies for getting meaningful work done that serves, renews, and strengthens our immediate communities and our broader society. Both approaches translate easily into broadly Christian and particularly Anabaptist frameworks. The circle way helps us think about the various levels and forms of denominational organization, from congregations to schools to the national delegate assembly. Whether concentric or overlapping, circles all share the same center: the trinitarian life of God that is actively guiding the cosmos toward the Great Shalom of salvation, justice, well-being, and reconciliation.

As a denomination, we have been reluctant to develop a thoroughgoing teaching and practice of the priesthood of all believers that actually sees each individual performing a priestly, leadership function. As long as "servant-leader" means things like regarding my needs as secondary to yours, either preserving or abandoning church institutions because they are institutions, doing other people's emotional work for them, or failing to make difficult decisions—all because I lead by serving—then servant leadership is a bad idea.

However, when we intentionally orient ourselves as baptized members of congregational communities toward being in the world in ways that build capacity for self-empathy, vulnerability, compassion, boldness, and creativity, then we will be ready to talk about servant leadership. Think about what could happen if we began to harness the truth and power in seemingly divergent christological moments ranging from Jesus' birth in a barn to the pain of Simon-Peter's denial, from raising

Lazarus to withstanding grueling temptation, from challenging lax temple practices to tenderly playing with children. All of these moments are part of defining how Jesus navigated his reality. I believe Jesus invirtes us to take our lives as seriously and to consider what might happen in our part of the church and through our participation in society if we reimagine and radically connect service and leadership in circles upon circles upon circles, claiming and sharing moral authority in God's beloved community.

Notes

1. There are some exceptions. David R. Brubaker, program director at Eastern Mennonite University, Harrisonburg, Virginia, roots his organizational theories and models in the Greenleaf tradition. John Stahl-Wert, of the Newton Institute and the Center for Serving Leadership also works in this tradition. Goshen College President Jim Brenneman also connects servant leadership to Greenleaf (see James F. Brenneman, "Culture for Service Leadership: A Paradox Worth Living" [Goshen College, 2011]. doi:https://www.goshen.edu/news/2011/08/31/culture-for-service-leadership-a-paradox-worth-living/ <25 July 2016>).

2. Robert K. Greenleaf, *Servant Leadership: A Journey Into the Nature of Legitimate Power and Greatness* (Mahwah, N.J.: Paulist Press, 1977), 1-2. In his writing, Greenleaf would hyphenate "servant-leader" to keep in tension the opposing connotations of the two words as if they form a koan. He did not hyphenate "servant leadership," however, perhaps because servant leadership assumes the presence of servant-leaders. Some sources capitalize the terms Servant-Leader and Servant Leadership. In what follows, I have preserved the capitalization when it appears in direct quotations.

3. Greenleaf, *Servant Leadership*, 3.

4. James W. Sipe and Don M. Frick, *Seven Pillars of Servant Leadership: Practicing the Wisdom of Leading by Serving* (Mahwah, N.J.: Paulist Press, 2009), xiv.

5. Don M. Frick, *Robert K. Greenleaf: A Life of Servant Leadership* (San Francisco: Berrett-Koehler Publishers, 2004), 5-6.

6. Sipe and Frick, *Seven Pillars*, 49.

7. Sipe and Frick, *Seven Pillars*, xiv.

8. Greenleaf, *Servant Leadership*, 5-6.

9. Sipe and Frick, *Seven Pillars*, 4.

10. Sipe and Frick, *Seven Pillars*, 5.

11. Sipe and Frick, *Seven Pillars*, 6.

12. Frick, *Robert K. Greenleaf*, 4.

13. Sipe and Frick, *Seven Pillars*, 126.

14. Sipe and Frick, *Seven Pillars*, 130.

15. One example is Harold Bauman's handbook intended to help Mennonite Church (MC) congregations fulfill the Delegate Assembly's 1981 statement titled

"Leadership and Authority in the Life of the Church." While "servant leaders" appears in the title, the book has zero references to Robert Greenleaf. See Harold E. Bauman, *Congregations and Their Servant Leaders: Some Aids for Faithful Congregational Relationships* (Scottdale, Pa.: Mennonite Publishing House, 1982).

16. Larry C. Spears, "Introduction: Tracing the Past, Present, and Future of Servant Leadership," in *Focus on Leadership: Servant-Leadership for the 21st Century*, 3rd ed., ed. Larry C. Spears (2002), 9-13

17. I offer this critique as an insider. I am part of an extended family that includes four generations of young adults educated in Mennonite colleges and universities. Along with lifelong exposure to Mennonite institutions of all kinds, I served on the Mennonite Education Agency's Board of Directors from 2010-2013.

18. Peter J. Dyck, "Service," *Global Anabaptist Mennonite Encyclopedia* (1989), http://gameo.org/index.php?title=Service&oldid=104389 <25 July 2016>.

19. Greenleaf, *Servant Leadership*, 67.

20. Harold S. Bender and Marlin E. Miller, "Priesthood of All Believers," *Global Anabaptist Mennonite Encyclopedia* (1989), http://gameo.org/index.php?title=Priesthood_of_all_believers&oldid=93326 <25 July 2016>.

21. Bender and Miller, "Priesthood of All".

22. Robert K. Greenleaf, *The Power of Servant Leadership*, ed. Larry C. Spears (San Francisco: Berrett-Koehler Publishers, 1989), 148.

23. Greenleaf, *The Power*, 148-149; Greenleaf, *Servant Leadership*, 80.

24. Greenleaf, *Servant Leadership*, 81-82.

25. Kay Pranis, *The Little Book of Circle Processes: A New/Old Approach to Peacemaking* (Intercourse, Pa.: Good Books, 2005), 3-4.

26. Chapter 17 in this volume describes the use of circle groups for discipline, for cultural understanding, and for building relationships among students and staff in the public school system of Madison, Wisconsin.

27. Christina Baldwin and Ann Linnea, *The Circle Way: A Leader in Every Chair* (Oakland, Calif.: Berrett-Koehler Publishers, 2010), 7, 10.

28. Baldwin and Linnea, *The Circle Way: A Leader in Every Chair*, 14. Baldwin and Linnea define hierarchy as "a system of organization that follows well-defined patterns of priority that allows the carrying out of clearly delineated tasks with little or no debate" (200).

29. Baldwin and Linnea, *The Circle Way: A Leader in Every Chair*, 11.

30. Sipe and Frick, *Seven Pillars*, 285.

31. Sipe and Frick, *Seven Pillars*, 114.

32. Christina Baldwin and Ann Linnea, "Basic Guidelines for Calling a Circle-Priesthood of All Believers," *The Circle Way* (2016), http://static1.squarespace.com/static/55597e72e4b0f7284bff49e0/t/56e340a1f8baf38bbe1d00f6/1457733793606/TCW+Guidelines+English.pdf <25 July 2016>. For the agreements, see Baldwin and Linnea, *The Circle Way: A Leader in Every Chair*, 67-69.

33. Baldwin and Linnea, *The Circle Way: A Leader in Every Chair*, 200-201.

CHAPTER ELEVEN

WHY THE ANABAPTIST ACADEMY SHOULD GO TO CHURCH

Gerald J. Mast

Embracing the Body of Christ

In his brilliant and defining account of race in church history and Christian theology, J. Kameron Carter concludes his book with a call for theologians to "speak from within the crises of life and death rather than in the scholastic universes and out of the disposition of scholastic reason."[1] In Carter's view, the abstractions of reason associated with the Western academy are identified with the whiteness of ancient Gnostic beliefs that associated salvation with the erasure of the body. Real human bodies display color and difference that contrast with the disembodied and universal spiritual unity Gnostics channeled in their battle against Jewish passion and particularity.[2]

Carter's observation about the link between whiteness and scholastic theology could be understood to apply more generally to the whiteness of the "liberal arts" academy as it is typically posed against technical or vocational schools in current debates about the mission and identity of Anabaptist educational institutions. For example, contemporary social theorists like Edward Said have demonstrated the identification of supposedly objective Enlightenment reason, as well as Western art and culture, with white colonial and imperial political projects, including liberal democracy and its supporting institutions.[3]

Institutions that seek to distinguish themselves as providing a broad-based liberal arts education rather than mere career training risk identifying themselves with the abstraction and "whiteness" of leadership paradigms that feature control and management as paths to upward mobility and higher status. Within this framework, study of the arts, humanities, and social sciences is justified as leverage for "out of the box" thinking required for leadership success in the competitive marketplace of global capitalism. By contrast, professional programs are often presented as providing more practical training in marketable skills that help guarantee high wage jobs and income security within that same marketplace.

So, whether students choose liberal arts based programs that prepare them for challenging leadership roles or professional programs that prepare them for a secure career path, they are nevertheless invited to see their education primarily as preparation for a path up and out of poverty and vulnerability. Theirs is then a flight from rather than an embrace of "the crises of life and death."

In response to this argument between the liberal arts and the professions, Anabaptist schools should embrace their roots in an alternative set of motivations for education rooted in the call to reconciliation and service. By featuring biblical studies and cross-cultural competencies as the linchpins of their educational curriculums, Anabaptist schools and colleges provide a promising alternative to either career-centered or elite-identified education. Faithful education in such an alternative context is experienced less as a unified abstraction enabling mastery of an orderly world and more as a risky adventure based in attachment to God's infinitely absorbing creation.[4]

In this short essay, I explore the possibility that Anabaptist educators can transcend the tension between liberal-arts grounded and career-focused models of education by embracing their identity as church schools whose educational practices are rooted in the life and body of Jesus Christ and therefore also in the existence and struggle of the church. The groundwork for an Anabaptist curriculum rooted in peace and conflict transformation has already been displayed in a number of publications.[5]

Moreover, Mennonite schools have mostly embraced their identity as peace church institutions by teaching restorative justice, peacebuilding, and conflict transformation across a variety of program platforms. Biblical studies or biblical theology typically plays a key role in general education at Mennonite schools, taking up the function of exploring first principles that is typically associated with philosophy in liberal arts colleges or with dogmatic theology in church-related schools.[6]

I propose to build on and strengthen these distinctive commitments in Mennonite education by renewing the attachment of the Anabaptist academy to the church of Jesus Christ as the defining site for the "crises of life and death" to which the gospel is a reconciling response.

Albert Meyer has characterized church schools as institutions that are understood to be part of the mission of a church.[7] My definition of a church school incorporates a reversal of this definition: schools that see the church as central to the mission of the academy. By this I do not mean that the church should be an arm of the academy; rather, the church should be a laboratory for the Anabaptist academy and the ground for its engagement with the knowledge of the world that God is reconciling through Jesus Christ.

Moreover, the academy should serve the church as a key resource for carrying out the church's mission in the world. This emphasis on the church as a kind of front row seat to the cosmically significant work of Jesus Christ in reconciling the whole creation shifts the focus of Anabaptist schools away from the struggle between liberal arts-based leadership preparation and self-actualization on the one hand and professionally focused skills acquisition and career advancement on the other. Anabaptist church schools offer the resources of the liberal arts and professional preparation within the adventurous context of service to others and the advancement of God's peaceable kingdom.

In sum, by going to church the Anabaptist academy can avoid the secularization of its mission into a mere conduit for effective leaders and workers for global capital. In this essay, I focus on one specific dimension of a church-going and church-centered academy: talking with college students about why they should go to church. This conversation features the church's role in forming lives of faith capable of walking in the weakness of Jesus Christ and embracing the life and death conflict that defines all active discipleship. I argue that inviting students into the crisis of the church as participant observers—scholars and followers of the way of Jesus Christ—is the central mission of Anabaptist schools.

Forming Lives of Faith

I published a book in 2012 entitled *Go to Church, Change the World: Christian Community as Calling.* In this book I urged readers to receive the life of the church as the primary vocational calling of all Christians—the calling we receive in baptism to be joined with Jesus Christ in his death and resurrection and thus with his body as it is present in the world today. The book argued that the practices of the church—reading and understanding the Bible together, offering and receiving baptism, joining together in the Lord's Supper, sharing resources and discernment, and serving the life of the world—are all activities by which we learn those habits of truth and excellence that the world needs to become transformed and holy, a dwelling place for God.[8]

In reframing this argument for college students in a number of settings, I have highlighted three reasons to go to church: First, students should go to church for themselves, their own happiness, and their own well-being. This claim is supported in studies reported by the American sociologist Robert Putnam that correlate church attendance with happiness and life satisfaction.[9] Going to church situates students within a network of meaning and purpose that transcends personal or romantic relationships on the one hand and academic or professional ties on the other hand.

Second, students should go to church for the world. This is because in the church we learn how to become reconciled to our enemies, a skill that the world needs perhaps more than any other skill to be saved from the war and violence that threaten our future.[10] Part of this reconciliation with enemies is making visible God's triumph over injustice and violence by involvement in movements for social change that express the human desire for well-being and peace.[11]

And third, students should go to church for God, because God delights in the gathering of God's people for worship and accountability and God is present where such gatherings take place. For those who want a life that has the capacity for miracles and surprises, there is no better place to go than where God's presence is persistently acknowledged—in church.[12]

These arguments highlight how church attendance and involvement can help college students relate personal and social well-being by forming students into faithful believers who are receptive to the reconciliation and service mission of the Anabaptist academy. In this essay, I develop two additional arguments for church attendance that embrace the "crises of life and death" by which Anabaptist learning remains firmly rooted in the vulnerable and broken body of Christ.

Witnessing the Weakness of the Church

College students should go to church not just because the church provides leverage for moral formation and humanization; they should also go to witness the failure and weakness and difficulty that are associated with the church of Jesus Christ. Alex Sider has written a book about how to receive the conflict-ridden and often disappointing history of the church doxologically; that is, as an occasion for praise and thanksgiving, rather than as a project of control or management of meaning. While Sider's book focuses on the way we tell the story of the church, his argument could be extended to the way that we discuss or display the weakness and failure of the church to one another and especially to college students.

Drawing on the picture of salvation history exhibited in the book of Hebrews, and by critiquing the work of modern political historians and theologians such as Troeltsch, O'Donovan, Volf, and Yoder, Sider argues that the salvation being brought about in the life of God's people is a gift received amid catastrophe and faithlessness. From Sider's work we can see that it is because we insist that God's work is being received and offered in the life of an often faithless and failing people that we can actually experience the gospel as both radical gift and plausible promise.[13]

The fallible church offers the gospel as radical gift when it acknowledges this gift as good news that we flawed and failing humans are only able to receive thankfully, rather than control strategically. The fallible church offers the gospel as plausible promise when it demonstrates that our weakness is a condition of possibility for exhibiting God's living city rather than being a compromise of perfection that threatens to sidetrack the march to Zion.

Such faith that is displayed amid the catastrophe of the church is displayed in Anna Jansz's letter to her son as found in the *Martyrs Mirror*.

Anna Jansz was a young adult Dutch Anabaptist martyr who made the transition from being a revolutionary Münsterite to a spiritualist Davidite and who before her execution at age twenty-nine on January 24, 1539 in Rotterdam left a written epistle for her son that has become a classic Anabaptist text.[14] In the letter she tells her son,

> Do not regard the great number, nor walk in their ways. . . . But where you hear of a poor, cast-off simple little flock, which is despised and rejected by the world, join them; for where you hear of the cross, there is Christ; from there do not depart.[15]

This comment is often regarded as a description of what is sometimes called the persecuted church—the church regarded as a threat to the established order. While that is certainly part of what is meant here, I also think that for Anna Janz this experience of a poor, cast-off flock included her experience as a Münsterite—which constituted a much larger part of her church experience than being affiliated with the group led by David Joris.

Moreover, both the Münsterites and the Davidites were failures not just in the sense of being persecuted by the authorities but also in the sense of representing quite visible moral and theological failures, including the lapse into polygamy and the use of the sword by the Münsterites as well as the sexual utopianism and esoteric enthusiasm of the Davidites.[16] And these radical church projects were also failures in the sense that they were not savvy enough to survive, as was the Mennonitism that eventually appropriated Anna's story and testimony for its martyr literature.

Anna's experience reflects in a dramatic and intense way the more deliberate earlier decision of Menno Simons in 1536 to finally leave his respectable position in the Catholic priesthood and join a completely discredited and fragmented Anabaptist group—"sheep without a proper shepherd" as he put it.[17] In Menno's conversion testimony, the violent and misguided actions of the Münsterite Anabaptists are responsible for ultimately convincing him to give up his comfortable and successful clerical career. Discussing the armed Anabaptist takeover of the Olde Klooster monastery that led ultimately to a massacre of these Anabaptists by the authorities, Menno reflects, "After this had transpired, the blood of these people, although misled, fell so hot upon my heart that I could not stand it, nor find rest in my soul."[18]

Of course, Menno also discusses the influence of many other Christian reformers such as Luther, Zwingli, Bucer, and Bullinger—all of them church leaders he regarded as partly right but also partly wrong. In other words, Menno Simons, like Anna Jansz, was converted to Anabaptist faith through the failure and weakness of the church and not by any exhibition of great spiritual success. This failure and weakness was experienced by Menno in all of the available options at the time: the Catholic faith of his youth, the Protestant Reformation that aroused his interest as a pastor, and the Anabaptist movement that he finally joined. Menno not only left a flawed and failing church, he also joined a church that he knew was in error.

So it is not surprising that in the early editions of Menno's writings, he described the Münsterite Anabaptists as "dear brothers who erred only a little when they sought to defend their faith with the sword."[19] While such statements were edited out of later editions of Menno's writings, they do accurately reflect that sometimes forgotten fact that the Mennonite church is named after someone who joined the Anabaptist movement primarily because of the dramatic mistakes, failures, and sins of the revolutionary and polygamous Münsterites, and was himself baptized by the former Münsterite—Obbe Phillips.

What does this all have to do with the church and college students? I'm suggesting that one reason we should encourage college students to go to church is so that they can discover how truly flawed and disastrous the church actually is. In fact, I think it's possible we should invite them to follow Anna Janz's advice: look for the cast-offs, the conflict-ridden, the failures, and the small, because that is where they might truly experience the gospel as a gift that is communicated in weakness.[20]

Our goal at church colleges should be to expose students to the difficulty of church history and life—so that our graduates are, like Menno, energized rather than scandalized by the failures of the church. Stories and testimonies like those of Anna and Menno invite students to invest their lives and learning in the human crises of their own time and place, to practice what Quentin Schultze has called downward mobility rather than upward mobility.[21] For students who respond to this invitation, the church offers a sort of internship opportunity to discover the complex and concrete human realities that the work of Jesus Christ is renewing and restoring through the power of weakness.

Remembering Who We Are in Conflict

Walking in weakness assumes knowledge of self and community that is carried in the experiences of the body, not just in the abstractions of the mind. Students should go to church, therefore, to remember who they are, to remember that they are baptized or to realize that they are not. Conflict is central to this bodily experience of knowing who we are.

Sara Wenger Shenk discusses the role of habit and ritual in bodily memory in her important book *Anabaptist Ways of Knowing*. In this book, Shenk draws on Paul Connerton to explain the transmission of communal conviction and history through practices that become habitual.[22] She discusses specific habits and rituals that have been part of Mennonite church life in the past—such as Bible study, singing together, simplicity in attire, bedtime prayers, communion, Sunday rest, and so on.[23] She identifies a decreasing regard for such practices in the church and urges a critical recovery of Anabaptist practices that renew the bodily knowledge of communally centered discernment and, to use Rebecca Chopp's terminology, "emancipatory transformation."[24]

Shenk urges a renewed partnership among families, churches, and schools to recreate a communal culture that values the Scriptures, strengthens family life, baptizes new believers, teaches discipleship, and prepares Christians to live as resident aliens—loyal first of all to God's peaceable reign. She suggests a number of bodily practices and celebrations that can help believers remember in their bodies who they are: Sabbath keeping, cultivating sacred spaces, engendering a unique identity, weaving relational networks, and writing and telling stories.[25]

I would add this to Shenk's list: engaging in harrowing church conflict. Part of what it means to be a baptized believer is to experience in our bodies the difficulty of salvation history, the memory of conflict and cross. At least in my experience of church, conflict has been as basic and routine as communion and Sabbath keeping, if not always as pleasant.

Ephraim Radner has written a large and rambling book on the often painful and divisive unity that marks the life of the church, including its capitulations to the bloodiest conflicts and crimes of history such as the U.S. Civil War and the German Holocaust. He argues that divisions and traumatic conflicts are unavoidable realities in the church, a truth that Christ announced when he said that he had not come to bring peace but division, dividing a household of five, two against three and three against two (Luke 12:51-53).[26]

Radner argues that the church's conflicts reflect the divided work of salvation that Jesus Christ displayed and accomplished: "Division is bound to Christ's very coming and presence," he writes, just as "separation also lies at the center of creation," when God divided light from darkness, waters and earth, day and night. Intrinsic to authentic and true reconciliation is the division that demands it.[27] Intrinsic to the resurrection is the death that is embraced by it. Citing *Martyrs Mirror* editor Thieleman van Braght's admonition, as summarized by Reformation historian Benjamin Kaplan, that "toleration is a greater threat to the soul than persecution," Radner concludes: "We are called to be one, but our life depends on the sharp edge of division."[28]

College students should be invited to go to church so that they can experience the life of Christ that depends on the sharp edge of division. The cosmic struggle for reconciliation that is on display in the church confirms that matters of great consequence are being worked out in the life of the church. These matters of great consequence often shake the life and organization of the church and demand reconsideration of such basic matters as the purpose and ground of the church, the means by which we know the truth of God's Word, and the relationship of the church to the world.

By taking up the conflicts of the church as opportunities to study such first order questions as the nature and future of the cosmos and the meaning of life within that cosmos, the Anabaptist academy can prepare students and graduates to remember the whole and unvarnished truth about their baptisms. That practice is the devastating and transformative division of their new life in Christ from the ruins of the fading conformist self, routed as this fading self now is by the power of Christian weakness. Seen and understood this way, the conflicts and failures of the church can be a source of renewal and hope rather than cynicism and disappointment. Moreover, from such a perspective the reconciliation of enemies that the church promises becomes a disruptive source of the world's salvation rather than a mere management of status quo-threatening conflict.

The exploration and study of conflict in the church thus provides critical knowledge for addressing the conflicts in the world—especially since conflicts in the church are usually channeling conflicts in the world. The church can be seen as a laboratory for understanding both the depth of division as well as the potential for reconciliation.

However, the life of the church provides crucial knowledge not only for the study of peace and conflict transformation. As a comprehensive historical, cultural, and political community that exhibits both the intransigence of human sinfulness and the strategies of weak power that God has chosen to defeat sin, the church also provides experiential and experimental knowledge of crucial topics. These include governance, leadership, economics, business, accounting, literature, art, design, music, communication, health care, social work, education, cultural studies, history, philosophy, law, politics, ethics, gender and sexuality studies, and so on. Because the church constructs and maintains structures such as church buildings, campground facilities, schools and hospitals, the knowledge and skills of architects, engineers, naturalists, nutritionists, and a host of other scientists are intrinsic to the church's existence and mission.

Sending our students to church provides an opportunity to enlist their gifts and knowledge in the challenging and humanizing call of Jesus Christ to make disciples of all nations. During the release of episode 7 of the *Star Wars* film series, I overheard two young men in the cafeteria line at Bluffton talk wistfully about how the world of *Star Wars* had captured their imagination. "I wish I could be a Jedi Knight," one of the young men said. "Yes, wouldn't it be great to have been born in a different galaxy?" his companion chimed in. At the lunch table I discussed these startling and intriguing student comments with my faculty colleagues. We acknowledged that these comments exhibited the boredom and dehumanization associated with the career and vocation paths identified with the marketplace of global capitalism.

Students yearn for a greater purpose than to earn money, acquire possessions, climb the corporate ladder, or achieve fame and status. Students desire a world-changing and life-consuming mission—such as that displayed in the training and purpose of the Jedi order in Star Wars. And they yearn to be born into another world—a world of wonder and cosmic marvel that transcends their own space and time.

Such a world is available to our students in the life and ministry of the church as it carries out the great commission and prepares its members to be ambassadors of Christ's peace. The church's schools should embrace the work of inviting and training such globally savvy and locally grounded ambassadors as the primary purpose that unites the entire curriculum.

I conclude with the words of a Mennonite college graduate, a young man named Jake Short who attended my church and was part of my Sunday school class during his four years as a Bluffton student. Jake Short describes his experience of connecting with local versions of the church throughout his college years, both in Bluffton and in Northern Ireland where he spent a semester immersed in peace and conflict studies as part of Bluffton's cross-cultural program. He discusses visiting numerous congregations, both Catholic and Protestant, during his studies in Northern Ireland: "The exploration along the way to finding a church home can be just as exciting and a good learning experience as finally discovering this church home."[29]

At the same time, Short found the courage for such exploration of the many forms taken by the global church from his firm rootedness in a particular congregation during his college years: "It is comforting to know, that even years later, I can still return to First Mennonite of Bluffton and call it 'home' and people welcome me with open arms. This is a reason to go to church, so there is always some place you can return to."[30]

Jake Short here expresses the experience of church as both adventure and safe harbor. The church is a promise for which you are looking; the church is a refuge to which you return. Both the promise and the refuge should be part of the church's appeal to the next generation of college students. Both the adventure and the safe harbor should be intrinsic to an Anabaptist academy immersed in the colorful "crises of life and death" more than in the white abstractions of scholastic reason.

Notes

1. J. Kameron Carter, *Race: A Theological Account* (New York: Oxford University Press, 2008), 377.
2. Carter, *Race*, 19-23.
3. Edward Said, *Orientalism* (New York: Vintage Books, 1979), 227.
4. Nancey Murphy, "A Theology of Education," in *Mennonite Education in a Post-Christian World*, ed. Harry Huebner (Winnipeg, Man.: CMBC Publications, 1998), 11.
5. J. Denny Weaver, "Teaching for Peace," in *Mennonite Education in a Post-Christian World*, ed. Harry Huebner (Winnipeg, Man.: CMBC Publications, 1998), 67-80; J. Denny Weaver and Gerald Biesecker-Mast, eds., *Teaching Peace: Nonviolence and the Liberal Arts* (Lanham, Md.: Rowman & Littlefield Publishers, Inc., 2003).

6. *Christ, Creation, and the Classroom*, Mennonite University Faculty Conference Presentations, Eastern Mennonite University, Aug. 7-9, 2008 (Goshen, Ind.: Mennonite Education Agency, 2008).

7. Albert J. Meyer, *Realizing Our Intentions: A Guide for Churches and Colleges with Distinctive Missions* (Abilene, Tex.: Abilene Christian University Press, 2009), 262.

8. Gerald J. Mast, *Go to Church, Change the World: Christian Community as Calling* (Harrisonburg, Va.: Herald Press, 2012), 17-18.

9. Robert Putnam, *American Grace: How Religion Divides and Unites Us* (New York: Simon and Schuster, 2010), 490-492.

10. This argument is developed more fully in Mast, *Go to Church*, 61-64, 68-78.

11. For an argument that the church is a socially-active alternative community in which members find support for social activism consistent with the way of Jesus Christ, see J. Denny Weaver, "The Socially Active Community: An Alternative Ecclesiology," in *The Limits of Perfection: Conversations with J. Lawrence Burkholder*, 2nd ed., ed. Rodney J. Sawatsky and Scott Holland (Waterloo, Ont.; Kitchener, Ont.: Institute of Anabaptist and Mennonite Studies, Conrad Grebel College; Pandora Press, 1993), 90-94.

12. Weaver, "Socially Active Community," 157-159.

13. J. Alexander Sider, *To See History Doxologically: History and Holiness in John Howard Yoder's Ecclesiology* (Grand Rapids, Mich.: William B. Eerdmans Publishing Co., 2011), 21-29.

14. C. Arnold Snyder and Linda A. Huebert Hecht, eds., *Profiles of Anabaptist Women: Sixteenth-Century Reforming Pioneers*, Studies in Women and Religion/Études sur les Femmes et la Religion (Waterloo, Ont.: Wilfrid Laurier University Press, 1996), 336-351.

15. Thieleman J. van Braght, *The Bloody Theater or Martyrs Mirror of the Defenseless Christians Who Baptized Only Upon Confession of Faith, and Who Suffered and Died for the Testimony of Jesus, Their Savior, from the Time of Christ to the Year A.D. 1660*, trans. Joseph F. Sohm (Scottdale, Pa.: Mennonite Publishing House, 1950), 454.

16. Willem de Bakker, Michael Driedger, and James Stayer, *Bernhard Rothman and the Reformation in Münster* (Kitchener, Ont.: Pandora Press, 2009), 147-182; Gary K. Waite, *David Joris and Dutch Anabaptism, 1524-1543* (Waterloo, Ont.: Wilfrid Laurier University Press, 1990), 122.

17. Menno Simons, *The Complete Writings of Menno Simons c.1496-1561*, ed. John Christian Wenger, trans. Leonard Verduin, with biography by Harold S. Bender (Scottdale, Pa.: Herald Press, 1956), 670.

18. Menno Simons, *Complete Writings*, 670.

19. Abraham Friesen, *Menno Simons: Dutch Reformer Between Luther, Erasmus, and the Holy Spirit a Study in the Problem Areas of Menno Scholarship* (Np: Xlibris, 2015), 147.

20. Thieleman J. van Braght, ed., *The Bloody Theater or Martyrs Mirror, Compiled from Various Authentic Chronicles, Memorials, and Testimonies*, trans. Joseph F.

Sohm (Scottdale, Pa.: Herald Press, 1987), 454.

21. Quentin Schultze, *Communicating for Life: Christian Stewardship in Community and Media* (Grand Rapids, Mich.: Baker Book House, 2000), 99.

22. Sara Wenger Shenk, *Anabaptist Ways of Knowing: A Conversation About Tradition-Based Critical Education* (Telford, Pa.: Cascadia Publishing House, 2003), 25.

23. Shenk, *Anabaptist Ways of Knowing*, 29-36.

24. Shenk, *Anabaptist Ways of Knowing*, 100.

25. Shenk, *Anabaptist Ways of Knowing*, 147-164.

26. Ephraim Radner, *A Brutal Unity: The Spiritual Politics of the Christian Church* (Waco, Tex.: Baylor University Press, 2012), 428.

27. Radner, *Brutal Unity*, 428.

28. Radner, *Brutal Unity*, 432.

29. Jake Short, personal correspondence (16 Oct. 2015).

30. Short, personal correspondence.

CHAPTER TWELVE

SEARCHING FOR SELF: COMMUNITY AS CONDUIT FOR GOD'S DEEPEST TRANSFORMATION

Sarah Ann Bixler

Introduction

Psychologists have talked much about the self. Anabaptist Mennonites have talked much about community but not so much about the self or the development of self within community. This essay imagines psychological and theological perspectives on the self within an Anabaptist-Mennonite experience of community. I propose that Mennonite education stands with great promise at the intersection of these approaches.

Educational psychologists have defined adolescence as a time when young people search for a sense of self. Erik Erikson, for example, located the stage of identity versus role confusion in adolescence, which he classifies as "the last stage of childhood."[1] He outlined the possibility for constructive navigation of this stage based on the ego's achievement of a sense of individuality, and introduced the concept of a psychosocial moratorium as important for this developmental progress.

Such a moratorium, "a prolongation of the interval between youth and adulthood," is marked by the avoidance of occupational commitments and the rejection of any learning not immediately interesting to the adolescent.[2] In the mid-twentieth century when Erikson wrote, adolescence ended about the time of high school graduation, after which the young adult would engage the subsequent task of intimacy vs. isolation. Currently, however, adolescence begins with puberty—as early as age eight—and extends as late as age thirty. Adolescence, then, encompasses most students in middle school, high school, and undergraduate institutions. As they search for a healthy and integrated sense of self, these students are navigating a critical period of time for the development of identity.

Participation in community requires an integrated and clearly developed sense of self. A healthy sense of self is affirmed in Scripture and emphasized in psychology. What distinguishes the development of the psychosocial self from the divinely illuminated self, however, is the transformation from the ego as primary to the ego operating in service of the self. As theology teaches, the self is the part of us that knows God. To this end, the distinctively theological perspective of the self articulated by Søren Kierkegaard and the insights of Christian educator James Loder help provide clarity about this mysterious process of transformation.

Additionally, recent findings in neuroscience highlight the importance of interpersonal relationships for the developing mind and its neural connections, which undergo substantial change as adolescents grow. Considering the importance of community for adolescent development, this paper identifies the enterprise of Mennonite education as a community that can act as a powerful conduit for God's deepest transformation of the self.

Where Is the Mennonite Self?

For Anabaptist Mennonites, known for a strong sense of community, a robust concept of the self has often been lacking and may invoke suspicion. Humility is highly valued, and believers are called to deny themselves to follow Jesus (Matt. 16:24), imitating Jesus who emptied himself (Phil. 2:7). The concept of self is often viewed as negative, equated with selfishness, and something to be repressed. The proposed corrective, then, is to deny one's self in service of Jesus who gave himself for us. While Christians must rightly seek to imitate Jesus, especially in distinguishing themselves from an individualistic society, the haste with which Mennonite adolescents are urged to deny their selves circumvents an important developmental process and bypasses a critical opportunity for God's transformation.

The concept of the self can be viewed in a variety of ways, some of which invoke moral interpretations. Edwin Friedman discusses the ambivalent regard for the self in American society generally, as demonstrated by the varied uses of the term in the English language. Sometimes "self" is simply descriptive, as in "self-expression," which generally carries a neutral tone. In other cases, the addition of "self" carries positive connotations, as in "self-assured" or "self-made." Other times the addition of "self" turns a neutral word into a negative one, as in "self-centered," "self-seeking" and "self-righteous."[3] Mennonites generally view the use of "self" in negative terms, lest one make the moral error of elevating self above the community.

The roots of this perspective may be traced back to Anabaptism's origins. Cornelius Dyck describes historic Anabaptist spirituality, which "was not an introspective cultivating of the life of the soul but a nurturing of a life of prayer, peace, integrity, humility, and communal relationships."[4] When Anabaptists broke from the Roman Catholic Church in the Radical Reformation, they articulated a new understanding of community that did not focus on the soul's interior life, which distinguished them from monasticism. For the early Anabaptists, "the restoration of ethics into personal and communal spiritual life was a primary goal . . . implemented only in and through a new body of believers."[5] In what was perhaps a reaction to the inwardness of monastic faith and the unethical behaviors they critiqued in the state church, Anabaptists traded an inward focus for their communal orientation.

This emphasis on community over self persists today. As an example, consider the place of "self" in Mennonite theology. A grammatical survey of the *Confession of Faith in a Mennonite Perspective* reveals the current theological usages of this term (see Appendix A: Instances of "Self" and "Selves" in *Confession of Faith in a Mennonite Perspective*). Not counting the use of self in an intensifier, such as in "Jesus himself," the *Confession of Faith in a Mennonite Perspective* includes five instances of a derivative of the singular "self" and sixteen instances of a word with the suffix "selves."[6] The many plural occurrences might be expected in a joint confessional statement. What is interesting, however, is the use of the singular "self."

Two of these instances describe God's gracious action on behalf of humanity: "God's infinite freedom and constant self-giving are perfect in faithful love" (Article 1: God) and "Humbling himself and becoming obedient unto death on a cross" (Article 2: Jesus Christ). Two other instances do not specifically refer to people, but humans may be inferentially included. The first references creation, which includes humanity: "All creation ultimately has its source outside itself" (Article 5: Creation and Divine Providence). The second refers to the church: "Patterning itself after the reign of God" (Article 10: The Church in Mission). Notably, the final instance uses self as an adjective in a negative way: "Use power selfishly, do violence, and become separated from God" (Article 7: Sin). Overall, in the *Confession of Faith*, for believers as individual or plural selves, the emphasis is on commitment or submission—whether to God, Christ, Scripture, or the churchly community.

Anabaptist Mennonites emphasize three core values: "Jesus is the center of our faith, community is the center of our lives, and reconciliation is the center of our work."[7] Palmer Becker articulates these tenets in his booklet, *What Is an Anabaptist Christian?* Not counting the reflexive pronoun "himself" that refers to God or Jesus, Becker mentions the concept of the individual self only twice. He describes the infamous Münsterites, who engaged in self-defense, to emphasize the importance of "unselfish forgiving" in reconciliation.[8] The self is notably absent in that Palmer makes no mention of the discipline of solitude and says nothing about cultivating inner spirituality in his twenty-three-page description of Anabaptist Christians. He mentions prayer only within the corporate context.[9] Rather than posing a critique of Becker's understanding, these observations simply indicate Anabaptist Mennonites' lack of engagement with the concept of the self.

In modernity, Western society became focused on the individual, an emphasis that has only increased with postmodernism. American society most certainly embodies this focus on the individual. As Eugene Peterson asserts, for example, "America is in conspicuous need of unselfing."[10] In the face of society's obsession with the self manifested as individualism, the Mennonite church has good reason to stress a theology of community.

However, participating in community involves an important psychological process that the church may overlook. Are Mennonite adolescents receiving the subliminal message that, as good disciples, they must first deny themselves and their own perhaps fragile identities, to belong to the faith community? Does humble behavior necessarily precede belonging to the church, to the extent that adolescents are encouraged to abandon completely their search for an innate sense of self? If so, the Mennonite church is doing a great spiritual and psychological disservice to the development of its young people. But Mennonite education may hold the potential for a corrective.

What Is the Self?

To understand the self from a uniquely Christian perspective, we turn to the disciplines of biblical studies and theology. In the New Testament, the word translated *self* is *anthropos*, which is the Greek word for a human being, either male or female depending on context. Twice New Testament epistles refer to the "old self," something that is crucified (Rom. 6:6) or put off in exchange for "the new self, created according to the likeness of God in true righteousness and holiness" (Eph. 4:22-24). The self is not static but transformed by Christ. Jesus is recorded as asking, "What does it profit them if they gain the whole world, but lose or forfeit themselves?" (Luke 9:25). Here the self is something essential to the person. Later, in the household codes of 1 Peter, women's beauty is described as coming from the "inner self," something positive and valued by God (1 Pet. 3:3-4).

Jesus empowers the concept of self by naming it as the very location of the kingdom of God. In Luke 17:20-21, he answers the Pharisees' question about the coming of the kingdom by saying, "The kingdom of God is not coming with things that can be observed; nor will they say, 'Look, here it is!' or 'There it is!' For, in fact, the kingdom of God is among you." The Greek word the NRSV translates as "among" can also be translated "within," which may be a better translation. This locates the kingdom of God as an internal reality. Additionally, discrepancy exists among versions of the Greek New Testament as to whether "you" is the Greek word *entos*, which is the second-person singular pronoun, or the second-person plural pronoun.

Either way, this passage could be interpreted to mean that the kingdom of God exists within the self. On plenty of other occasions, to be sure, Jesus describes the kingdom of God as an external reality. A close look at his language in Luke 17, however, suggests that the kingdom of

God is not limited to external reality. God's kingdom is also within the self.

Søren Kierkegaard affirms the internal reality of the self grounded in God. In his theological work, *A Sickness unto Death*, he describes various forms of despair, "a sickness in the spirit, in the self."[11] Such "despair over oneself" ensues as long as one seeks "to tear his *[sic]* self away from the Power which constituted it," a self that lives without consciousness of its spiritual being.[12] The self must undergo transformation so that "the self is grounded transparent in the Power which posited it" and becomes "a self face to face with Christ." In this new state of being, the self is in touch with what John Howard Yoder called the "grain of the universe."[13] In this way, Kierkegaard writes, "Despair is completely eradicated by [the self] relating itself to its own self and by willing to be itself the self is grounded transparent in the Power which posited it."[14] This theological perspective compels Mennonite education to facilitate consciousness of the spirit-self.

God alone has the power to expose the true spirit-self. A close look at Kierkegaard's conclusion clarifies this distinction: "By relating itself to its own self and by willing to be itself, the self is grounded transparently in the Power which constituted it."[15] Every time Kierkegaard mentions this phrase, he includes the curious modifier *durchsichtig*, translated "transparently" in English. This German word conveys the image of transparency, a see-through quality in which the self becomes transparent to its true ground, not merely reflecting but acting as a clear lens through which a center outside of oneself is seen.[16]

The concept of *durchsichtig* can similarly be understood in terms of its English translation, whereas transparent means "allowing light to pass through so that objects behind can be distinctly seen."[17] This suggests that God illuminates the spirit-self, which can be distinctly seen only by allowing itself to be grounded in God. Christ is the medium through which God's light passes, illuminating the spirit-self; as Kierkegaard puts it, "the more conception of Christ, the more self."[18]

Furthermore, groundedness in God is a work of divine action, something neither a community nor a person can solely achieve. Gerhard Schreiber insightfully interprets Kierkegaard as saying, "Rather, the self's proper relation to God as ground is to *let itself be grounded.*"[19] This, then, becomes the essential task of Mennonite education in relation to the self: to create an environment whereby learners can let their selves become grounded in God through Christ, thereby experiencing the transforming power of the Holy Spirit. Mennonite education does not by its own agency cause learners to find their selves but rather leads them to encounter God who illuminates the self.

The Adolescent Self

The self in despair as described by Kierkegaard represents a conflict that, according to James Loder, requires transformation to heighten consciousness of its spirit-self.[20] Of particular relevance for Mennonite education, Loder identifies adolescence as a pivotal moment for experiencing the Spirit's transformation. In this developmental stage, new levels of cognitive, personal, and social awareness collide to create a perfect storm in which the experience of spiritual conversion is suddenly possible. This can result either in the self-sufficient hardening of the ego, which usurps the self and turns it away from God, or "the transformation of the entire ego struggle by the power of the Spirit, a transformation not developmentally possible before this period [of adolescence]."[21]

Furthermore, as Kenda Creasy Dean points out, "The unformed selves of adolescents can make room for Christ in ways that are difficult for hardened, formed egos."[22] Whether or not adolescence is the *first* time this is possible can be debated, but either way, adolescence undoubtedly marks a *prime* time for God to transform the ego in service of the self, the part of oneself that knows God. This self is marked by wholeness and unity rather than individualism and subjectivism. Such transformation occurs through conscious awareness and spiritual attunement to the movement of God's Spirit stirring within.

Loder adds this important theological perspective to developmental psychology by clarifying the relationship between ego and self. What Loder fails to adequately address, however, is the role of the community in the experience of individual transformation. Although lacking a theological framework, Erik Erikson's psychosocial life cycle theory recognizes the essential role of society in identity formation. Throughout his work, he highlights the interplay between the individual ego and its social context. Identity formation occurs in the context of one's ego, which is unconscious but has a definite social dimension.[23] The human ego binds together one's inner and outer lives.[24] This is what makes Erikson's use of the term psycho*social* identity so important. For Erikson, ego identity is "a defined ego within a social reality."[25] Discovering one's ego identity is not an individualistic task nor can it be accomplished in isolation. It depends on "the mutual complementation of ethos and ego, of group identity and ego identity."[26] When Erikson published and taught his psychosocial theory in the mid-twentieth century, he was working from intuition. Interestingly, his conclusions about ego development are now corroborated by recent findings in neuroscience.

In his most recent edition of *The Developing Mind,* the interpersonal neurobiologist Daniel Siegel discusses social impact on individual identity. He demonstrates how "our relational connections shape our neural connections. This interactive process occurs throughout the lifespan."[27] Adolescence represents a crucial time of neurological pruning, where pathways that are not used go out of service. It is possible to recreate these pathways later in life, but it is much more difficult and takes a great deal of work. Interaction with others shapes the pruning process; the mind adapts itself, socially based on the functioning of those around it.

Furthermore, the important capacity for internal integration may be "derived initially from attachment relationships, and later shaped by individuals' ongoing involvement with parents, teachers, and peers."[28] These relationships can contribute to, or hinder, the development of what Siegel calls the relational self. Thus a context of community not only influences the self, but is integral to its health and wholeness. When one observes the confluence of theological perspectives with the observations from developmental psychology and neuroscience, another example comes into view of an empirical science reflecting the grain of the universe for those who have eyes to see.

Community as Conduit for Transformation of Self

If social context is so important for ego and identity formation, what role might the Mennonite educational community play in God's transformation of the ego in service of the self, so that the self can let itself be grounded transparently in God who constituted it?[29] Given the theological importance of God's action in this transformational process, as well as the required social context for identity and mind development, Mennonite education is poised for a critical role as *conduit* for God's deepest transformation of the self. A conduit is an entity that conducts, as in physics where a conduit transmits some form of energy. Metal is a conduit of electricity, for example, as it transmits that energy from one object to another. In a similar manner, Mennonite education can serve as a conduit of God's transformation, setting up a channel of heightened spiritual awareness through which God's Spirit touches the adolescent.

Mennonite education is not the source of spiritual transformation of the self. Rather, it provides the environment in which this can happen by cultivating learners' awareness of God's presence within the self. Although it is not the only community through which this transformation occurs, Mennonite education is a significant one because adolescents spend more time in school than in church or possibly at home, especially undergraduates. Moreover, education builds on the premise of expanding worldviews and providing exposure to new ideas. One of the express purposes of Mennonite education is transformation.[30] When students enroll in school, they expect to encounter something new—in essence, they expect to undergo some sort of transformation. Mennonite education is a prime setting in which God's transformation can occur.

Erikson emphasizes the importance of a moratorium for adolescent identity formation, of which Mennonite education can provide a theologically appropriate version. In this "world between childhood and adulthood," Erikson envisions a permissive holding environment that tolerates the adolescent exercising extreme subjectivity, experimenting with non-normative ideologies, and exploring potential commitments.[31] He suggests that social institutions, one of which could be Mennonite education, might promote identity formation by "offering those who are still learning and experimenting a certain *status-of-the-moratorium,* an apprenticeship or discipleship."[32]

While Erikson's conception of a moratorium as "free-role experimentation" does not completely correspond with a theology of Christian discipleship, it resonates with the Mennonite perspective of identity-forming community. Erikson writes, "The young adult gains an assured sense of inner continuity and social sameness" that bridges what one was as a child and is about to become, reconciling one's self-conception with the community's recognition.[33]

From a faith perspective, Mennonite education offers adolescents a moratorium-like holding environment through opportunities to focus intentionally on receiving one's self, engage in practices that help that transformation, and experience the faith community's affirmation of the newly recognized self in Christ. Unlike Erikson's version, however, adolescents are not necessarily affirmed in their reluctance to make commitments or refusal to stake their identity on the Christ who calls and redefines them.

Mennonite education can use spiritual practices to cultivate identity formation and an integrated sense of self. Integrating faith across programs of curricular study helps adolescents integrate their spiritual selves with their academic selves, facets of the self that are sometimes disconnected. For this reason, Siegel prefers the plural term *selves* to the singular *self*. One of the particular tasks of adolescence, he explains, is the "integration of selves across time and role relationships. . . . to achieve coherence of the self" rather than disintegration.[34] Although Siegel calls them "mindsight skills," he essentially points toward spiritual practices to promote integration. He explains, "Mindful awareness practices and other forms of meditation . . . transform the functioning of the prefrontal cortex" and promote neural interconnectedness.[35]

Through such intentional opportunities for reflection, Mennonite education can guide students through deep inquiry into their multifaceted selves and discover how the working of God within can unite and transform the entire self. Such reflective practices promote an integrated or interconnected sense of self that encompasses past and present selves into a whole, poised to move into God's future calling.

Kierkegaard insists that knowledge must exercise such reflection, an essential self-referential component. He writes, "The increasing degree of knowledge corresponds with the degree of self-knowledge, that the more the self knows, the more it knows itself."[36] Education that privileges the amassing of subject knowledge over the knowledge of self as subject must be reframed to acknowledge that learning "is as much about who one wants *to be* as what one demonstrably comes to *know*."[37] In this context, education seeks to resolve the dissonance between self and knowledge and between self and community. In doing so, education can "become an occasion for new insight and the heightening of consciousness," which Loder associates with transformation.[38]

While internal integration is important, so also is the healthy development of the relational self.[39] Based on their guiding theology, Mennonite schools strive to embody compassion and nonviolence. Rather than a competitive environment, Mennonite education can represent a healthy, collaborative learning community. Such a community upholds the diversity of individual selves while bringing them together in compassionate relationality. As John Roth states, "Healthy communities will always need to balance the inevitable diversity of individual differences and the constant reality of change with a deeper sense of coherence and a shared commitment to a larger whole."[40] This dialectic of self and community, when tended in a compassionate and collaborative context by Mennonite educators, invites the possibility for God's transformation.

Indeed, an understanding of one's self is an integral part of being in community. Jesus' articulation of the second greatest commandment, "Love your neighbor as yourself" (Matt. 22:39), implies a foundational love of oneself. Psychology tells us that when we do not have compassion for ourselves, we cannot exercise compassion for others.[41] Understanding and loving oneself is an integral part of loving others in community, whether that community is primarily defined as social or spiritual. Dietrich Bonhoeffer affirms this in his two-fold warning, "Let him [sic] who cannot be alone beware of community," and, "Let him [sic] who is not in community beware of being alone."[42]

Indeed, this embodiment of the second greatest commandment flows out of the first. The necessary result of loving God with all of one's being is the ability to love oneself and others. Similarly, Bo Karen Lee explains that in experiencing the presence of God,

> one begins to see oneself as the object of God's delight, and from there, become a God-bearer, learning to see others in the same way. Only at that point is the individual able to see the other as equally embraced by the delight of God. With this new perception, the face of the other is transformed and given new beauty.[43]

Being in God's presence facilitates love of oneself and others. Delighting in the other is the display of God in us, the deepest form of love, borne from the recognition of one's self grounded in God. Because of this, nurturing the self makes an essential contribution to the Mennonite ideal of community.

Conclusion

As we have seen, the Anabaptist Mennonite focus on community can act as an obstacle as well as a means to God's transformation. Adequate attention to the self must be balanced with the emphasis on community, and Mennonite education holds great potential as an environment in which this can occur. Scripture affirms that the kingdom of God is within the self, although not exclusively, and Kierkegaard calls us to allow the self to be grounded in the power that constituted it, which is God.

This is the experience of transformation, of which Mennonite education can be a conduit for adolescents who inhabit a prime time for this spiritual transformation of the self. In providing a spiritual moratorium for adolescents, Mennonite education offers a community that practices and cultivates reflection, integration, compassion, and love for God, oneself, and others. As Eugene Peterson affirms, "The self is only *it*self, healthy and whole, when it is in relationship, and that relationship is always dual, with God and with other human beings."[44] In this context, God can transform the ego in service of the self—a transformation that happens at the deepest level of the self, with the Mennonite educational community serving as its conduit.

Appendix A: Instances of "Self" and "Selves" in *Confession of Faith in a Mennonite Perspective* (1995)

"God's infinite freedom and constant self-giving are perfect in faithful love" and "Love their neighbors as themselves" (Article 1: God)

"Humbling himself and becoming obedient unto death on a cross" (Article 2: Jesus Christ)

"All those who open themselves to the working of the Spirit" (Article 3: Holy Spirit)

"We commit ourselves to persist and delight in reading, studying, and meditating on the Scriptures" (Article 4: Scripture)

"All creation ultimately has its source outside itself" and "Entrust ourselves to God's care" (Article 5: Creation and Divine Providence)

"Use power selfishly, do violence, and become separated from God" and "Making gods of creation and of ourselves" and "We open ourselves to the bondage of demonic powers" (Article 7: Sin)

"Commit themselves to follow Christ" and "Join themselves to Christ" (Article 9: The Church of Jesus)

"Patterning itself after the reign of God" (Article 10: The Church in Mission)

"Commit themselves to follow Jesus" and "Commit themselves to follow Christ" (Article 11: Baptism)

"Recommit ourselves to the way of the cross" (Article 12: The Lord's Supper)

"Commit themselves to give and receive counsel" and "Separated themselves from the body of Christ" (Article 14: Discipline in the Church)

"Yield ourselves to God" and "Putting ourselves more completely into the hands of God" (Article 18: Spirituality)

"Commit ourselves to tell the truth" (Article 20: Truth)

Notes

1. Erik H. Erikson, *Identity: Youth and Crisis* (New York: W. W. Norton & Co., 1968), 155.

2. Erik H. Erikson, *Identity and the Life Cycle*, 111.

3. Edwin H. Friedman, *A Failure of Nerve: Leadership in the Age of the Quick Fix*, ed. Margaret M. Treadwell and Edward W. Beal (New York: Seabury Books, 1999), 175.

4. Cornelius Dyck, ed. and trans., *Spiritual Life in Anabaptism* (Scottdale, Pa.: Herald Press, 1995), 23.

5. Dyck, *Spiritual Life*, 22.

6. *Confession of Faith in a Mennonite Perspective* (Scottdale, Pa.: Herald Press, 1995).

7. Palmer Becker, *What Is an Anabaptist Christian?* Missio Dei: Exploring God's Work in the World, 18 (Elkhart, Ind.: Mennonite Mission Network, 2008), 2.

8. Becker, *What Is an Anabaptist Christian?* 11, 17.

9. Becker, *What Is an Anabaptist Christian?* 11.

10. Eugene H. Peterson, *Where Your Treasure Is: Psalms That Summon You from Self to Community* (Grand Rapids, Mich.: William B. Eerdmans Publishing Co., 1985), 3-4.

11. Soren Kierkegaard, "The Sickness Unto Death: A Christian Psychological Exposition for Edification and Awakening," in *Fear and Trembling and the Sickness Unto Death*, reprint, trans. Walter Lowrie (Princeton, N.J.: Princeton University Press, 1974), 146.

12. Kierkegaard, "Sickness Unto Death," 159.

13. John H[oward] Yoder, "Armaments and Eschatology," *Studies in Christian Ethics* 1 (1988): 58.

14. Kierkegaard, "Sickness Unto Death," 147, 244.

15. Kierkegaard, "Sickness Unto Death," 262.

16. George Pattison, *Kierkegaard's Upbuilding Discourses: Philosophy Literature, and Theology* (New York: Routledge, 0202), 101.

17. *Oxford Dictionaries*, s.v. "Transparent."
18. Kierkegaard, "Sickness Unto Death," 245.
19. Gerhard Schreiber, "Christoph Schrempf: The 'Swabian Socrates' as Trans. of Kierkegaard," in *Kierkegaard's Influence on Theology, Tome I: German Protestant Theology*, ed. Jon Steward, Kierkegaard Research: Sources Reception and Resources, vol. 10 (Burlington, Vt.: Ashgate, 2012), 304.
20. James E. Loder, "Transformation in Christian Education," *The Princeton Seminary Bulletin* 3, no. 1 (1980): 16.
21. James E. Loder, *The Logic of the Spirit: Human Development in Theological Perspective* (San Francisco: Jossey-Bass, 1998), 205.
22. Kenda Creasy Dean, *Almost Christian: What the Faith of Our Teenagers Is Telling the American Church* (New York: Oxford University Press, 2010), 81.
23. Erikson, *Identity: Youth and Crisis*, 218.
24. Erik H. Erikson, *Insight and Responsibility* (New York: W. W. Norton & Co., 1994), 148.
25. Erikson, *Insight and Responsibility*, 224.
26. Erikson, *Identity and the Life Cycle*, 23.
27. Daniel J. Siegel, *The Developing Mind: How Relationships and the Brain Interact to Shape Who We Are*, 2nd ed. (New York: The Guilford Press, 2012), 15.
28. Siegel, *The Developing Mind*, 349.
29. Kierkegaard, "Sickness Unto Death," 262.
30. See John D. Roth, *Teaching That Transforms: Why Anabaptist-Mennonite Education Matters* (Scottdale, Pa.: Herald Press, 2011).
31. Erikson, *Identity and the Life Cycle*, 175.
32. Erikson, *Identity and the Life Cycle*, 175.
33. Erikson, *Identity and the Life Cycle*, 120.
34. Siegel, *The Developing Mind*, 348.
35. Siegel, *The Developing Mind*, 304.
36. Siegel, *The Developing Mind*, 164.
37. John Bransford, et al., "Learning Theories and Education: Toward a Decade of Synergy," in *Handbook of Educational Psychology*, 2nd ed., Patricia A. Alexander and Philip H. Winne (New York: Routledge, 2012), 218.
38. Loder, "Transformation," 16.
39. Siegel, *The Developing Mind*, 35.
40. Roth, *Teaching That Transforms*, 105.
41. Marshall B. Rosenberg, *Nonviolent Communication: A Language of Life*, 2nd ed. (Encinitas, Calif.: PuddleDancer Press, 2003), 129.
42. Dietrich Bonhoeffer, *Life Together* (New York: HarperSanFrancisco, 1954), 78.
43. Bo Karen Lee, "The Face of the Other: An Ethic of Delight," *Ogbomoso Journal of Theology* 16, no. 1 (2011): 25.
44. Peterson, *Where Your Treasure Is*, 8.

Part Four
Literature from the Margins

Part Four: Literature from the Margins

One implication of locating Mennonite education in the narrative of Jesus is to make that education marginal education. Notice that marginal does not mean unimportant. Rather, marginal means that it is not identified by, with, or in the so-called mainstream of American society. When that is the case, marginal can signify great importance. It indicates issues or perspectives missed by the mainstream. And when the marginal is compared with the mainstream, we catch an idea of what can be—but is not always—the identifying characteristic of the group.

Fiction often portrays characters in settings on the margin. The very fact that the portrayal is of characters on the margin is what makes the fiction interesting, certainly more intriguing that the commonplace. Part Four has two chapters that analyze writings by characters on the margins. In a sense the Mennonite authors in the fiction or memoirs discussed are two times marginal. First of all, they are marginal because they are Mennonite writers—and Mennonites are in some sense marginal to North American society. But further, the writers themselves are marginal to the majority Mennonite tradition, and this marginality is visible in their writings.

The chapter by Rebecca Janzen compares a Mennonite writer on the margin with a Mormon author, who belongs to another group that is marginal in terms of North American society. This comparison of marginal women presents some interesting parallels. In her treatment of these authors, Janzen avoids a common approach, namely to critique the marginal voices precisely because they do not represent the majority. By avoiding that pitfall, Janzen is able to use the marginal voices to say something important to the majority.

Daniel Shank Cruz's chapter deals with the marginal church in a different way. His concern is the inability of Mennonites to figure out how far to go in welcoming people who identify as LBGTQ into Mennonite Church USA—and the schisms that follow the disagreement. Without specifically taking sides in this debate, Shank Cruz uses literary analysis of a set of short stories not related to the LGBTQ conversation to offer a suggestion on how Mennonites might move beyond this disagreement.

THIRTEEN

LEARNING TO LISTEN IN GREG BECHTEL'S "SMUT STORIES"

Daniel Shank Cruz

Mennonite literature is frequently socially activist and is thus explicitly, though informally, educational. It has valuable things to teach the Mennonite community about dealing with perplexing stories, something that is especially needed now in yet another era of official schisming, this time around the question of how welcoming to be of LGBT (Lesbian, Gay, Bisexual, and Trans) individuals. In literature, most Mennonite authors do not explicitly address official Mennonite institutions, which allows their work to be a conceptual space that offers room for outsider perspectives and for open dialogue on controversial topics that might not be possible in official settings. As an example, this chapter uses short stories seemingly unrelated to the LGBT conversation to address that issue.

In the past Mennonite literature has been proactive about investigating issues that Mennonite institutions have had difficulties addressing in a timely manner. For example, North American Mennonite literature's seminal text, Rudy Wiebe's 1962 novel *Peace Shall Destroy Many*, examines the hypocritical use of various forms of violence in the Mennonite community. Di Brandt's and Julia Spicher Kasdorf's poetry from the 1980s and 1990s sheds light on the issue of sexual abuse, especially

Brandt's *questions i asked my mother* and Kasdorf's *Sleeping Preacher*. Miriam Toews's recent novel *All My Puny Sorrows* and Wiebe's recent novel *Come Back* are sensitive portrayals of clinical depression and suicide. And Jan Guenther Braun's 2008 novel *Somewhere Else* depicts the struggle of a lesbian protagonist trying to remain in the church.[1]

My goal in this chapter is to describe how a recent piece of Mennonite literature has something to say about how the two sides of the LGBT-inclusion debate, and, indeed, the sides of any fractious community issue, might approach one another. However, rather than doing what one might expect and focusing on what queer Mennonite literature[2] has to say regarding the current strife in Mennonite Church USA, I will use a set of short stories by Greg Bechtel[3] that deal with the nature of stories themselves and how we should encounter and interpret them.

It may seem odd to bring literature to bear on a theological issue. Nonetheless, the question of the relationship of Mennonite literature to institutional Mennonitism has been an important one in the field since at least the publication of John L. Ruth's *Mennonite Identity and Literary Art* in 1978. Ruth argues that literature should serve the church, calling for "the imaginative courage for the literary artist to become involved in the very soul-drama of his [sic] covenant-community."[4] The work of Mennonite writers often performs this task even though its creators may no longer be in the theological community, and we can learn from the stories they tell. While they may not be the active participants in the community for which Ruth calls, readers of their work can still observe what their literature has to say to the more official community.

Since Ruth's time of writing, Mennonite writers have insisted that their work be judged according to literary standards, not theological ones, and that it be independent from the faith community's guidelines of what is proper, and with good reason. I am not calling for that to change, and frankly I disagree with a fair amount of what Ruth has to say in *Mennonite Identity and Literary Art* about how writers should view their work as a form of service.[5] But he is right that artists have important messages for the faith community, and in light of the present crisis I think it is time to give the writers a hearing and to see whether they offer any solutions in an informal way.

One way of seeing the struggle over LGBT inclusion/exclusion is as one between conflicting stories. There is the traditional church story that defines same-sex relationships as sin versus the LGBT community's story of being a marginalized people, and thus one that deserves inclusion in light of Jesus' concern for the oppressed, especially since the one certain place of refuge in a harsh world should be the church. Instead of sincerely listening to one another, it seems that each side has simply been talking past the other.

There is a real need to listen to each other's stories. If we could listen as family members rather than viewing each other as combatants in a theological debate, the conversation would be healthier, whether or not the outcomes would differ. Bechtel's interrelated series of short stories, "The Smut Story (I)," "The Smut Story (II)," and "The Smut Story (III)" are useful for teaching us how to perform this listening.[6]

In an interview with Sofia Samatar, Bechtel, an ethnic Mennonite, acknowledges that "a Mennonite influence shows up" in his writing even though he is not a theological Mennonite. One way this background is evident in his writing is that he thinks about his work in ethical terms. He tells Samatar that having a "sense of uncertainty" when crafting stories is "an ethical necessity" to keep from "oversimplify[ing]" his characters and their perspectives.[7] I think it is fair to say that both sides of the inclusion/exclusion debate oversimplify the other. However, as I will show, the "Smut Stories" teach us that the sense of uncertainty Bechtel mentions is essential for us as readers or hearers of stories to maintain as well. Taking this approach allows us to be open to what we might hear instead of forcing narratives to fit our preconceived notions of them.

Bechtel's stories occupy a relatively unmapped space in Mennonite literature as speculative fiction, that is, fiction that is in some way not mimetic. This fiction takes place in a story world that is not our own, whether because it is in the future, or in an alternative reality, or in space or some other non-Earth setting.[8] Bechtel asserts to Samatar that Mennonitism and speculative fiction share similarities because they both emphasize "a certain *in-the-world-but-not-of-the-world* . . . self-consciously alienated from the mainstream" outlook (italics in the original).[9]

This is the case in the "Smut Stories," as their narrators all belong to groups on the fringes of their society. One of speculative fiction's strengths is that it offers visions for what the world can be rather than of what it is, and the "Smut Stories" do this in their narrative slipperiness, which functions as a kind of openness, and in their characters' insistence on loving actions, especially in "The Smut Story (II)" and "The Smut

Story (III)." The stories are speculative in that they take place partly in the future, offering hope that society will develop into a more open place than it is currently.

The three stories are sprinkled throughout Bechtel's 2014 short story collection *Boundary Problems*. This placing of the stories at seemingly random spots in the book rather than side by side[10] immediately teaches readers that encountering stories requires hard work. The "Smut Stories" do not make sense individually but only when read as a whole. Similarly, it is important to remember that both sides of the inclusion/exclusion debate have legitimate claims to the Anabaptist-Mennonite story and that this tradition loses something significant when the combatants choose to emphasize their differences rather than what they share.

The larger story the three stories tell is further complicated by their misleading titles: "The Smut Story (III)" is actually the first of the stories printed, and its events take place before those in the other two stories even though it is numbered as "III" rather than "I." Likewise, "The Smut Story (I)" is the last of the three stories printed in the collection and is the concluding one of the set plot-wise even though it is numbered as "I." On the surface this misnumbering of the stories might feel like an annoying postmodern fiction gimmick but, aside from being a subtle nod to the notion that the last shall be first and the first shall be last in one of the stories' numerous biblical allusions, it also suggests that sometimes stories re-order our world if we let them, and we need to be open as readers or listeners to this possibility. The process of piecing the three stories together is a reminder that one must be an active listener or reader to do a story justice.

The three stories illustrate the diversity that terms such as "narrative" or "story" denote as they each use the form of a different genre. The first to appear in Bechtel's book, "The Smut Story (III)," is a transcript of a 2010 press conference, the second printed, "The Smut Story (II)," is a personal letter written in 2015, and "The Smut Story (I)," the last to appear and the last chronologically, is an excerpt from an introduction to a new edition of a collection of scholarly essays called *The Smut Story* published in 2059.

The varied generic nature of the stories teaches us that we need to keep an open mind about what a story might entail. We may think we know what the story will be, and this close-mindedness leads to an inability to be changed by the story, and in the case of the inclusion/exclusion debate to harmful caricaturing of those on the opposite side. But when we set aside pre-conceived notions we allow room for transformation to occur.

The titles of the stories also play with readers' expectations because they are not actually explicitly "smut[ty]." At their core, the three stories are all about trying to determine what happened during "the Mother's Day Affair," an open mic reading at an Edmonton coffeehouse in 2009.[11] The press conference in "The Smut Story (III)" is about its aftermath, the letter that is the second story in the sequence is an attempt by one of the audience members to describe the reading to his then-infant daughter, and the essay collection introduced in "The Smut Story (I)" at the end of the trilogy examines how the events of that night have spawned a movement of people known as "Smutsters" who hold rituals that mimic the reading.[12]

The central element of the reading was a story told by someone of indeterminate gender variously referred to throughout the stories as "T.," "Tia," or "Tio" Boop.[13] While there is general agreement that Boop's story included erotic elements—it is the "smut story" of the title—audience members are unable to agree about the content of the story, and thus Boop's narrative itself never actually gets included in the three stories. The hearers cannot reproduce a definitive version of the story because they are all awestruck by Boop's body, which is so dazzling that it transcends gender.[14]

Boop's beauty and subsequent vanishing before any of the audience members can ask Boop about Boop's story echoes Jesus' quick disappearance in Luke 24 after revealing himself to several followers on the road to Emmaus. Boop is never seen again, but Boop's story is so inspirational that some of its hearers decide to move in together and live in community.[15] From this original community, which is reminiscent of the early Christian community in Acts 2, the Smutster movement develops over the next fifty years.

The Smutsters are very much like a faith community in two ways.[16] First, they hold meticulously choreographed rituals that commemorate and mimic the 2009 reading where Boop appeared. As a part of these readings, they always leave a spot open where Boop's story would occur with the hope that Boop will reappear.[17] This practice is an obvious allusion to the practice of leaving an empty chair for Elijah during a Passover

Seder. This element of the "Smut Stories" is significant because it reminds us that we never know where or when a representative of the divine might appear, thus we must practice openness to others rather than being close-mindedly dogmatic. In the heat of the inclusion/exclusion debate it is easy to forget that both sides are sincerely seeking to be faithful to their vision of God and thus easy to close ourselves off from whatever revelations they may have.

Sadly, the second way the Smutster movement is akin to a faith community, and one way in which it is reminiscent of the current state of affairs in Mennonite Church USA, is that conflicts among Smutsters about the proper ways to observe their rituals lead to schisms within the movement.[18] The "Smut Stories" are about trying to reconstruct a story that is central to a movement that it inspires and the conflict within the movement as a result of squabbles regarding this reconstruction. Similarly, the LGBT inclusion/exclusion debate may be read as a conflict about two versions of the same story. The Smutsters are akin to Christians in that rather than bonding together over their belief in the importance of a founding event they split up into factions who squabble about doctrine.

This element of the "Smut Stories" is especially Mennonite. As Ruth writes, unfortunately one of the essential elements of the Mennonite "stor[y]" is "[t]he apparently inevitable Mennonite schismatic process."[19] Schisming is what Mennonites do,[20] and it is happening again. The question thus becomes, if this fragmenting must happen, how can we do it in a healthy way? If the model of open listening found in the "Smut Stories" did not lead to reconciliation in Mennonite Church USA's case, it might at least lead to a more peaceful breaking apart than is currently occurring or enable healthy conversation after the separations.

Aside from the biblical allusions in Bechtel's stories evincing their subtly Mennonite character, these allusions reveal that the stories are in a sense a re-telling of the Christian story. Their speculative nature encourages speculation about what the Christian community could be like if it were more open to present-day prophets. The name of the central character of the final printed story, "The Smut Story (I)," Eva, who is the addressee of the letter from the second story and the one responsible for the coagulation of the Smutster movement via her propagation of the story of the "Mother's Day Affair," is significant because it points to the possibility of a new beginning by referencing the first biblical woman, Eve.

This new beginning is symbolized by Eva's farm, which includes "a spacious garden [. . . with] fruit-bearing trees," and a lack of "fences" around it. The Smutsters and their primary antagonist, Peter Smith, are able to be reconciled there.[21] The farm is like a revised, healed Garden of Eden, open to everyone.[22] It reminds us as readers that a better future is possible despite our currently fallen state.

Similarly, two of Boop's possible names, "Tia" and "Tio," are Spanish for "aunt" and "uncle," which is significant in the stories because Boop's narrative leads to the creation of a family, the Smutsters. Mennonites are also a family,[23] and while being a part of a family is not always easy, this bond is something that often seems forgotten in the inclusion/exclusion debate. The "Smut Stories" do not offer a completely utopian vision because there are the aforementioned schisms among the Smutsters, but they do argue that a more peaceful way of being in community is possible.

"The Smut Story (I)," the essay collection introduction that is the last of the three stories printed, also teaches through its form that true listening requires a willingness to offer a hearing to all perspectives on an issue. The story is ten pages long, but more than half of it is taken up by sixteen footnotes. The main text takes up nineteen inches of page space while the notes take up thirty-six inches even though they are printed in a smaller font size.

Furthermore, the content of the notes is more interesting than the body of the story itself because they contain the history of the Smutster movement, which, as previously explained, is an essential element of the stories. Without these footnotes, the three stories' shared narrative falls apart, thus it is necessary for us as readers to take the time to peruse them. This deliberateness is a key component of the listening philosophy the stories advocate.

Similarly, Mennonite understandings of Jesus have traditionally emphasized the necessity of being on the margins of society, of being in the world but not of it, and "The Smut Story (I)" reminds us that being on the margins is an exciting place to be because it allows us to see the world in a way that those ensconced in the center are blind to as long as we are open to doing so. Bechtel's stories teach us the kind of deliberate listening that helps this kind of seeing.

I am drawn to the way that Bechtel's work entices me to focus on making connections between disparate stories rather than focusing on their differences. Reading Bechtel's stories becomes a kind of meditation or contemplation because they are so difficult. One is forced to listen because they do not lend themselves to easy interpretation. This listening opens us up to thoughts and experiences we may not have otherwise encountered. Unfortunately, the openness that the "Smut Stories" advocate has not been especially present in the debate over LGBT inclusion within the church, and honestly I am at a point where I despair that it ever will. But if there is hope for it to happen, new models other than the ones that are currently failing are necessary. Bechtel provides us one such model. The "Smut Stories" really are socially active literature.

Notes

1. Rudy Wiebe, *Peace Shall Destroy Many* (Toronto: McClelland, 1962); Di Brandt, *questions i asked my mother* (Winnipeg, Man.: Turnstone Press, 1987); Julia Kasdorf, *Sleeping Preacher* (Pittsburgh, Pa.: University of Pittsburgh Press, 1992); Miriam Toews, *All My Puny Sorrows* (San Francisco: McSweeney's, 2014); Rudy Wiebe, *Come Back* (Toronto: Knopf, 2014); Jan Guenther Braun, *Somewhere Else* (Winnipeg, Man.: Arbeiter Ring Publishing, 2008).

2. Aside from Braun's novel, examples of the ever-expanding field of queer Mennonite literature include Stephen Beachy, *boneyard* (Portland, Ore.: Verse Chorus Press, 2011); Christina Penner, *Widows of Hamilton House* (Winnipeg, Man.: Enfield & Wizenly, 2008); Lynnette Dueck, *boundary problems* (Vancouver, BC: Press Gang Publishing, 1992).

3. The three "Smut Stories" are from Greg Bechtel, *Boundary Problems* (Calgary, Alberta: Freehand Books, 2014).

4. John L. Ruth, *Mennonite Identity and Literary Art* (Scottdale, Pa.: Herald Press, 1978), 70.

5. Ruth may have changed his position on this issue as well. According to Julia Spicher Kasdorf, in conversation Ruth has "told [her] that he would not write the lectures that became *Mennonite Identity* in quite the same way now" and that he appreciates how Mennonite literature has developed. Julia Kasdorf, "Dreams of the Written Character," in *The Measure of My Days: Engaging the Life and Thought of John L. Ruth*, ed. Reuben Z. Miller and Joseph S. Miller (Telford, Pa.: Cascadia Publishing House, 2004), 32.

6. For an account of how poetry, both Mennonite and not, "teaches [us] how to listen," see Anita Hooley Yoder, "I've Read Too Much Poetry for That: Poetry, Personal Transformation and Peace," *CrossCurrents* 64, no. 4 (December 2014): 463.

7. Greg Bechtel, "Interview with Greg Bechtel," by Sofia Samatar, *Journal of the Center for Mennonite Writing* 7, no. 3 (2015): https://mennonitewriting.org/jour-

nal/7/3/interview-greg-bechtel/#all.

8. Other examples of Mennonite speculative fiction include Keith Miller's novels *The Book on Flying* (Stafford, UK: Riverhead Books, 2009) and *The Book on Fire* (New York: Immanion Press, 2009), Sofia Samatar's novel *A Stranger in Olondria* (Easthampton, Mass: Small Beer Press, 2013), and the short story by Casey Plett, "Portland, Oregon," in *A Safe Girl to Love* (New York: Topside Press, 2014), 93-121.

9. Bechtel, "Interview." One helpful aspect of Bechtel's stories is that they model talking to a different tradition through their interaction with non-Mennonite speculative fiction. I encountered Bechtel's book as a piece of Mennonite literature, but what draws me to write about it is that it takes me out of the tradition to other valuable texts (which is an example of the kind of teaching that Mennonite literature can do that I am talking about) that I have discovered in my continuing search for narratives that speak to me. "The Smut Story (III)" begins with an epigraph from the Canadian science fiction writer Candas Jane Dorsey's 1996 essay "Being One's Own Pornographer." When I saw this epigraph I became tremendously excited because Dorsey's essay, which I first came across while doing research on the novelist and literary critic Samuel R. Delany for my dissertation, is one of the best pieces of literary criticism I have ever read.

Much of the essay is devoted to discussing some of Delany's sexually explicit fiction, especially his 1994 novel *The Mad Man* (Candas Jane Dorsey, "Being One's Own Pornographer," *ParaDoxa* 2, no. 2 (1996): 191-203; Samuel R. Delany, *The Mad Man* (New York: A Richard Kasak Book, 1994).) Although Delany has no connection to Mennonites whatsoever, *The Mad Man* is one of the most Anabaptist texts I have ever read in terms of its insistence on paying attention to those on the margins of society. Several of its central characters are homeless men, a group that I had never seen depicted in fiction before I read it even though my primary reading (and, as a literary critic, writing) interest is fiction from and about the margins. Dorsey's essay responds to Delany's willingness to confront seemingly taboo subjects, and Bechtel's stories respond to Dorsey's essay by also advocating this openness.

Boop's mysterious story discussed below is also called "Being One's Own Pornographer" and includes an epigraph from Dorsey's essay (Bechtel, *Boundary Problems*, 52-53). Bechtel's references to Dorsey and the Bechtel-Dorsey-Delany-Anabaptism connection show that we never know where stories that impact us will come from, and so we need to have the openness that the "Smut Stories" advocate.

10. There are two unrelated stories between each of the three "Smut Stories." "The Smut Story (III)" is the third story in *Boundary Problems*, "The Smut Story (II)" is the sixth story, and "The Smut Story (I)" is the ninth story, the second-to-last story in the book.

11. Bechtel, *Boundary Problems*, 50.

12. Bechtel, *Boundary Problems*, 169n.

13. Bechtel, *Boundary Problems*, 50, 104, 166.

14. Bechtel, *Boundary Problems*, 53.

15. Bechtel, *Boundary Problems*, 106.

16. Another way that the Smutsters are like Anabaptists is that their name was given to them by outsiders as a term of derision (Bechtel, *Boundary Problems*, 169n).

17. Bechtel, *Boundary Problems*, 169-70n.

18. Bechtel, *Boundary Problems*, 170n.

19. Ruth, *Mennonite Identity*, 19-20.

20. Fred Kniss, *Disquiet in the Land: Cultural Conflict in American Mennonite Communities* (New Brunswick, N.J.: Rutgers University Press, 1997) offers a history of a number of official Mennonite schisms.

21. Bechtel, *Boundary Problems*, 168n, 174n.

22. My thanks to M. L. DeLaFleur for proposing this reading in a conversation.

23. One may question whether it is appropriate to apply lessons from a Canadian Mennonite's work to a church issue in the U.S., but I believe that doing so is justifiable because of this family connection. While place is vital in some of the other stories from *Boundary Problems* (most notably "The Everett-Wheeler Hypothesis"), the fact that "The Smut Story (III)" and "The Smut Story (II)" take place in Edmonton is incidental to the rest of their content; this setting does not affect the validity of their lessons for those in other locales.

Furthermore, while this essay does not afford room for a full discussion of the border issue in Mennonite literature, I will note that it is common practice for Mennonite literary critics to discuss Canadian writers and writers from the U.S. together in their work rather than observing the strict divide between Canadian literature and U.S. literature that is present in the field of literary studies as a whole. I would argue that Mennonitism's familial nature has played a major role in bridging this divide.

FOURTEEN

MENNONITE AND MORMON WOMEN'S LIFE-WRITING

Rebecca Janzen

Introduction

In this chapter, I will discuss Mormon and Mennonite books that fall into the categories of memoir and fictional life writing. The works in question are Joanna Brooks' *The Book of Mormon Girl* and Miriam Toews' *Irma Voth*.[1] Both works speak from the margin of their respective religious traditions. Analysis of these works can help us with peace education.

It is often in the reading from the margin that we can explore the most devastating effects of unjust structures of power. This introduction points out that when reading literary works, it is important to pay attention to representations of the margins, that is, to that which is not mainstream. Seeing what the margins have to say about the mainstream has some similarities to Felipe Hinojosa's call in his chapter of this book to study Mennonite history from the outside in.

I understand that peace education teaches about unjust structures of power and considers how they might be transformed. The structures of power I have in mind are social and religious institutions like schools, unions, churches and intentional communities that directly or implicitly encourage and enforce divisions based on race, class, gender, ability, sexual orientation, and more. In my view, these divisions are unjust. Reading from the margins is one way to expose the injustice.

In literary studies, education for peace examines how structures of power are reflected in works of a variety of genres. It then encourages us to focus on how the literary works imaginatively dismantle these structures and thus how we might enact similar change in the non-literary universe. In other words, this approach to peace education moves from reading to taking action to effect social transformation. Changing these structures, then, is the reason for developing education for peace.

The Book of Mormon Girl is a memoir, in the genre of creative nonfiction, and *Irma Voth* is a novel that mimics this genre. Many of the commonalities between the texts, in particular those that demonstrate the effects of unjust structures of power, pertain to the lived and embodied experiences of the protagonists.

In this chapter, as I examine the questions of belonging, history, purity and sacrament in both works, I relate these themes to the ways the individual bodies of Joanna, in Brooks' memoir, and Irma, in Toews' novel, participate in the physical and historical movements of their communities. I will suggest that we imagine how the representation of the experiences of these young women parallel one another.[2] This exercise will, I argue below, allow us to circumvent many issues that would arise if we were to emphasize the Mennonite or Mormon aspects of the texts.

This approach will then allow us to consider representations of broader unjust structures of power, and connect to our own lives the ways the texts propose to transform these structures through creative acts of storytelling and the visual arts.[3] To prepare the way for analysis of the two texts, I first provide a bit of background on Mormons, who are lesser known to Mennonites, and then contrast my approach with identity studies.

Mennonites and Mormons

This discussion deals with Mennonite and Mormon literature. I assume some familiarity with Mennonites but briefly review Mormonism. The official name of the Mormon Church is the Church of Jesus Christ of Latter-day Saints, often abbreviated to LDS Church. Other groups also claim the name Mormon but the LDS with headquarters in Salt Lake City, Utah, is by far the largest and most mainstream.

The LDS church and the Mennonite churches that subscribe to the *Confession of Faith in a Mennonite Perspective*[4] and other non-plain Mennonite groups differ in their theological beliefs and religious practices. Brooks explains one of the fundamental differences through an object lesson she received as a child about "the Mormon belief that the human body is a transitory habitation for a spirit being that existed before this life and will exist afterward." Her father demonstrated the idea by suggesting that the spirit is like a glove that exists before and after the hand or body is put inside of it.[5]

In addition to theological differences, the LDS church is much larger and more bureaucratic than Mennonite Church USA or the US Conference of Mennonite Brethren Churches.[6] The LDS church also officially encourages Mormons to keep journals.[7] Given this emphasis, there is a huge Mormon presence online, particularly in blogs, which are often called the "Bloggernacle."

Further, because the LDS church, for some, is doctrinally more discriminatory toward women than most Mennonite churches, there is a treasure trove of Mormon feminist blogs and a series of excellent memoirs of life in the LDS church by women who acknowledge both the positive and negative aspects of their upbringing.[8]

Nonetheless, because Mennonites and Mormons both have a sense of being different from wider society, they have developed some similar cultural practices. Even though both groups have a missionary bent, there is the predominance of a certain ethnic group in both churches, which means that power often tends to be held by people with a recognizable collection of surnames. In both churches, men predominate in leadership positions, although the specifics differ. Women in leadership is a contested issue in the male-led LDS church.[9]

Women function as leaders in more progressive Mennonite denominations, although they still disproportionately take care of children, cook food, clean, and are subject to any number of comments that reflect people's surprise with women in leadership. Men still lead conservative or evangelical Mennonite churches, regardless of denominational affiliation. Members of the LDS church dedicate one Sunday a month to fasting and sharing testimonies.[10] More evangelical Mennonites also likely have testimonies and more progressive Mennonites would discuss their lives in terms of their faith journeys or their stories.

Other historical and cultural similarities also appear, given the desire for both groups of separation from society. W. Cole Durham's article "Church and State," in the *Encyclopedia of Mormonism*[11] explains that Mormons are less separate then they once were, that is, before Utah joined the United States in the late nineteenth century. Mennonites, too, are no longer as separate. Both groups, it should be added, are the product of religious persecution. As a result, both churches are invested in some version of triumphalist historical narratives in which they overcome it.[12]

Mennonites trace their history to the sixteenth-century Radical Reformation in Europe and the ensuing centuries of migration and persecution. For their part, Mormons trace their history to the Second Great Awakening in early nineteenth century in the United States, with persecution faced in the eastern part of the country. They, too, migrated, in their case, from New York to Ohio, Illinois, Nebraska, and finally to Utah. Some continued on to Mexico and to Canada.

This history means that Mormons often describe themselves as a peculiar people.[13] Mennonites will find that this terminology about peculiarity resonates with them. The *Confession of Faith in a Mennonite Perspective* reminds us that "Conformity to Christ necessarily implies nonconformity to the world."[14] More conservative and plain Mennonites adopt this edict to an even higher degree. Indeed, historically both groups have encouraged a specific form of dress. The LDS church continues to officially emphasize modesty.[15] Brooks' memoir explains some of the subtler practices encouraged by leaders in her childhood in the 1970s and 1980s: "No playing with face cards. No masks, even on Halloween. No two-piece bathing suits. No dating a non-Mormon; no dating before age sixteen. No R-rated movies. For Mormon women: no working outside the home."[16] Mennonites will find many of these rules familiar. As we can see, both groups have evolved in their relationship with broader society.

Although Mennonites and Mormons may still suffer some discrimination, it is no longer the majority of their experience. For this reason, it is crucial to read narratives that counter the focus on persecution and redemption in a specific period in history. Counter narratives, moreover, help us understand the structures of power at play within the churches; in other words, they can shed light on religious practices that may differ from the claims of religious doctrine. These religious practices, I believe, mirror societal practices. It is our task to critique these represented structures and, through imaginative works of literature, ponder how these structures can be transformed.

Irma Voth and *Book of Mormon Girl* represent experiences of religious practice rather than faithful adherence to religious doctrine. Some writers have critiqued such books on the basis of whether, or how well, they represent a majority Mennonite or Mormon identity.[17] Rather than engaging with this perspective, I follow reviewers like Valerie Weaver-Zercher. She engages with Brooks' work from a Mennonite perspective and notes the similarities between Mennonite and Mormon practice.[18] This critical perspective encourages us to engage with structures of power in both churches rather than engage religious doctrine. This approach will allow us to pursue the peace education that exposes unjust structures and to envision alternatives.

Identity Studies

In is important to distinguish the methodology that focuses on practices, which is followed below, from identity-based studies, an approach common in the academy. Identity-based studies privilege any category of identity, such as Mennonites, Mormons, or women, or gender studies and queer studies. These areas, and others, have been significant in decolonizing the academy. Identity-based approaches make academic inquiry a space for engaging with material and subjects beyond the interests and approaches of a parade of white men that dominate academia. At the same time, methodology that focuses on practices can align with concerns raised in identity studies about sexist religious and cultural practices.

Further, these identity-focused areas of study, which have not yet been exhausted, often mean that scholars from one area find it difficult to converse with scholars in another.[19] Robert Zacharias has edited a collection titled *After Identity: Mennonite Writing in North America.*[20] It deals with questions, oversights, and possibilities that arise from an identity-based approach. The collection brings Mennonite studies into conversation with broader areas of inquiry.[21] In line with that approach, I follow historian Felipe Hinojosa, who calls for a relational approach that puts Mennonite studies in conversation with other areas of inquiry.[22] Hinojosa's keynote address at the conference that produced this book, now its fourth chapter, expanded the audience's understanding of what it means to be Mennonite.

Several Marxist scholars have taken the challenge to identities studies to a further degree. Eve Mitchell established that identity politics, and by extension identity-based studies, are primarily bourgeois politics.[23] That is, they respond only to the needs of people from a certain social grouping. If we use these areas of study, Mitchell goes on to explain, we will only ever be able to transform the conditions of a small sector of the population. Mennonite studies, then, could only transform the situation of Mennonites, more specifically, the limited number of Mennonites who are this area's primary authors and subjects of inquiry.[24]

Charles Hatfield advocates completely recasting the particular in *The Limits of Identity*. He expounds upon the trouble with identity in Latin American studies by examining foundational works in the field. In his view, imagining an "alternative future in terms that are no longer identitarian might . . . provide the necessary vocabulary for correcting the region's most grievous material injustices."[25]

Michael Rectenwald adds that the trouble with identity politics is that it "pretends to deal with collectivities but instead works to individualize and to condemn."[26] He and Mitchell suggest that to effect transformation, which is, I repeat, the desired outcome of peace education, the particular must dialogue with the universal. Brooks describes this tendency among Mormons in the following way:

> We could identify other Mormons just by the sound of their names: older men named Rulon, Larue, or Lavell; older women named LaVera. Some of us named Brigham or Spencer for modern prophets. . . . Some even had well-known Mormon last names like Allred, Hatch, Rigby, Ricks, Tanner, Cannon, and Young.[27]

Mennonites will understand being able to recognize the surnames of one another as a comforting, if troubling, practice. Mormons, as Brooks goes on to state:

> loved to see one another . . . out and about in the confusion of the greater world we traversed each day . . . [to] speak the familiar language of our people, a language of modern prophets and apostles,

small Utah towns, church auxiliaries, missions and missionaries.[28]

For Mennonites, finding other Mennonites and speaking the same language, knowing particular acronyms and locations that loom large in the Mennonite imagination if not necessarily in terms of population, is the Mennonite game. As much as these practices are comforting, when they are replicated academically in Mennonite or Mormon studies, they are somewhat limiting. So, to have more forceful effects, these areas of study that focus on particularities must dialogue with the universal, or at least with other particularities. For greater impact, then, we can see that the findings in identity studies need to be put in dialogue with other identities.

The Role of the Body

In Brooks and Toews' works, we will consider the embodied as a particular and as a universal. Thus we will pay attention to identity but not center exclusively on it. This allows us to draw our attention to passages in Brooks' work such as this one: "As I wrote, agnostic Catholics, reform Jews, gay Christian girls, even stone-cold atheists, gave me a hard look, then nodded, and said, 'Yes, I recognize something familiar in the story you are telling.'"[29] Her particular, then, as Hatfield has suggested in Latin American studies, can have universal implication.

The universal in these works, as I have already stated, can be thought of in relation to the protagonists' bodies. To relate their bodies to one another, my analysis follows what the feminist philosopher Gail Weiss terms *intercorporeality*. Her book *Body Images* states that the human body exists in relationship with other bodies and that the individual becomes a subject through an exchange with the bodies and body images of others.[30] I believe that focusing on these relationships will allow us to relate the literary works to one another.

In this way, I also follow literary critic Christopher Breu, who has called for a sensual or corporeal politics. In his recent work, which focuses on the portrayal of fluid relationships between bodies in literature, he states that such attention allows us to circumvent identity. By engaging with English-language fiction from the twentieth century, he encourages us to find "an alternate aesthetic organized around attending to the materiality of the body" that would counter what he calls neoliberal ideals that ignore the body.[31] Such attention would move beyond the unjust understanding of bodies as commodities that can make a profit for large corporations.

Memoir and Life Writing

Memoirs and first-person narrative fiction that mimic memoir are powerful literary genres and so are ideal for moving from the embodied and particular to the universal and to transformation. As Nancy K. Miller asserts in a concise survey of both genres, any autobiographical narrative is told in the spirit of truth, and fiction may also include truth.[33] For this reason, it is appropriate to study Brooks' memoir alongside of Toews' novel. In this vein, other critics have noted that these genres are effective in the classroom. Former high school teachers Dawn Latta Kirby and Dan Kirby explain that it is because these works' narrate "*meaningful moments* that connect to a reader's life experience. Writers of C[ontemporary] M[emoir] use a compelling first-person voice and create detailed word-pictures for their readers."[33] The first-person voice relates to the rise in popularity of Vine, Snapchat, selfies, and Instagram at the time of this writing in 2016.

Brooks and Toews: History, Belonging, and Purity

Brooks' memoir, *The Book of Mormon Girl*, is superior to any selfie and will promote understanding of another religious group and critical thinking. It describes her life in the LDS church, growing up as part of a very devout family in Orange County, California. Her father was a bishop and gave her some of her most important spiritual instruction. Her mother was also very committed to the church and worked diligently in genealogy, which is crucial to Mormon theology and its understanding of the afterlife.

Miriam Toews' *Irma Voth* conflates the author's experience as the character Esther in the film *Stellet Licht* [*Silent Light*] and a fictionalized version of her childhood in Steinbach, Manitoba. *Irma Voth* more closely relates to other aspects of Toews' work, such as *A Complicated Kindness*,[34] than to the experiences of Low German Mennonites in Mexico.

Toews' novel describes the events in Irma's life from Irma's perspective. From the novel we learn that she was born in Canada but that after her older sister Katie mysteriously disappeared, the family fled to the Mennonite colonies near Cuauhtémoc, in the Mexican state of Chihuahua. Irma married a Mexican man called Jorge, who was a drug runner, and who eventually disappeared from their home in Campo Siete (Village Seven) Irma also participated in a film called *Campo Siete* as a translator and fixer for an eccentric film director from Mexico City. When the film was over and her husband had left, Irma left Campo Siete for Mexico City with her two younger sisters, Aggie and Ximena.

A central theme in both works is the notion of belonging. For example, Brooks reflects on a Mormon youth week at Brigham Young University, where she got to be a cheerleader. She recalls: "I waved my pom-pom because I was not afraid of polygamy, sacred underwear, or the idea of eternal godhood, and neither were the fifteen thousand youth in flammable sateen outfits moving in majestic precision in the field around me."[35] Her physical movements and dress affirm that Mormonism is particular, if not perhaps also peculiar. Its theological ideas lead to unique religious practices and gatherings.

Brooks' profound sense of belonging wavers as she pursues graduate education and begins to adopt more liberal beliefs. Despite this absent sense of belonging, she recognizes that she has been shaped by, and longs to participate in, Mormonism. She states: "I am not an enemy and I will not be disappeared from the faith of my ancestors. I am the descendant of Mormon pioneers."[36] She alludes to the fact that her family migrated from the eastern United States to Utah; this heritage gives her significant credibility in the LDS church and lends weight to her refusal to be cast as someone opposed to it.

Another central issue in both literary works is the question of history. Brooks describes the past from a Mormon perspective: "We inherit not only the glorious histories of our ancestors, but their human failings too, their kindness, their tenderness, and their satisfaction with easy contradictions . . . their sparkling differences, and their human failings." Ancestors, who are important in Mormon thinking, live on in Brooks' life. She continues, "Sometimes, even in my own tradition, I feel a long way from home."

She finally comes home to herself, and makes peace with her place in her tradition, when she tells her story to a weeklong workshop, called Camp Courage, designed for activists to tell their own stories about why equality matters.[37] This hyper-particular meditation on Mormonism would be identifiable to Mormon readers; we can see that from her perspective, there are many aspects of her church that should be changed in order for her to feel like she belongs. Such changes, such as abandoning institutional sexism and discrimination against gay people, she might argue, would also create a more just environment. We would do well to follow her example of storytelling and then use our own stories to implement changes in our own structures, whatever and wherever they might be.

Toews' work also focuses on the questions of history and belonging. It describes the history of Mennonites in Mexico in the following way:

> They'd been offered this land for cheap and they decided to accept the offer and move everyone from their colony in central Canada down to Mexico where they wouldn't have to send their kids to regular school or teach them to speak English or dress them in normal clothing. Mennonites formed themselves in Holland five hundred years ago after a man named Menno Simons became so moved by hearing Anabaptist prisoners singing hymns before being executed by the Spanish Inquisition that he joined their cause and became their leader. Seven Mennonite men traveled from Manitoba to the Presidential Palace in Mexico City to make a deal.[38]

Mennonites, in Irma's view, are backwards, strange, unwilling to integrate and deeply rooted in their history. She does not feel at home there.[39] Irma's version of Mennonite history, like Brooks' version of Mormon history, is based on movement and migration. There are other similarities that involve some sort of connection to spiritual or genealogical ancestors. If we can imagine these two young women's fictionalized experiences in relationship with one another, we realize that their problems are not unique.

One of the reasons both works give for feeling alienated within the community where they are supposed to belong is its sexism and emphasis on purity. This structure of power in religious contexts manifests itself in policing the young girls' bodies. Both note that their religions are inherently sexist. Brooks turns to specific examples in LDS doctrine, where as she began to menstruate, and sat in church "silent and bleeding . . . the boys my age stood before the congregation in clean white shirts to prepare and pass the white bread and tap water that was the sacrament."[40] This contrast between men's role in charge of the sacrament and women's bodies as painful, suggests that institutional sexism metaphorically manifests itself in her body. She almost becomes like the pure water that she is not allowed to distribute. Indeed, she recounts that her childhood goal was to: "be so pure and clear, no one would know [she] was even here."[41]

Toews' work presents another kind of sacrament and purity. Irma eventually realizes that her family moved to Mexico not because Katie had disappeared but because her father killed Katie. In other words, she realized that her father moved to Mexico to take advantage of its culture of impunity.[42] Irma then told her younger sister Aggie about this realization. In response to this staggering example of violence, Aggie painted a mural of the Voth family praying before a meal.[43] Katie's body is at the center of the table and they are praying before and, one imagines, eating the murdered woman. This parallels Katie and Jesus Christ, and Katie's body is metaphorically sanctified.

> Irma also ridicules the Mennonite desire for purity and invisibility. She tells us that we [Mennonites] live like ghosts . . . sometimes, those countries [where we live] decide they want us to be real citizens . . . and then we pack our stuff up in the middle of the night and move to another country where we can live purely but somewhat out of context.[44]

But what does this purity mean if murder can go unpunished? The Mennonites are not, as Toews' novel ironically suggests, living purely or out of context.

Conclusion

Each literary text demonstrates the particularities of injustice; my analysis has moved from the particular drawing parallels between the two texts in the related issues of belonging, history, and purity. By focusing on the ways these topics manifest themselves in Joanna and Irma's bodies, we can relate Brooks' memoir to Toews' work of creative non-fiction. We realize that these works allude to broader sexist cultural practices and the ways society polices women's bodies.

At the same time, as we pay attention to the religious particularities in both works, we realize that these issues do not pertain only to women, or only to Mennonites, or only to Mormons. Thus, our reading does not fall into what Mitchell describes as a bourgeois politics that only transforms a single sector. This perspective, as adapted in my interpretation of peace education, approaches literature through a focus on the body. It suggests that Joanna, in Brooks' memoir, mirrors Irma, in Toews' work. If we imagine them with Weiss' intercorporeality and Breu's corporeal politics we can imagine that their experiences shape one another.

As they do so, we can imagine that they counter a religious culture that values their bodies for their purity, and societies that value them for their sexuality, and we can place them in an alternative history where they are not ghosts and will not be disappeared. This would correct some of what Breu critiques as the neoliberal commodification of the body and perhaps moves toward what Hatfield desires, which is correcting injustice. In this vein, I conclude with Brooks' particular words, realizing that Mennonite could be substituted for Mormon, and encourage us to imagine their universal application: "I want room at the table for all the gay and lesbian Mormons who feel like they can't go home for dinner, and room for all the Mormon parents who don't know how to let them in the door."[44]

Notes

1. Joanna Brooks, *The Book of Mormon Girl: A Memoir of an American Faith* (New York: Free Press, 2012); Miriam Toews, *Irma Voth* (New York: Harper, 2011). Other examples of this genre include Elna Baker, *The New York Regional Mormon Singles Halloween Dance: A Memoir*, reprint (New York: Plume, 2010); Nicole Hardy, *Confessions of a Latter-Day Virgin: A Memoir* (New York: Hyperion, 2013), and Rhoda Janzen, *Mennonite in a Little Black Dress* (New York: St. Martin's, 2010).

2. Brooks' memoir elaborates on the Mormons, who for her, maintain sexist and homophobic elements. Nevertheless, she remains committed to them. In contrast, Toews' work negatively portrays Mennonites as backwards, strange, and willing to harbor murderers. Thus, the comparison between the two works on the basis of their religious experience is inexact; the works arrive at different conclusions about their religious and cultural milieu.

3. *Irma Voth* is set among Mennonites in Mexico, who belong to a variety of church groups. The Voth family's religious practices in the novel differ significantly from the church groups to which Mennonites in Mexico adhere (such as Old Colony, *Kleingemeinde*, or *Conferencia Misionera Evangelica*). For this reason, I compare events in this novel to the larger Mennonite groups with which Toews and this collection's readers may be familiar, such as the Mennonite Church USA and the

Canadian and U.S. Conferences of Mennonite Brethren Churches.

4. *Confession of Faith in a Mennonite Perspective* (Scottdale, Pa.: Herald Press, 1995).

5. Brooks, *Book of Mormon Girl*, 155, 1.

6. Other differences become visible in analysis of Mitt Romney's faith statement during his 2008 campaign for president. In this speech he stated, "I believe that Jesus Christ is the Son of God and the Savior of mankind." Mitt Romney, "Transcript: Mitt Romney's Faith Speech," *NPR*, 6 December 2007, http://www.npr.org/templates/story/story.php?storyId=16969460 <19 July 2016>. Significant differences between Mormons, Evangelicals, and other Christians arise in the meaning of these terms, particularly in the Mormon idea of pre-mortal existence in a spirit world and the return to the spirit world after death. According to LDS doctrine, "Jesus is the Firstborn of the Father in the spirit and is the Only Begotten of the Father in the flesh," who atones for "the sins of mankind." In Mormon understanding, after death, with body and soul reunited, righteous people live in one of three kingdoms of glory based on their level of obedience. "Basic Doctrines," in *LDS.Org* (2016), https://www.lds.org/manual/basic-doctrines/basic-doctrines?lang=eng <19 July 2016>.

These beliefs form the basis of the Mormon concept of eternal families and eternal progression in deity for each faithful person. The additional revelation to which Mormons subscribe has led to widespread discrimination against Mormons in their past. For comparisons of Mennonites and Mormons see for example Glenda Evon Miller, "A Comparison of the Mennonite and Mormon Colonies in Northern Mexico," MA thesis (El Paso, Texas: University of Texas-El Paso, 1993) or Janet Bennion, *Desert Patriarchy: Mormon and Mennonite Communities in the Chiluahua Valley* (Tucson, Ariz.: University of Arizona Press, 2004). The LDS church also has a very active online presence and has provided much of the information about LDS doctrine for this chapter.

7. "'How Will Keeping a Personal Journal Bless Me and My Family," *LDS.Org* (2016), https://www.lds.org/youth/learn/ss/marriage-and-family/journal?lang=eng <19 July 2016>.

8. For more information about Mennonites and gender see Carol Penner, ed., *Women and Men: Gender in the Church* (Scottdale, Pa.: Mennonite Publishing House, 1998). For information about sexual violence in Mennonite contexts see Ruth Krall, *The Elephants in God's Living Room: Clergy Sexual Abuse and Institutional Clericalism*, 4 vols. (N.p.: Enduring Space, 2012-2014). http://ruthkrall.com/wp-content/uploads/downloads/2015/09/The-Elephants-in-Gods-Living-Room-Vol-1-%C2%A9.pdf. For more information about Mormon feminism and gender in the LDS church, see for example the *Feminist Mormon Housewives* blog, 2016, http://www.feministmormonhousewives.org.

9. For more information about these debates see for example Lisa Butterworth, "Episode 83: Meet Kate Kelly," *Feminist Mormon Housewives Podcast*, 7 October 2013, http://feministmormonhousewivespodcast.org/episode-83-meet-kate-kelly/<19 July 2016>, an interview with a woman who founded the organization,

called "Ordain Women." See also this article about the Wear Pants to Church Movement in the LDS Church, Timothy Pratt, "Mormon Women Set Out to Take a Stand, Through Pants," *New York Times*, 19 Dec. 2012, A25.

10. Chapter 25: Fasting," in LDS.Org (2011), 144-148. https://www.lds.org/manual/gospel-principles/chapter-25-fasting?lang=eng.

11. W. Cole Durham, "Church and State," in *Encyclopedia of Mormonism*, ed. Daniel H. Ludlow (New York: Macmillan, 1992), 281-283.

12. See for example Mennonite histories such as Steven Nolt and Harry Loewen, *Through Fire and Water: An Overview of Mennonite History*, rev. ed. (Scottdale, Pa.: Herald Press, 2010); see Mormon histories such as Reid L. Neilson and Matthew J. Grow, *From the Outside Looking in: Essays on Mormon History, Theology, and Culture* (Oxford, UK: Oxford University Press, 2016), or Thomas Cottam Romney, *The Mormon Colonies in Mexico*, with new introduction (Salt Lake City, Utah: University of Utah Press, 2005).

13. Wilford E. Smith, "'Peculiar' People," in *Encyclopedia of Mormonism*, ed. Daniel H. Ludlow (New York: Macmillan, 1992), 1072-1074.

14. *Confession of Faith*, 65.

15. "Modesty," LDS.Org (2016), https://www.lds.org/topics/modesty?lang=eng <19 July 2016>.

16. Brooks, *Book of Mormon Girl*, 16.

17. A 2012 review of Brooks' work from a Mormon perspective is Blair Hodges, The Book of Mormon Girl, *By Common Consent*, 17 May 2012, http://bycommonconsent.com/2012/05/17/review-joanna-brooks-the-book-of-mormon-girl-stories-from-an-american-faith-2/. This review emphasizes Brooks' faith as expressed by her memoir, and concludes that religious practice and Mormon sacred elements comprise a common thread.

18. Valerie Weaver-Zercher, "*The Book of Mormon Girl*, by Joanna Brooks," review of *The Book of Mormon Girl*, *The Christian Century*, 25 Oct. 2012, 39-40.

19. It would be helpful, for instance, if scholars in Mennonite studies were familiar with scholarship in Latin American and Latino/a studies, given the growing number of Latino/a congregants in the Mennonite church, and growing numbers of Mennonites in Latin America. As an additional note, Latino/a is a term that refers to people who come from Mexico, Central America, South America, and the Caribbean and who live in the United States. It may also refer to people whose families come from these regions but are born in the U.S. The census typically uses the word *Hispanic* to refer to this community.

20. Robert Zacharias, ed., *After Identity: Mennonite Writing in North America* (University Park, Pa.: Pennsylvania State University Press, 2015). At the same time, the book privileges Mennonite writing from a very limited understanding of what it means to be Mennonite and so, I believe, there is more work to be done. A significant number of the contributions to this work come from people who work at Mennonite institutions, including Hildi Froese Tiessen (emerita, Conrad Grebel University College), Ann Hostetler (Goshen College) and Jeff Gundy (Bluffton University). Others, such as Daniel Shank Cruz, whose work forms part of this collection, engage

primarily with writing from a Mennonite perspective for a Mennonite audience.

21. Mormon Studies has a longer history of engaging with the surrounding world than Mennonite studies. For more information about this, see Michael J. Hunter's multi-volume edited collection, *Mormons and Popular Culture: The Global Influence of an American Phenomenon* (Santa Barbara, Calif.: Praeger/ABC-CLIO, 2013), which brings popular culture and Mormonism together. The Mormon studies program at Claremont Graduate University offers a fresh perspective on Mormon identity. See for example Patrick Q. Mason, "The Continuing Relevance of Mormon Studies: We're Certainly not in 2012 Anymore, but Mormonism Continues to Make the News," *Claremont Mormon Studies Newsletter* 11 (Fall 2014): 1-2.

22. See Felipe Hinojosa, *Latino Mennonites: Civil Rights, Faith and Evangelical Culture* (Baltimore, Md.: Johns Hopkins University Press, 2014). Hinojosa calls for a relational Mennonite studies, in which Mennonites would engage with other areas of inquiry to a higher degree. He reminds us of the many kinds of Mennonites in the world. In addition to Latino/a (see note 19), Chicano/a is a term that refers to Mexican-Americans or people in the Southwestern United States whose families became American when the U.S. acquired new territory in 1848 after the end of the Mexican-American war.

23. Eve Mitchell, "I Am a Woman and a Human: A Marxist-Feminist Critique of Intersectionality Theory," *Unity and Struggle*, 12 Sept. 2013, http://unityandstruggle.org/2013/09/12/i-am-a-woman-and-a-human-a-marxist-feminist-critique-of-intersectionality-theory/>. <19 July 2016>

24. Mennonite studies has focused on the experiences of white "ethnic" Mennonites. Felipe Hinojosa's *Latino Mennonites*, challenges this tendency from Latino/a studies. Drew G. I. Hart's *Trouble I've Seen: Changing How the Church Views Racism* (2015) similarly challenges Anabaptist and other Christians from African-American studies. Stephanie Krehbiel's brilliant dissertation "Pacifist Battlegrounds: Violence, Community, and the Struggle for LGBTQ Justice in the Mennonite Church USA" (2015) similarly draws on early work in feminism and Mennonite studies to engage with violence and peace from a new perspective.

25. Charles Hatfield, *The Limits of Identity: Politics and Poetics in Latin America* (Austin, Texas: University of Texas Press, 2015), 109. Hatfield observes that the subject, which he calls the particular, does not need "to be *everywhere* or *everyone* in order to be universal and make universal claims but rather that *anyone anywhere* who has a belief is already committed to its universality" (5, emphasis in text). For him, understanding that the particular is already universal could lead to transforming injustice. We can extend his work to suggest that in Mennonite studies, or in Mormon studies, moving beyond terms of identity could similarly allow us to explore broader unjust structures of power in literary works and as we critique them from these particularities, to realize that we are already engaging with the universal.

26. Michael Rechtenwald, "What's Wrong with Identity Politics (and Intersectionality Theory)? A Response to Mark Fisher's 'Exiting the Vampire Castle (and Its Critics)'," *The North Star*, 2 Dec. 2013, http://www.thenorthstar.info/?p=11411 <19 July 2016>

27. Brooks, *Book of Mormon Girl*, 16.

28. Brooks, *Book of Mormon Girl*, 16-17.

29. Brooks, *Book of Mormon Girl*, 187.

30. Gail Weiss, *Body Images: Embodiment as Intercorporeality* (New York: Routledge, 1999), 3. Weiss' intercorporeality is based on Merleau-Ponty's pioneering notion of *écart* [divergence] and his work on intersubjectivity in *The Visible and the Invisible: Followed by Working Notes*, ed. Claude Lefort, trans. Alphonso Lingis (Evanston, Ill.: Northwestern University, 1968). For him and other philosophers in the phenomenological tradition, the individual becomes a subject through a relationship with the object. In other words, the subject depends on its sensual relationships with the objects that surround it to develop a sense of self, and it becomes an individual subject through relationships with objects (132-136).

31. Christopher Breu, *Insistence of the Material: Literature in the Age of Biopolitics* (Minneapolis: University of Minnesota Press, 2014), 123-124.

32. Nancy K. Miller, "The Entangled Self: Genre Bondage in the Age of Memoir," *Publication of the Modern Language Association* 122, no. 2 (March 2007): 538.

33. Dawn Latta Kirby and Kirby Dan, "Contemporary Memoir: A 21st-Century Genre Ideal for Teens," *English Journal* 99, no. 4 (March 2010): 23, emphasis in text. Kirby and Kirby conclude, in a way that is significant for our project here, that "The mental engagement required by C[ontemporary] M[emoir] as a genre may promote self-awareness, multicultural understandings, and critical thinking." "Contemporary Memoir," 28. This particular genre, then, would seem ideal for teaching and for thinking critically about how to do the necessary work for justice.

34. Carlos Reygadas, dir., *Stellet Licht [Silent Light]*, DVD (Mantarraya, Bac and No Dream Films, 2007); Miriam Toews, *A Complicated Kindness* (New York: Counterpoint, 2005).

35. Brooks, *Book of Mormon Girl*, 82.

36. Brooks, *Book of Mormon Girl*, 160.

37. Brooks, *Book of Mormon Girl*, 28, 160, 177-180.

38. Toews, *Irma Voth*, 12.

39. Historians would agree with most of this statement. Approximately 6,000 Mennonites moved to Mexico from Manitoba and Saskatchewan in the 1920s. They moved because the governments of these provinces insisted that they send their children to English language public schools—instead of to their church run village schools, which were in German. For them this was such a serious violation that they began to look for a new homeland. They moved after their leaders met with Mexico's president, Álvaro Obregón, in 1921, and he agreed to give them the freedoms they desired in education and other areas. For more information about Mennonites in Mexico, see Harry Leonard Sawatzky, *They Sought a Country: Mennonite Colonization in Mexico* (Berkeley, Calif.: University of California Press, 1971). For a more recent ethnographic history of Low German Mennonites in the Americas, see Royden Loewen, *Village Among Nations: "Canadian" Mennonites in a Transnational World, 1916-2006* (Toronto: University of Toronto Press, 2013).

40. Brooks, *Book of Mormon Girl*, 92. In the LDS church, priesthood means

being able to distribute the sacrament, which, for Mormons, is bread and water, during their sacrament meetings or church services. It also means that one is eligible for other positions in the lay-led LDS church. "Sacrament," *LDS.Org* (2016), https://www.lds.org/topics/sacrament?lang=eng <19 July 2016>.

41. Brooks, *Book of Mormon Girl*, 65.

42. For more information about the culture of impunity in the Mexican context, see Oswaldo Zavala, "Imagining the U.S-Mexico Drug War: The Critical Limits of Narconarratives," *Comparative Literature* 66, no. 3 (Summer 2014): 340-360. For more information about sexual violence, the Mennonite church and institutional complicity, see the work of Stephanie Krehbiel, Ruth Krall, or Carol Penner.

43. Toews, *Irma Voth*, 230.

44. Toews, *Irma Voth*, 12.

45. Brooks, *Book of Mormon Girl*, 200.

Part Five
Peace and Conflict Studies

Part Five: Peace and Conflict Studies

Some Fellow Travelers

Since the rejection of violence that Christians observe in the story of Jesus is reflected in the grain of the universe, it is visible to those outside of Christian faith who have eyes to see . Two notable examples are Hindu Mahatma Gandhi and Muslim Khan Abdul Ghaffar Khan, called Badshah Khan. Gandhi's orchestration of nonviolent action in the struggle for Indian independence is well known. Less well know is the work of Badshah Khan, a Pashtun Muslim from Afghanistan who came from a long tradition of vengeance killings. Khan realized that such killings only continued a cycle of violence. He swore himself to nonviolence and raised a nonviolent force of 100,000 men that figured prominently in the struggle for Indian independence. Gandhi and Khan were close friends and lived and worked together during the independence struggle. Because of the effectiveness of Khan's movement, his nonviolent force experienced some of the worst violent repression by the British. Both Gandhi and Khan were bitterly disappointed when independence led to partition of Muslims from Hindus.[1]

Although Jesus' name was not appealed to by Gandhi and Khan, their nonviolent efforts aligned with the grain of the universe. Christians can make tactical alliances with such movements without settling the underlying disagreements about their ultimate identities. Such alliances can continue as long as there is agreement on tactics that do not challenge the underlying commitment of loyalty to Jesus and the reign of God.

These tactical alliances can form with any number of projects. Mennonite Central Committee, for example, partners with people of various religious groups in their work with refugees and peace building. Practitioners of Mennonite education can thus find tactical allies and work with and learn from those who assert no religious identity in their practices and from those in other religious traditions. There are many avenues for cooperation on projects where interests intersect, and any number of practices, which under another name, reflect the grain of the universe.

The chapters in Part Five portray research and education that point to the grain of the universe revealed in the story of Jesus, but without appealing specifically to Christian faith. Lowell Ewert's chapter describes the three facets of international law that would make the world more peaceful if applied. While it is unrealistic to think that nations will actually implement these laws, their existence at least makes people more aware of injustices. Ewert recognizes these limitations. At the same time he believes that including international law in the Mennonite curriculum for peace and conflict studies would contribute to the wider awareness of what peace entails. Rudi Kauffman's chapter demonstrates one specific limitation. He uses empirical evidence to demonstrate that just war rhetoric, despite its claimed intention to limit warfare, in practice does not work. The fact that empirical evidence makes this point is another oblique reference to what is visible in the grain of the universe for those with eyes to see, namely that rejecting violence is the best way for people to live. But as was true with Ewert's observations, the idea of a just war provides a norm with which to critique the practices of nations. Since just war terminology is the common parlance used by political leaders to justify their resorts to military force, teaching ways to critique just war theory belongs to the Mennonite peace curriculum.

Note

1. For Badshah Khan's story, see Eknath Easwaran, *Nonviolent Soldier of Islam: Badshah Khan, a Man to Match His Mountains* (Tomales, Calif.: Nilgiri Press, 1999) and Amitabh Pal, *"Islam" Means Peace: Understanding the Muslim Principle of Nonviolence* (Santa Barbara, Calif.: Praeger, 2011), 97-123.

CHAPTER FIFTEEN

PEACE STUDIES AND INTERNATIONAL LAW

Lowell Ewert

Introduction

The advancement of peace across a broad spectrum of activities is one of the distinct markers of both the theology and practice of Mennonites. As the first chapter of this book demonstrated, there is a compelling biblical and theological justification for pacifism and for resistance to the call to join military campaigns or professions that may require the use of weapons, force and coercion.

However, as important as are refusing the military and the use of violent coercion, equally important are other dimensions of the practice of peace. Mennonites have responded with compassion, humility, and service in a desire to find creative solutions to injustice and violence. This peace work has occurred under such structures as Mennonite Central Committee, Mennonite Disaster Service, and Mennonite Economic Development Associates. Mennonites have been instrumental in fostering the practice of restorative justice and conflict mediation programs.

This wide-ranging peace work functions with only minimal awareness, if any, of its relationship to international principles recognized by many nations. It is the thesis of this chapter that international humanitarian law, human rights standards, and international criminal prosecution provide an additional layer of meaning for such peace activity. On occasion, appeal to each of these three areas of international law explicitly serves a function to protect innocent civilians impacted by conflict, making the restoration of peace more likely. To the extent that these three move the process in a less violent direction, they reflect the grain of the universe.

This chapter suggests that Mennonite-related peace and conflict programs could advance their causes by appealing to and working with international institutional structures that have at their core minimizing violence and war, and maximizing the opportunities for peace. It follows that Mennonite peace studies programs should then teach courses in international law. It also follows that greater attention to international law may also increase the impact of the work of many Mennonite agencies serving the poor, marginalized, and vulnerable.

Law of War, Human Rights, and International Criminal Prosecution

When attempting to understand how international law intersects with notions of peace, there is an added layer of complexity that makes this analysis far more challenging than a simple comparison of domestic law with peace. International law lacks a formal mechanism that develops and "passes" legislation that becomes law. There is no global parliament that manages a universally agreed process for law "creation." For example, when identifying what international law is, the International Court of Justice reflects a diffuse notion of law when it specifies not one, but four sources of law—international conventions and treaties, international custom, general principles of law recognized by civilized nations, and the teachings of highly qualified publicists.[1] Given how fluid especially the last three sources of law listed are, one can be forgiven for not knowing what international law is, when a principle has become law, or whether the conclusion of your highly qualified publicist defining law will be consistent with that of my expert.

Despite this lack of specific definition, it is accepted that the entire field of international law is designed to replace "war by a system of peaceful co-existence and co-operation among States (and other subjects of international law) based on institutions, procedures and rules of conduct."[2] The ultimate goal is clear even if the specific legal framework or roadmap is not. It is important to understand that international law is a very different species from domestic law because international law loses its greatest possible benefit for peace when we incompletely understand it. International law does its job best to benefit humanity by the way it establishes an operating system and a normative framework, not just a punitive one.

> As an operating system, international law provides the framework for establishing rules and norms, outlines the parameters of interaction, and provides the procedures and forums for resolving disputes among those taking part in these interactions. In contrast, international law as a normative system provides direction for international relations by identifying the substantive values and goals to be pursued. If the operating system designates the "structures" . . . that help channel international politics, then the normative system element gives form to the aspirations and values of the participants of the system.[3]

This means that international law is prescriptive in that it enumerates what is allowed and what is not. But it is more. It also paints a picture of the kind of world that the "international system" (which does not exist as one coherent entity) has agreed is the shared aspirational goal. And even this perceived aspirational goal is further complicated because the "shared" nature of the goal is not really universally shared because there is no parliament or court that determines whether all ideals are shared.

It is within this vague context that three subsets of international law—the law of war (or what is also interchangeably referred to as humanitarian law), human rights, and international criminal prosecution function to promote or support peace. While general international law is most commonly thought to regulate relations between nations, these three subsets of law have a different function and operate primarily to shield individuals who otherwise have no or limited protection.

The Law of War

The law of war is not one document or treaty. The term *law of war* includes reference to a collection of legal documents such as the Geneva Conventions, subsequent Protocols as well as a variety of other international codes and documents that are commonly understood to regulate organized armed violence. Because the law of war evolved or developed separately, it has emerged piecemeal from different sources. Therefore humanitarian law can at times seem to be a mishmash of inconsistent or even conflicting principles which have as a common overarching goal the regulation of war. While this regulation has been mostly in the public consciousness since World War II, it is not a new concept.

Contrary to common belief, there has almost always been some customary or legal restraint on the waging of war. The notion of total and unlimited war has been the exception, not the norm. The development of limits has been most recognizable during the twentieth century. Specific prohibitions concerning warfare were promulgated to establish limits on destruction and to raise the bar for protection of civilians from a very minimal level to a level of death and mayhem that nation states could tolerate. The problem has been, however, that this threshold of protection given to noncombatants and civilians has often been so low that it appeared no limits existed when in fact there were some.

Two factors make the law of war an important consideration when contemplating how to build peace after violent conflict. First, before the adoption of these minimal standards, individuals were considered essentially as property of the nation of their citizenship and had almost no standing to claim protection if their country did not advocate on their behalf. In other words, individuals who faced the risk of attack from their own government had no recourse. These victims were subject to arbitrary maltreatment with complete legal impunity for the state perpetrators. The law of war put an end to this impunity. The law of war sets a minimum threshold of protection that a state should uphold. Those who violate these minimum standards can be guilty of war crimes, a prospect that even the worst human rights violators do not take lightly.

Second, the law of war seeks to regulate killing and destruction to make the eventual restoration of peace more likely. In international law, war is assumed to be a temporary condition, not a permanent one. "[W]ar is a transitional state. Therefore, it must be conducted in a way that will not make a return to peace impossible, and will not cause irreparable harm."[4] Irreparable harm is caused when persons are killed and things destroyed that are not necessary to accomplish a military objective. This notion of harm recognizes that the human and physical infrastructure that supports life will need to be rebuilt after the war, and therefore only what is necessary to accomplish a military objective should be destroyed. To this end, the law of war generally forbids the deliberate destruction of roads, hospitals, water systems, schools, food supplies, dams, power systems, or places of worship that have no significant military value and which are essential for the survival of the civilian population.

Irreparable harm is also the result of gratuitous violence that has no military necessity, which makes it more difficult to restore peace after a war is concluded. The prohibition of gratuitous violence is based on the notion that following the conclusion of hostilities, warring parties will understand and accept the fact that soldiers and combatants die and that military bases and equipment will be destroyed. In other words, former enemies will be able to move psychologically beyond what has been perceived as "necessary" death even if it was their brother or sister killed. Additionally, the destruction of military property or other accoutrements of the war effort will be understood as legitimate targets of war, and former enemies will again be able to leave peacefully with, or beside, each other.

In contrast, deliberate attacks on children, the elderly, the disabled, or other noncombatants will be far harder to excuse, forgive, or understand, making a peace agreement harder to negotiate or sustain. In recent years we have seen how the narratives of innocent victims of gratuitous violence have taken on a life of their own in places such as the Balkans, Gaza, Lebanon, Syria, and Iraq. These narratives then seem to justify new rounds of war, even making new wars seem necessary to obtain what is deemed to be justice or revenge.

Skeptics often dismiss the impact of the law of war as a sham that excuses or justifies war. However, it is worth recognizing that the law of war aims to insert a sense of minimal humanity into the most inhumane of situations, namely, war. For example, even amid a brutal war in Afghanistan that appeared to have few limits, hospitals were generally protected by all sides, at least until the United States airstrike October 2015 that killed and injured dozens.

Even this tragedy, however, underscores the significance of humanitarian law as the United States did not claim the right to bomb hospitals, and maintained that the hospital in question was bombed accidentally. With this explanation, the principle limiting war was actually affirmed even as the safety of this particular hospital was compromised. In this way, we see that

> this battle for humanity is not always won. Yet each partial success means that a prisoner will not have been tortured or put to death, a hand grenade not blindly lobbed into a crowd, a village not bombed into oblivion: that in a word, man has not suffered unnecessarily from the scourge of war.[5]

It therefore behooves people of peace to seek to better use the protections contained in the law of war even if one finds repugnant the underlying notion that a certain amount of killing and destruction is lawful. People of peace do victims of war a disservice and are complicit in their suffering when they ignore the benefits the law of war can provide to those caught in armed conflict.[6]

International Human Rights

A similar argument can be made concerning international human rights law which was developed with the aspiration of promoting peace. The Universal Declaration of Human Rights, adopted by the United Nations General Assembly on 10 December 1948, has anchored the modern day human rights—or I might say, peace—movement. The Declaration was based on the notion, radical at the time, that respect for human rights would sustain peace and make wars less likely. Keep in mind that when the Declaration was adopted, the world had just come out of a horrible period, experiencing two world wars in less than two generations.

In response, the drafters of the Universal Declaration believed that a solution to the scourge of war was needed. In their minds, war would be less likely if three kinds of rights would be protected: first, civil and political rights that Western liberal democracies tend to favor (similar to the U.S. Bill of Rights or the Canadian Charter of Rights and Freedoms); second, economic and social rights favored by cocialist nations (right to food, education, health care, a job, an adequate standard of living, etc.); and third, group rights favored by traditional societies (self-determination, rights of the community).

As such, the Declaration's thirty short articles can be understood as the recipe for peace and the antidote to war. War will be less likely, the visionary drafters of the Declaration hoped, if civil, political, economic, social and cultural human rights are respected. The Declaration thus describes what it takes to sustain peace.

But the peace impact of respect for human rights has a ripple effect far greater than merely the possible aversion of war. Human rights can also transform society. Some examples illustrate. First, 1998 Nobel Prize winner for Economics, Amartya Sen, has argued that respect for basic civil and political rights (vote, petition, organize, free press, etc.) will make famine less likely as societies will be able to adapt to changing circumstances. People will not starve as a result. Second, other commentators would claim that "[h]elping to educate people about human rights may ultimately be as important, or even more important, for their health than any specific AIDS educational program."[7] In other words, human rights, especially for women who often lack the right to control their own bodies, are more important than condoms to fight the spread of AIDS. Third, since a refugee is someone who feels a well-founded fear of persecution, there would be no refugees if human rights were protected.

Last, it is my contention, as yet unproved, that violations of civil and political human rights create conditions that result in more harm from natural disasters than in contexts where basic civil rights are respected. This hypothesis stems from the belief that respect for civil and political rights enables a society to hold power accountable and learn from its past. For example, if the damage caused by a disaster was magnified because corruption in the construction of homes, buildings, bridges or other infrastructure made these structures less durable, those responsible can be held to account and changes made. If the disaster was made worse because of bad building codes or improper societal or governmental processes or decisions, society going forward can learn from these mistakes and take steps to mitigate the potential impact of future disasters. One cannot hold power accountable and create a learning society in a totalitarian state. Thus, if a peaceful society is one that incorporates compassion and most effectively affirms access to the basic necessities of life, opportunity, and dignity for all, then "peace" work cannot be separated from "human rights" work.

International Criminal Prosecution

The third subset of international law designed to support peace and make its restoration more likely is international criminal prosecution. It is represented by the International Criminal Court or other tribunals such as those with jurisdiction in Rwanda, the former Yugoslavia, or Lebanon. While some would argue that violations of human rights and war crimes can be negotiated away at a peace conference or during a reconciliation process, others would suggest that it is not so easy.

> Historical injustices cast a long shadow. Their effects can linger long after the perpetrators and their victims are dead. They haunt the memories of descendants, blight the history of peoples, and poison relations between communities. They are the root cause of many existing inequities. Historical grievances have provided people with a justification for enmity, a reason for seeking revenge. They are at the heart of some of the bloodiest struggles and deeds in both historical and contemporary times.[8]

One can see evidence of the long-term impact of perceived unresolved injustices in conflicts such as those involving the Serbs and Kosovars. Slobadan Milosevic successfully appealed to memory going back to the fourteenth century to mobilize Serb nationalism that eventually led to the war in the Balkans in the 1990s. The Rwandan genocide, leaving almost one million people dead, was encouraged by a sense of historical injustice. The conflicts currently playing out in the Middle East between Sunnis and Shiites, the Israelis and Palestinians, the Kurds and the Turks, to name a few conflicts, are deeply rooted in a sense of historical injustice. Unaddressed historical injustices tend to act like an untreated flesh-eating disease that continues to eat away at its host until it is destroyed.

It is within this toxic context that international criminal courts attempt to increase the likelihood of peace. International courts

> contribute to a process of national reconciliation by substituting individual guilt for collective guilt, provide justice for victim communities, re-establish the legal order in post-conflict environments, provide a forum for truth-telling that creates an authoritative and shared record of history, deter future crimes by strengthening legal enforcement procedures, and raise the normative level of acceptable behavior.[9]

Courts perform this peacemaking function in multiple ways. First, courts can determine who should be held accountable. For example, at Nuremberg it was determined that not every German was guilty of war crimes. Only those senior military and political leaders who orchestrated the Holocaust were culpable. Therefore, it was not the German people who should be punished but only a few of its Nazi leadership.

Second, national courts may build on the notion of national accountability but hold others accountable as well. That was the outcome of the Auschwitz trials, which involved 6,500 defendants and which confronted the German people with a historical record documenting that thousands of ordinary Germans were complicit in horrific crimes too.[10] Something rotten in Germany needed to be excised.

Third, the decisions of criminal courts also affirm for victims of massive crimes that their victimhood was not their fault and that they did not deserve their fate.

Fourth, legal criminal decisions construct memory and are moments of truth that force societies to confront their past in a way that few other political decisions do.[11] If a legitimate criminal court says otherwise, no longer can one claim that an act was self-defense, justified, or regrettable but excusable.

Last, the threat of international criminal prosecution has a ripple effect. The justification the United States used for refusing to ratify the establishment of the International Criminal Court—the potential criminal prosecution of its representatives—is evidence that the promise of criminal prosecution concerns the powerful. One can only imagine what the impact of a more robust international criminal system would have on the seemingly intractable conflict between Israel and its Palestinian neighbors. All sides would have much to worry about if criminal jurisdiction were expanded to include them. Violence would likely be reduced if the courts were empowered to work effectively.

In Summary

These three subsets of international law all lie on a continuum. The law of war or humanitarian law, designed to ensure that the restoration of peace will be more likely following the end of hostilities, is on one end, and at the other end of the continuum is human rights law which asserts the claim that protection of human rights will make war less likely. Thus both the law of war and human rights law have a common aim, reducing or eliminating the impact of violent, organized conflict. In the middle of this continuum is international criminal prosecution, which serves to make the goal of the other two subsets of law more impactful. By adjudicating the "rules" of violence, criminal prosecution is both attempting to limit the violence of war while also emphasizing the human rights of individuals. Violations of the law of war are punished as are grave breaches of human rights. In this way, criminal prosecution empowers the other two areas of law to be more effective.

Conclusion

The premise of this chapter is that the law of war, human rights, and international criminal prosecution all contribute to creating the structures that enable the formation of a peaceful, stable, and just society. While I do not believe that these legal regimes alone are sufficient for peace, I also believe that peace and justice are impossible without them. Even though the world lacks supranational institutions that can effectively enforce these subsets of international law, their formal existence does contribute—if sometimes marginally—to peace in the world. They hold up an ideal, which enables bringing international pressure to bear on offenders, and they raise the norm for judging behaviors.

In my view, the traditional Mennonite practice of giving short shrift to the way that the law of war, human rights and international criminal prosecution can serve the interests of the vulnerable abdicates an important opportunity to build peace. Just because law is perceived to be weak, inconsistent, or rendered unenforceable by the powerful does not make it irrelevant. Challenging law to function better as an operating and normative system serves the cause of peace. Peace and conflict studies programs and the civil society agencies that serve the global poor and marginalized would be more impactful if they more explicitly acknowledged how international legal structures contribute to peace theory and worked to make these structures function more effectively.

Notes

1. Statute of the International Court of Justice, "Article 18," http://www.icj-cij.org/documents/index.php?p1=4&p2=2&p3=0 <1 Aug. 2016>

2. Daniel Thurer, *International Humanitarian Law: Theory, Practice, Context*, 3rd ed. (The Hague, Netherlands: Hague Academy of International Law, 2011), 39.

3. Charlotte Ku and Paul F. Diehl, "International Law as Operating and Normative Systems: An Overview," in *International Law: Classic and Contemporary Readings*, ed. Charlotte Ku and Paul F. Diehl (Boulder, Col.: Lynne Rienner Publisheers,

2009), 3.

4. Francoise Bouchet-Saulnier, *The Practical Guide to Humanitarian Law* (Lanham, Md.: Rowman & Littlefield Publishers, 2002), 7.

5. Frits Kalshoven and Liesbeth Zegveld, *Constraints on the Waging of War: An Introduction to International Humanitarian Law* (Cambridge, UK: Cambridge University Press, 2011), 280-281.

6. It is important to understand the difference between the law of war and traditional just war theory. The law of war regulates warfare, but it does not ipso facto determine if a war is "just," as do the theorists who debate the criteria for when a war can be engaged. However, there is some parallel between the law of war and the discussion among just war theorists about the conduct of a just war once it has been engaged. A detailed discussion about their differences and possible parallels is the subject for another essay.

7. Harvard Professor Jonathan Mann, quoted in Mark E. Wojik, "On the Sudden Loss of a Human Rights Activist: A Tribute to Dr. Jonathan Mann's Use of International Human Rights Law in the Global Battle Against AIDS," *The John Marshall Law Review* 32, no. 1 (Fall 1998): 129.

8. Janna Thompson, *Taking Responsibility for the Past: Reparation and Historical Justice* (Cambridge: Polity Press, 2002), vii.

9. Matthew Brubacher, "Striking a Balance: Humanitarian, Peace and Justice Initiatives," *The Conrad Grebel Review* 28, no. 3 (Fall 2010): 9-10.

10. Rebecca Wittmann, *Justice: The Auschwitz Trial* (Cambridge, Mass.: Harvard University Press, 2005), 5-6.

11. Mark Osiel, *Mass Atrocity, Collective Memory, and the Law* (New Brunswick, NS: Transaction Publishers, 2000), 2-3.

CHAPTER SIXTEEN

ONLY JUST WAR: THE BROKEN LOGIC OF NECESSARY EVIL AND FUNCTIONAL VIOLENCE

Rudi Kauffman

Introduction

The justification of war, whether calling it "just" or merely "justified," has a long history. At its best, it is held up as the only realistic and reasonable way to moderate the horrors of war. At its worst, it becomes part of the long and painful tradition of justified violence. Complicating the dubious history of justified violence in its various other forms, just war theory is particularly problematic because of the inconsistent and convoluted combination of theological, political, and legal influences that produced it.

Rather than focusing on the traditional debates about the limits of ethical behavior in war, this chapter works with the accepted criteria, to investigate the empirical impacts of adhering to just war theory. This is exploratory in nature, so there is a brief description of methodology followed by an application of the proposed method to three recent military engagements by the United States. In preparation, the first section of the chapter sketches the just war criteria.

In a very general sense, the identification of the rules that define just war criteria is an assertion that some wars or approaches to war are 'better" than others. Of course, the understanding of "better" has varied widely, and the theory itself has little clarity on this issue.

Development of Just War Criteria

In its Christian iteration, just war theory has developed over more than 1,500 years. The first major argument for the compatibility of war and Christianity came in the fourth century from North Africa from Augustine of Hippo. Augustine's concern was for the soldier's spiritual well-being. Augustine rejected fighting in self-defense and made the soldier's innocence dependent on obedience to his sovereign who in turn was duty bound to God. On the sovereign's side, Augustine's theory forbade conquest and emphasized protection of the weak.

The theory was substantially and durably altered some 800 years later with Thomas Aquinas' commentary in *Summa Theologica*. Writing from a much more powerful and politically robust Christendom, Aquinas altered the spiritual/religious focus of Augustine to permit the more pragmatic interest of an empire, including self-defense. Expounding on Augustine, Aquinas developed the three foundational principles of *jus ad bellum* (justification for going to war) that are central in just war theory today: legal authority, a just cause, and right intent.

Both Augustine and Aquinas clearly prioritize spiritual absolution before God. These three foundational criteria are designed to delineate the process by which a warrior can avoid damnation. The spiritual point is moot for secular humanists who assert that a just war serves humanitarian objectives.

In the sixteenth century, Francisco de Vitoria developed two addition criteria for a just war. Writing at the request of the Spanish crown to justify the conquest of indigenous populations in the Americas, Vitoria went beyond Scripture and oriented his discussion of just war theory toward human experience. His first addition was the requirement that war making be a last resort. The second requirement focused on proportionality, a recognition that war must have the hope of some greater good because of its tremendous evil. The idea of proportionality has since expanded to include the requirement of reasonable hope of success.

The work of Francisco Suárez built on the hints of humanism that began in Vitoria's work. Suárez ascribed proper authority in large part to the consent of the governed rather than the natural result of holding office. While Suárez's work in the sixteenth and early seventeenth century began to move more robustly to a focus on human well-being than salvation, Hugo Groitus showed a more complete embrace. Grotius not only attended to the conditions to start war but began describing the conditions by which a war might be conducted. Grotius suggested that a just war must inflict the minimum damage necessary to accomplish military objectives, focus on targets that contribute to the outcome of the war, and avoid civilian targets.

The varying spiritual/secular and secular foundations that drove the development of just war theory have largely yielded to secular-humanist understandings in contemporary political and legal writing. In the past 150 years, the advent of new weapons, acknowledgement of mass murder, and development of new technologies have motivated leaders to consider ways to avoid the most heinous acts of war. The laws of war have thus been developed by politicians, lawyers, warriors, and ethicists, with human rights being substituted for the will of God as the basic criterion for a just war.

The formal codification of just war theory began in earnest in the 1860s with the Lieber Code during the United States Civil War. In rapid succession, a number of pacts and statements of principle were adopted focusing on non-combatants and treatment of prisoners. The most recent, full iteration of principles concerning the conduct of war is found in the Charter of the United Nations. Among other things, this charter firmly establishes the United Nations as the "legitimate" or "proper" authority for authorization of war.[1]

Empirical Methodology

In light of the long history and varying objectives that shaped just war criteria, it is only sensible to consider how existing requirements serve the current focus on humanitarian outcomes. A robust study requires the development of a new literature and new voices, well beyond what is possible in this brief discussion. The remainder of the chapter draws on my 2012 dissertation but focuses on different data and analyses illuminating the same disturbing problems with just warmaking.

> **Justness of War – Defining Terms**
>
> 1) **Proper Authority**
> *Strong form:* Endorsed by the UN Security Council
> *Weak form:* Endorsed by a durable intergovernmental organization
>
> 2) **Just Cause**
> *Strong form:* Objectives were exclusively self-defense or aiding the victim of aggression
> *Weak form:* Objectives included self-defense or aiding the victim of aggression
>
> 3) **Differentiation of Targets**
> *Strong form:* Targeting decisions focused on *solely* military targets
> *Weak form:* Targeting decisions focused only on dual-use and military-combatant facilities
>
> 4) **Proportionality**
> *Strong form:* Strategic & tactical decisions minimize total harm and do not use banned weapons
> *Weak form:* Strategic decisions avoid damage and casualties and do not use of banned weapons

The dissertation itself represents the full universe of conflicts between 1960-2000. During that period, wars meeting the criteria for just war correlated with the worst interstate conflict outcomes. Non-just war conflicts yielded better results. Non-intervention, even in the face of genocide, correlated with the best outcomes. However, the data does not support the generalizing of these results to other eras.

To undertake such a study, two concepts must be defined: the justness of wars and the justness of outcomes. Because of the quantity of literature in both legal and political science disciplines surrounding international human rights and human rights law, the most data exist for the justness of outcomes.

The obvious candidate to represent the justness of outcomes is the Human Development Index (HDI). The United Nations and a range of NGOs use it as a quick estimate of the development of a country. It is based on three indicators: life expectancy at birth, literacy rate, and per capita Gross Domestic Product (pcGDP). For the brief analysis found here, life expectancy at birth and education indicators are derived from the UNESCO Institute for Statistics[2] and per capita gross domestic product (pcGDP) data is used from the Groningen Growth and Development Center at the University of Groningen, the Netherlands in conjunction with the Conference Board.

Measuring the relative justness, or perhaps "justifiability," of conflicts is somewhat more challenging. The idea of justness has an inherent element of subjectivity, which means that the meaning and importance of findings must be properly tempered and contextualized. To quantify (that is, to assign numbers to) the concept of justness, adherence to just war principles is evaluated on the basis of four areas most prominent in international law: Proper Authority, Just Cause, Differentiation of Targets, and Proportionality. In each case, the principle will be evaluated as either complying with the most robust interpretation of the idea (the "strong form" of a given just war requirement), a moderate level of compliance (called compliance in the "weak form"), or non-compliance.

The Application Questions

Proper Authority

In classical just war theory, proper authority is derived from divine mandate. As noted above, Suárez introduced the concept of proper authority being derived from democratic consent,[3] a perspective that is reinforced in the United Nations Charter.[4] For this reason, in its strongest form, proper authority arises solely from the United Nations as indicated by a formal resolution of the Security Council.

In the weak form, proper authority is simply derived from theory and practice rather than formal treaty. The contemporary call for democratic support of war as a source of proper authority would suggest that the endorsement of any durable intergovernmental institution is more appropriate than countries acting unilaterally.[5] This is upheld, or at the least not overturned, by the dearth of prosecutions against countries that have initiated war with the support of regional entities.

Strong form of question: Was the country's role in the war formally endorsed by the UN Security Council?

Weak form of question: Was the country's role in the war formally endorsed by a durable intergovernmental institution?

Just Cause

Just cause is also clearly defined in international law. The strongest case for just cause is in response to unprovoked aggression. According to the Charter of the United Nations, Chapter 1, Article 51, "Nothing in the present Charter shall impair the inherent right of individual or collective self-defense if an armed attack occurs against a Member of the United Nations." This concept of "collective self-defense" has been broadly interpreted to mean intervention on behalf of a state that has been targeted by unprovoked aggression.

The weak form of just cause allows for ulterior motives as long as right intent remains a substantial and overt part of the logic. Note that "right intention," is differentiated by some legal scholars from "right motives." Terry Nardin asserts, "[an] agent's intention is what he chooses to do; his motive is the disposition and desires that explain his choice."[6]

Strong form of question: Did the stated objectives clearly and solely conform to permissible intentions (self-defense, aiding a state that is the victim of aggression)?[7]

Weak form of question: Did the stated objectives include permissible intentions (self-defense, aiding a state that is the victim of aggression)?

Other Military Targets

Differentiation of military targets from non-combatants has been important in the development of just war criteria since the 1860s. The various treaties allow only viable combatant military assets as targets. The wounded (nonviable military asset), infirm (nonviable military asset), civilians (non-military asset), and non-combatant military (non-combatant military asset) personnel are never to be targeted directly and targeting should minimize the harm that comes to these groups even when attacking legitimate military assets. In the strongest form, respect for this principle would dictate that no such assets are targeted. In the weak form, it would demand that all targets at least have some clear, valuable connection to the military apparatus or the ability to support ongoing war-making activities.

Strong form of the question: Were targeting decisions made to target *solely* military targets? (No targeting of dual-use facilities, civilian facilities, or non-combatant military facilities such as hospitals or prisoners-of-war.)

Weak form of the question: Were all targeting decisions clearly focused on military and military-combatant related facilities? (Avoiding unnecessary harm to civilian, prisoners of war, and non-combatant; associated facilities; but including dual use facilities.)

Proportionality

Finally, there is the issue of proportionality. Proportionality and target differentiation are cited as the underlying reasons for bans on specific weapons, most notably nuclear, biological, and chemical weapons. In international law, such bans are the clearest and most prevalent voicing of the proportionality requirement.

In the strong form, both the non-use of illegal weapons and a concerted effort to avoid unnecessary harm must be evident. An example would be choosing to take part in ground operations which might be higher risk to the opposing force's troops in an effort to avoid the collateral damage associated with a high altitude bombing campaign.

In the weak form, illegal weapons remain proscribed but there would be evidence that the opposing state made decisions to curtail unnecessary violence. An example would be ceasing hostilities after a victory even though continuing would heigthen the advantage.

Strong form of question: Did strategic and tactical decisions represent a clear effort to minimize total harm *and* refrain from the use of banned weapons (under the strictest interpretation upheld in international court) and tactics?

Weak form of question: Did strategic decisions avoid damage and casualties that were not necessary to achieve stated military objectives (most notable in cases where an advantage was not pressed when it would have been militarily feasible resulting in lives and or property being spared) *and* refrain from the use of banned weapons and tactics?

With these four concepts in place, it is possible to offer some initial analysis of the impact on local populations in situations that supposedly met just war criteria. I investigate three potential or actual humanitarian interventions in the post-Cold War era. During the administration of President Bill Clinton, the United States had three opportunities to intervene and responded in three different ways. In the instability in Somalia, the United States engaged in a largely just manner. The United States did not intervene in the genocide in Rwanda. The United States engaged with questionable justness in the fracturing of the Balkans.

Three Case Studies

Somalia

Following a coup d'état, the United States special forces led an international coalition in an effort to restore order, particularly in the capital of Mogadishu. Since the expedition was under the auspices of a United Nations Security Council resolution, the action represented strong form compliance with the proper authority requirement. In terms of just cause, the United Nations resolution noted a "humanitarian tragedy . . . exacerbated by the obstacles being created to the distribution of humanitarian assistance."[8] Thus it appears accurate to suggest that the intervention met the strong form of just cause as well.

Differentiation of targets is somewhat more difficult and analysis requires some greater background information.[9]

Mohammed Farrah Aidid, who eventually declared himself president, had been managing the allocation of international humanitarian aid in Mogadishu in ways to strengthen his own militias and weaken opposing factions. The United Nations intervention was to insure food for the entire population, and it was in the course of providing security for food distributions to underserved populations that the United Nations forces began taking significant causalities.

When the United States force began to suffer casualties, President Clinton sent in special forces units to arrest or kill the militias and their leadership. During a mission to arrest a high-level aid to Aidid, the soldiers serving the warrant came under attack. An extensive battle erupted between militias and the military personnel who were trying to extricate themselves from the city. At least 1,000 and as many as 2,000 Somalis died, with 19 United Nations soldiers killed.

Ultimately, the question of targeting and proportionality is extremely difficult to explain. It appears that one of the failures of just war theory is the desperation of forcing people to make life-and-death decisions. In this case, the initial mission was solely and appropriately on target as it was executing a legal warrant and there was no intentional targeting of civilians. It seems that once a soldier is engaged in a firefight, strategic "targeting" of civilians is unlikely, but civilians are nonetheless unnecessarily put into harm's way because distinguishing between threats and civilians is difficult. In short, it appears that this situation meets the strong form of the targeting requirement because there is no evidence that there was an effort to target anything but military targets. However, it raises questions about proportionality.

The first piece of the proportionality requirement is the use of illegal weapons. The United Nations forces appear to have complied wholly with conventions regarding banned weapons. However, the exposure of civilians to an active firefight suggests that a better approach was warranted. Evaluating the degree of failure is no small thing. On its face, it appears that there was an effort to be proportional, but that the degree, danger, and strength of the opposition was significantly underestimated. It would be difficult to say that there was no effort properly to tailor the strategic decisions to meet military objectives—but also difficult to say that every possible caution was taken. This appears to be an example of compliance in the weak form. As a whole, the intervention in Somalia meets the four criteria for a just war intervention.

Rwanda

Although the story of Rwanda deserves considerable attention, it has little relevance to the inquiry concerning just interventions except to recognize that it was truly horrible. With an estimated 800,000 deaths, it was at least the equal, in scope and intensity, of the other incidences that precipitated interventions by the United States. However, likely because of the experience of failure in Somalia, the United States chose to avoid engagement in Rwanda, even though *jus ad bellum* criteria would have labeled it a just intervention.

The Balkans

The situation in the Balkans was complex due to both the internal dynamics and larger geopolitical implications. Following the fragmentation of Yugoslavia, Serbia and the Serbian people maintained close ties to Russia while, particularly during the Bosnian war, the United States was sympathetic to the plight of the Bosnians and outspokenly critical of Serbian ethnic cleansing. Consequently, as the various ethnic groups began jostling for power, there was substantial disagreement on the UN Security Council about how or if intervention might happen.

Sympathy with the Bosnians along with reports of "ethnic cleansing" and memories of Rwanda were sufficient to push the Clinton administration toward action. Because of the impasse at the United Nations Security Council, and in light of ongoing atrocities, the United

States chose to move forward with an intervention with the approval of NATO which, in turn cited an earlier statement from United Nations Security Council. This constitutes compliance with the weak form of proper authority.

Regarding the cause, there was ample evidence that powerless parties were being harmed, including Kosovar Albanians, which means that there is reason to believe that involvement was at least partly justified. However, unlike the situation in Somalia where ulterior motives were difficult to identify, the decision to use NATO and to bypass the United Nations afforded the United States a number of tactical benefits that would be hard to ignore. Particularly in light of the non-intervention in Rwanda, there is an appearance that the cause of the war may have been, at least in part, to shore up NATO and draw a line in the sand for Russia. This would have yielded not only some geographical benefits for the United States (allies in Eastern Europe and associated military bases), but it served to give purpose and definition to a powerful alliance that had been searching for meaning after the Cold War. For these reasons, the war is scored as being in compliance with the weak form of just cause.

Compliance of the Conflicts to Just War Theory

1) **Somalia** – Meets just war criteria
    Proper Authority – Strong Form Compliance
    Just Cause – Strong Form Compliance
    Targeting – Strong Form Compliance
    Proportionality – Weak Form Compliance

2) **Rwanda** – Non-intervention
    Just Cause was present

3) **The Balkans** – Does not meet all just war criteria
    Proper Authority – Weak Form Compliance
    Just Cause – Weak Form Compliance
    Targeting – Weak Form Compliance
    Proportionality – Non-compliance

Perhaps in response to the pain of the Somalia experience or as a result of domestic politics, the United States explicitly chose to minimize its own risk in the Balkans by avoiding the use of ground troops. This decision has significant impact in the areas of targeting and proportionality—decreasing risk for the warrior meant higher risk to civilians and non-combatants. A number of targeting errors led to disproportionate civilian losses, which drew the ire not only of Russia and Serbia but also Amnesty International.[10] Appealing to international norms of war, Tania Voon makes a strong case that NATO simply failed to meet its basic obligations in areas associated with targeting and proportionality.[11]

It is still possible to argue that targeting compliance was consistent in the weak form because there is no evidence of *intent* to hit purely civilian targets. Nonetheless, because of multiple instances of wrong targeting and the possibility to avoid such errors,[12] it seems appropriate to say that the basic requirements of proportionality were not met.

Conclusions

The question, then, lies in the relative success of these interventions. The intervention in Somalia was a legitimate effort at a just war, Rwanda is an example of genocide with no intervention, and the Balkans are an example of an unjust intervention. The aftermath of these experiences sheds considerable light. Somalia is in utter disarray, such that there are literally no reliable data regarding economic and literacy indicators. Missing data makes formal mathematical models difficult, but for the purposes of this analysis, it is sufficient to say that Somalia has been thoroughly destroyed and shown few signs of significant improvement. Somalia's economic system, civil society, and political structures all appear to be thoroughly crushed. In 1990, Somalia had a life expectancy nearly thirteen years higher than Rwanda's, but in 2005 Rwanda's rate had passed Somalia's. At least in this case, it appears that intervention does not correlate with markedly better outcomes.

For Rwanda and Kosovo/Serbia, the results show some reason for optimism. As just noted, without intervention, Rwanda shows a meteoric rise in life expectancy. To be sure, some of this is reversion to the mean, which is to say, it is a rise to the level of life expectancy common throughout the world. Managing AIDS, violence, and health care all contributed to this change—a growth that Somalia did not share.

To stabilize and accurately reflect the various populations, the data for Kosovo and Serbia is derived from an average of the life expectancies of the states of the former Yugoslavia (Bosnia and Herzegovina, Croatia, Montenegro, Serbia, and Slovenia) which is referred to as the "Balkans" in the accompanying figure. The life expectancy data shows a noticeable decline around the period of war, but a recovery that stabilizes between 74-75 years.[13] This suggests that intervention produced no dramatic shift—either positive or negative—in state capacity to provide for health care nor in standard of living surrounding health care.

The economic data uses standardized dollars and is adjusted for purchasing power parity (so that one dollar can roughly be equated to one US dollar in 2015). After experiencing a precipitous decline in pcGDP in the year of the conflict, 1994 (to $337.42), Rwanda has seen a steady and significant improvement ever since, more than doubling to $820.18 in 2005.[14] Using the same averaging method, the states of former Yu-

	Somalia (Conflict - 1993)	Rwanda (Conflict - 1994)	Balkans (Conflict - 1999)
pcGDP	No data		
Literacy	No data		
Life expectancy			

goslavia show a slow recovery after struggling to recover from the turmoil and violence of the disintegration of Yugoslavia and the preceding war with Bosnia. Though not a meteoric economic boom, as was experienced by Rwanda, it is within range of normal economic growth relative to other states in Eastern Europe over this time period.

Meaningful interpretation of reported literacy rates is challenging because of sparse data and because available data is difficult to interpret. Based on UNESCO numbers, the Balkans have a literacy rate over 99 percent consistently throughout the time in question; consequently, no meaningful analysis can be derived from the slight reported variations. Though sparse, Rwanda's data shows a pre-genocide rate of just under 75 percent (measured in 1991). It rose to over 77.5 percent in 2000, after which it remained largely stagnant until 2010.[15]

Even with this small snapshot, it is quite evident that the just war experience of Somalia ultimately led to the worst outcomes. On its face, it appears that among these three cases the best outcomes may well be associated with non-intervention. This is particularly notable because the non-intervention was associated with a much higher total human cost and the resolution was anything but peaceable. Ultimately, these three cases appear to suggest that a "just war" is actually the worst possibility for the people. Because Rwanda and the states of former Yugoslavia are from such markedly different regions with such markedly different baseline demographics, there is no definitive statement regarding the relative value of unjust or just interventions. Rwanda's remarkable post-genocide boom is impressive relative to Yugoslavia's relative stagnation; however, it is unclear precisely what forces drive this difference.

Whatever the case, seeking explanations for this phenomenon and exploring its generalizability certainly merits further study. A few tentative explanations are worthy of consideration. First, it is possible that the same mechanisms that make just war appear humane actually lead to situations which sap popular support. Somalia's failure is as much the result of the international community withdrawing as it is a result of the international community's actions when it was present. Put plainly, it is possible that the prevalence of democracies makes it impossible to sustain a just war to its proper conclusion. The United States could sustain high-altitude bombing of Serbia because Americans will tolerate unintended killing of others rather than loss of their own soldiers. The United States could not sustain a solution in Somalia because its citizens simply were not prepared to engage in the long difficult work of fighting justly.

If the previous explanation is a macro-political systems perspective, it is possible that an even broader view could be behind the failure. Using the comment by J. Denny Weaver in the first chapter of the book, the seeming failure of just war intervention may actually illuminate something of the grain of the universe. War in any form runs counter to that grain and thus cannot have a fully righteous outcome. Perhaps the outcome suggested by the empirical data is actually all in the nature of war.

An unjust war makes no pretense of trying to set things right and so avoids the pitfalls of mission drift and entanglement. Without worrying about careful rules of engagement, a warrior can claim success and leave to allow the situation to resolve. But a so-called just war appears little better. When one becomes involved in the ways that a just war requires, the brokenness is compounded and the intervening force becomes entrapped in the conflict, which actually contributes to the pain with every effort to ameliorate it.

Put another way, perhaps war is like clubbing a baby seal. If a person has decided to do so, there is no benefit in clubbing the seal gently or using a small stick. The deed itself has specific parameters that must be met. When clubbing a seal, it will end up dead, and avoiding this outcome means failure. It is possible that war is fundamentally about destroying the other. In this case, there is no gentle destruction. Notably, this leaves ample room for non-intervention and perhaps even an exploration of non-war responses to situations.

In the case of Kosovo, one might imagine an entirely different recovery profile—as measured by the HDI, relationships among the ethnic groups, perhaps even in Russo-American relations. If the ten-year-long, nonviolent movement initiated by Kosovars had not been ignored by the international community,[16] it is relatively easy to imagine the support and success that Rwanda felt being amplified in the Balkans. Ultimately, whether viewing the world wars of the twentieth century or the Cold War that defined the second half, there is ample reason to believe that only peace can be won. The greatest military victories appear only to make space to bring justice into the following peace.

Though not definitive, it is painfully obvious that the three cases presented here challenge the assumptions of just war advocates. Those who lament the lack of military intervention in Rwanda must ask themselves how and where they have seen such responses lead to success. Even at its best, violence is radically over-trusted by those who look to justify war. Perhaps General Sherman was correct that, "War is cruelty. There is no use trying to reform it; the crueler it is the sooner it will be over."[17] It is essential that those constructing the theological and theoretical frameworks to justify war consider their enterprise in light of the real costs and benefits it visits upon humanity.

It may be that the empirical data sketched in this chapter is anomalous and that there are countervailing benefits to developing critera, as named by Lowell Ewert in the previous chapter, namely that what just war criteria accomplish is to establish conditions for the restoration of peace and enable gross violators later to be held accountable. On the other hand, it may be that its original purpose is still its defining characteristic. Perhaps just war theory is merely a salve for the warriors and the powerful. It was created to ensure justification before God; its purpose now been secularized, allowing murder to be justified before the people, the press, and the courts. If this is the case, just war theory is not merely a problem because it is language that justifies war. It actively contributes to the misery of the powerless so that the powerful who wage war might feel vindication.

Notes

1. John Howard Yoder's extended survey of these changes argues that changes were usually in the direction of lessening the criteria as a restraint. Rather than limiting war, it has become the language used to justify the war a leader wants to pursue. See John Howard Yoder, *When War is Unjust: Being Honest in Just-War Thinking*, 2nd ed. (Maryknoll, N.Y.: Orbis, 1996), 1-70.

2. UNESCO Institute for Statics, "Data Centre," *Unitred Nations Educational, Scientific, and Cultural Organization* (2015), http://data.uis.unesco.org/Index.aspx <11 Aug. 2016>.

3. This is a clear illustration of the foundational shift which occurred in the Enlightenment and ultimately shaped the understanding of the purpose and nature of just war theory. Where God was previously the highest power, humanity is now lifted up as the great norm. Broad human consensus has quite literally supplanted God.

4. The United Nations, *Charter of the United Nations* (1945), Ch. VII.

5. Examples of durable intergovernmental institutions would include NATO and the Warsaw Pact. Non-qualifying endorsements would include "coalitions of the willing" (not durable) or Amnesty International (not an intergovernmental organization).

6. Terry Nardin, "Introduction," in *Nomos XLVII—Humanitarian Intervention*, ed. Terry Nardin and Melissa Williams (New York: New York University Press, 2006), 10.

7. Note that "solely" means that all evident objectives of the intervening state are either self-defense or aiding a state that is the victim of aggression. In the strong form, no other objective is permissible; in the weak form, other objectives are permissible as long as the objectives include one of the claimed just causes.

8. United Nations Security Council, *Resolution 794* (New York: United Nations Security Council, 1992).

9. Here my sources for the over arching narrative surrounding the activities of the

United Nations and the United States in Mogadishu in 1993 is Mark Bowden, *Black Hawk Down: A Story of Modern War* (New York: Signet Books, 1999), and the series of interviews by the PBS news show, Frontline, *Ambush Mogadishu* (Frontline—PBS, 1998).

10. Amnesty International, "NATO /Federal Republic of Yugoslavia: 'Collateral Damage' or Unlawful Killings? Violations of the Laws of War by NATO During Opereration Allied Force" (2000).

11. Tania Voon, "Pointing the Finger: Civilian Casualities of NATO Bombing in Kosovo Conflict," *American University International Law Review* 16, no. 4 (2001): 1083-1113.

12. Voon, "Pointing the Finger," 1095-1099.

13. UNESCO Institute for Statics, "UNESCO Institute."

14. UNESCO Institute for Statics, "UNESCO Institute."

15. UNESCO Institute for Statics, "UNESCO Institute."

16. James H. Satterwhite, "Nonviolent Political Movements as Missed Opportunity in Kosovo," in *Teaching Peace: Nonviolence and the Liberal Arts*, ed. J. Denny Weaver and Gerald Biesecker-Mast (Lanham, Md.: Rowman & Littlefield Publishers, Inc., 2003), 89-101.

17. Norman K Risjord, *The Civil War Generation* (Lanham, Md.: Rowman & Littlefield, 2002), 143.

Part Six
Local Applications

Part Six: Local Applications

Part Six presents chapters in two areas where Mennonite education poses a significant challenge to wide spread assumptions in North American society. Stated generally, these areas are the application of violence and the science of evolution. Each area has implications for Mennonite education, and individual professors and practitioners can address these areas. This statement requires some elaboration.

In the public mind and in the United States national ethos, there is an unquestioned axiom that violence is effective, that violence works to solve problems. But when political scientists, sociologists, and historians are honest, they can tell a different story. They can point to the cyclical nature of violence and its ineffectiveness. A few examples illustrate. World War II continued a cycle that began with the widely recognized, harsh conditions forced on Germany by the victorious powers after World War I that fostered a bitter climate in which the Nazi agenda could fester.

The cycle is clear in arms races, as each side says that it needs more weapons to counter the weapons on the other side. The cycle is quite visible in the responses to terrorist attacks. The attacks are originally stimulated by a perceived wrong, which leads a smaller group to feel that their only way of convincing the other side of truth is by a violent act. However, the side attacked never recognizes the justice of the cause of the attackers. Its adherents respond with greater violence, which then provokes the other side to yet more attacks. This cycle is clearly visible in the ever-widening scope of United States efforts to fight a "war on terror."

At a local level, consider the riots which erupted after unarmed African-American men died at the hands of white police officers. These riots spring from longstanding feelings of betrayal by police forces, which are epitomized by the shootings. Martin Luther King Jr. famously said "A riot is the language of the unheard."¹ But as King also said, riots accomplish nothing positive. They provoke the police to don riot gear and engage in harsh tactics to quell the riot. Eventually the energy of riots expends itself, but resentment remains and continues to fester until it bursts forth again.

At the level of one-on-one confrontation, consider the small boy bullied on the play ground, who threatens to get his big brother to attack the bully. The bully may bring his friends, and the escalation continues in the streets.

Such examples make it possible for those with eyes to see that violence is cyclical. Rather than being the effective problem solver of unquestioned public faith, at one remove or another, violence actually provokes more violence. De-escalating a conflict and/or pursuing a resolution with nonviolent means accomplishes much more than mirroring the violence one hates. Although theological language is not used, political and social scientists and historians who point to the cyclical nature of violence are performing analysis that aligns itself with the grain of the universe revealed in Jesus.

Three chapters in Part Six describe ways that individuals can interrupt the cycle of violence.

Chapter 17 concerns restorative justice, which poses an alternative to retributive justice. The criminal justice system in the United States and in many countries of the world is based on retributive justice. Retributive justice focuses on determining the guilt or innocence of a person accused of a crime and then to apply appropriate punishment to the guilty. Justice is declared done when the process was fair that led to the determination of guilt or innocence, and appropriate punishment was administered to a person judged guilty. The deed committed by the guilty party is presumed to be against society, with officials of government managing the process in the name of society (often referred to in court as "the people"). These government authorities, who act in the name of the people, carry out the prosecution and administer the eventual punishment. Fines levied as punishment are paid to the state. A guilty party who pays the fine or serves time in prison is said to have "paid his or her debt to society."

For our purposes here, two things are worthy of particular note in retributive justice. First, it focuses on punishment. In other words, it is vengeance oriented—harm committed by an offender is balanced by pain inflicted on the offender. Second, note that retributive justice focuses on the offender. It does nothing for the victim who was wronged. That person is a spectator to the trial process that determines guilt or innocence. Even a fine levied on the guilty party goes to the state and not to the victim of the crime.

In contrast, as the name indicates, restorative justice aims to restore a broken relationship, and it works with all parties involved. It focuses on the victim and what the victim needs for restoration, and it envisions the offender and how the offender might be helped. In some cases, as a part of the process of restoration, the offended party may sometimes reach the point of offering forgiveness to the offender. The process of restoration may never be wholly completed, but its focus is quite different from retributive justice.

Applying the principles of restorative justice does not require the reform of an entire system. Individuals can work with these ideas at whatever level they occupy—from teachers in a classroom to principals applying it to a school to a superintendent putting it in place for an entire school district. A police officer could apply it in his or her patrolling, a lawyer can work for restorative outcomes in cases, an individual judge can remand cases to a restorative justice program. Knowledgeable church people can establish a program and request cases from a local judge. Possibilities are many.

The practice of restorative justice does not emerge from starry-eyed idealism. Significant research shows that practices of restorative justice actually work. They lower recidivism rates and keep conflicts from escalating. Because it works, some cities have established programs where cases can be remanded to practitioners trained in applying restorative justice. Schools have begun to use restorative principles. In Chapter 17, Lonna Stoltzfus describes the application of restorative justice practices in the public school system of Madison, Wisconsin.

Chapter 18 by J. Denny Weaver discusses forgiveness. Forgiveness is understood as the process whereby a victim lets go of the anger against a perpetrator. Holding on to anger gives the offense and the offender power over the victim. With the release of anger, the one offended ceases being a victim and is once again in charge of his or her own life.

Forgiveness may or may not lead to reconciliation. Forgiveness involves offering a small gift to the offender and is thus another way of expressing love for an enemy or of changing the situation to break a cycle of violence. Research by social scientists and psychologists in the practices of forgiveness demonstrate that it does in fact allow the one who forgives to live a healthier life. Thus for both restorative justice and for forgiveness, there is research evidence that shows these practices work in the wider world. They are thus additional examples in which the results of research done apart from theological considerations agree with the grain of the universe made visible in the nonviolent life of Jesus.

The third chapter in this section deals with the "pacifist's dilemma," the well-known question posed to pacifists, namely, "What would you do if a man with a gun came after your mother/wife/daughter?" This question assumes the seemingly universal faith in violence to solve problems and is assumed by the questioner to refute completely any pacifist argument. Zachary Walton's chapter describes some of the techniques he uses in a college classroom to show students the problematic logic of the question, and ultimately to bring students to question the prevailing assumptions about the efficacy of violence to solve problems.

It is a commonplace to say that we live in a scientific age. It seems equally obvious that Mennonite students should thus study science at all levels of their education from the elementary grades through college. The more complicated questions concern the attitude Mennonites should take toward science and the relationship of biblical studies and theology to science.

Approaching the question of the relationship of the Bible and theology to science is to enter a realm of controversy in the United States and to a lesser extent in Canada. Although scientists in overwhelming numbers support the evidence of an extremely old earth and cosmos (more than 13 billion years) and the evolution of human beings from lesser species, in a recent poll 46 percent of the population in the United States believed in an earth no more than 10,000 years old and that human beings were created by God in their present form. About fifteen percent accept the idea that evolution occurred and was guided by God, and the remainder accept evolution without God. In Canada perhaps a fifth of the population rejects evolution and accepts the idea of a young earth and a creationist view of human origins. This data means that in North America, large numbers of people reject the findings of modern science, and assert that the Bible contradicts the findings of science.[2]

Global warming is a second issue where a significant portion of the public disputes scientific findings. Many branches of science have contributed to the idea that global warming is occurring. Again, overwhelming majorities of scientists have concluded that this warming is caused by human activity while in a recent poll only 57 percent of the population accepted that idea. The remainder of the population attributed global climate change to natural causes. Traditionally conservative Christians have not accepted the idea that human beings are causing global warming, but there is some indication that that stance is beginning to change.[3]

Christians who oppose evolution and believe in a young earth and Christians who refuse to accept human contributions to global warming cite the Bible or theology as the foundation of their positions. This means that for these Christians, there is a conflict between the Bible and the findings of modern science.

I represent and write from a much different perspective—one that accepts and is comfortable with the findings of modern science. And I believe that when the limits of both science and theology are recognized, there need be no conflict between science and religion, and in particular, between science and the kind of Mennonite education represented in this volume. This statements needs an explanation.

I understand limits on science in two ways. I assume that God exists, and I assume that in some way God is responsible for the existence of the cosmos and everything in it. This means, I believe, that there should not be a conflict between the findings of science and what we can know about God who is the origin of all that is. With this statement I limit science to the extent that I reject the idea that science disproves the existence of God. More on this in a moment.

The second limit concerns recognizing that our model of the cosmos is just that—it is a model, not absolute truth. The observations of science reflect our current understanding of the world and the cosmos. Our present scientific answers provide models for describing the world around us. But these models are not absolutes. Since the models that describe the world have changed in the past, in some distant time, new and different models may emerge.

Two examples. In my youth, when I studied chemistry, I learned that an atom consisted of a nucleus (consisting of neutrons and protons) with electrons circling this nucleus. In more recent years, this model has been entirely abandoned and replaced by several more complex models. Rather than assuming neutrons and protons as the fundamental particles, scientists now think neutrons and protons are made of quarks, which are the fundamental particles.

At the cosmic level, long ago one ancient model of the cosmos pictured a flat earth with domes over it containing the astral bodies. The movement of these domes supplied the motion of the sun and moon, stars and planets. This model reflected the experience of people standing on the earth and looking up at the sky. Then as early as four centuries before Christ, philosophers such as Aristotle figured out that the earth was spherical, but they still thought it was stationary. Our language yet today reflects this cosmology, when we speak of the sun, moon, and planets rising and setting. Not until 1543 did astronomer Nicholas Copernicus propose the model eventually adopted, that of the rotating earth orbiting around the sun. Today our model of the universe would shock Copernicus. It describes an immense cosmos whose size seems virtually impossible to imagine (91 billion light years across) and even our entire galaxy is far from the center of this cosmos.

My point here is to say that models or pictures of the world and the cosmos have changed over the course of human history. Currently we are working with a model that works with what we know and observe in our time. However, we need to remember that it is not an absolute; it is rather a model and at some future time this model too may be abandoned and replaced by a different picture of the cosmos.

With these observations in mind, I suggest that Anabaptist theologian Nancey Murphy provides a way of understanding the compatibility of modern science and theology, including the acceptance of evolution and even a belief in the nonviolence of God. One comment describes the hierarchy in which Murphy arranges the sciences and the way that they relate to each other. At the lowest or subatomic level, physics studies atoms and the behavior of their constituent particles at the most basic or elemental level of reality. At the next level, chemistry deals with the preparation and properties of compounds made of atoms, followed by biology that studies whole organisms, including human beings.

Murphy describes a branching of the hierarchy at the level of humans. On one branch, the discipline of psychology deals with the behavior of individuals and sociology with groups, while the discipline of ethics establishes and evaluates criteria for behavior. On the other branch of the hierarchy, in the natural sciences, cosmology studies the physical universe. Murphy suggests that theology belongs at the top of each branch of this pyramid of ways of knowing about or describing the world.

At each level in the hierarchy, scientists can proceed without knowing all details in the previous level. For example, a chemist can process chemical equations of atoms without having to know how many quarks are in the nucleus of atoms. Or a biologists can analyze the function of water in the human body without dealing with water's composition of atoms of oxygen and hydrogen. Each of these sciences or ways of studying the world deals well with questions within its level. However, at the borders between these levels, questions appear that can only be answered at the next level below or above in the hierarchy. Our primary concern here is with the top of the hierarchy involving cosmology and theology.

At its level, theology asks questions and seeks answers, just as these are pursued in the preceding levels in the hierarchy. However, as do the other disciplines, theology has limits. It should not try to answer questions that properly belong to ways of knowing in the preceding levels. It can pose answers to ultimate questions about the nature of reality that appear at the borders of theology and the other ways of knowing, but theology cannot intercede in a lower realm and determine answers for scientists in their discipline. Examples here concern questions about the origin and age of the universe. In her chapter to follow, Angela Horn Montel discusses these limits in terms of the difference between methodological materialism and philosophical materialism.

In the science of cosmology, scientists observe the immense, almost incomprehensible size of the cosmos, and note that it is still expanding. By calculating its rate of expansion and the size it has reached, they arrive at an approximate age for the cosmos. Cosmologists believe that the expansion started with a gigantic explosion a bit more than 13 billion years ago. In popular language, this is called the "big bang theory."

There appears to be no definitive answer to the origin of the so-called "Big Bang" nor why it happened. Theology can posit one kind of answer—that the big bang originated with God, the eternal being. This answer is a hypothesis. Many cosmologists respond differently. They explain the big bang without God—suggesting that the cosmos may be involved in some kind of never-ending expansion and contraction—meaning matter is eternal. But this answer is also a hypothesis.

At this point, the limits of both cosmology and theology become visible. To posit eternal God as first cause with matter being created is not less logical than denying the existence of God and seeing matter as eternal. Theology should not reach down and attempt to tell cosmologists the age of the earth and to deny the reality of their observations, as do the young earth creationists, who claim that counting numbers of generations in the first chapters of Genesis puts the age of the earth at six to ten thousand years. But neither can cosmology reach into the realm of theology and claim to have proven that there is no God because God does not appear in a telescope. Theology's answer does not prove the existence of God nor definitively explain the origin of the cosmos. But for those who are willing to listen, Christian theology does make a meaningful observation about the physical world.[4]

It is possible to understand that this God of the "Big Bang" is the nonviolent God who is revealed in Jesus, and whose story was sketched in the first chapter of this book. This God is also compatible with the idea of evolution, as is also visible in Nancey Murphy's understanding. She is concerned to provide an understanding of God that is in accordance with the revelation of God in the nonviolence of Jesus, but that also envisions God's providential control of all reality while preserving human freedom and the freedom of creation. If creation and human beings are genuinely to have freedom, then God must not use coercion and must be nonviolent.

Murphy's argument assumes and works with modern scientific observations, but encompasses them within the reign of God. Within atoms, the location and movement of any one particle is random and unpredictable, while the behavior of matter as a whole is predictable. Murphy uses this randomness within predictability as an analogy for the image of God as creator who allows the freedom of creation. The characteristics of the expanding universe after the so-called Big Bang have allowed life to develop on our planet. Minute variations in conditions on earth would have rendered impossible life on earth as we know it. Theology at the top level of the pyramid of ways of knowing offers God as an explanation—from a Christian perspective—of the source of the universe, and within this universe humans could evolve in the image of the creator God.

The God of this process is the God who limited God's own power to allow the freedom of creation to develop, and to allow human beings the freedom to cause harm to the earth and to themselves. The noncoercive, nonviolent character of God is thus intrinsic to the process that created human beings by allowing them to evolve. It is also the case that God has to "suffer" the consequences, sometimes deadly consequences, of the freedom given to creation and to human beings. Those consequences include the careless human activity producing global warming.

This brief discussion has certainly not resolved all possible questions concerning the relationship of science, the Bible, and theology. It has however shown that future Mennonite education need not fear the findings of science for questions of human origins and the origins of the cosmos. By extension, Mennonite education can accept the findings of science in the area of global warming and can urge students to work at lessening the human contribution to this harm that threatens our planet. A peace church understanding of God is most certainly compatible with findings of science, when science and theology each recognize the limits of what they can know.

The final chapter of this book deals with one of these controversial questions in an educational setting. Angela Horn Montel discusses the teaching of evolution to students who enter the classroom assuming that it is incompatible with their Christian faith.

Notes

1. Comment came in an interview with Mike Wallace on *60 Minutes*. For a transcript of the interview, see http://www.cbsnews.com/news/mlk-a-riot-is-he-language-of-the-unheard/.

2. In fact, hundreds of millions of dollars are being spent to teach this anti-evolution, young earth, creationist view of human origins. In northern Kentucky there is the Creationist Museum which features dinosaurs and human beings living together. This museum and the website "Answers in Genesis" are dealt with in Angela Montel's chapter to follow. Most recently a replica of Noah's Ark opened with much media fan fare, and featuring multiple Mennonite and Amish contributions to the construction. Gene Stowe, "Ark Replicates Genesis: Craftsmen Follow Biblical Blueprint to Build Creation Museum Attraction," *Mennonite World Review* 94, no. 15 (19 July 2016): 1, 12; Emily McFarlan Miller, "At Ark Encounter, a 'Biblical Worldvierw' on Display," *Mennonite World Review* 94, no. 15 (19 July 2016): 12.

3. A Google search turns up various commentaries and discussions of Evangelicals and global warming.

1. For Nancey Murphy's philosophy of science, see Murphy, *Reconciling Theology and Science: A Radical Reformation Perspective* (Kitchener, Ont and Scottdale, Pa.: Pandora Press, co-published Herald Press,1997); Nancey Murphy and George F. R. Ellis, *On the Moral Nature of the Universe: Theology, Cosmology, and Ethics* (Minneapolis: Fortress Press, 1996).

SEVENTEEN

RESTORATIVE JUSTICE IN SCHOOLS

Lonna Stoltzfus

Introduction

Restorative justice, a social movement deeply rooted in age-old religious and cultural traditions, is an approach to justice that seeks to address the needs of those impacted by crime and wrongdoing, involving the individuals and community with a stake in the situation. While restorative justice and conventional justice both desire to hold wrongdoers accountable, restorative justice recognizes that punishment is often ineffective, and seeks to help wrongdoers understand the harm they have caused and encourages them to repair that harm to the extent possible. Howard Zehr, pioneer in the field of restorative justice since the beginning of the movement in the 1970s, and co-director of the Zehr Institute for Restorative Justice at Eastern Mennonite University [EMU], articulates these key understandings of restorative justice:

- Crime is a violation of people and of relationships.
- Violations create obligations.
- The central obligation of justice is to put right or restore the broken relationships.[1]

Restorative justice grows from the belief that people are fundamentally interconnected. When crime is committed, that web of relationships is disrupted. Thus, a restorative approach to justice calls us to attend to the needs of people who have been harmed and to work at restoring the relationships. At the same time, the approach recognizes that because of the nature of that web, people who cause harm may also have needs, and that damaged relationships, a disrupted web, may be both a cause and an effect of crime.

Restorative processes allow those who have been harmed opportunities to tell their stories and identify their needs, and they provide an opportunity for those who have caused harmed to understand the impact of their actions and to take steps to repair the harm. Such processes are intentionally collaborative and inclusive. They provide voice, respect, and dignity for everyone with a stake in the situation.

Restorative justice reflects beliefs Mennonites hold dear, of right relationships, just communities, and nonviolence. Mennonite institutions, including EMU's Center for Justice and Peacebuilding and Zehr Institute for Restorative Justice and Mennonite Central Committee (the social-action arm of the Mennonite church), have been instrumental in articulating the theory of restorative justice and in developing, implementing, and teaching processes which bring this theory to life in local settings and across the globe. The restorative justice movement continues to grow rapidly as a common sense, effective and moral approach to crime and other wrongdoing across various segments of society. It is being implemented in a variety of settings, including criminal and juvenile justice systems, schools, and faith communities.

Terminology

Terminology for restorative justice philosophy and practice varies. In this essay, I use *restorative justice* to describe the philosophy of a particular understanding of and response to crime and other wrongdoing. *Restorative practices* is then the term used to describe the various processes rooted in and that apply the principles of restorative justice. Some of these practices may be used more proactively. One such practice is the Circle process discussed in the following section. The remainder of this chapter discusses the application of restorative justice in school settings. Particular examples come from the Madison (Wisconsin) Metropolitan School District, in which I am employed.

Restorative Practices in Schools

Many years of research and experience have shown that punitive approaches to discipline in schools are not effective in producing the wanted outcomes. In addition to not "working," punitive, exclusionary discipline has a negative and disproportionate impact on students of color. It also increases the possibility of school dropout and the potential for youth to become involved in the juvenile/criminal justice system, a trajectory commonly referred to as the school-to-prison pipeline.

As many school districts are rethinking their discipline policies and practices and searching for effective alternatives, restorative practices are gaining recognition. Among the potentially positive impacts on school discipline is the alleviation of disparities based on race. A growing body of evidence points to the effectiveness of restorative practices in reducing unwanted behavior, maintaining safe learning environments, and decreasing racial disparities in school discipline. Such research includes a Rutgers University study[2] that explores the impact of restorative practices by teachers in the classroom, and an evaluation of the Oakland Unified School District's comprehensive restorative justice program.[3] A guidance package released jointly by the U.S. Departments of Education and Justice advocates for the continued development of restorative practices in schools.[4]

Restorative practices in schools focus on developing healthy relationships and creating peaceful, just, and equitable learning communities. More than being a set of strategies and skills, a restorative approach in schools involves a shift in culture. It is a way of being that must have deep roots in the values inherent in restorative justice and particular practices such as Circle process. Without this understanding, so-called restorative practices can be implemented in ways that are out of alignment with restorative justice values and may continue to perpetuate, or even deepen, alienation, inequity, and injustice. Principled implementation of restorative practices often requires not only a change in practice but a fundamental shift in beliefs and values.[5]

While each school or district engaging in restorative practices does so in ways that fit its unique context, there is often movement toward implementation of practices for the whole school based on a tiered model. The bottom or universal tier includes all members of the school community. In this tier, proactive practices focus on the critical elements of developing and maintaining strong, healthy relationships and a sense of belonging for each member of the classroom or school community. When positive relationships and a sense of belonging in a community are lacking, the likelihood increases of challenging and hurtful behaviors. Further, if interpersonal connections are negative or do not exist at all, there are obvious challenges inherent in trying to restore and repair relationships and a sense of belonging to a community. Thus investing in the development of positive, trusting, and respectful relationships among students, and between adults and students, both decreases the incidence of behaviors that damage relationships and community and increases the will and ability to repair those when needed.

Repairing harm and restoring relationships is the second tier of work. This tier may also include the use of restorative practices to address other difficult situations that arise.

Finally, the third tier involves the reintegration of students who have been excluded from school (for example, those who have been expelled or incarcerated) back into the school community after an extended absence, or intensive support through restorative processes.

As more schools seek to become restorative communities, several specific practices are gaining recognition and use. *Restorative conversations*, sometimes called restorative dialogues or restorative chats, can be used to address relatively simple situations in which behavior negatively impacts others. These conversations allow students and adults to reflect on what happened, who was harmed or impacted, and what is needed to repair that harm, areas Zehr identified as fundamental to explore in a restorative justice approach.[6]

Restorative conversations typically take place between an adult and only one or two students. They can happen immediately or relatively quickly in response to a situation and with little or no preparation. Such conversations may become almost second nature as adults learn to adopt a restorative approach, and gain comfort and skill with the structure of the conversation. In addition to encouraging students to reflect on their behavior and its impact on others, and to repair harm, restorative conversations can help adults to build understanding of the situation and possible contributing factors. These conversations can deepen empathy, respect, and trust between students and adults

The core practice being used in many schools is *Circle process*, sometimes referred to as peacemaking Circles, restorative Circles, or by the specific purpose of the Circle (e.g., community-building Circle, conflict

Circle, re-entry Circle). The Circle process has roots in values that foster positive human interaction and relationships and in the teachings of indigenous groups in many parts of the world. Carefully structured and intentional, the Circle relies on a number of elements including seating, the use of a talking piece, attention to identifying values and generating shared guidelines, carefully chosen guiding questions, and consensus decision-making to create a space for people to interact and communicate with authenticity, respect, and equal power and voice.[7]

In some ways simple and intuitive, the process of the Circle is at the same time nuanced, deep, and counter-cultural. It allows people to speak, listen, and understand in ways that may not typically happen in other settings or with other processes. Circle is an extremely flexible process and may be used for a wide range of situations and topics, including building relationships, resolving differences, discussing difficult topics, teaching and learning, repairing harm, providing support, and facilitating reentry.

In a growing number of middle and high schools, a group of students is trained in restorative justice and Circle keeping. Representative of the demographics of the school as a whole, these students learn important skills and have opportunity to be positive leaders in their school community and beyond.

Some communities and schools have a youth court (or peer- or teen court) to address behaviors that would otherwise be grounds for arrest and lead to involvement with the court system. While youth courts may be more, or less, restorative based on the language and model used, at their best they aim to help referred youth explore the harm caused in a situation and what is needed to make amends. In addition, they often explore contributing factors and needs of the referred student. They are a direct effort to keep youth out of the juvenile justice system, and students who successfully follow through on agreements remain out of the formal system.

Some schools create a Peace Room to serve as the physical hub of much of the restorative work.

The next section illustrates restorative justice in schools with stories from the Madison, Wisconsin, Metropolitan School District.

Restorative Justice in Schools of Madison, Wisconsin

Tier One Examples

At the universal level, classroom Circles are often used for community building, establishing classroom norms, welcoming new students, problem-solving, talking about difficult topics, developing social and emotional skills, and teaching and learning.

AVID—Advancement Via Individual Determination—is an effort to close the educational opportunity gap by preparing students for college, especially students typically underrepresented in higher education. In high school, AVID students join a cohort in ninth grade and stay with the same teacher and group of students throughout high school for their AVID experience. They become a family of sorts. One such group was often not working in ways that demonstrated full commitment to AVID expectations nor treating each other with the respect and care they all deserved as part of their group.

The teacher requested a series of Circles to build their community, reflect openly on concerns, and work together to make commitments to academic behaviors in line with AVID philosophy and personal interactions needed to strengthen the sense of an AVID community. A staff member and a student co-kept the Circle. The student was himself a senior AVID student, and a trained Circle Keeper. The Circle was initially challenging, with students demonstrating many of the behaviors of concern during the first rounds. But the structure of the process encouraged the students to interact in different ways than they often did outside of Circle. They came to listen respectfully without interrupting when others spoke, which created space for them to engage in meaningful dialogue around the concerns, and to make personal commitments and mutual agreements for their class that changed the course of their engagement and relationships.

At another Madison high school, a staff member was asked to lead a problem-solving Circle in a class that was experiencing chronic classroom climate issues. But unexpected things sometimes happen when people come together in authentic ways. The focus of this Circle quickly and spontaneously changed to one of giving and receiving support around the death of a local African American teen who had been fatally shot by a white police officer in the city two months before. There was grieving, laughter, and a strong sense of community in this group of students from many different walks of life. The previously identified issues of concern resolved themselves as a result of the students being able to process deeper feelings and needs. (Immediately following the shooting, this school, and others around the city, had also offered Circles for students to help process their grief and anger, and a bit later, to consider possible social actions to take and to talk about experiences related to race.)

Tier Two Examples

The second tier involves situations where more significant harm has been done (fight, harassment, vandalism), or there is conflict. Circles are used to bring together those involved in the situation to explore what has happened, to process feelings, and to determine how things can be made right or what agreements and support are needed to move forward constructively.

During lunch one day, a small group of students were dancing in an out-of-the-way hallway. Another student came quickly around the corner and nearly ran into them. Tempers flared, and racially offensive language was exchanged that could have resulted in suspensions on both sides (the group of students was Latino; the single student was African American). A staff member intervened before a fight broke out, and the decision was made to invite the students to participate in Circle together. If they could talk through the situation, resolve the conflict peacefully, and follow through with any agreements made, none would be suspended.

Student Circle Keepers, with staff support, led the Circle. Students who not long before had been ready to fight shared their perspectives of and feelings about the situation and listened respectfully to each other. They each voluntarily apologized for their part in it and for the hurtful words they had said; they agreed to put the conflict to rest. Then they returned to class and finished the school day. Relationships were repaired, lost instruction time was minimized, and school order and safety were maintained.

In another situation, a conflict erupted between two students at a city bus stop. It became physical, resulting in one of them losing bus privileges for the remainder of the semester. The young man, white, and with a cognitive disability, had used racially offensive and hurtful language in speaking to the young woman of color. He had already been suspended that year for use of offensive racial language which was considered harassment. Because city bus stops are outside the jurisdiction of the school, the school would not be involved in a disciplinary response in this incident. The school did, however, intervene to help create understanding, repair relationships, and try to prevent similar situations in the future.

In planning the intervention, the school staff involved were unsure whether the male student would be able to appropriately participate in Circle with the female student. Thus they planned a Circle that did not include the young woman and invited another student who had not been involved to participate. Because he was African American, had a brother with a disability, and was a trained Circle Keeper, he had a valuable perspective to offer. In the Circle the student involved in the incident gained understanding of how his behavior and language was hurtful and inappropriate. He also was able to share how some of his negative feelings and beliefs grew out of hurtful interactions he experienced when he was younger.

School staff then decided it would be appropriate to bring the young woman together with him to work through the situation. At that time, he sincerely apologized for how he had hurt her; she developed understanding and empathy for him and ultimately advocated successfully on his behalf for the reinstatement of his bus privileges. There were no more known incidents that year in which the young man used racially charged language with another student.

Tier Three Example

A few students each year are out of school for an extended time due to hospitalization or treatment, expulsion, or incarceration. A re-entry Circle offers an opportunity to bring together the student, parent or caregiver, key school staff, and supportive people in the community to welcome the student back and help to create a positive and successful transition.

Staff

As students are experiencing the power of Circles, staff are as well. Increasingly, staff groups are engaging in Circle to deepen their relationships and connections, identify and reflect on shared values as educators (especially important when the work is challenging, and shifts in thinking and practice are required), engage in critical and challenging conversations around racial bias and equity, and resolve conflict. In addition, a district level group of staff charged with supporting students and schools when there is a critical incident such as a death also sits in Circle following these situations. They reflect on the personal and cumulative impact of providing such support and undergird each other in this work.

Implications for Mennonite Education

Mennonites have made and continue to make significant contributions to the restorative justice movement. Our theology, values and practices regarding relationships and community, and particular institutional efforts have often supported this work. It is a gift that Mennonites have the privilege of offering a world in desperate need of justice and healing. Eastern Mennonite University has taken another step in leading this work by offering an interdisciplinary concentration in Restorative Justice in Education (RJE) for students pursuing an MA in Education, the first restorative justice program in a graduate teacher education program in the country. EMU also offers a certificate in RJE for non-graduate degree students.

In these programs, K-12 educators are being explicitly trained to be leaders in restorative justice work in public and private schools. We know that this approach holds great promise for impacting school discipline, including the racial disparities involved in school discipline, as well as other outcomes. How much broader and deeper might the impact be if more Mennonite institutions of higher education considered adding courses in restorative justice and practices for aspiring teachers, social workers, and church leaders as a way of sharing the good news of right relationships, peace, equity, and justice?

At the same time that many around the country and around the globe are benefiting from Mennonite contributions, there is room for growth of understanding and practice in our own institutions, churches, schools, and homes. Establishing and maintaining a sense of belonging in a community may seem almost second nature for many Mennonite communities, yet as the church grows and changes, some among us do not yet feel this sense of belonging. We care deeply about the peaceful resolution of conflict yet often find ourselves "resolving" our differences by denying them or parting ways with those with whom we disagree.

Here I echo the concerns expressed by Hannah Heinzekehr's chapter in this book. In our own institutions, faith communities, and homes, individuals have been deeply wounded; that harm and the resulting needs have not always been recognized or attended to adequately. The issues related to LGBTQ inclusion are a visible current example of our own failure to respond to differences lovingly. The way we have often addressed situations of sexual misconduct of leaders in our churches and institutions exemplifies our shortcomings in acknowledging harm and supporting healing.

In addition to being something we offer to a world in need, restorative justice can be, must be, an intentional and consistent way of being for ourselves as well. Restorative practices as a way of being together in community can strengthen the healthy development of individuals and of our communities, and the integrity of our work and witness in the world. Restorative justice principles and restorative practices build strong and healthy relationships and communities in which hierarchies are flattened, each person is included and valued, each voice is heard, difficulties are resolved openly and constructively, and the needs of those harmed are identified and met.

Some of this work already happens because of what we believe and who we are together at our best, whether or not we know to call it restorative justice. Using and teaching these practices more intentionally in our schools, from kindergarten to college and seminary, would be a natural expression of our values, help to create stronger, healthier, more inclusive communities, and prepare our children, youth, and young adults to be leaders in this critical and hopeful work of peace and justice in the world.

Notes

1. Howard Zehr, *The Little Book of Restorative Justice* (Intercourse, Pa.: Good Books, 2002), 21.

2. Anne Gregory, Kathleen Clawson, Alycia Davis, and Jennifer Gerewitz, "The Promise of Restorative Practices to Transform Teacher-Student Relationships and Achieve Equity in School Discipline," *Journal of Educational and Psychological Consultation* (4 Nov. 2014), http://www.tandfonline.com/doi/pdf/10.1080/10474412.2014.929950 <4 Aug. 2017>

3. Sonia Jain, Henrissa Bassey, Martha A. Brown, and Kalra Preety, "Restorative Justice in Oakland Schools: Implementation and Impacts" (2014), http://www.

ousd.org/cms/lib07/CA01001176/Centricity/Domain/134/OUSD-RJ%20Report%20revised%20Final.pdf <11 April 2016>.

4. Catherine E. Lhamon and Jocelyn Samuels, "Dear Colleague Letter on the Nondiscriminatory Administration of School Discipline" (2014), http://www2.ed.gov/about/offices/list/ocr/letters/colleague-201401-title-vi.pdf <11 April 2016>.

5. Kathy Evans, "Restorative Justice in Education—Possibilities but Also Concerns" (2014), http://emu.edu/now/restorative-justice/2014/06/26/restorative-justice-in-education-possibilities-but-also-concerns/ <11 April 2016>.

6. Zehr, *Little Book of Restorative Justice*, 21.

7. Carolyn Boyes-Watson and Kay Panis, *Circle Forward: Building a Restorative School Community* (St. Paul, Minn.: Living Justice Press, 2015).

EIGHTEEN

FORGIVENESS: PSYCHOLOGY, JESUS, AND THEOLOGY

J. Denny Weaver

In October 2006, the United States and much of the world was shocked when a shooter opened fire in the Old Order Amish school of West Nickel Mines in Lancaster, Pennsylvania, and killed five children and wounded five others. Then the nation looked on in amazement as the Amish announced that they had forgiven the shooter and reached out with material assistance to his wife.[1] This story constitutes a graphic example of the kind of forgiveness that we see modeled by Jesus in the story of the woman taken in adultery and exhibited by the father in the parable of the prodigal son. (Both texts are discussed below.)

Understanding forgiveness has important implications for the way we think about God as well as for our relationships with others. Forgiveness involves another aspect of breaking a cycle of violence, and it presents another place to discover the grain of the universe.

Forgiveness in Psychology

Psychologists talk about forgiveness quite apart from discussion of the story of Jesus or of theology. In fact, according to recent research in psychology, practicing forgiveness is a healthy activity in and of itself.

The common expression is "forgive and forget," but that is not what forgiveness means in psychology.[2]

As understood in psychology, forgiveness means to let go of the anger that a person feels toward the individual or group or institution that has committed the wrong. A person who carries that anger is allowing the wrong to control the emotions. For example, someone may say, "Because this individual wronged me, I will never be able to _____." The claim is that because of a wrong received, a person can never again be happy or visit a certain place or engage in a specific activity or any number of other things. Advice columns in daily newspapers, for example, frequently feature letters from people who have refused to speak to a parent or sibling or one-time friend because of some offense, real or imagined. This angry person is carrying a psychological burden that impacts that way he or she lives. And in this case, the psychologist says, the person wronged is giving the perpetrator control over emotions or actions. Forgiveness means to let go of the anger so that it no longer controls emotions or actions. This process of letting go allows the individual to be free of the burden of anger being carried. It means moving from the state of being a victim to taking control of ones life. The result is improved psychological health of the one who forgives.

A typical program of forgiveness in psychology begins by acknowledging that the person has indeed been wronged. And it involves recognizing the burden that comes with carrying the anger, along with a desire to be free of this burden. The process of forgiveness then requires offering a small, unmerited gift to the perpetrator. This gift may be as small as saying, "I forgive," but it is the beginning of the process of letting go of the anger toward the perpetrator.

If the perpetrator acknowledges his or her harm committed, reconciliation may sometimes occur between victim and perpetrator. If the perpetrator does not acknowledge the wrong committed and reconciliation does not occur, the one offering forgiveness is nonetheless keeping that possibility open. But even if there is no reconciliation, the goal of forgiveness is for the person harmed to become free of the burden of anger that binds and controls.

This kind of forgiveness certainly does not mean "forgetting." In fact, the statement "I forgive" is a clear recognition that a wrong was committed. It means that despite that wrong, the individual will work at letting go of anger toward the perpetrator. Offering forgiveness does not mean that a perpetrator is absolved of accountability for the wrong committed. On the contrary, true forgiveness means recognizing who is responsible. With forgiveness, restoration is required whenever possible;[3] but forgiveness can occur even if the perpetrator refuses to accept responsibility. For reprehensible deeds, the perpetrator who receives forgiveness may need to be confined. The point is that forgiveness is not about how serious the wrong was or whether the perpetrator confesses and offers restitution. Forgiveness concerns the one who practices forgiveness. And it is practiced for the health of this individual whether or not the perpetrator expresses remorse and offers restitution.

To be emphasized is that this practice of forgiveness can be very difficult. For serious offenses, the one wronged may need to repeat the process many times, each time with a bit more success. In essence, this kind of forgiveness is a way of life, a way to live without retaliating and without holding grudges about what has happened. Psychologists describe this ability to practice forgiveness, that is, to live without built-up anger, as one of the keys to happiness.

A word of caution is also in order. In cases of horrendous offenses, forgiveness may in fact seem impossible. It is important to remember Robert Enright's statement that "forgiveness is a choice," which is also the title of his book. In the case of horrendous offenses, it may take a long time for someone to reach the point of wanting to forgive. A choice not to forgive must be honored. An offended person can start or stop and restart the process a number of times. No one else can decide for another that forgiveness is appropriate, and no one should be coerced or shamed into attempting the process of forgiveness. Further, forgiveness does not mean trusting the offender. In cases such as spousal abuse or sexual assault or pedophilia, appropriate safeguards must be in place to protect the one who has forgiven.[4]

In a final comment on forgiveness as understood in psychology, note that forgiveness practiced by the one who forgives occurs apart from punishment of the perpetrator. The significance of this comment becomes clear in what follows.

Forgiveness and Jesus

This description of forgiveness from psychology is reflected in the narrative of Jesus. The first part of John 8 has a story of forgiveness. The scribes and Pharisees brought a women to Jesus who had been caught in adultery. They pointed out that the law of Moses called for stoning such a woman and asked Jesus what he thought. His answer was that the one without sin should throw the first stone. They all left. With none left to condemn her, Jesus said that he also would not condemn her. But he did not ignore the sin. He told her not to do it again. Although the term *forgiveness* is not used, I suggest that this is a story of forgiveness without punishment. She was admonished not to sin again, but this sin was not held against her. She was forgiven.

The well-known Parable of the Prodigal Son presents forgiveness without punishment. The prodigal had demanded his inheritance, and then ran off to a far country where he wasted his money in riotous living. Flat broke and feeding pigs, he finally decided to return home and offer to work as a hired hand. But when he was still a great distance away, his father saw him. Forgetting all elderly dignity, the father ran to greet the returning prodigal, welcomed him, and proclaimed a great feast in celebration.

It is clear that the father had long waited with open arms to welcome the prodigal home. There was no word of punishment for wasted money nor a process by which the prodigal would need to earn his way back. He was simply welcomed with open arms. This is forgiveness without punishment. It was not entirely free to the prodigal, however. He had to acknowledge his fault and commit to make a change. In contrast to the father, the older brother complained about the welcoming celebration. A desire for punishment of the returned prodigal is certainly implied in the complaint.

Forgiveness and Love of Enemies

In Chapter 1, we observed that in the Sermon on the Mount, Jesus said, "Love your enemies." This love is not the romantic love of affection. Rather we saw that it meant not to retaliate in kind, not to respond to evil or violence with the same kind of evil or violence. It means to respond to evil or confrontation by changing the situation. Jesus gave three examples of responses that do not mirror evil—turn the other cheek, give underwear with outerwear, and go the second mile. Such responses diffuse a situation and have the potential to change a tense relationship. Sayings from Paul and Peter express the same idea, namely rather than responding to evil with evil, one should respond to evil with good.

I believe that the practice of forgiveness as described here is another way to express love of enemies by acting to change the situation. Offering the unmerited gift to the offender is returning good for evil. The act of letting go of anger—that is, of forgiving—certainly benefits the one who forgives, but by offering the unmerited gift to the offender, the possibility is open of a restored relationship. Thus I suggest that the practice of forgiveness is another dimension of Jesus' statement "Love your enemies" and of Paul and Peter's injunctions to "return good for evil."

Forgiveness has yet another link to chapter 1. We saw that working with the nonviolent Jesus was to be in line with the "grain of the universe." Retaliating against violence and evil with more of the same continues a cycle of violence, while loving enemies and returning good for evil—that is, working with the grain of the universe—changes the situation and reduces violence. In this chapter we have talked about the practice of forgiveness as another example of expressing love of enemy and changing the situation. And with forgiveness, there is research evidence from psychology to show that practicing forgiveness really does improve the health of the one who practices it. Research in psychology done without reference to Christian ethics has demonstrated the truthfulness of the practice of forgiveness.

What psychologists have discovered through their research corresponds to what Christians can find in the teaching of Jesus. Forgiveness is another example of the grain of the universe, another example that the nonviolence of the Christian story is not an abstract principle that exists apart from Jesus and is then read back into the story. Rather, we read the story and come to the understanding that rejection of violence is intrinsic to that story. And since God is revealed in Jesus, it is apparent that nonviolence characterizes God and the reign of God and God's means of acting in the world.

When we know that Jesus' rejection of violence reflects the God who created the universe, we can then observe that the truth of the rejection of violence is visible in the world. Thus rejecting violence, loving enemies, returning good for evil, practicing forgiveness, are the best ways to live in God's universe. Research in psychology can demonstrate the benefit of practicing forgiveness, but the ultimate validation of forgiveness comes from the narrative of Jesus in whom God is revealed.

Forgiveness in Atonement Images

The inherited atonement motifs present an image of God distinctly different from Jesus who forgave without punishment or from offering the unmerited gift in the practice of forgiveness. In the inherited understandings of atonement, in particular for the satisfaction and penal substitution motifs, God can forgive sinners because Jesus has first paid the price for sins. For the satisfaction motif, sinners have offended God's honor and distorted the order of the universe. God cannot forgive until satisfaction is made for that sin. But since God sent Jesus to die on our behalf to pay the satisfaction we (sinners) owed to God, God can indeed forgive those who repent and turn to God.

Similarly, for penal substitution, God cannot forgive until the penalty demanded by God's law has been paid. Since Jesus was punished in our place, the penalty demanded by the law was satisfied, and God can then forgive sinners who avail themselves of Jesus' sacrifice. God cannot forgive those who do not accept Jesus' sacrifice on their behalf. Stated differently, God holds onto God's anger and withholds forgiveness until compensation has been paid to God and sinners have appropriated it for themselves.

Now consider these inherited atonement images in light of the description of forgiveness in psychology. In satisfaction and substitutionary atonement images, God uses or sanctions violence, and God holds on to anger until God's justice has been satisfied. God arranged for Jesus to die to fulfill a divine need, whether for satisfaction of honor or to pay the penalty demanded by God's law. In other words, for these atonement images, God's forgiveness depends on God's prior sanctioning of violence against Jesus. These atonement images link forgiveness to divine violence. Compared with psychology, while human forgiveness is depicted as letting go of anger, God holds on to anger, exacting punishment or satisfaction on Jesus, before forgiveness can occur. In these images of forgiveness, God acts differently from humans. Humans offer the unmerited gift of forgiveness to the perpetrator, whereas God demands punishment as the basis of forgiveness.

Recall the narrative of Jesus sketched in Chapter 1. It says nothing about his death satisfying a debt owed to God or paying the penalty of God's law. The narrative climaxes with resurrection while the satisfaction images ignore it entirely. These atonement images feature a vengeful God, who has Jesus killed to satisfy God's justice. It stands in contrast to the nonviolent God from the Old Testament whose story continues in Jesus, as described in Chapter 7.

When we read the Gospels, we see that Jesus' life, his actions, and his teaching, made present the reign of God. These actions challenged the legitimacy of the religious authorities. These authorities generated a plot to have him killed. Evil powers, represented by the religious leadership in Jerusalem and above all by the Roman empire, put him to death on a cross. But after three days, God raised him from the dead. Rather than picturing a God who demands death as the price of forgiveness, the God of this story restores life and is revealed in Jesus as the source of live.

This outline of the life of Jesus presents the story as one in which the powers of evil that killed Jesus are overcome or defeated by the resurrection. In classic language this is the atonement image of Christ the Victor or Christus Victor. In the early church, Christus Victor described a confrontation in the cosmos between God and Satan. However, I have brought the confrontation down to earth and visualized it between Jesus, who represents the reign of God, and Rome and the religious leadership, who represent the powers of evil. Because my version uses the story of Jesus, it is a narrative Christus Victor.

When looked at from the point of view of the activity of God, narrative Christus Victor is a nonviolent atonement image. The evil that killed Jesus was perpetrated by humans while God acted to restore life. Restoring life stands in sharp contrast to the role of God in satisfaction atonement, where God needed a death and sent Jesus to be killed to supply that death. Narrative Christus Victor is thus *nonviolent atonement*, the name I have come to use for this motif.[5]

Compare the violence based divine forgiveness of the satisfaction motifs with God's forgiveness as depicted in nonviolent atonement. All human beings are involved in the forces of evil in the world. These are powers with which the Romans and religious leaders cooperated in killing Jesus. It is thus possible to say that all human beings have been involved with the powers that killed Jesus. But when these powers killed Jesus, God responded by raising Jesus from the dead.

Resurrection then poses an invitation to join in and live in the story of Jesus and participate in the reign of God, including a future resurrection. In the language used for psychology, God has let go of anger against those who cooperated with the evil powers that killed Jesus and has offered the gift of fellowship with God. No punishment is involved as the prior basis for this forgiveness. This offer of forgiveness is an unmerited, free gift, given to sinful humanity by a gracious God. God lets go of anger against sinful humans and forgives. This is divine forgiveness without exacting punishment.

This divine forgiveness in nonviolent atonement reflects the same impulse that human forgiveness does as described by psychologists. God offers unmerited forgiveness to sinners, which can be understood as parallel to the impulse of forgiveness by human beings as described in psychology.

Synthesis

The parable of the Prodigal Son (Luke 15:11-32) brings together this discussion of atonement images and forgiveness. It is a story that portrays forgiveness as letting go of justifiable anger. The prodigal wasted his inheritance and returned home in a desolate state, to offer to work as a hired hand. But the father welcomed him back to the family with open arms and proclaimed a great feast in celebration. Meanwhile, the older brother was angry.

The figures of father and prodigal reflect the impulses of nonviolent atonement. The father is an image of God, who has been sinned against by humankind; the prodigal who offended the father and the family is like sinful humans who sinned against God by participating in the death of Jesus. But as God restored Jesus to life and offers grace to sinners without exacting a penalty or compensation, the father welcomes the son without penalty and proclaims a great celebration of his return to the family. Meanwhile, from the reaction of the older brother, it appears that he believes the returning prodigal should have to do some kind of penance, such as work as a servant until wasted money has been repaid. The older brother's reaction aligns itself with the satisfaction images of atonement.

Forgiveness and Restorative Justice

Restorative justice seeks to restore relationships that have been broken by the perpetrator of harm. Restorative justice works with all sides of the problem, the victim or victims who have suffered harm, and the perpetrator(s) of that harm.

As discussed in this chapter, forgiveness concerns the victim. Forgiveness describes a process that leads to the psychological healing of the victim, who ceases being a victim. By letting go of anger against the perpetrator, the victim becomes stronger and healthier. As part of the process, the victim—the one practicing forgiveness—offers an unmerited gift to the perpetrator, who may or may not receive it. The ultimate outcome may be full restoration and reconciliation of victim and offender. This goal of full restoration and reconciliation may be difficult to achieve and long in coming, but it can begin with the gift offered by the victim.

But in some, even many instances, forgiveness may not lead to restoration. Important to realize is that forgiveness serves first of all the health and well-being of the person offended. Forgiveness is what enables the victim to cease being a victim and become someone whose psyche is no longer dominated by anger at the perpetrator. As victims let go of anger, they gain control of their lives, and anger at the perpetrator no longer controls them. Their emotions are no longer controlled by the offender, and ceasing to be a victim does not depend on the response of the perpetrator. Forgiveness is the work of the one who forgives. It involves letting go of anger toward the perpetrator, but not necessarily a restoration of trust. Safeguards may remain permanently in place.

Notes

1. The story of the shooting at the West Nickel Mines school, along with a general introduction to the Old Order Amish, appears in Donald B. Kraybill, Steven M. Nolt, and David L. Weaver-Zercher, *Amish Grace: How Forgiveness Transcended Tragedy* (San Francisco: Jossey-Bass, 2007).

2. The description of the practice of forgiveness in this chapter follows Robert D. Enright, *Forgiveness is a Choice: A Step-by-Step Process for Resolving Anger and Restoring Hope* (Washington, D.C.: American Psychological Association, 2001). The discussion to follow draws on material in Chapter 5 of J. Denny Weaver, *God Without Violence: Following a Nonviolent God in a Violent World* (Eugene, Ore.: Cascade Books, 2016).

3. At this point, the practice of forgiveness intersects with the practice of restorative justice described in the introduction to Part Six and in Chapter 18. In language similar to that used in this chapter, Howard Zehr's seminal book on restorative justice describes forgiveness as "letting go of the power the offense and the offender have over a person. It means no longer letting the offense and offender dominate." Howard Zehr, *Changing Lenses: A New Focus for Crime and Justice*, 3rd ed., A Chris-

tian Peace Shelf Selection (Scottdale, Pa.: Herald Press, 2005), 47.

4. See Enright, *Forgiveness is a Choice*, 37-39, 41-42, 74, 133.

5. For an extended development of the motif called narrative Christus Victor, see the first three chapters of J. Denny Weaver, *The Nonviolent Atonement*, 2nd ed., greatly rev. and expanded (Grand Rapids, Mich.: William B. Eerdmans Publishing Co., 2011). For a discussion of this motif as nonviolent atonement and directed to a popular audience, see the first three chapters of Weaver, *God Without Violence*.

CHAPTER NINETEEN

TEACHING THE "PACIFIST'S DILEMMA"

Zachary J. Walton

Introduction

Okay, you are a pacifist. "What would you do if a criminal, say, pulled a gun and threatened to kill your wife?"[1] The assumption behind the question is that there are two, and only two, options: either do nothing or kill the attacker.

Many readers of the book in hand have likely faced this hypothetical situation from an interlocutor, often within minutes or even seconds of the beginning of a conversation about war and peace. Students in my communication classes frequently appeal to this hypothetical situation to support military conflict. In the telling, minor variations may appear in details. For example, the "innocent" in the situation may be not only my wife but also a mother or daughter or sister yet always female and pictured as absolutely helpless, mere objects in the scene. Such variations, however, are relatively inconsequential to the underlying argumentative structure and the foundational logic of the posed hypothetical situation.

Regardless of the specific details, the inquisitor assumes that the situation as presented serves as an absolutely airtight case. The example presents what I call "the pacifist's dilemma." In this chapter, I will outline how I approach this "dilemma" in my communication classes.

To the interlocutor, the "answer" to the pacifist's dilemma seems so self-evident, so obvious, so beyond question that the hypothetical situation itself functions more like a rhetorical question than an actual question. It is an example of what philosopher Richard Rorty calls a conversation-stopper, meaning an utterance meant to shut down debate rather that encourage argument.[2]

This ubiquitous hypothetical situation is a dilemma in at least two senses. For one, it is parallel in function and structure to other thought scenarios, such as the prisoner's dilemma and the trolley problem, which are designed to pose highly abstract moral situations rarely, if ever, actually faced in real-world situations.[3] Second, for the individual committed to nonviolence, it is also a dilemma because we know the fundamental assumptions are incorrect, yet it is challenging concisely and convincingly to expose the fundamental faulty assumptions of the scenario in the moment in the classroom.

There's a good chance that when a student poses the question in class, the questioner believes he or she has conclusively ended and won the argument and is not expecting a serious response. In addition, I am usually faced with an audience of other student onlookers and a sense that if I cannot provide a legitimate counter-argument, there may be little reason for them thoughtfully to consider the possibility of nonviolence as a viable personal commitment and political option.

Therefore, encountering the pacifist's dilemma in the classroom requires ability to respond carefully and succinctly in the moment in improvisational ways pedagogically appropriate to students' deep-seated ideological commitments. Indeed, a factor that motivated me to study in the communication discipline was the challenge of responding to this argument in a convincing way. In doing so, I had the opportunity to study rhetorical criticism, argumentation studies, and other persuasive approaches to discourse. As a result, I have the opportunity to teach a wide-ranging set of classes in which I can easily integrate the pacifist's dilemma as a pedagogical tool.

In this chapter, I will share some of my approaches in responding to the pacifist's dilemma in pedagogical contexts. For this discussion, I will consider the rhetoric of thought experiments and how I integrate elements of rhetorical theory and criticism into my classes to challenge students to investigate the argumentative structure and assumptions implicit in the hypothetical situation.

I suggest that encountering the pacifist's dilemma serves as an important pedagogical opportunity to help students become more complex thinkers and to question assumptions and arguments that they carry around in everyday life. It also serves as a basis for challenging them to dig more deeply into their already given notions of the place of violence in our culture. The discussion works because it is familiar and most students believe that they already know the answer—that there are only two possibilities and that only the use of lethal violence is morally permissible and responsible. But once the alternative approaches are presented in a credible light, this can spark students' moral imaginations. I have found that when I add a number of alternatives and complexities to the well-known pacifist dilemma, students are far more receptive to discussions of nonviolence and just peacemaking without falling back on this unrealistic and logically inconsistent hypothetical situation.

Thought Experiments

Thought experiments—the type of hypothetical argumentation that characterizes the pacifist's dilemma—are highly, though not obviously, rhetorical in nature. By "rhetoric," I mean something that goes beyond mere ornamentation or stylistics. Rather, contemporary rhetorical theorists and critics such as myself suggest that the framing of any given discourse is intrinsic to its meaning and influences our perception. Put another way, the structure and assumptions intrinsic in any symbolic exchange direct our attention in one direction or another. In the case of the pacifist's dilemma, it may be in ways that obfuscate other possible responses other than passive non-engagement or lethal response.

Communication scholar Kenneth Burke has been instrumental in redefining our understanding of the term *rhetoric* as foundational to human symbol. One of Burke's key conceptions is the notion of "terministic screens." Since any given terminology is "a reflection of reality," he famously argued, that terminology is by its very nature "a selection of reality; and to this extent it must function as a deflection of reality." For Burke, the use of any particular set of terms functions like a color filter on a camera by allowing some concepts or ideas to be foregrounded while forcing others into the background.[4] The terms that one uses direct attention in one way or another. These are not biases that one could simply choose to do without. "Since we can't say anything without the use of terms," Burke notes, any terms we use will "necessarily constitute a corresponding kind of screen; and any screen necessarily directs the attention to one field rather than another."[5]

With this conceptual framework of rhetorical influence in view, I first ask my students, what terministic screens might be at work in the pacifist's dilemma? How do the details of the dilemma and what the dilemma omits shape our perception of possible responses as, again in Burke's words, the "spinning out of possibilities implicit in our particular choice of terms?"[6]

My first move would be to examine the rhetorical construction of the question itself in specific examples of the presentation of the pacifist's dilemma. I ask students to notice and analyze the most prominent elements often foregrounded while also noting what possibilities and details are pushed into the background and how these conception frames might influence the perception of the dilemma and our response to the situation.

The first step in rhetorical analysis is to have students classify the pacifist's dilemma by discursive genre. Is it an example? A metaphor? An analogy? A narrative? Once we place it in genre, we can note the common structures shared among other devices in that genre and how the pacifist's dilemma might deviate from those common elements. I help students to define the pacifist's dilemma as a hypothetical thought experiment rather than a real-world example that could be the building block for inductive reasoning.

Fantastical thought experiments, such as the pacifist's dilemma, regularly appear in everyday argumentation when real examples are not possible. Such hypotheticals have a long history in Western thinking, Plato's allegory of the cave being one of the most well-known and significant. Other popular and contemporary ethical and psychological thought experiments include the well-known trolley problem and the prisoner's dilemma, but there are many others. These thought experiments attempt to demonstrate argumentative or philosophical principles where a real example is not available or unrealistically feasible to test.

I do not oppose thought experiments *per se*, and there are good reasons to think that thought experiments are intrinsic to the moral reasoning process. However, thought experiments become problematic when the low material and ethical realism common to thought experiments comes to characterize and justify real-world violence, which is the case with the pacifist's dilemma. My objection is that the highly speculative and abstract parameters of the pacifist's dilemma are easily confused as a concrete and common ethical conundrum with a self-evident answer. In other words, I do not object to using Plato's allegory of the cave to illustrate philosophical principles but think it would be a poor guide to spelunking.

In my experience, nearly all of my students are familiar with the pacifist's dilemma; if not the specifics, than the general outlines of the situation artificially generate a false dilemma between tragic non-involvement or a lethal response. However, their easy confidence in responding to it lacks any comparable personal experience or parallel real-life example in their everyday lives. When pushed, none of my interlocutors can provide a situation from their lived experience that shares any but the roughest outline with the pacifist's dilemma.

I have found that once I add a proper amount of alternatives and complexities to the pacifist dilemma that many know so well, students are far more receptive to discussions of nonviolence and just peacemaking without falling back or relying on this unrealistic and logically inconsistent hypothetical situation as a conversation-stopper. In this case, it is not hard to see how far the pacifist's dilemma is linked to what Walter Wink calls "the myth of redemptive violence," the idea that violence is the ultimate problem solver, and the fundamental narrative that informs a lifetime consumption of violent television, film, video games, and other elements of violent popular culture.[7]

After having assigned Wink's short essay, I use a classroom exercise that easily demonstrates the prevalence of the myth of redemptive violence. I ask my students to name every movie, TV show, comic book, and so forth, in which the protagonist uses violence to defeat an aggressive antagonist and thus save or defend the lives of innocents. The answers can easily fill one or more dry-erase boards with examples. I then ask them, out of the list they've created, to identify which depict the protagonist "getting the girl" at the conclusion of the narrative; I'll say more about this shortly.

Then I ask them to fill the board with every movie, TV show, and more in which a conflict generated by an aggressor is resolved by the protagonist or protagonists using means other than violence. Often the board is nearly empty and might include only one or two examples. This procedure is especially useful when the violent movies are visible on the same black or dry erase board as the small list of alternatives. Students can see the ongoing repetition of the violent stories they have been told through these media compared with the very few ways of thinking about alternatives to violence.

This classroom exercise is a variation of cultural theorist Slavoj Zizek's claim that our ideological horizon is framed in such a way that it is easier to imagine total extinction of life on this planet than to imagine viable alternatives to the ideological horizon of capitalism.[8]

The pacifist's dilemma shares the same drawbacks of other fantastical thought experiments meant to draw out moral or ethical connections. Few respondents have direct experience with the scenarios. A 2014 article argues that these types of hypothetical thought experiments

> are low in mundane realism because it is hard to imagine how that could happen in real life . . . [and also] are low in psychological realism because the implausibility of the scenario[s] decouples moral reproach from judgments of immorality—a link that is fundamental to the way people experience moral situations and commonly observed in other research.[9]

Indeed, there is a growing body of academic work, produced by contemporary moral philosophers and psychologists, which suggests that these hypothetical thought experiments provide little to no useful information regarding the processes of human moral reasoning or ethical decision making. Such is the case with the pacifist's dilemma as it is commonly deployed to respond to the issue of violent situations at the individual level.

The Significance of Address

Rather than a useful guide for pragmatic action in responding to instances of interpersonal violence, the pacifist's dilemma and other moral thought experiments tell us more about the teller of the tale rather than the respondent or the moral issue itself. In an extensive study of the rhetorical nature of thought experiments, communication scholar

Lawrence Souder found that variations in the specific details of individual thought experiments tend to "reflect certain goals and self images" of the narrator and the audience.[10] In other words, much like Burke's notion of terministic screens, the details of any given thought experiment, and the perspective and knowledge of the characters and their motivations, all play a consequential, or even central, role in the ideological horizon from which dialogue partners participate in the communicative exchange.

First, note that in almost every case, the pacifist's dilemma is posed from the second-person perspective: "What would you do?" In facing the pacifists, we rarely hear the encounter narrated from an abstracted third-person perspective and only rarely from the first-person perspective. The phrasing of the pacifist's dilemma in the second person encourages subjects to relate to the conditions of their world in particular ways.[11]

To demonstrate, notice the ideological shifts that accompany a change in the perspective in which the dilemma is posed: "What should the onlooker do?" "What would I do?" or "What would we do?" From the standpoint of Anabaptist epistemology, the latter communally focused rephrasing seems particularly apt. From a broader ideological perspective, in the case of the pacifist's dilemma, except for the innocent and helpless victim, the address of "you" strips out all social background and character, including the social embeddedness or relationship of the attacker in relation to the other participants in the setting, as well as the material and ideological setting of the scene. The setting is an argumentative framework closer to the logical fallacy of the *ad hominem* attack—one that calls into question the character of the individual addressed rather than the substance of his or her argument.

Further, the dualistic phrasing of the question constitutes an additional logical fallacy—the "loaded question"—functionally equivalent to a statement such as, "have you stopped cheating on your taxes?"[12] The "you" is phrased in close proximity to the singular choice. Indeed the pacifist's dilemma is premised on, and the interlocutor is expecting, that the only possible response to the question is either yes or no to the use of lethal violence. It also assumes that the response to the attacker must necessarily be lethal and that a non-lethal response is both unrealistic and ineffective. Certainly the challenge assumes that non-defense will certainly permit the worst to happen.[13] A response of yes or no to lethal violence makes the pacifist either an irresponsible coward or a hypocrite who secretly would use violence in extreme circumstances.

The Contribution of Details

Influential rhetoric scholars Chaim Perelman and Lucie Olbrechts-Tyteca note that "to create emotion, it is essential to be specific. General notions and abstract schemes have few effect on the imagination."[14] In the case of the pacifist dilemma, we can identify the specifics that attempt to generate emotion, as well as where the account lacks certain details, which suggests the attempt to suppress emotional reaction.

I ask my students; "what details are commonly present in these scenarios and what details are absent or left in the abstract? What is known, assumed, and unknown?" For example, the pacifist's dilemma does not permit me to know the motivations of the attacker, nor anything else about him or her. The scenario does not permit me to know or consider the layout of my surroundings, or my relative skill with the weapon of choice. I cannot know if I have a previous relationship with the attacker or know his or her name or story. As John Howard Yoder notes, lack of detail presented in the situation

> excludes the possibility that the other party might have reasons for behaving in the way I perceive to be wrong. There is no room for the possibility that the offender might be a Jean Valjean, only looking for bread for his hungry children in the home of someone who has more bread than needed.[15]

Lacking all detail in regards to the conditions and players in the situation expresses a profound epistemological hubris insofar as the incredible complexity of human nature and character can be reduced to a single label "attacker," or "criminal." As with any argumentative exchange, exposing the emotionally loaded language is a helpful corrective.

After noting the absence of salient details in the hypnotical scenario, I encourage my students to consider adding the missing elements of the situation. Indeed, I state, the addition of these "inconsequential" details should not alter the basic moral calculus of the situation or the basic argumentative structure of the thought experiment. Let's, I suggest, simply add some details, such as giving the attacker a name. Perhaps a background story and motivation grounded in something relatable? Or at least something comprehensible? Or something that would snap the picture of the attacker into sharp emotional clarity? Perhaps something like this: "You see that your mother is about to attack a young child. You have a gun in your hand. Do you shoot your mother to save the child?" In this case, simply adding specificity substantially shifts the perspective.

Noting the amount of detail often missing in the pacifist's dilemma permits us to discern a number of common elements often present. For example, one detail that seems to be common in the pacifist's dilemma is that the attacker is always moving in the situation. The onlooker, the "you" is nearly always described as "standing," or looking on in some way, giving the impression of having the space of logical deliberation and reason in contrast to the single-minded forward momentum and destructive force of the attacker. This gives the impression that the attacker is pre-programmed to do the very worst, somehow closer to an impersonal force or natural disaster rather than a real person. We also note that the victim, while having the specificity of being directly connected to the onlooker, is always static, frozen in place and situated to bear the maximum force of the attacker's aggression, functioning in the situation more like an object rather than a person.

Connected with this lack of detail is the specificity of sex and gender roles of the players in the situation. I hardly ever know the attacker's name in the pacifist's dilemma, but I nearly always know that his sex is male. Gender assumptions occur frequently in the dilemma, with the picture often painted as one man attacking a woman or, less often, a child. I welcome students to apply any sort of physical characteristics they would like but they have to note them.

The results: nearly universally, students describe the attacker as a male and the passive victim as female. This description certainly opens the door for a discussion of gendered assumptions, which I encounter in my course Gender, Race, and Communication. We also discuss how patriarchal discourse often serves to infantilize women and render them passive objects for male desire and protection. We observe the connection of femininity with passivity and helplessness, which by necessity requires patriarchal protection. Here, "woman," "wife," "daughter," or "grandmother" is equated with weakness and helplessness. She is an object that relies on masculine aggression and intervention and patriarchal protection for survival.[16]

Simply adding some detail about the victim to constitute her as more than a prop in the situation may alter the perceived moral calculus considerably. For example, I can say that I have spoken with my wife and that she has reported not wanting to be defended by lethal force, so I have to take her consent into account. I have found that this response in particular tends to put students back on their heels. Most have never considered the victim in the situation to be more than furniture in the setting rather than a person with thoughts, feelings, or philosophical and theological commitments. Students are challenged by the notion of consent. They are quite familiar with running their ethical frameworks though an individualistic framework of consent in a contractual sense of relationality with others. The question thus becomes, "Can I protect another person from violence without that person's consent, or even when the person opposes a violent defense?"

This is also an opportunity to discuss the distorted picture of masculinity at play in the pacifist's dilemma in which masculinity is connected with violence. Not only is the attacker always a man, it is also assumed that the defender is also a man. The assumption here is that "If I do not respond to the brutal threat in a brutal way, I will not be a man," a response that fits the very definition of an *ad hominem* logical fallacy.

War, Roles, and Metaphors

"Metaphors can kill." With this provocative statement, George Lakoff began his 1991 essay "Metaphor and War; the Metaphor System Used to Justify War in the Gulf." For Lakoff, metaphorical descriptions are not simply an extra gloss added to accurately depict an objective situation, but rather metaphors serve as an unconscious framing system for our interpretations of reality, and thus, of the imaginative options for action. Lakoff writes,

> Reality exists. So does the unconscious system of metaphors that we use without awareness to comprehend reality. What metaphor does is limit what we notice, highlight what we do see, and provide part of the inferential structure that we reason with. Because of the pervasiveness of metaphor and thought, we cannot always stick to discussions of reality in purely literal terms.
>
> There is no way to avoid metaphorical thought, especially in complex matters like foreign-policy.[17]

Here, metaphors are neither intrinsically good nor bad but play a pivotal role in human cognition. We cannot help but reach for metaphorical frameworks when discursively organizing perceptions and interpretations. In and of itself this is neither positive nor negative, yet our metaphorical constructions can frame reality in such a way that other options or ways of understanding happenings in the world can fade into the background.

Lakoff draws attention to a dominant structure of metaphorical thought when it comes to thinking about war, what he calls the fairytale of the just war.

> Cast of characters: a villain, a victim, and a hero. The victim and the hero may be the same person.
>
> The scenario: A crime is committed by the villain against innocent victim (typically an assault, theft, or kidnapping). The offense occurs due to imbalance of power and creates a moral imbalance.... The villain is inherently evil, perhaps even a monster, and thus reasoning with him is out of the question. The hero is left with no choice but to engage the villain in battle. The hero defeats the villain and rescues the victim. The moral balance is restored. Victory is achieved. The hero, who always acts honorably has proven his manhood and achieved glory. The sacrifice was worthwhile. The hero receives acclaim, along with the gratitude of the victim and the community.[18]

It is not difficult to discern that a number of elements already discussed in regards to the pacifist's dilemma make their appearance in the metaphoric structure of Lakoff's "fairy tale of just war." Most saliently, much like the pacifist's dilemma, we see three absolute, distinct, and irreconcilable roles in Lakoff's fairytale of just war. The absolutely corrupt villain poised to do as much damage as possible without discernable motivations, the passive victim with no agency, and the active onlooker/intervener, in this case a "hero." Much like in the pacifist's dilemma, the hero is rational, the enemy cannot be reasoned or negotiated with, and must be defeated by the hero.[19] In the case of the first Gulf War, reasoning with the enemy was not an option because "you just do not reason with a demon, nor did you enter in negotiations with him. The logic of the metaphor demands that Saddam [Hussein] be irrational.[20]

According to Lakoff, the metaphors used to define, organize, and execute the first Gulf War definitively framed the perception and discourse of the military conflict. If one is engaging in analytical reasoning from one domain (the potentially violent interpersonal situation of the pacifist's dilemma) to another (war between nation-states), who is analogically playing what role? Not only can the details not be imported or transported from one domain to the other, even the basic ethical parameters posed by the pacifist's dilemma resist analogical transference from hypothetical to real-world military conflicts. For example, is a pre-emptive military strike—such as was the justification for the use of military force in the second Gulf War—the moral equivalent of invading the attacker's home and destroying his family before an attack takes place?[21] Or perhaps, "a comparison on the individual level might be a man entering my house to fight my wife because he fears my neighbor might sometime want to attack his home."[22]

Lakoff notes that the metaphorical structure of the "fairytale of the just war" conceals the profound differences between violent interpersonal situations between individuals and militarized conflict between nation-states. Much like Burke's dictum mentioned toward the beginning of this chapter—that language can conceal as much as it can reveal—Lakoff notes how the just war fairytale attempts to finesse the profound differences between the situation outlined in pacifist's dilemma and war by drawing on a common dramatic metaphoric structure with clear heroes, villains, and moral imperatives.

Lakoff also notes that in this metaphorical construction, the line between the state and the individual confrontation is blurred and perhaps even nonexistent.

> The State-as-Person metaphor highlights the ways in which states act as units, and hides the internal structure of the state. Class structure is hidden by the metaphor, as is the ethnic composition, religious rivalry, political parties, the ecology, the influence of the military and corporations (especially multinational corporations).[23]

Much like in the first Gulf War, here we see the pacifist's dilemma not as usually deployed to justify the legitimacy of violence at the personal level but rather to justify modern warfare.

Demonstrating the disjuncture between the pacifist's dilemma and military conflict is a straightforward affair in the classroom. One way is to provide an extensive list of actions that have been taken during wars—pre-emptive military strikes, the capture and abuse of prisoners of war in the form of "enhanced interrogation techniques," firebombing of civilian populations, use of atomic weapons against civilian populations, unmanned drone strikes—and invite students to attempt to draw direct parallels to the situation outlined in the pacifist's dilemma. Who, for example, plays the role of the innocent passive victim or the rational onlooker ready to intervene in the instance of thermonuclear exchange between nation-states?

Other Considerations

One need not look very hard to find a plethora of situations and arguments that intersect with the issues discussed here. Tragically, it is becoming all too common in our discourse to hear calls that violence in the form of mass shootings must be met with violence, both from "legitimate authority" in the increasing militarization of police forces throughout the country or though political calls to overturn gun control laws and put guns in the hands of as many citizens as possible. The answer to mass killings, it seems, is to attempt to add guns to every situation.

However, when applied to real-world situations, this mentality of more guns seems to fly in the face of evidence. Indeed, in all cases of mass shootings over the past thirty years, a study by Mark Follman shows that one cannot find a single instance of an armed civilian successfully intervening with lethal force to stop a mass shooting.[24] Not only is the pacifist's dilemma highly speculative and has little connection to real-world situations, this study suggests there seems to be little to no empirical evidence of pragmatic efficacy of impromptu lethal responses to violent interpersonal encounters.

Space prevents me from fully exploring more of the common faulty assumptions that undergird the pacifist's dilemma. Among some common assumptions are these: that "illegitimate" violence can only be met with and constrained by more violence; that onlookers to violent acts have the ability to instantly discern the entirety of the moral calculus of an emotionally charged situation with detachment and reason and act accordingly; that reactive violence on the part of an armed onlooker has a higher probability of success in the moment compared to the attacker, who may well have the element of surprise; and that violence on the part of the third-party onlooker is far more likely to be used with precision and not injure or kill other innocent participants in the situation.

Finally, we have not explored the fact that in addition to the two responses assumed in the pacifist's dilemma, there are actually five other possible outcomes. These included responses buttressed by "real world" examples that show ways to respond successfully to the intruder without violence. An honest dialogue concerning war, peace, and nonviolence must dwell on such considerations.

That all of these assumptions can be at work in every-day American public discourse and are not seriously questioned by the majority of the culture is a testament to the durability and deep-seated nature of the ideology at work in the pacifist's dilemma.

Conclusion

In this chapter, I've addressed only a small portion of the creative and pedagogically valuable ways of responding to the pacifist's dilemma in the classroom. Again, I am not opposed to the use of thought experiments in the classroom. One advantage to using the pacifist's dilemma in the classroom is that it provides opportunity to open the conversation to students who are first encountering issues of peace and violence and allows them to enter the conversation.

Through the lens of rhetorical theory and criticism, we noted that many elements of the pacifist's dilemma are ripe for careful and thoughtful analysis that can provide fertile ground for classroom discussion. Rather than a trap, I argue that the pacifist's dilemma represents an opportunity for teaching our students complexity of thought and how to carefully consider how our use of metaphors and stories can shape our reasoning. Rather than an obstacle, the pacifist's dilemma actually poses an opportunity for sharing the gospel of peace that constitutes the heart of Mennonite education.

Notes

1. John Howard Yoder, with, Joan Baez, et al., *What Would You Do?: A Serious Answer to a Standard Question*, expanded ed. (Scottdale, Pa.: Herald Press, 1992), 11. Yoder's short text has been instrumental in shaping my thoughts in regards to this question. His discussion considers a number of different perspectives and answers to the hypothetical situation outlined here and more comprehensively considers and

integrates peace church theology as an approach to answering the hypothetical question; I have limited my discussion to the rhetorical and argumentative elements of the dilemma. I must also note, as was already stated in note 1 of Chapter 1, the revelations regarding Yoder's personal life and shameful treatment of women adds complexity to any contemporary use Yoder's texts. Although I continue to make my own use of what I learned from his writing, I recognize and am distressed by the profound gulf between Yoder's incisive scholarship and his personal misdeeds.

2. Richard Rorty, "Religion as a Conversation-Stopper," in *Philosophy and Social Hope* (New York: Penguin, 1999), 168-74.

3. In the simplest scenario of the prisoners' dilemma, two prisoners are held separately with no means of communication between them. Prosecutors lack evidence to convict both, but hope to sentence each to a minimum penalty. Each prisoner is offered a choice. Remain silent or implicate the other. If each remains silent, each will receive a one-year sentence. If one implicates the other, he will go free and the other will receive a three-year sentence. But if each implicates the other, each will receive a two-year sentence. The dilemma is that rational self-interest would call for betraying the other but that actually they would be better off cooperating.

The simplest version of the trolley problem concerns an out-of-control trolley that is approaching five people suspended on the track. "You," the one addressed, are standing by a lever that would throw a switch to route the trolley to a track where only one person is suspended. The dilemma—do nothing and allow five people to be killed, or take action that would contribute to the death of one person. Both hypothetical situations, while heuristically useful in considering broad ethical approaches, share the similarity of being so abstracted from every-day experience that they provide little to no ethical guidance in responding to actual violent situations the average person might encounter. In addition, like the pacifist's dilemma, much like the prisoner's dilemma and the trolley problem, they allow only binary responses (e.g. in the case of the trolley problem, "Do you throw the switch or not?") in a tightly closed systems; constraints one is highly unlikely to encounter "in the wild."

4. Kenneth Burke, *Language as Symbolic Action: Essays on Life, Literature, and Method* (Berkeley, Calif.: University of California Press, 1966), 45.

5. Burke, *Language as Symbolic*, 50.

6. Burke, *Language as Symbolic*, 46.

7. Walter Wink, "Facing the Myth of Redemptive Violence," *Ekklesia*, 15 Nov. 2014, http://www.ekklesia.co.uk/content/cpt/article_060823wink.shtml <15 Aug. 2016>.http://www.ekklesia.co.uk/content/cpt/article_060823wink.shtml <15 Aug. 2016>.

8. Taylor Astra, dir., *Zizek!* DVD (United States: Zeitgeist Films, 2005).

9. Christopher W. Bauman, et al., "Revisiting External Validity: Concerns About Trolley Problems and Other Sacrificial Dilemmas in Moral Psychology," *Social and Personality Psychology Compass* 8 (2014): 540.

10. Lawrence Souder, "What Are We to Think About Thought Experiments?" *Argumentation* 17, no. 2 (June 2003): 214.

11. Phrasing the pacifist's dilemma in the second person is connected with the

theory of interpellation and the constitution of audiences. For discussion of the work of critical theorist Louis Althusser on constituting audiences, see Maurice Charland, "Constitutive Rhetoric: The Case of the Peuple Québécois," *Quarterly Journal of Speech* 73, no. 2 (0133-50 1987): 203-17.

12. In argumentative circles, one traditional and unfortunately common example of a "loaded question" is "Have you stopped beating your wife?" I refrain from using this example here and absolutely avoid its use in the classroom setting due to its patriarchal worldview, heteronormative assumptions, and violent imagery.

13. Yoder et al., *What Would You Do?* 25.

14. Chaim Perelman and Lucie Olbrechts-Tyteca, *The New Rhetoric* (Notre Dame, Ind.: University of Notre Dame Press, 1969), 147.

15. Yoder, et al., *What Would You Do?* 17.

16. Yoder, et al., *What Would You Do?* 18.

17. Lakoff George, "Metaphors and War: The Metaphor System Used to Justify War in the Gulf" (University of California, Berkeley: EScholarship, 1992), 26. http://eprints.cdlib.org/uc/item/9sm131vj <15 Aug. 2016>.

18. Lakoff, "Metaphor and War: The Metaphor System Used to Justify War," 6.

19. Lakoff, "Metaphor and War: The Metaphor System Used to Justify War," 6.

20. Lakoff, "Metaphor and War: The Metaphor System Used to Justify War," 15.

21. Yoder, et al., *What Would You Do?* 20.

22. Yoder, et al., *What Would You Do?* 21.

23. Lakoff, "Metaphor and War: The Metaphor System Used to Justify War," 21.

24. Mark Follman, "More Guns, More Mass Shootings—Coincidence?" *Mother Jones*, no. 15 Dec. (2012), http://www.motherjones.com/politics/2012/09/mass-shootings-investigation. <15 Aug. 2016>.

CHAPTER TWENTY

BRINGING CHRISTIAN STUDENTS TO PEACE WITH DARWIN

Angela Horn Montel

In the beginning was the Word, and the Word was with God, and the Word was God. He was in the beginning with God. All things came into being through him, and without him not one thing came into being
—John 1:1-3

In the sciences was the word, and the word was with controversy, and the word was *evolution*. It was in the beginning with God's creation. All things came into being through it, and without it not one thing came into being.[1]

The War on Science

In my discipline of biology, the Word with a capital "W" is *evolution*. The grand theory of evolution unites all of biology to the extent that, as the evolutionary biologist Theodosius Dobzhansky famously stated, "Nothing in biology makes sense except in the light of evolution."[2] One could extend Dobzhansky's observation to encompass many of the other scientific disciplines, including cosmology, geology, and nuclear physics; all of these sciences are unified in the evidence that they provide for an ancient Earth, dating to around 4.6 billion years old and fostering the development of the first single-cell, prokaryotic life as early as 3.8 billion years ago.

The general public and American scientists were asked the same Gallup Poll questions in surveys conducted five years apart, the general public being surveyed in 1991 and the scientists in 1996. In the surveys, 40 percent of the general public agreed with the statement that, "Man evolved over millions of years from less developed forms of life, but God guided the process, including the creation of man." An identical percentage of scientists from disciplines as diverse as biology and mathematics agreed with the same statement.

The stark difference between scientists and other members of society, however, can be seen in the percentages that selected the other two alternatives offered to the participants. Greater than half (55 percent) of American scientists agreed with the statement, "Man evolved over millions of years from less developed forms of life. God had no part in the process." In contrast, only 9 percent of the general public affirmed this statement. Instead, 46 percent of the general public embraced the idea that, "Man was created pretty much in his current form at one time within the past 10,000 years," while only 5 percent of scientists agreed.[3]

The implications of each of these statistics merit discussion, but for this chapter I want to emphasize the 40 percent figure. Fully 40 percent of scientists were willing to agree that "God guided" the evolution of humans from other life forms. In 2002, when the Ohio State Board of Education was confronted with the issue of whether or not to include intelligent design in the public school science curriculum, the University of Cincinnati's Internet Public Opinion Laboratory polled Ohio science professors. Eighty-four percent of the respondents answered in the affirmative to the question, "Do you think accepting the theory of evolution is consistent with believing in God?"[4] Many scientists apparently do not see a conflict between religious beliefs and the theory of evolution.

In my undergraduate general education biology classroom, filled with earnest Christian youth anxious to take a stand for their faith, the Word with a capital "W" is *creationism* or the neocreationism that masquerades under the guise of "intelligent design." No one seems to have told these young folks that religious belief and acceptance of evolutionary theory can peacefully coexist. Some of them arrive in my classroom fortified for the war against secular explanations for life on Earth. It is certainly a war. And it frightens me.

Individual scientists and scientific organizations such as the National Center for Science Education[5] have invested endless resources, both intellectual and financial, to maintain the integrity of the science education that is received by young people in our country. At the same time, individuals and organizations such as Ken Ham's Answers in Genesis[6] have spent many millions of dollars to fight the concept of evolution. From Ohio, where I live and teach, one can drive just a few minutes over the border into Kentucky and visit Ham's 70,000-square foot Creation Museum,[7] "designed by a former Universal Studios exhibit director." There one can observe modern *Homo sapiens* (whose oldest know fossil remains date from around 200,000 years ago) and dinosaurs (which according to the fossil record became extinct 65 million years ago) coexisting.

At the Creation Museum, one can also visit a planetarium where their website boasts the visitor can experience "a spectacular gravity-defying spaceflight, a thrilling ride billions of light years away to the vast outer regions of our universe."[8] Young-Earth creationists believe that the Earth is only around 6,000 years old—a figure arrived at by counting all the generations of people listed in Genesis. Since the "vast outer regions of our universe" are more than 6,000 light years away, how does a young-Earth creationist reconcile their existence?

One explanation proffered by creationists (with a fascinating nod to an *old* Earth and universe) is the "biosphere model," which suggests that the six, twenty-four-hour days of creation apply only to the creation of the Earth's biosphere, allowing the actual Earth itself (and the universe) to be billions of years old. "In this view, God made the stars before Day Four (even billions of years prior), but the stars did not become visible upon the surface of the earth until Day Four, for the Earth's atmosphere was opaque up to that point."[9] Another explanation invokes the theory of general relativity to allow days on Earth to be equivalent to eons elsewhere in the universe. A third, long-popular explanation is that the speed of light was much, much faster in the past.

A fourth explanation posits stretching of space that carried the light with it in a miraculous act of God.[10] These explanations are either not supported by our current scientific understanding or are impossible to test scientifically because they involve miracles.

A fifth explanation is that God made the universe *appear* to be billions of years old by instantaneously allowing light from galaxies billions of light years away to reach our planet at the time of its creation 6,000 years ago. This last explanation presents a disturbing image of God. As Kenneth Miller puts it in his book, *Finding Darwin's God*, it makes God out to be a charlatan who "deliberately rigged a universe with a consistent—but fictitious—age to fool its inhabitants."[11]

If readers are confused by the barrage of creationist propaganda, they are not alone. Writes Darrel Falk, author of *Coming to Peace with Science*, "As our young people go to college and study, they will incorrectly perceive that they need to make a decision that is focused not so much on whether to pick up their cross and follow Jesus but on whether astronomy, astrophysics, nuclear physics, geology, and biology are all very wrong."[12] Given the war that is being waged against my discipline in the name of God, how am I as a pacifist Christian biologist to bring Christian youth to peace with Darwin?

A Pacifist Response

I cannot pretend to have this immense question answered completely. I am constantly revising my approach and second-guessing myself. What follows outlines my current approach on this journey.

Since evolution is pervasive in biology, in my general education biology classes I try to incorporate various evolutionary concepts throughout the semester, such as the endosymbiosis theory, which suggests that eukaryotic cells obtained internal organelles like mitochondria by engulfing ancient aerobic bacteria. But of course until I actually use the word *evolution* my students' defenses are not on full alert.

Toward the end of the term we begin our unit on evolution in earnest. It is here that I consistently use the term evolution as I attempt to show how all of the biology that we have studied unites in the theory of evolution. And it is at this point that I distinctly feel that some of the students begin to view me as the prototypical amoral and atheistic scientist. After all, some of my students have heard, perhaps even from the pulpit, that many of the evils of society, including racism, can be blamed on Darwin's theory of evolution, or they have attended workshops on how to challenge anyone who presents them with the theory of evolution.

One approach would be to say that since my course is a science course and since creationism is religion and not science, we will not discuss creationism. In recent years, I have tried to avoid this separatist approach. Since many of my non-science majors may never again be presented with the evidence for evolution unless they specifically seek it out in later life, I must not skimp on my presentation of the evidence for evolution. However, I have an obligation to incorporate a discussion of creationism into my classroom, not only because students are amazingly attentive to such material but also because, like Darrel Falk, I am concerned that a deep chasm is opening up between science and religion that leaves young people confused.

To begin the discussion, I introduce students to the various positions on a creation/evolution continuum, a tool developed by the National Center for Science Education (NCSE).[14] Positions range from the "flat earthers," who despite scientific evidence to the contrary believe that the Earth is flat because the Bible refers to "the four corners of the Earth," to atheist evolutionists, who embrace evolutionary theory and believe that matter alone, in the absence of spirit, can account for the appearance of life on Earth. I present the concept of intelligent design, as outlined in Michael Behe's book *Darwin's Black Box*,[13] and then point out the scientific arguments against intelligent design, thus exposing it as another form of creationism. I explain the position of "theistic evolutionism," a middle ground occupied by those who believe that evolution is the mechanism by which the creator brought about life on Earth.

In this discussion, I try to be very clear that acceptance of evolution does not rule out belief in a creator. To this end, I attempt to explain the difference between *methodological* and *philosophical* materialism.[15] All scientists use methodological materialism in conducting their research. In other words, they use only material (matter and energy) as explanations for their observations. When scientists come to a question for which science does not currently have an answer, they do not halt their research and simply state that God did it and we cannot explain it; instead they assume that there can be a "material" explanation. Many past "unknowns" in our world, such as the tides or solar eclipses, were once attributed directly to the hand of God, but we now have material explanations for these phenomena.

Philosophical materialism goes a step further than methodological materialism. Philosophical materialism states that not only do scientists look for materialistic explanations, but material is the only thing that exists. It denies a spiritual dimension to the world. To be a scientist, one must apply *methodological* materialism to one's studies, but one does not have to assume *philosophical* materialism to be a scientist. In fact, by definition, science does not accept supernatural explanations and therefore cannot prove or disprove the existence of God.[16]

Unfortunately, some scientists mistakenly use the fact of evolution to argue for the absence of a creator. Ironically, creationists themselves set up the perfect scenario for scientists who espouse philosophical materialism to argue against the existence of God. Creationists do this when they search for God in the apparent inadequacies of nature. For example, Kenneth Miller recalls in *Finding Darwin's God* when a well-known creationist used to poke fun at the lack of transitional fossils between four-legged, terrestrial organisms and whales by showing comical drawings that were half-cow, half-whale. But, subsequently in the 1990s scientists unearthed amazing transitional fossils showing several species that are intermediate between whales and terrestrial mammals.[17]

Intelligent design creationist Michael Behe has claimed that biochemical pathways such as the blood clotting cascade are too complex to have evolved and therefore had to be designed by a "designer." Since publication of his book (and actually even before its publication), science has assembled much evidence that such pathways could have gradually evolved by co-opting existing proteins for new functions. With each new materialistic explanation, the creationist must retreat to the next gap in our knowledge to search for God. And when that gap, too, is filled by science, the philosophical materialists are standing ready to falsely assert that once again science has disproved the existence of God.

And this is exactly what the creationists and some of my students fear: that accepting the scientific explanation for life will leave them with a powerless God who is out of a job. To illustrate to my students that they need not fear for their faith when they accept reason, I introduce my students to several scientists and theologians who go beyond the god-of-the-gaps theology and write from the perspective of theistic evolution, including John Haught, Nancey Murphy, and Ken Miller. For example, in his book *God After Darwin* theologian John Haught writes,

> For if ultimate reality is conceived of . . . as self-emptying, suffering love, we should already anticipate that nature will give every

appearance of being in some sense autonomously creative . . . Since it is the nature of love, even at the human level, to refrain from coercive manipulation of others, we should not expect the world that a generous God called into being to be instantaneously ordered to perfection. Instead, in the presence of the self-restraint befitting an absolutely self-giving love, the world would unfold by responding to the divine allurement at its own pace and in its own particular way.[18]

We readily accept that God has granted free will to us as humans. Would we not expect God to do the same with the rest of creation?

In one of my courses, I had my students read the entire book *Coming to Peace with Science* by biologist and evangelical Christian Darrel Falk. In addition to doing a marvelous job of explaining the evidence for evolution, it emphasizes that the Bible's purpose is to bring people to God; it is not meant to be a science textbook. In the book, Falk also points out that God could not have spoken in the language of evolution to the prophets of the Bible considering that society at the time would not have comprehended such concepts and the inclusion of such concepts would have detracted from the central message that God is loving.

Although I have not yet found time in class to explain the concept to my students, many writers have suggested that the indeterminacy at the level of subatomic particles means that we can never know everything about nature. We cannot know, for example, when a particular radioactive atom will decay, thus resulting in a DNA mutation, which is the raw material upon which natural selection works. This leaves room for the divine hand to function within natural laws. Such divine guidance would not be detectable to scientists and would allow for divine nudging.

So, does this discussion bring my students to peace? Not all of them. But, in the essays I have had them write to explain where they would place themselves on the NCSE creation/evolution continuum, many of my students express profound relief to have been introduced to the concept of theistic evolutionism/evolutionary creationism. "Until now I thought there were only two views on evolution," writes one of my students. "Either it was all science and there was no God or God created everything and science had nothing to do with it. Now I know that it is possible for them both to be right." Such expressionos of students coming to peace with their faith and with Darwin are very encouraging to me.

However, even if I could dedicate my entire course to the creation/evolution debate, some students would still leave the course with conflict in their minds. Questions that still remain are how to incorporate the stories of Adam and Eve or of Noah's flood or concepts of the human soul into a worldview that encompasses gradual human evolution from less intelligent life forms over millions of years. Such questions will require reading and soul searching beyond my course. But, I do hope that the seeds of a desire to learn more are planted and that my students can grow a faith that is strong enough to accept that the Word of God can encompass the word *evolution*.

A creation that has taken billions of years to "unfold by responding to the divine allurement" can be all that more miraculous and awe-inspiring. Students need to recognize that an owl or an epiphytic plant or even a fungal species that is on the verge of extinction due to habitat destruction took several thousand or million years to evolve into the distinct species it is today. To recognize the interwoven dependencies within ecosystems, whose intricacies scientists have only begun to understand, is also important to developing a deeper appreciation for the creation.

Endless examples illustrate these interwoven dependencies. In the past I have described to my students the discovery that a species of tropical ants not only cultivates a fungus to feed itself, but the ants also play host to a species of bacteria that produces antibiotics that prevent the overgrowth of a parasitic fungus that would otherwise destroy the ants' fungal garden.[19]

During my last sabbatical, I attended a seminar where a speaker suggested that herpes viruses that many children acquire during childhood (not the venereal kind but species such as HHV6 or EBV) may confer protection from bacterial infection or even cancer. Since we house these viruses for life once they have infected us, the speaker was suggesting that the viruses are maintaining the immune system in a slightly activated state, and he coined the term "benevogens" (in contrast to "pathogens") to describe this relationship between us and the viruses.

More recently, to help my students develop a better understanding of the co-evolutionary dance between us and our resident microbes (known as our "microbiome"), I have had my microbiology students read the book *Missing Microbes* by Martin Blaser. In his book, Blaser lays out an argument that overuse of antibiotics may be altering the composition of microbes inhabiting our gut and skin surfaces, causing our immune system to be more "twitchy," as he says, and altering the contribution microbes make to our metabolism. This may have contributed to the recent increased rates of ailments such as allergies, asthma, type I diabetes, and even obesity.[20] A full understanding of the symbiotic relationships that have evolved among living creatures is beyond our grasp. The creative power of the creation is nearly incomprehensible.

In other sections of my courses, I emphasize an understanding of how human population growth threatens the rest of creation, how humans have disrupted the balance in the carbon cycle to bring about global climate change, how the burning of fossil fuels creates acidic precipitation, and how other environmental issues such as eutrophication must be addressed. The creativity of the creation is being challenged in ways not seen in the nearly four-billion-year history of life on Earth. The intricate relationships that evolved over millions of years are being altered or destroyed. In Genesis 1 we are repeatedly reminded that "God saw that it was good" in reference to each stage of creation. Perhaps an understanding of a creation to which we are inextricably linked by the very sequences of our DNA held in every cell in our body can further inspire our stewardship of God's good creation.

Notes

1. This chapter is an updated and expanded version of Angela Horn Montel, "How Does the Creativity of the Incarnated Word of God Shape the Discovering and Understanding of the Creation in My Discipline and in My Classroom?" in *Creation, Christ, and the Classroom: Mennonite University Faculty Conference Presentations* (Goshen, Ind.: Mennonite Education Agency, 2008), 83-88. Used by permission.

2. Theodosius Dobzhansky, "Nothing in Biology Makes Sense Except in the Light of Evolution," *The American Biology Teacher* 35, no. 3 (March 1973): 125-29.

3. Larry Witham, "Many Scientists See God's Hand in Evolution," *The Washington Times*, 11 April 1997, A8.

4. George Bishop, "Majority of Ohio Science Professors and Public Agree: 'Intelligent Design' Mostly About Religion," *National Center for Science Education*, 15 October 2002, http://ncse.com/creationism/general/ohio-scientists-intelligent-design-poll <18 Aug. 2016>.

5. "National Center for Science Education," https://ncse.com/ <18 Aug. 2016>.

6. Ken Ham, "Answers in Genesis," https://answersingenesis.org/ <18 Aug. 2016>.

7. "Creation Museum," http://creationmuseum.org/ <18 Aug. 2016>.

8. "Creation Museum."

9. Danny R. Faulkner, "A Proposal for a New Solution to the Light Travel Time Problem," *Answers in Genesis*, 24 July 2013, https://answersingenesis.org/astronomy/starlight/a-proposal-for-a-new-solution-to-the-light-travel-time-problem/ <18 Aug. 2016>.

10. Faulkner, "A Proposal."

11. Kenneth R. Miller, *Finding Darwin's God* (New York: HarperCollins, 1999), 80.

12. Darrel Falk, *Coming to Peace with Science: Bridging the Worlds Between Faith and Biology* (Downers Grove, Ill.: InterVarsity Press, 2004), 25.

13. Eugenie Scott, "The Creation/Evolution Continuum," *National Center for Science Education* (2000), http://www.ncseweb.org/resources/articles/9213_the_creationevolution_continu_12_7_2000.asp <18 Aug. 2016>.

14. Michael Behe, *Darwin's Black Box: The Biochemical Challenge to Evolution* (New York: Free Press, 1996).

15. Scott, "The Creation/Evolution Continuum."

16. To explore this topic further, I would suggest consulting Amir D. Aczel, *Why Science Does not Disprove God* (New York: William Morrow, 2014).

17. Miller, *Finding Darwin's God*, 264.

18. John Haught, *God After Darwin* (Boulder, Col.: Westview Press, 2000), 53.

19. C. R. Currie, et al., "Fungus-Growing Ants Use Antibiotic-Producing Bacteria to Control Garden Parasites," *Nature*, no. 398 (22 April 1999): 701-704.

20. Martin J. Blaser, *Missing Microbes: How the Overuse of Antibiotics is Fueling Our Modern Plagues* (New York: Henry Holt, 2014).

CONCLUSION

Using a brief sketch of the narrative of Jesus, this book has attempted to demonstrate how living in that narrative has the potential to expand the scope of our worldview into a wide-ranging theological-ethical outlook that can accommodate virtually anything in the curriculum of Mennonite schools, colleges, and universities. But the discussion in this book is only a beginning. Teachers, professors, and their students will write the next chapters, either in classrooms or in applying the learnings in life beyond those classrooms.

This book is only a beginning in another way as well. Much more could be said, both in expanding the chapters included here and in writing about issues beyond those discussed here. I mention several in no particular order of importance.

Much could be written about economics—economic disparity and the widening gap between rich and poor, the impact of international trade agreements, the impact of international corporations, banking practices, and more.

This book has little discussion of examining history from a nonviolent perspective, as in analyzing wars to explore opportunities missed for peace and what would have been alternatives to war.

The book features few discussions of current world trouble spots—Palestine and the Middle East, the refugee crisis precipitated by the war in Syria, problems in central Africa, North Africa, and many more that we could name.

332 / Conclusion

In discussing the relationship of the peace church to government and the social order, I was acutely aware that the book contains no discussion of how different these issues feel in the cultural mosaic of Canada in contrast to the ethos in the United States that is shaped by a tangible civil religion and the claim of American exceptionalism. That difference has a number of implications for theology and the way Christians live.

The book concerns education for the peace church, but there is little discussion of nonviolent techniques and of nonviolent lifestyles.

How to apply a nonviolent focus on the relationship of people in the management of church institutions—schools, publishing enterprises, conferences, national bureaucracy—in light of difficult decisions about hiring and retaining employes needs a great deal of further discussion.

There could be much more discussion of research in science and science application as well as guiding students through avoiding entanglements in military applications.

This book has very little discussion of technology, its development, its uses, and its abuses.

Although the book concerns education, there is little discussion of the science of pedagogy and of teaching techniques.

No discussion of music and the arts appears in these pages.

The book contains no mention of the importance of cross-cultural education and the importance of studying languages other than English.

This list could go on. But listing additional topics does not indicate the inadequacy of this book's collection of essays. No book can say everything. Rather, this list of additional topics points to the viability of the future of Mennonite education. It will be lively and there is much to do.

For those with the imagination and willingness to see, the assumption that the way of Jesus reflects the grain of the universe has the potential to bring new or additional understandings and research in disciplines across the school, college or university curriculum. For every discipline, whether in the liberal arts or an applied or professional discipline, one can ask how the grain of the universe is visible or can be made visible in it. The intent is not to proscribe the practice of a discipline but rather to bring new insight or to add an additional layer of meaning and interpretation to what is known or practiced in a discipline. The only limit to this discussion is the scope of the scholar's or practitioner's imagination.

This sense of the grain of the universe means that there should be continual dialogue between theologians, ethicists, theoreticians, and practitioners in disciplines such as public education, social work, criminal justice, restorative justice, conflict resolution, economics and finance, counseling and psychology, medicine, international development, and more. It may not always be appropriate to refer to theology in the professional exercise of such disciplines, but it is certainly possible for practitioners to shape their practice in line with the grain of the universe. In this practice, the continual interaction and dialogue of theoreticians-theologians and practitioners is essential.

In fact, the conversation between theologians and ethicists and practitioners is a specific expression of the fact that ethics and theology constitute two sides of the same proverbial coin. Recall that theology talks about the meaning of Jesus' story and ethics gives the lived version of that story. Claiming that theologians-ethicists and practitioners should be in continual dialogue gives expression to the two sided reality of theology and ethics that reflect the narrative of Jesus.

On to the abundant future of Mennonite education.

BIBLIOGRAPHY

Aczel, Amir D. *Why Science Does not Disprove God*. New York: William Morrow, 2014.
Alexander, Michelle. *The New Jim Crow: Mass Incarceration in the Age of Colorblindness*. Rev. ed. Foreword by Cornel West. New York: The New Press, 2012.
Allen, James. *Without Sanctuary: Lynching Photography in America*. Santa Fe, N.M.: Twin Palms Publishers, 2000.
Alvarez, Luis. "From Zoot Suits to Hip Hop: Towards a Relatioinal Chicana/o Studies." *Latino Studies* 5, no. 1 (2007): 53-75.
Ambush Mogadishu. Frontline—PBS, 1998.
Amnesty International. "NATO /Federal Republic of Yugoslavia: 'Collateral Damage' or Unlawful Killings? Violations of the Laws of War by NATO During Opereration Allied Force," 2000.
Augsburger, Myron. "Unity with Diversity in CCCU." *Mennonite World Review*, 29 September 2015, http://mennoworld.org/2015/09/29/the-world-together/unity-with-diversity-in-cccu/.
Augustine. *De Musica*.
Baker, Elna. *The New York Regional Mormon Singles Halloween Dance: A Memoir*. Reprint ed. New York: Plume, 2010.
Bakhtin, Mikhail. *Problems of Dostoevsky's Poetics*. Ed. Caryl Emerson. Theory and History of Literature. Minneapolis: University of Minnesota Press, 1984.
Baldwin, Christina, and Ann Linnea. "Basic Guidelines for Calling a CirclePriesthood of All Believers." *The Circle Way* (2016), http://static1.squarespace.com/static/55597e72e4b0f7284bff49e0/t/56e340a1f8baf38bbe1d00f6/1457733793606/TCW+Guidelines+English.pdf <25 July 2016>.
———. *The Circle Way: A Leader in Every Chair*. Oakland, Calif.: Berrett-Koehler Publishers, 2010.
"Basic Doctrines." In *LDS.Org*, https://www.lds.org/manual/basic-doctrines/basic-doctrines?lang=eng <19 July 2016>, 2016.
Bauman, Christopher W., A. Peter McGraw, Daniel M. Bartels, and Caleb Warren.

"Revisiting External Validity: Concerns About Trolley Problems and Other Sacrificial Dilemmas in Moral Psychology." *Social and Personality Psychology Compass* 8 (2014): 536-554.

Bauman, Harold E. *Congregations and Their Servant Leaders: Some Aids for Faithful Congregational Relationships*. Scottdale, Pa.: Mennonite Publishing House, 1982.

Beachy, Stephen. *boneyard*. Portland, Ore.: Verse Chorus Press, 2011.

Bechtel, Greg. *Boundary Problems*. Calgary, Alberta: Freehand Books, 2014.

———. "Interview with Greg Bechtel," by Sofia Samatar, *Journal of the Center for Mennonite Writing* 7, no. 3 (2015): https://mennonitewriting.org//journal/7/3/interview-greg-bechtel/#all.

Becker, Palmer. *What Is an Anabaptist Christian?* Missio Dei: Exploring God's Work in the World, 18. Elkhart, Ind.: Mennonite Mission Network, 2008.

Behe, Michael. *Darwin's Black Box: The Biochemical Challenge to Evolution*. New York: Free Press, 1996.

Bender, Harold S., and Marlin E. Miller. "Priesthood of All Believers." *Global Anabaptist Mennonite Encyclopedia* (1989), http://gameo.org/index.php?title=Priesthood_of_all_believers&oldid=93326 <25 July 2016>.

Bender, Harold S., and Nanne van der Zijpp. "Apocrypha." *Global Anabaptist Mennonite Encyclopedia Online* (1953), http://gameo.org/index.php?title=Apocrypha&oldid=119941.

Bennett Smith, Alyssa. *Grace at the Table: A Resource for Understanding the Polity of Mennonite Church USA*. http://mennoniteusa.org/wp-content/uploads/2015/06/Grace-at-the-Table.pdf.

Bennett-Smith, Alyssa. "Grace at the Table," 25 June 2016.http://mennoniteusa.org/menno-snapshots/grace-at-the-table/.

Bennion, Janet. *Desert Patriarchy: Mormon and Mennonite Communities in the Chiluahua Valley*. Tucson, Ariz.: University of Arizona Press, 2004.

Biesecker-Mast, Susan, and Gerald Biesecker-Mast, eds. *Anabaptists and Postmodernity*. With a foreword by J. Denny Weaver. The C. Henry Smith Series, vol. 1. Telford, Pa.: Pandora Press U.S.; copublished with Herald Press, 2000.

Bishop, George. "Majority of Ohio Science Professors and Public Agree: 'Intelligent Design' Mostly About Religion." *National Center for Science Education*, 15 October 2002. http://ncse.com/creationism/general/ohio-scientists-intelligent-design-poll <18 Aug. 2016>.

Bixler, Benjamin. "Prophetic Challenges in Dialogue with Popular Culture." Unpublished master's thesis. Harrisonburg, Va.: Eastern Mennonite Seminary, 2013.

Blackmon, Douglas A. *Slavery by Another Name: The Re-Enslavement of Black Americans from the Civil War to World War II*. New York: Doubleday, 2008.

Blaser, Martin J. *Missing Microbes: How the Overuse of Antibiotics is Fueling Our Modern Plagues*. New York: Henry Holt, 2014.

Bonhoeffer, Dietrich. *Life Together*. New York: HarperSanFrancisco, 1954.

Bouchet-Saulnier, Francoise. *The Practical Guide to Humanitarian Law*. Lanham, Md.: Rowman & Littlefield Publishers, 2002.

Bowden, Mark. *Black Hawk Down: A Story of Modern War*. New York: Signet Books, 1999.

Boyarin, Daniel. *Border Lines: The Partition of Judaeo-Christianity*. Philadelphia: University of Pennsylvania Press, 2004.

Boyes-Watson, Carolyn, and Kay Panis. *Circle Forward: Building a Restorative School Community*. St. Paul, Minn.: Living Justice Press, 2015.

Brandt, Di. *questions i asked my mother*. Winnipeg, Man.: Turnstone Press, 1987.

Bransford, John, Reed Stevens, Schwartz Dan, Andy Meltzoff, Roy Pea, Jeremy Rosehelle, Nancy Vye, Pat Jubl, Philip Bell, Brigid Barron, Byron Reeves, and Nora Sabelli. "Learning Theories and Education: Toward a Decade of Synergy." In *Handbook of Educational Psychology*, 2nd ed., Patricia A. Alexander and Philip H. Winne, 209-244. New York: Routledge, 2012.

Braun, Jan Guenther. *Somewhere Else*. Winnipeg, Man.: Arbeiter Ring Publishing, 2008.

Brenneman, James F. "Culture for Service Leadership: A Paradox Worth Living." Goshen College, 2011. https://www.goshen.edu/news/2011/08/31/culture-for-service-leadership-a-paradox-worth-living/ <25 July 2016>.

Breu, Christopher. *Insistence of the Material: Literature in the Age of Biopolitics*. Minneapolis: University of Minnesota Press, 2014.

Brooks, Joanna. *The Book of Mormon Girl: A Memoir of an American Faith*. New York: Free Press, 2012.

Brubacher, Matthew. "Striking a Balance: Humanitarian, Peace and Justice Initiatives." *The Conrad Grebel Review* 28, no. 3 (Fall 2010): 7-21.

Burke, Kenneth. *Language as Symbolic Action: Essays on Life, Literature, and Method*. Berkeley, Calif.: University of California Press, 1966.

Burkholder, Jared S. "How Peacemaking Helps Frame the Context of Anabaptism, Sexuality, and Higher Education." https://pietistschoolman.com/2015/10/06/how-peacemaking-helps-frame-the-context-of-anabaptism-sexuality-and-higher-education/.

Burkholder, Jared S., and David C. Cramer, eds. *The Activist Impulse: Essays on the Intersection of Evangelicalism and Anabaptism*. Eugene, Ore.: Pickwick Publications, 2012.

Butterworth, Lisa. "Episode 83: Meet Kate Kelly." *Feminist Mormon Housewives Podcast*, 7 October 2013, http://feministmormonhousewivespodcast.org/episode-83-meet-kate-kelly/ <19 July 2016>.

Carter, J. Kameron. *Race: A Theological Account*. New York: Oxford University Press, 2008.

"Chapter 25: Fasting." In *LDS.Org*, 144-148, 2011.https://www.lds.org/manual/gospel-principles/chapter-25-fasting?lang=eng <19 July 2016>.

Charland, Maurice. "Constitutive Rhetoric: The Case of the Peuple Québécois." *Quarterly Journal of Speech* 73, no. 2 (0133-50 1987): 203-17.

Christ, Creation, and the Classroom. Mennonite University Faculty Conference Presentations, Eastern Mennonite University, Aug. 7-9, 2008. Goshen, Ind.: Mennonite Education Agency, 2008.

The Chronicle of the Hutterian Brethren, vol. 1. Ed. and trans. Hutterian Brethren. Rifton, N.Y.: Plough Publishing House, 1987.

Coleman, Will. "Tribal Talk: Black Theology in Postmodern Configuration." *Theology Today* 50, no. 1 (April 1993): 68-77.

Cone, James H. *God of the Oppressed*. Rev. ed. Maryknoll, N.Y.: Orbis, 1997.

Confession of Faith in a Mennonite Perspective. Scottdale, Pa.: Herald Press, 1995.

Copeland, M. Shawn. *Enfleshing Freedom: Body, Race, and Being*. Minneapolis: Fortress Press, 2010.

Cramer, David C. "Mennonite Systematic Theology in Retrospect and Prospect." *The Conrad Grebel Review* 31, no. 3 (Fall 2013): 255-273.

"Creation Museum." http://creationmuseum.org/ <18 Aug. 2016>.

Crossan, John Dominic. *God and Empire: Jesus Against Rome, Then and Now*. New York: HarperCollins, 2007.

Currie, C. R., J. A. Scott, R. C. Summerbell, and D. Malloch. "Fungus-Growing Ants Use Antibiotic-Producing Bacteria to Control Garden Parasites." *Nature*, no. 398 (22 April 1999): 701-704.

de Bakker, Willem, Michael Driedger, and James Stayer. *Bernhard Rothman and the Reformation in Münster*. Kitchener, Ont.: Pandora Press, 2009.

Dean, Kenda Creasy. *Almost Christian: What the Faith of Our Teenagers Is Telling the American Church*. New York: Oxford University Press, 2010.

Delany, Samuel R. *The Mad Man*. New York: A Richard Kasak Book, 1994.

Dobzhansky, Theodosius. "Nothing in Biology Makes Sense Except in the Light of Evolution." *The American Biology Teacher* 35, no. 3 (March 1973): 125-29.

Dorsey, Candas Jane. "Being One's Own Pornographer." *ParaDoxa* 2, no. 2 (1996): 191-203.

Dueck, Lynnette. *boundary problems*. Vancouver, BC: Press Gang Publishing, 1992.

Durham, W. Cole. "Church and State." In *Encyclopedia of Mormonism*, ed. Daniel H. Ludlow, 281-283. New York: Macmillan, 1992.

Dyck, Cornelius J., William E. Keeney, and Alvin J. Beachy, trans. and eds. *The Writings of Dirk Philips 1504-1568*. Classics of the Radical Reformation, vol. 6. Scottdale, Pa.: Herald Press, 1992.

Dyck, Cornelius, ed. and trans. *Spiritual Life in Anabaptism*. Scottdale, Pa.: Herald Press, 1995.

Dyck, Peter J. "Service." *Global Anabaptist Mennonite Encyclopedia* (1989), http://gameo.org/index.php?title=Service&oldid=104389 <25 July 2016>.

Easwaran, Eknath. *Nonviolent Soldier of Islam: Badshah Khan, a Man to Match His Mountains*. Tomales, Calif.: Nilgiri Press, 1999.

Enright, Robert D. *Forgiveness is a Choice: A Step-by-Step Process for Resolving Anger and Restoring Hope*. Washington, D.C.: American Psychological Association, 2001.

Epp, Charles R., Steven Maynard-Moody, and Donald Haider Markel. *Pulled Over: How Police Stops Define Race and Citizenship*. Chicago: The University of Chicago Press, 2014.

Erikson, Erik H. *Identity and the Life Cycle*. New York: W. W. Norton & Co., 1959.

———. *Identity: Youth and Crisis*. New York: W. W. Norton & Co., 1968.

———. *Insight and Responsibility*. New York: W. W. Norton & Co., 1994.

Evans, Kathy. "Restorative Justice in Education—Possibilities but Also Concerns," http://emu.edu/now/restorative-justice/2014/06/26/restorative-justice-in-education-possibilities-but-also-concerns/ <11 April 2016>, 2014.

Falk, Darrel. *Coming to Peace with Science: Bridging the Worlds Between Faith and Biology*. Downers Grove, Ill.: InterVarsity Press, 2004.

Faulkner, Danny R. "A Proposal for a New Solution to the Light Travel Time Problem." *Answers in Genesis*, 24 July 2013, https://answersingenesis.org/astronomy/starlight/a-proposal-for-a-new-solution-to-the-light-travel-time-problem/ <18 Aug. 2016>.

Feminist Mormon Housewives blog, 2016, http://www.feministmormonhousewives.org <19 July 2016>.

Follman, Mark. "More Guns, More Mass Shootings—Coincidence?" *Mother Jones*, no. 15 Dec. (2012), http://www.motherjones.com/politics/2012/09/mass-shootings-investigation <15 Aug. 2016>.

Frick, Don M. *Robert K. Greenleaf: A Life of Servant Leadership*. San Francisco: Berrett-Koehler Publishers, 2004.

Friedman, Edwin H. *A Failure of Nerve: Leadership in the Age of the Quick Fix*. Ed. Margaret M. Treadwell and Edward W. Beal. New York: Seabury Books, 1999.

Friesen, Abraham. *Menno Simons: Dutch Reformer Between Luther, Erasmus, and the Holy Spirit: A Study in the Problem Areas of Menno Scholarship*. Np: Xlibris, 2015.

Gilbreath Edward. *Birmingham Revolution: Martin Luther King Jr.'s Epic Challenge to the Church*. Downers Grove, Ill.: IVP Books, 2013.

"Global Christianity—a Report on the Size and Distribution of the World's Christian Popoulation." *Pew Research Center*, 19 December 2011, http://www.pewforum.org/2011/12/19/global-christianity-exec/.

Gollner, Philipp. "How Mennonites Became White: Religious Activism Cultural Power, and the Limits of Race." In *Good White Christians:How Immigrants Shaped Race, Changed America—and Lost Their Flavor*. Ph.D. diss., Philip Collner. University of Notre Dame, 2016.

Goossen, Rachel Waltner. "'Defanging the Beast': Mennonite Responses to John Howard Yoder's Sexual Abuse." *The Mennonite Quarterly Review* 89, no. 1 (January 2015): 7-80.

Graybill, Beth E. "'Finding My Place as a Lady Missionary': Mennonite Women Missionaries to Puerto Rico, 1945-1960." *Journal of Mennonite Studies* 17 (1999): 152-173.

Greenleaf, Robert K. *The Power of Servant Leadership*. Ed. Larry C. Spears. San Francisco: Berrett-Koehler Publishers, 1989.

———. *Servant Leadership: A Journey Into the Nature of Legitimate Power and Greatness*. Mahwah, N.J.: Paulist Press, 1977.

Gregory, Anne, Kathleen Clawson, Alycia Davis, and Jennifer Gerewitz. "The Promise of Restorative Practices to Transform Teacher-Student Relationships and Achieve Equity in School Discipline," *Journal of Educational and Psychological Consultation*, (4 Nov. 2014), http://www.tandfonline.com//doi/pdf/10.1080/10474412.2014.929950 <4 Aug. 2017>.

Gross, Leonard, and Jan Gleysteen. *Colonial Germantown Mennonites*. With a foreword by John L. Ruth. Telford, Pa.: Cascadia Publishing House, 2007.

Ham, Ken. "Answers in Genesis." https://answersingenesis.org/ <18 Aug. 2016>.

Harder, Leland, ed. *The Sources of Swiss Anabaptism: The Grebel Letters and Related Documents*. Classics of the Radical Reformation, vol. 4. Scottdale, Pa.: Herald Press, 1985.

Hardy, Nicole. *Confessions of a Latter-Day Virgin: A Memoir*. New York: Hyperion, 2013.

Hart, Drew G. I. "Anablacktivism: Following Jesus the Liberator and Peacemaker in the Twenty-First Century." In *A Living Alternative: Anabaptist Christianity in a Post-Christendom World*, ed. Joanna Harader and A. O. Green, 203-217. Garden City, New York: Etelloc Publishing, 2014.

Hatfield, Charles. *The Limits of Identity: Politics and Poetics in Latin America*. Austin, Texas: University of Texas Press, 2015.

Haught, John. *God After Darwin*. Boulder, Col.: Westview Press, 2000.

Hinojosa, Felipe. *Latino Mennonites: Civil Rights, Faith and Evangelical Culture*. Baltimore, Md.: Johns Hopkins University Press, 2014.

Hodges, Blair. The Book of Mormon Girl. *By Common Consent*, 17 May 2012, http://bycommonconsent.com/2012/05/17/review-joanna-brooks-the-book-of-mormon-girl-stories-from-an-american-faith-2/.

Holland, Scott. "How Do Stories Save Us? Two Contemporary Theological Responses." *Conrad Grebel Review* 12, no. 2 (Spring 1994): 131-153.

Horsch, John. *Modern Religious Liberalism: The Destructiveness and Irrationality of the New Theology*. Scottdale, Pa.: Fundamental Truth Depot, 1921.

Houser, Gordon. "The Top 10 Most Influential Mennonites." *The Mennonite*, June 2014, 53.

"'How Will Keeping a Personal Journal Bless Me and My Family." *LDS.Org* (2016), https://www.lds.org/youth/learn/ss/marriage-and-family/journal?lang=eng <19 July 2016>.

Hubmaier, Balthasar. *Balthasar Hubmaier: Theologian of Anabaptism*. Trans. and ed. H. Wayne Pipkin and John H. Yoder. Classics of the Reformation, vol. 5. Scottdale, Pa.: Herald Press, 1989.

Huebner, Chris K. *A Precarious Peace: Yoderian Explorations on Theology, Knowledge, and Identity*. With a foreword by Stanley Hauerwas. Scottdale, Pa.: Herald Press, 2006.

Hunter, J. Michael, ed. *Mormons and Popular Culture: The Global Influence of an American Phenomenon.* Santa Barbara, Calif.: Praeger/ABC-CLIO, 2013.

Hut, Hans. "On the Mystery of Baptism." In *The Radical Reformation*, ed. Michael G. Baylor, 152-171. Cambridge: Cambridge University Press, 1991.

Jain, Sonia, Henrissa Bassey, Martha A. Brown, and Kalra Preety. "Restorative Justice in Oakland Schools: Implementation and Impacts," http://www.ousd.org/cms/lib07/CA01001176/Centricity/Domain/134/OUSD-RJ%20Report%20revised%20Final.pdf <11 April 2016>.

Janzen, Rhoda. *Mennonite in a Little Black Dress.* New York: St. Martin's, 2010.

Jennings, Willie James. *The Christian Imagination: Theology and the Origins of Race.* New Haven & London: Yale University Press, 2010.

———. "The Fuller Difference: To Be a Christian Intellectual." *Fuller Magazine*, https://fullerstudio.fuller.edu/the-fuller-difference-to-be-a-christian-intellectual/.

Juhnke, James C. "Gemeindechristentum and Bible Doctrine: Two Mennonite Visions of the Early Twentieth Century." *Mennonite Quarterly Review* 57, no. 3 (July 1983): 206-221.

———. *Vision, Doctrine, War: Mennonite Identity and Organization in America 1890-1930.* Mennonite Experience in America, vol. 3. Scottdale, Pa.: Herald Press, 1989.

Kalshoven, Frits, and Liesbeth Zegveld. *Constraints on the Waging of War: An Introduction to International Humanitarian Law.* Cambridge: Cambridge University Press, 2011.

Kasdorf, Julia Spicher. "The Autoethnographic Announcement and the Story." In *After Identity: Mennonite Writing in North America*, ed. Robert Zacharias, 21-36. University Park, Pa.: Penn State University Press, 2015.

Kasdorf, Julia. "Dreams of the Written Character." In *The Measure of My Days: Engaging the Life and Thought of John L. Ruth*, ed. Reuben Z. Miller and Joseph S. Miller, 29-37. Telford, Pa.: Cascadia Publishing House, 2004.

———. *Sleeping Preacher.* Pittsburgh, Pa.: University of Pittsburgh Press, 1992.

Kaufman, Gordon D. *In Face of Mystery: A Constructive Theology.* Cambridge, Mass.: Harvard, 1993.

Kierkegaard, Soren. "The Sickness Unto Death: A Christian Psychological Exposition for Edification and Awakening." In *Fear and Trembling and the Sickness Unto Death.* Reprint, trans. Walter Lowrie, 141-278. Princeton, N.J.: Princeton University Press, 1974.

Kirby, Dawn Latta, and Kirby Dan. "Contemporary Memoir: A twenty-first-Century Genre Ideal for Teens." *English Journal* 99, no. 4 (March 2010): 22-29.

Klaassen, Walter. "Anabaptist Hermeneutics: Presuppositions, Principles and Practice." In *Essays on Biblical Interpretation: Anabaptist-Mennonite Perspectives*, ed. Willard Swartley. Text-Reader Series, 5-10. Elkhart, Ind.: Institute of Mennonite Studies, 1984.

Kniss, Fred. *Disquiet in the Land: Cultural Conflict in American Mennonite Communities*. New Brunswick, N.J.: Rutgers University Press, 1997.

Krall, Ruth. *The Elephants in God's Living Room: Clergy Sexual Abuse and Institutional Clericalism, 4 Vols*. N.p.: Enduring Space, 2012-2014. http://ruthkrall.com/wp-content/uploads/downloads/2015/09/The-Elephants-in-Gods-Living-Room-Vol-1-%C2%A9.pdf.

Kraybill, Donald B., Steven M. Nolt, and David L. Weaver-Zercher. *Amish Grace: How Forgiveness Transcended Tragedy*. San Francisco: Jossey-Bass, 2007.

Ku, Charlotte, and Paul F. Diehl. "International Law as Operating and Normative Systems: An Overview." In *International Law: Classic and Contemporary Readings*, ed. Charlotte Ku and Paul F. Diehl. Boulder, Col.: Lynne Rienner Publisheers, 2009.

Lakoff, George. "Metaphor and War: The Metaphor System Used to Justify War," 1992.

Lee, Bo Karen. "The Face of the Other: An Ethic of Delight." *Ogbomtoso Journal of Theology* 16, no. 1 (2011): 15-31.

Levine, Amy-Jill. *The Misunderstood Jew: The Church and the Scandal of the Jewish Jesus*. New York: HarperOne, 2006.

Lhamon, Catherine E., and Jocelyn Samuels. "Dear Colleague Letter on the Nondiscriminatory Administration of School Discipline," http://www2.ed.gov/about/offices/list/ocr/letters/colleague-201401-title-vi.pdf <11 April 2016>, 2014.

Liechty, Daniel, ed. and trans. *Early Anabaptist Spirituality: Selected Writings*. With a preface by Hans J. Hillerbrand. Classics of Western Spirituality. Mahwah, N.J.: Paulist Press, 1994.

Loder, James E. *The Logic of the Spirit: Human Development in Theological Perspective*. San Francisco: Jossey-Bass, 1998.

———. "Transformation in Christian Education." *The Princeton Seminary Bulletin* 3, no. 1 (1980): 11-25.

Loewen, Royden. *Village Among Nations. "Canadian" Mennonites in a Transnational World, 1916-2006*. Toronto: University of Toronto Press, 2013.

Machinist, Peter. "Nahum." In *The Harper Collins Bible Commentary*. Rev. ed., James L. Mays, 665-667. New York: HarperCollins, 2000.

MacMaster, Richard K. *Land, Piety, and Peoplehood: The Establishment of Mennonite Communities in America, 1683-1790*. Mennonite Experience in America, vol. 1. Scottdale, Pa.: Herald Press, 1984.

Manzullo-Thomas, Devin. "Mennonites, Evangelicals, and the Sexuality Debate in Christian Higher Ed." Blog entry, https://pietistschoolman.com/2015/08/12/mennonites-evangelicals-and-the-sexuality-debate-in-christian-higher-ed-devin-manzullo-thomas/.

Marpeck, Pilgram. *The Writings of Pilgram Marpeck*. Ed. and trans. William Klassen and Walter Klaassen. Classics of the Reformation, vol. 2. Scottdale, Pa.: Herald Press, 1978.

Martens, Paul. "How Mennonite Theology Became Superfluous in Three Easy Steps: Bender, Yoder, Weaver." *Journal of Mennonite Studies* 33 (2015): 149-166.
Mason, Patrick Q. "The Continuing Relevance of Mormon Studies: We're Certainly not in 2012 Anymore, but Mormonism Continues to Make the News." *Claremont Mormon Studies Newsletter* 11 (Fall 2014): 1-2.
Mast, Gerald J. *Go to Church, Change the World: Christian Community as Calling.* Harrisonburg, Va.: Herald Press, 2012.
———. "Sin and Failure in Anabaptist Theology." In *John Howard Yoder: Radical Theologian*, ed. J. Denny Weaver, foreword by Marva J. Dawn, afterword by Lisa Schirch, 351-370. Eugene, Ore.: Cascade Books, 2014.
Mast, Gerald J., and J. Denny Weaver. *Defenseless Christianity: Anabaptism for a Nonviolent Church.* Foreword by Greg Boyd. Telford, Pa.: Cascadia Publishing House; copublished with Herald Press, 2009.
Menno Simons. *The Complete Writings of Menno Simons c.1496-1561.* Ed. John Christian Wenger and trans. Leonard Verduin, with biography by Harold S. Bender. Scottdale, Pa.: Herald Press, 1956.
Mennonite Church General Assembly. "Biblical Interpretation in the Life of the Church." Adopted June 18-24, 1977, Estes Park, Colorado. Appendix I in *Slavery, Sabbath, War and Women: Case Issues in Biblical Interpretation*, Willard M. Swartley, 235-249. Scottdale, Pa.: Herald Press, 1983.
Mennonite Church USA. "Hope for the Future," http://mennoniteusa.org/what-we-do/undoing-racism/hope-for-the-future/.
Mennonite Education Agency. "Hope for the Future," http://www.mennoniteeducation.org/OurWork/Pages/Hope-for-the-Future.aspx.
"The Mennonites." *Third Way*, http://thirdway.com/mennonites/ <1 Aug. 2016>.
Merleau-Ponty, Maurice. *The Visible and the Invisible: Followed by Working Notes.* Ed. Claude Lefort. Trans. Alphonso Lingis. Evanston, Ill.: Northwestern University, 1968.
Meyer, Albert J. *Realizing Our Intentions: A Guide for Churches and Colleges with Distinctive Missions.* Abiline, Tex.: Abilene Christian University Press, 2009.
Miller, Emily McFarlan. "At Ark Encounter, a 'Biblical Worldview' on Display." *Mennonite World Review* 94, no. 15 (19 July 2016): 12.
Miller, Glenda Evon. "A Comparison of the Mennonite and Mormon Colonies in Northern Mexico." MA thesis. El Paso, Texas: University of Texas-El Paso, 1993.
Miller, Keith. *The Book on Fire.* Stafford, UK: Immanion Press, 2009.
———. *The Book of Flying.* New York: Riverhead Books, 2004.
Miller, Kenneth R. *Finding Darwin's God.* New York: HarperCollins, 1999.
Miller, Nancy K. "The Entangled Self: Genre Bondage in the Age of Memoir." *Publication of the Modern Language Association* 122, no. 2 (March 2007): 537-548.
Mitchell, Eve. "I Am a Woman and a Human: A Marxist-Feminist Critique of Intersectionality Theory." *Unity and Struggle*, 12 Sept. 2013, http://unityand-

struggle.org/2013/09/12/i-am-a-woman-and-a-human-a-marxist-feminist-critique-of-intersectionality-theory/ <19 July 2016>.

"Modesty." *LDS.Org* (2016), https://www.lds.org/topics/modesty?lang=eng <19 July 2016>.

Molina, Natalia. *How Race Is Made in America: Immigrants, Citizenship, and the Historical Power of Racial Scripts*. Oakland, Calif.: University of California Press, 2013.

Montel, Angela Horn. "How Does the Creativity of the Incarnated Word of God Shape the Discovering and Understanding of the Creation in My Discipline and in My Classroom? In *Creation, Christ, and the Classroom: Mennonite University Faculty Conference Presentations* (Goshen, Ind.: Mennonite Education Agency, 2008), 83-88

———. "Violent Images in Cell Biology." In *Teaching Peace: Nonviolence and the Liberal Arts*, ed. J. Denny Weaver and Gerald Biesecker-Mast, 223-234. Lanham, Md.: Rowman & Littlefield Publishers, Inc., 2003.

Murphy, Nancey C. *Reconciling Theology and Science: A Radical Reformation Perspective*. Kitchener, Ont. and Scottdale, Pa.: Pandora Press, co-published Herald Press, 1997.

Murphy, Nancey. "A Theology of Education." In *Mennonite Education in a Post-Christian World*, ed. Harry Huebner, 1-16. Winnipeg, Man.: CMBC Publications, 1998.

Murphy, Nancey, and George F. R. Ellis. *On the Moral Nature of the Universe: Theology, Cosmology, and Ethics*. Minneapolis: Fortress, 1996.

Murray, Stuart. *Biblical Interpretation in the Anabaptist Tradition*. Studies in the Believers Church Tradition. Kitchener, Ont.: Pandora Press, 2000.

Nardin, Terry. "Introduction." In *Nomos XLVII—Humanitarian Intervention*, ed. Terry Nardin and Melissa Williams, 1-30. New York: New York University Press, 2006.

"National Center for Science Education." https://ncse.com/ <18 Aug. 2016>.

Neilson, Reid L., and Matthew J. Grow. *From the Outside Looking in: Essays on Mormon History, Theology, and Culture*. Oxford, UK: Oxford University Press, 2016.

Nelson-Pallmeyer, Jack. *Jesus Against Christianity: Reclaiming the Missing Jesus*. Harrisburg, Pa.: Trinity Press International, 2001.

Newsom, Carol A. *The Book of Job: A Contest of Moral Imaginations*. Oxford; New York: Oxford University Press, 2003.

Nolt, Steven, and Harry Loewen. *Through Fire and Water: An Overview of Mennonite History*. Rev. ed. Scottdale, Pa.: Herald Press, 2010.

Olson, Dennis T. "Biblical Theology as Provisional Monologization: A Dialogue with Childs, Brueggemann and Bakhtin." *Biblical Interpretation* 6, no. 2 (April 1998): 162-180.

Oppel, Richard A. Jr., Sheryl Gay Stolberg, and Matt Apuzzo. "U.S. to Criticize Baltimore Police Over Racial Bias." *The New York Times*, 10 Aug. 2016, A1, A13.

Osiel, Mark. *Mass Atrocity, Collective Memory, and the Law.* New Brunswick, NS: Transaction Publishers, 2000.

Oxford Dictionaries, http://www.oxforddictionaries.com/us/definition/american_english/transparent <14 Dec. 2015>.

Pal, Amitabh. *"Islam" Means Peace: Understanding the Muslim Principle of Nonviolence.* Santa Barbara, Calif.: Praeger, 2011.

Pattison, George. *Kierkegaard's Upbuilding Discourses: Philosophy Literature, and Theology.* New York: Routledge, 0202.

Penner, Carol, ed. *Women and Men: Gender in the Church.* Scottdale, Pa.: Mennonite Publishing House, 1998.

Penner, Christina. *Widows of Hamilton House.* Winnipeg, Man.: Enfield & Wizenly, 2008.

Pereira, Jairzinho Lopes. *Augustine of Hippo and Martin Luther on original sin and Justification of the Sinner.* Gottingen: Vandenhoeck & Ruprecht, 2013.

Perelman, Chaim, and Lucie Olbrechts-Tyteca. *The New Rhetoric.* Notre Dame, Ind.: University of Notre Dame Press, 1969.

Peterson, Eugene H. *Where You Treasure Is: Psalms That Summon You from Self to Community.* Grand Rapids, Mich.: William B. Eerdmans Publishing Co., 1985.

Plett, Casey. "Portland, Oregon." In *A Safe Girl to Love*, 93-121. New York: Topside Press, 2014.

Pranis, Kay. *The Little Book of Circle Processes: A New/Old Approach to Peacemaking.* Intercourse, Pa.: Good Books, 2005.

Pratt, Timothy. "Mormon Women Set Out to Take a Stand, Through Pants." *New York Times*, 19 December 2012, A25.

Putnam, Robert. *American Grace: How Religion Divides and Unites Us.* New York: Simon and Schuster, 2010.

Radner, Ephraim. *A Brutal Unity: The Spiritual Politics of the Christian Church.* Waco, Tex.: Baylor University Press, 2012.

Rectenwald, Michael. "What's Wrong with Identity Politics (and Intersectionality Theory)? A Response to Mark Fisher's 'Exiting the Vampire Castle (and Its Critics)'." *The North Star*, 2 December 2013, http://www.thenorthstar.info/?p=11411 <19 July 2016>.

Reygadas, Carlos, director. *Stellet Licht [Silent Light].* DVD. Mantarraya, Bac and No Dream Films, 2007.

Riedemann, Peter. *Peter Riedemann's Hutterite Confession of Faith.* John J. Friesen. Classics of the Radical Reformation. Scottdale, Pa.: Herald Press, 1999.

Rieger, Joerg. *Christ and Empire: From Paul to Postcolonial Times.* Minneapolis: Fortress Press, 2007.

Risjord, Norman K. *The Civil War Generation.* Lanham, Md.: Rowman & Littlefield, 2002.

Romney, Mitt. "Transcript: Mitt Romney's Faith Speech." NPR, 6 Dec. 2007, http://www.npr.org/templates/story/story.php?storyId=16969460 <19 July 2016>.

Romney, Thomas Cottam. *The Mormon Colonies in Mexico*. With a new introduction. Salt Lake City, Utah: University of Utah Press, 2005.
Rorty, Richard. "Religion as a Conversation-Stopper." In *Philosophy and Social Hope*, 168-74. New York: Penguin, 1999.
Rosenberg, Marshall B. *Nonviolent Communication: A Language of Life*. 2nd ed. Encinitas, Calif.: PuddleDancer Press, 2003.
Roth, John D. *Stories: How Mennonites Came to Be*. Scottdale, Pa.: Herald Press, 2006.
———. *Teaching That Transforms: Why Anabaptist-Mennonite Education Matters*. Scottdale, Pa.: Herald Press, 2011.
Ruth, John L. *Mennonite Identity and Literary Art*. Scottdale, Pa.: Herald Press, 1978.
"Sacrament." *LDS.Org* (2016), https://www.lds.org/topics/sacrament?lang=eng <19 July 2016>.
Said, Edward. *Orientalism*. New York: Vintage Books, 1979.
Samatar, Sofia. *A Stranger in Olondria*. Easthampton, Mass: Small Beer Press, 2013.
Sanders, John. *The God Who Risks: A Theology of Providence*. Downers Grove, Illinois: InterVarsity Press, 1998.
Satterwhite, James H. "Nonviolent Political Movements as Missed Opportunity in Kosovo." In *Teaching Peace: Nonviolence and the Liberal Arts*, ed. J. Denny Weaver and Gerald Biesecker-Mast, 89-101. Lanham, Md.: Rowman & Littlefield Publishers, Inc., 2003.
Sawatsky, Rodney J. "What Can the Mennonite Tradition Contribute to Christian Higher Education?" In *Models for Christian Higher Education: Strategies for Success in the Twenty-First Century*, ed. Richard T. Hughes and William B. Adrian, 187-199. Grand Rapids, Mich.: William B. Eerdmans Publishing Co., 1997.
Sawatzky, Harry Leonard. *They Sought a Country: Mennonite Colonization in Mexico*. Berkeley, Calif.: University of California Press, 1971.
Schlabach, Theron F. *Peace, Faith, Nation: Mennonites and Amish in Nineteenth-Century America*. The Mennonite Experience in America, vol. 2. Scottdale, Pa.: Herald, 1988.
Schreiber, Gerhard. "Christoph Schrempf: The 'Swabian Socrates' as Trans. of Kierkegaard." In *Kierkegaard's Influence on Theology, Tome I: German Protestant Theology*, ed. Jon Steward. Kierkegaard Research: Sources Reception and Resources, Vol. 10. Burlington, Vt.: Ashgate, 2012.
Schultze, Quentin. *Communicating for Life: Christian Stewardship in Community and Media*. Grand Rapids, Mich.: Baker Book House, 2000.
Schwehn, Mark R. *Exiles from Eden: Religion and the Academic Vocation in America*. New York: Oxford University Press, 1993.
Scott, Eugenie. "The Creation/Evolution Continuum." *National Center for Science Education* (2000). http://www.ncseweb.org/resources/articles/9213_the_creationevolution_continu_12_7_2000.asp <18 Aug. 2016>.
Seibert, Eric A. *Disturbing Divine Behavior: Troubling Old Testament Images of God*. Minneapolis: Fortress Press, 2009.

Seiling, Jonathan. "Solae (Quae?) Scripturae: Anabaptists and the Apocrypha." *The Mennonite Quarterly Review* 80, no. 1 (Jan. 2006): 5-34.

Sharp, Gene. *The Methods of Nonviolent Action*. The Politics of Nonviolent Action, vol. 2. Boston: Porter Sargent Publishing, 1973.

———. *Waging Nonviolent Struggle: Twentieth Century Practice and Twenty-First Century Potential*. N.p.: Porter Sargent Publishers, Inc., 2005.

Shearer, Tobin Miller. "Conflicting Identities: White Racial Formation Among Mennonites, 1960-1985." *Identities* 19, no. 3 (2012): 268-284.

———. *Daily Demonstrators: The Civil Rights Movement in Mennonite Homes and Sanctuaries*. Baltimore, Md.: Johns Hopkins University Press, 2010.

Shenk, Sara Wenger. *Anabaptist Ways of Knowing: A Conversation About Tradition-Based Critical Education*. Telford, Pa.: Cascadia Publishing House, 2003.

Short, Jake. Personal correspondence, 16 Oct. 2015.

Showalter, Shirley Hershey. "Deep Calls to Deep: Spirituality and Diversity at Goshen College." In *Education as Transformation: Religious Pluralism, Spirituality and a New Vision for Higher Education in America*, ed. Victor Kazanjian and Peter Laurence. New York: Peter Lang, 2000.

Sider, J. Alexander. *To See History Doxologically: History and Holiness in John Howard Yoder's Ecclesiology*. Grand Rapids, Mich.: William B. Eerdmans Publishing Co., 2011.

Siegel, Daniel J. *The Developing Mind: How Relationships and the Brain Interact to Shape Who We Are*. 2nd ed. New York: The Guilford Press, 2012.

Sipe, James W., and Don M. Frick. *Seven Pillars of Servant Leadership: Practicing the Wisdom of Leading by Serving*. Mahwah, N.J.: Paulist Press, 2009.

Smith, Wilford E. "'Peculiar' People." In *Encyclopedia of Mormonism*, ed. Daniel H. Ludlow, 1072-1074. New York: Macmillan, 1992.

Snyder, C. Arnold, and Linda A. Huebert Hecht, eds. *Profiles of Anabaptist Women: Sixteenth-Century Reforming Pioneers*. Studies in Women and Religion/Études sur les Femmes et la Religion. Waterloo, Ont.: Wilfrid Laurier University Press, 1996.

Souder, Lawrence. "What Are We to Think About Thought Experiments?" *Argumentation* 17, no. 2 (June 2003): 203-217.

Spears, Larry C. "Introduction: Tracing the Past, Present, and Future of Servant Leadership." In *Focus on Leadership: Servant-Leadership for the Twenty-First Century*. 3rd ed. Larry C. Spears, 1-16, 2002.

Spronk, Klaas. *Nahum*. Historical Commentary on the Old Testament. Kampen, The Netherlands: Kok Pharos Publishing House, 1997.

Stassen, Glen H., and Michael L. Westmoreland-White. "Defining Violence and Nonviolence." In *Teaching Peace: Nonviolence and the Liberal Arts*, ed. J. Denny Weaver and Gerald Biesecker-Mast, 17-36. Lanham, Md.: Rowman & Littlefield Publishers, Inc., 2003.

Statute of the International Court of Justice. "Article 18," http://www.icj-cij.org/documents/index.php?p1=4&p2=2&p3=0. <1 Aug. 2016>.

Stoner, Andre Gingerich. "Our Victim Mentality." *Mennonite World Review*, 28 May 2012, 5.
Stowe, Gene. "Ark Replicates Genesis: Craftsmen Follow Biblical Blueprint to Build Creation Museum Attraction." *Mennonite World Review* 94, no. 15 (19 July 2016): 1, 12.
Stutzman, Ervin R. *From Nonresistance to Justice: The Transformation of Mennonite Church Peace Rhetoric, 1908-2008*. Scottdale, Pa.: Herald Press, 2011.
Taylor Astra, director. *Zizek!* DVD. United States: Zeitgeist Films, 2005.
Thiessen, Janis. "Communism and Labor Unions: The Changing Perspective of Mennonites in Canada and the United States." *Direction* 38, no. 1 (Spring 2009): 181-202.
Thompson, Janna. *Taking Responsibility for the Past: Reparation and Historical Justice*. Cambridge: Polity Press, 2002.
Thurer, Daniel. *International Humanitarian Law: Theory, Practice, Context*. 3rd ed. The Hague, Netherlands: Hague Academy of International Law, 2011.
Tiessen, Hildi Froese. "After Identity: Liberating the Mennonite Literary Text." In *After Identity: Mennonite Writing in North America*, ed. Robert Zacharias. University Park, Pa.: Penn State University Press, 2015.
Toews, Miriam. *All My Puny Sorrows*. San Francisco: McSweeney's, 2014.
———. *A Complicated Kindness*. New York: Counterpoint, 2005.
———. *Irma Voth*. New York: Harper, 2011.
Toews, Paul. *Mennonites in American Society, 1930-1970: Modernity and the Persistence of Religious Community*. The Mennonite Experience in America, vol. 4. Scottdale, Pa.: Herald Press, 1996.
———. "The Quest for the Mennonite Holy Grail: Reflections on 'The Mennonite Experience in America's Project." *Direction* 26, no. 1 (Spring 1997): 43-61.
Tracy, David. *Blessed Rage for Order: The New Pluralism in Theology*. New York: Seabury Press, 1975.
———. *Dialogue with the Other: The Interreligious Dialogue*. Grand Rapids, Mich.: William B. Eerdmans Publishing Co., 1991.
UNESCO Institute for Statics. "Data Center." *Unitred Nations Educational, Scientific, and Cultural Organization* (2015), http://data.uis.unesco.org/Index.aspx <11 Aug. 2016>.
United Nations Security Council. *Resolution 794*. New York: United Nations Security Council, 1992.
The United Nations. *Charter of the United Nations*, 1945.
van Braght, Thieleman J., ed. *The Bloody Theater or Martyrs Mirror, Compiled from Various Authentic Chronicles, Memorials, and Testimonies*. Trans. Joseph F. Sohm. Scottdale, Pa.: Herald Press, 1987.
———. *The Bloody Theater or Martyrs Mirror of the Defenseless Christians Who Baptized Only Upon Confession of Faith, and Who Suffered and Died for the Testimony of Jesus, Their Savior, from the Time of Christ to the Year A.D. 1660*. Trans. Joseph F. Sohm. Scottdale, Pa.: Mennonite Publishing House, 1950.

Van Dyk, Leanne. "Vision and Imagination in Atonement Doctrine." *Theology Today* 50, no. 1 (April 1993): 4-12.
Voon, Tania. "Pointing the Finger: Civilian Casualities of NATO Bombing in Kosovo Conflict." *American University International Law Review* 16, no. 4 (2001): 1083-1113.
Waite, Gary K. *David Joris and Dutch Anabaptism, 1524-1543*. Waterloo, Ont.: Wilfrid Laurier University Press, 1990.
Weaver, J. Denny. *Anabaptist Theology in Face of Postmodernity: A Proposal for the Third Millennium*. Foreword by Glen Stassen. C. Henry Smith Series, vol. 2. Telford, Pa.: Pandora Press U.S., copublished Herald Press, 2000.
———. *God Without Violence: Following a Nonviolent God in a Violent World*. Eugene, Ore.: Cascade Books, 2016.
———. "The Jewish Jesus and the Doctrine of Discovery," https://dofdmenno.org/2015/11/03/the-jewish-jesus-and-the-doctrine-of-discovery/
———. *The Nonviolent Atonement*. 2nd ed., greatly rev. and expanded. Grand Rapids: William B. Eerdmans Publishing Co., 2011.
———. *The Nonviolent God*. Grand Rapids, Mich.: William B. Eerdmans Publishing Co., 2013.
———. "The Socially Active Community: An Alternative Ecclesiology." In *The Limits of Perfection: Conversations with J. Lawrence Burkholder*. 2nd ed. Rodney J. Sawatsky and Scott Holland, 71-94. Waterloo, Ont.; Kitchener, Ont.: Institute of Anabaptist and Mennonite Studies, Conrad Grebel College; Pandora Press, 1993.
———. "Teaching for Peace." In *Mennonite Education in a Post-Christian World*, ed. Harry Huebner, 67-80. Winnipeg, Man.: CMBC Publications, 1998.
———. "Theology in the Mirror of the Martyred and Oppressed: Reflections on the Intersections of Yoder and Cone." In *The Wisdom of the cross: Essays in Honor of John Howard Yoder*, ed. Stanley Hauerwas, Chris K. Hauerwas, Harry J. Huebner, and Mark Thiessen Nation, 409-429. Grand Rapids: William B. Eerdmans Publishing Co., 1999.
Weaver, J. Denny, and Gerald Biesecker-Mast, eds. *Teaching Peace: Nonviolence and the Liberal Arts*. Lanham, Md.: Rowman & Littlefield Publishers, Inc., 2003.
Weaver-Zercher, Valerie. "*The Book of Mormon Girl*, by Joanna Brooks." Review of *The Book of Mormon Girl*. *The Christian Century*, 25 Oct. 2012, 39-40.
Weiss, Gail. *Body Images: Embodiment as Intercorporeality*. New York: Routledge, 1999.
Whitehead, Alfred North. *Process and Reality*. Corrected ed. New York: Free Press, 1978.
Wiebe, Rudy. *Come Back*. Toronto: Knopf, 2014.
———. *Peace Shall Destroy Many*. Toronto: McClelland, 1962.
Williams, George Huntston, and Angel M. Mergal, eds. *Spiritual and Anabaptist Writers: Documents Illustrative of the Radical Reformation*. The Library of Christian Classics, vol. 25. Philadelphia: The Westminster Press, 1957.

Williams, Timothy, and Joseph Goldstein. "Censure of Baltimore Revives Zero-Toolerance Policing Doubt." *The New York Times*, 11 August 2016, A1, A114.

Wink, Walter. "Facing the Myth of Redemptive Violence." *Ekklesia*, 15 November 2014, http://www.ekklesia.co.uk/content/cpt/article_060823wink.shtml <15 Aug. 2016>; http://www.ekklesia.co.uk/content/cpt/article_060823 wink.shtml <15 Aug. 2016>.

Witham, Larry. "Many Scientists See God's Hand in Evolution." *The Washington Times*, 11 April 1997, A8.

Wittmann, Rebecca. *Justice: The Auschwitz Trial*. Cambridge, Mass.: Harvard University Press, 2005.

Wojik, Mark E. "On the Sudden Loss of a Human Rights Activist: A Tribute to Dr. Jonathan Mann's Use of International Human Rights Law in the Global Battle Against AIDS." *The John Marshall Law Review* 32, no. 1 (Fall 1998): 129-139.

Yoder, Anita Hooley. "I've Read Too Much Poetry for That: Poetry, Personal Transformation and Peace." *CrossCurrents* 64, no. 4 (Dec. 2014): 454-465.

Yoder, John H[oward], trans. and ed. *The Legacy of Michael Sattler*. Classics of the Radical Reformation, vol. 1. Scottdale, Pa.: Herald Press, 1973.

———. "Armaments and Eschatology." *Studies in Christian Ethics* 1 (1988): 43-61.

———. *The Jewish-Christian Schism Revisited*. Ed. Michael G. Cartwright and Peter Ochs. Grand Rapids, Mich.: William B. Eerdmans Publishing Co., 2003.

———. *Preface to Theology: Christology and Theological Method*. With an introduction by Stanley Hauerwas and Alex Sider. Grand Rapids, Mich.: Brazos Press, 2002.

———. *The Priestly Kingdom: Social Ethics as Gospel*. Notre Dame, Ind.: University of Notre Dame Press, 1984.

———. *To Hear the Word*. 2nd ed. Eugene, Ore.: Cascade Books, 2010.

———. *When War is Unjust: Being Honest in Just-War Thinking*. 2nd ed. Maryknoll, N.Y.: Orbis, 1996.

Yoder, John Howard, with, Joan Baez, Tom Skinner, Leo Tolstoy, and others. *What Would You Do?: A Serious Answer to a Standard Question*. Expanded ed. Scottdale, Pa.: Herald Press, 1992.

Zacharias, Robert, ed. *After Identity: Mennonite Writing in North America*. University Park, Pa.: Pennsylvania State University Press, 2015.

Zavala, Oswaldo. "Imagining the U.S-Mexico Drug War: The Critical Limits of Narconarratives." *Comparative Literature* 66, no. 3 (Summer 2014): 340-360.

Zehr, Howard. *Changing Lenses: A New Focus for Crime and Justice*. 3rd ed. A Christian Peace Shelf Selection. Scottdale, Pa.: Herald Press, 2005.

———. *The Little Book of Restorative Justice*. Intercourse, Pa.: Good Books, 2002.

THE INDEX

A

Abraham (Patriarch), 27, 32-33, 129, 132, 137
Abuse, sexual, 17, 41, 49n4, 157, 213, 235n8
African Americans, 49, 56, 80, 98, 89. *See also* Church, Black; Black Theology; Womanist Theology
After Identity: Mennonite Writing in North America, 227
All My Puny Sorrows, 214
Alvarez, Luis, 91, 96
Amish, Old Order, 43, 146, 294
Anabaptism/Anabaptist, 17, 115, 152, 216
"Anabaptist Vision," 75
    and Apocrypha, 141, 145-149
    contemporary, 97, 160, 164, 279
    hermeneutics, 78, 115-116, 117-123
    and education, 99-109, 164, 181-184, 188-191, 310
    and "priesthood of all believers," 173
    and the self, 194-197
    and servant leadership, 164, 170, 178
    sixteenth-century, 43, 62, 67, 78, 114, 147-149, 156,185-187, 232
    theology, 58, 77- 84
    See also *Martyrs Mirror*
Anabaptist Ways of Knowing, 77, 188
Anna Jansz, 186-187
Answers in Genesis, 322-23
Apocrypha, 20, 136, 141-150
    Anabaptist use of, 13, 147-150
Aristotle, 279
Augsburger, Myron, 107
Atonement theology, 47, 115, 299-301
Aquinas, Thomas, 257
Augustine of Hippo, 257

B

Bakhtin, Mikhail, 99, 102-105
Balkans, 249, 252, 264-269
Baptism, 152, 160, 173, 184
Barak, 126-127
Bechtel, Greg, 214-16, 218-220, 221n9
Becker, Palmer, 197
Behe, Michael, 324-325
Bender, Harold S., 75, 174
Berry, Malinda Elizabeth, 41, 154

351

Bible
  Anabaptist interpretation of, 116-123
  Old Testament, 25, 32, 103, 118-122, 137-138, 141, 300
  Old Testament violence, 13, 20, 50n4, 115-116, 125-129
Biblical Interpretation in the Anabaptist Tradition, 117
Black Church. *See*, Church, Black
Black Theology, 26, 56-58, 80, 84
Blaser, Martin, 327
Bluffton University, 12, 18, 101, 155, 190-191
Body Images, 229
Bonhoeffer, Dietrich, 204
Book of Mormon Girl, 223-224, 227, 230
Bosnia. *See* Balkans
Boundary Problems, 216
Brandt, Di, 213-214
Braun, Jan Guenther, 214
Brenneman, Laura L., 115, 147
Brethren, Church of, the, 43, 115
Breu, Christopher, 229, 234
Brooks, Joanna, 223-234
Brunk, George R., Bishop, 155
Burke, Kenneth, 306-307, 310, 315
Burkholder, Jared, 107

C

Calvin, John, 173
Carter, J. Kameron, 59n1, 82-84, 181
Chalcedon. *See* Christology. Chalcedon
Changing Lenses, 157, 302n3
Chávez, César, 93-95
Christendom, 76-81, 257
Christology, 55-57
  Chalcedon, 47, 56

Constantinople, 55
  life of Jesus, separated from, 47, 56
  New Testament, 55
  Nicea, 47, 55
Church
  beyond the church, 45-46
  Black, 75-84
  as community, 123, 152-153, 196-198
  Early, 25-26, 47, 54-57
  and education, 18, 44, 182-185, 202
  Established, 43-45, 78
  and farm workers, 95
  as flawed, 13, 153, 156-163, 185-191
  Latino, 88-89
  Leadership, 173-175, 178-79
  and LGBTQ, 18, 214-215 220
  Marginal, 210, 223
  peace church, 18, 43-44, 57, 114-115, 170, 183, 282
  and sexuality, 17-18, 41, 157, 292
  White, 45, 75-76, 81, 88-91, 181
  as witness to the world, 17, 41-42, 76, 82-83, 99, 152, 291, 332
Church of Jesus Christ of Latter Day Saints. *See* Mormons
Church Women United, 93
Circle way, 176-179, 284-291
Come Back, 214
Coming to Peace with Science, 323, 326
Confession of Faith in Mennonite Perspective, 160, 196-197, 205, 225-226
Complicated Kindness, 239

Copeland, M. Shawn, 81-84
Conquest of Palestine, 120, 126, 132-133
Constantinople. *See* Christology, Constantinople.
Copernicus, Nicolaus, 279
Cosmos. *See* Science, cosmos
Council of Christian Colleges and Universities [CCCU], 101
Creation, 14, 42, 66, 144, 148, 182-183, 197, 281-282, 320-321, 326-328
    in Genesis, 129-131, 137, 139n2, 189, 328
    Creationism, young earth, 277, 281, 321-325
    and intelligent design, 321, 324-325
Cruz, Daniel Shank, 210

D

Daniel (book), 136-138, 141, 144-145
David Joris, 147, 186
David (King), 27, 127, 134-135
Darwin, Charles, 169, 323-326
Darwin's Black Box, 324
Dean, Kenda Creasy, 200
Deborah, 126
De León, Lupe, 89, 93
Delano, California, 87, 91-93, 96
Denck, Hans, 77, 148
De Vitoria, Francisco, 257-258
Developing Mind, 201
Discipleship, 62, 84, 171, 188, 202
    as Anabaptist characteristic, 77, 81, 118, 122, 183
Dobzhansky, Theodosius, 320
Doctrine of Discovery, 56, 59n1
Dyck, Cornelius J., 196

E

Eastern Mennonite University [EMU], 101, 106, 283-284, 291
Ecclesiology. *See* Church
Elisha, 134
Encyclopedia of Mormonism, 226
Enuma Elish, 129-130
Enright, Robert, 296
Enfleshing Freedom, 81
Enlightenment, 64-66, 81, 182, 270n3
Erikson, Erik, 194-195, 200-203
Eucharist. *See* Lord's Supper
Evolution, 14, 21, 59n3, 274, 277-279, 282-282, 320-328
Exiles from Eden, 64
Exodus (from Egypt), 126-128, 132
Ewert, Lowell, 243, 270

F

Falk, Darrel, 323-326
Finding Darwin's God, 323, 325
First Nations, 44, 83
Flood, Great, 126, 128, 131, 139n3, 327
Follman, Mark, 316
Forgiveness, 54, 147
    in atonement images, 299-301
    by Jesus, 28, 36-37, 47, 296-297
    and love of enemies, 297-298
    in Prodigal Son, 294, 297, 301
    in psychology, 294-296
    in restorative justice, 21, 276-277, 301-302
Fox, George, 170, 174
Frick, Don, 166-168

G

Gandhi, Mahatma, 242

Gay. *See* LGBTQ
General Conference Mennonite Church, 94-95, 97n2
Gideon, 133-134
Global warming, 277-278, 282
God After Darwin, 325
God, nonviolence of. *See* Nonviolence, of God
Goossen, Rachel Waltner, 157
Go to Church, Change the World, 184
Goshen College, 88, 93, 101, 106, 157
Goshen, Indiana, 87, 91-93, 96
Grace College, 107
Grain of the universe, 16, 19, 21, 45-46, 49, 199, 201, 242-243, 246, 258, 275-277, 294, 298, 332-333
Greenleaf, Robert K., 164-176
Grotius, Hugo, 258

H
Ham, Ken, 322
Harding, Vincent, 75
Hart, Drew G. I., 41, 44, 58, 115, 160
Hatfield, Charles, 228, 229, 234
Haught, John, 325
Hegel, Georg Wilhelm Friedrich, 64, 68
Heinzekehr, Hannah, 41, 153, 292
Heinzekehr, Justin, 58
Hermeneutical community, 77-78, 118
Hershberger, Guy F., 94-96
Hinojosa, Felipe, 41, 45, 59, 104, 115, 158, 223, 227-228
Holland, Scott, 71n7, 104
Homosexuality. *See* LGBTQ
Holocaust, German, 188, 253
Houser, Gordon, 157
Huebner, Chris, 71n7, 79-81, 84

Huerta, Dolores, 93
Humanitarian law. *See* International law, Law of war
Human rights. *See* International law, Human rights

I
Identity studies, 224, 227-229
International criminal prosecution. *See* International law, Criminal prosecution
International law, 20, 243, 246-248, 251-254
    Criminal prosecution, 246-247, 251-254
    Human rights, 246-254
    Law of war, 247-250, 253-254
Irma Voth, 223-224, 227, 230
Isaac (Patriarch), 132
Isaiah, 14, 27-28, 32, 37, 106, 127, 154
Islam. *See* Muslim

J
Jael, 127
Janzen, Rebecca, 210
Jennings, Willie James, 105-106
Jeremiah, 37, 135, 138
Jesus,
    birth, 26-27, 178
    and the church, 152, 162, 173, 179, 182-185, 197, 205
    coninuing Israel's history, 116, 125, 137-138
    death, 39-40
    as disruptive, 70, 192
    and economics 32, 137
    and forgiveness, 28, 36-37, 47, 296-301
    identified by narrative, 18-19, 25-43, 54-55, 117, 137, 171, 210, 217

healings and restorations, 28-29
healing the withered hand, 29
   as human, 34-35, 56, 121-122
   and humility, 195, 197, 205
   literary parallels, 217, 233
   mission of, 27-28, 152-153, 187, 190
   nonviolence of, 33-36, 44, 48, 57, 115, 125, 137, 242, 281, 297
   "proved," 58
   reveals God, 49, 55, 58, 102, 121-122, 125, 138, 298
   and resurrection, 40-41
   and Sabbath, 29-30
   and Samaritans, 30-31, 175
   as saving story, 189, 198
   sayings, 33-38, 198, 204, 215
   and servant leadership, 169, 171
   as source for theology/ethics, 41-42, 54, 61, 76-77, 81-84, 89, 114-115, 119-122, 195, 323, 331, 333
   and temple cleansing, 36-37
   and women, 30-32, 131, 294, 296-297
Jonah, 103, 119-122, 134-135
Joshua, 119-122, 126, 132-133
Jude, 141, 143
Judges (book), 126, 133
Just war theory, 20, 243, 256-270, 312, 315
Justice
   restorative. *See* Restorative justice
   retributive. *See* Retributive justice

K

Kasdorf, Julia Spicher, 88, 213-14
Kauffman, Rudi, 243
Khan, Abdul Ghaffar (Badshah), 242
Kierkegaard, Soren, 195, 199-200, 203

King, Martin Luther, Jr., 75, 274
Kirby, Dan and Dawn Latta, 230
Klaassen, Walter, 118
Kosovo nonviolent movement, 269

L

Lakoff, George, 313-315
Lancaster Mennonite Conference [LMC], 108, 157
Latino/a, 44, 56, 289
   Mennonites, 20, 44, 59, 87-91, 94, 96, 236n19
   Latino Mennonites: Civil Rights, Faith, and Evangelical Culture, 88
Law of war. *See* International law, law of war
LGBTQ, 18, 20, 41, 97n2, 106, 153, 157, 161, 211-215, 218, 220, 292
Lederach, John Paul, 156
Lesbians. *See* LGBTQ
Limits of Identity, 228
Lord's Supper, 152, 184
Luther, Martin, 173-174

M

Madison, Wisconsin, 276, 284, 287-290
Margins/marginal, 82, 246, 254
   and African Americans, 44-45, 56, 75, 115
   Biblical interpretation from, 20, 68, 114-116, 121-123, 146-147
   and Latino/a, 44-45, 59
   literary interpretation from, 210-211, 223-224
   and LGBTQ, 41, 215
   and Mennonites, 44, 56-58, 61, 219, 246
   and women, 20

Marpeck, Pilgram, 72n20, 148-149
Martyrs Mirror, 149, 159, 185, 189
Mast, Gerald J., 19, 41. 153. 158
Mennonite Brethren, 94-95, 225
Mennonite Central Committee [MCC], 94-97, 242, 245, 284
Mennonite Church USA, 159-164, 234n3
   and abuse, 17
   Conflict, 157-163, 218
   LGBTQ, 18, 97n2, 108, 157, 161, 211, 214, 237n24
   privilege, 159
   and race, 162
   structure, 160-161, 225
Mennonite Education Agency, 99, 106
Mennonite Experience in America [Series], 50n6, 91
Mennonite General Assembly, 118-119
Mennonite Identity and Literary Art, 214
Menno Simons, 67, 69, 147, 173, 186-187, 232
Metaphysics, 62-63, 66-70
Meyer, Albert, 183
Meyer, Jocele T. 93-94, 96
Miller, Kenneth, 323, 325
Miller, Nancy K. 230
Minority Ministries Council, 88, 93, 96
Missing Microbes, 327
Mitchell, Eve, 228, 234
Molina, Natalia, 91
Montel, Angela Horn, 280, 282
Mormons, 20, 210, 223-234
Münsterites, 186-187, 197
Murphy, Nancey, 279, 281, 325
Murray, Stuart, 77, 117
Muslim, 57, 242

N

Nahum, 128, 134-135
National Center for Science Education [NCSE], 322-326
National Farm Worker Association; 93
National Farm Worker Ministry, 93
Native Americans. *See* First Nations
Nehemiah, 103
Newsom, Carol, 103-104
Nicea. *See* Christology, Nicea/Nicene Creed.
Nicene Creed. *See* Christology, Nicea/Nicene Creed.
Nineveh, 120, 128, 134-135
Nonviolence/nonviolent, 19-20, 47-49, 58, 62, 69, 203, 284, 331
   Activism, biblical, 14, 35, 48, 54, 116, 134, 136,
   Activism, contemporary, 48, 156, 162, 242, 269, 275, 305, 332
   Atonement image, 300-301
   Defined, 48
   of God, 19, 29, 115-116, 125, 129-138, 281, 300
   Jesus, 19, 28, 33-37, 43-45, 54, 62, 114-115, 137-138, 242, 275, 277, 281, 297-298
   Menno Simons, 67
   Old Testament, 29, 129-136
   and pacifist dilemma, 305-306, 308, 317
   Reign of God, 28, 35-36, 39-40, 48

O

Obbe Philips, 187
Obrechts-Tyreca, Lucie, 311
(Old) Mennonite Church, 88, 94, 97n2, 155

Old Testament. *See* Bible, Old Testament,

P

Pacifism, 71, 79, 115, 119, 245
Pacifist's dilemma, 20, 277, 304-317
Peace Shall Destroy Many, 213
Perelman, Chaim, 311
Peterson, Eugene, 197, 205
Plato, 102, 307-308
Pluralism, 20, 57-58, 70,
Precarious Peace, 79
Priesthood of all believers, 13, 154, 165, 173-175, 178
Process thought, 19, 58, 62-64. 68. 70
Prodigal Son. *See* Forgiveness, Prodigal Son.
Pseudepigrapha, 141, 144-147
Putnam, Robert, 184

Q

Quakers, 115, 170, 174
questions i asked my mother, 214

R

Race: A Theological Account, 59n1, 82
Racism, 43, 48-49, 58, 90, 96, 159, 176, 323
  and Jesus, 30-32, 47, 54
  Church silent on, 56, 58, 59n1, 115
Radner, Ephraim, 188-189
Rectenwald, Michael, 228
Redekop. Calvin, 160
Relativism. *See*, Pluralism
Restorative Justice, 13, 19, 21, 33, 156-158, 176, 183, 245, 275-277, 301, 333
  and forgiveness, 301-302
  in schools, 283-294

Retributive justice, 13, 275-276
Roth, John, 77, 101, 105-106, 204
Ruth (book), 103
Ruth, John L., 214, 218
Rwanda, 252, 262-269

S

Said, Edward, 181
Schultze, Quentin, 187
Schwehn, Mark, 58, 64-69
Samaritans. *See* Jesus and Samaritans
Samatar, Sofia, 215
Schirch, Lisa, 156
Schleitheim Confession, 156. *See also* Anabaptism, sixteenth-century
Schreiber, Gerhard, 199
Science, 69, 274, 277
  and the Bible, 130, 139n2 and 3
  branches of, 279-280
  cosmos, 130, 144, 174, 178, 189, 277-282, 300
  limits of, 278-279
  public distrust of, 21, 277, 321-323
Septuagint, 142
Serbia. *See* Balkans
Sermon on the Mount, 14, 33-35, 37, 114, 119, 297
Servant leadership, 13, 20, 154, 164-179
Servant Leadership: A Journey, 164-166
Shenk, Sara Wenger, 77-78, 81, 84, 188
Short, Jake, 191
Showalter, Shirley, 106-107
Sider, J. Alexander, 185
Siegel, Daniel, 201, 203
Sipe, James, 166-170
Slave, Slavery

Biblical, 34, 39, 126, 132
United States, 56, 74-75, 115
Sleeping Preacher, 214
Somalia, 262-268
Somewhere Else, 214
Souder, Lawrence, 310
Spears, Larry, 170
Star Wars, 190
Suárez, , Francisco, 258
Summa Theologica, 157
Sword and Trumpet 155-156

T

Teaching Peace, 19
Thiessen, Janis, 94
Tiessen, Hildi Froese, 91-92
Tillich, Paul, 102
Toews, Miriam, 214, 223-224, 229-234
Toews, Paul, 92
Tracy, David, 99, 102-105
Two-kingdom theology, 155-157

V

Violence/violent, 62, 78, 197, 233, 245
   accommodated, 56
   in atonement, 299-300
   cyclical, 34-36, 47, 242, 274-276, 294, 297-298
   defined, 47-48
   God, 125-129, 299-300
   in international law, 246-249, 253-254
   in just war, 20, 256-270
   national, 18, 21, 74, 184, 306, 308
   Old Testament, 20, 115-116, 125-129, 137
   in pacifist dilemma, 305-308, 317
   Sexual, 158, 213-214, 235n8
   structural/systemic, 48
   White, 75
Virginia Conference, 155

W

Weaver, J. Denny, 12, 19, 84, 86n29, 106, 116, 146, 155, 268, 276
Weber, Max, 64-65
Weiss, Gail, 229, 234
Wesley, John, 173
West Nickel Mines, 294
What is an Anabaptist Christian?, 197
White Privilege, 41, 159-160
White supremacy, 75-83, 95, 115
Whiteness, 77, 83-84, 90, 96, 105-106, 181-182
   Mennonites and, 75-77, 96, 106
Whitehead, Alfred North, 63, 68-70
Wiebe, Rudy, 88, 213-214
Wink, Walter, 308
WMSC, 93
Womanist theology, 58, 84, 106
Woolman, John, 170
Worldview, 42, 55-59, 70, 156, 202, 327, 331. *See also* Science, cosmos
Wyse-Rhodes, Jackie, 116

Y

Yoder, John Howard
   abuse, 18, 49n4, 157-158
   and grain of the universe, 45, 199
   theology of, 49n4, 66, 79, 140n7, 270n1, 311, 317n1

Z

Zacchaeus, 33
Zacharias, Robert, 227
Zehr, Howard, 157, 283, 286
Zizek, Slavoj, 309

THE CONTRIBUTORS

Malinda Elizabeth Berry is Assistant Professor of Theology and Ethics at Anabaptist Mennonite Biblical Seminary.

Benjamin Bixler is a PhD student in Hebrew Bible at Drew Theological School and Graduate Division of Religion.

Sarah Ann Bixler is a PhD student in Practical theology/Christian Education at Princeton Theological Seminary.

Laura L. Brenneman is a Sessional Faculty member at Anabaptist Mennonite Biblical Seminary and Eastern Mennonite Seminary and Visiting Lecturer at the University of Illinois Urbana-Champaign.

Daniel Shank Cruz is Assistant Professor of English at Utica College.

Lowell Ewert is Director of Peace and Conflict Studies at Conrad Grebel University College, affiliatred with the University of Waterloo.

Drew G. I. Hart is Assistant Professor of Theology at Messiah College.

Hannah E. Heinzekehr is Executive Director of The Mennonite, Inc.

Justin Heinzekehr is Director of Institutional Research and Assessment and Assistant Professor of Bible and Religion at Goshen College.

Felipe Hinojosa is Associate Professor of History at Texas A&M University.

Susan Schultz Huxman is President of Eastern Mennonite University.

Rebecca Janzen is Assistant Professor of Spanish at the University of South Carolina.

Rudi Kauffman is former Associate Professor of Restorative Justice at Bluffton University.

Gerald J. Mast is Professor of Communication at Bluffton University.

Angela Horn Montel is Professor of Biology at Bluffton University.

Lonna Stoltzfus is Lead for Restorative Practices in the Madison (Wisconsin) Metropolitan School District.

Zachary J. Walton is Associate Professor of Communication at Bluffton University.

J. Denny Weaver is Professor Emeritus of Religion at Bluffton University.

Jackie Wyse-Rhodes is Assistant Professor of Religion at Bluffton University.

www.ingramcontent.com/pod-product-compliance
Lightning Source LLC
Chambersburg PA
CBHW050200240426
43671CB00013B/2194